Information Systems for You

Stephen Doyle

Revised Edition

Stanley Thornes (Publishers) Ltd.

Text © Stephen Doyle 1995, 1996
Cartoon illustrations © Stanley Thornes (Publishers) Ltd 1995, 1996

First published in 1995 by
Stanley Thornes (Publishers) Ltd
Ellenborough House
Wellington Street
CHELTENHAM GL50 1YW

Revised edition published 1996

   99 00 01 / 10 9 8

A catalogue record for this book is available from the British Library

ISBN 0 7487 2809 0

Typeset by GreenGate Publishing Services, Tonbridge, Kent
Printed and bound in Great Britain by Redwood Books, Trowbridge, Wiltshire

Contents

Introduction

The aim of the book

The aim of this book is to build up your knowledge of information systems and information technology and also to develop your skills in these areas. By the time you reach the end of the course you should know about IT and IS and be able to use the skills and knowledge you have acquired to solve your own problems. It is not necessary to study the chapters in the same sequence that they are presented in the book. However, if you study them in another order, you may encounter terms that were covered in previous chapters.

The starting point

Since many of the questions, tasks, projects, etc. involve a knowledge of wordprocessing, spreadsheet and database software you should make sure that you know what they are and how to use them at a basic level. Many students will have used these before and will be fully familiar with them. If you haven't used them and don't know what they are you will need to look at Chapter 28 on wordprocessing, Chapter 29 on spread-sheets and Chapters 9 and 31 on databases.

Syllabus coverage

This book has been written to cover all the Information Systems and Information Technology syllabuses in the UK. The book also covers the National Curriculum in Information Technology. Some of the text also provides useful background material for students taking the Intermediate GNVQ in Information Technology.

How to use the book

The book is divided into two sections with the first part covering the material for the examination and the second part covering the coursework. Chapters 1 to 26 cover the theoretical part of the syllabus, although they do include a variety of practical tasks. Chapters 27 to 34 are coursework chapters and the aim of these chapters is to help you to gain skills and knowledge about software and to apply these to your own coursework. Coursework is important for both the National Curriculum Tests and the GCSE. If you want to know more about what the coursework involves, look at Chapter 27 which provides advice about coursework.

At the end of most chapters there is a Test Yourself section where you will be tested on material covered in the chapter.

A section called 'Things To Do' is also included. This includes a variety of problems including some examination style questions. These have been graded with the easiest questions at the start.

There are projects, called Investigations, in some chapters which allow you to do some research on a particular topic and use your skills to present your findings. These projects will also add to your overall knowledge of Information Technology and Information Systems in general.

Questions within the text

To help you understand concepts as you come to them, questions have been included within the text. This means that you do not have to wait till the end of a chapter before trying a question.

Skills building exercises

These exercises are scattered throughout the book and provide opportunities to build your skills in the use of hardware and software to solve real problems.

Icons

Icons indicate that a particular skill is being developed. Here are the icons along with the name of the skill that is being developed:

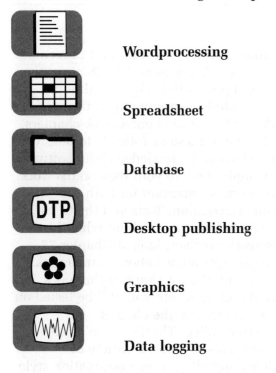

Wordprocessing

Spreadsheet

Database

Desktop publishing

Graphics

Data logging

Investigations

Investigations provide an opportunity to carry out a project on a particular topic or topics. In this book, investigations have an icon with a magnifying glass at the side of them. The aim of these investigations is to develop or reinforce your knowledge of the subject as well as to use a variety of skills in finding the information out and then presenting it.

Making use of IS/IT in other subjects

In many schools and colleges IS/IT is not taught as a separate subject but instead is taught in other lessons. For instance you may learn about how to access information held on CD-ROM while doing your GCSE history coursework or you might learn about sensors while performing an experiment which looks at the heat liberated during a chemical reaction. If you are doing the course in this way then you will need to make sure that you cover all the parts of the syllabus. You would be advised to get a copy of your syllabus and use it as a checklist to make sure that you have covered everything. You should not consider IT/IS as a subject in its own right since the knowledge and skills can be usefully applied to all subject areas and all aspects of your everyday life.

Advice on coursework

A chapter at the start of the coursework section of the book (Chapter 27) provides hints and tips as well as answers to questions you might have such as:

- What software can I use?
- How much do I write?
- Can my teacher help me?
- Do you get marks for your English?
- What is entailed in the coursework?

Also discussed is the difference between IT Tasks (sometimes called resource tasks) and Systems Tasks (sometimes called capability tasks).

The icons for the two different types of task are as follows:

There are some suggestions from several examination boards for each type of task.

Glossary

There is a glossary at the back of the book. This is a sort of dictionary of computer words, with their meanings. If you find a term that you do not understand you can do one of two things to help you find what it means. First, you could turn to the glossary and look it up. Here you will find a brief explanation of what it means. However, if you want a fuller explanation, use the index to find the relevant chapters.

Looking up words in the glossary will reinforce your knowledge of the subject. You will find that several of the smaller examination questions will ask you what is meant by certain computer terms. It is a good idea to try to learn some of the words in the glossary along with their meanings.

Learning the glossary

Find some paper or cardboard and cut it into rectangular pieces about the size of a playing card. Take two cards at once. Write a computer term on one card and its meaning on the other (see Figure 1). Shuffle all the cards and then try to match the terms with their meanings. Check them using the glossary.

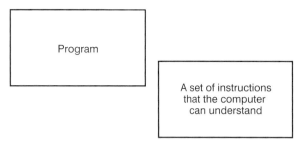

Figure 1 *Make up revision cards like these*

Acknowledgements

Thanks to Sarah Wilman and Louise Watson of Stanley Thornes for their encouragement and help in producing this book.

Thanks are due to the following for permission to use material:

George Thomas and Dr Martin Wynn of
    HP Bulmer Ltd
Philip Harris Education
DRS Data & Research Services plc
SIMS Education Services Ltd
Cambridgeshire Software House
GST Software Products
Elizabeth Segall of The Centre for World
    Development Education
City of Lverpool Community College;
CompuServe

The Data Protection Registrar
IBM

Thank you also to the following examinations boards which gave permission for the use of their questions:

Midland Examining Group
Northern Examinations & Assessment Board
Northern Ireland Schools Examinations &
    Assessment Council
Royal Society of Arts
Southern Examining Group
University of London Examinations &
    Assessment Council
Welsh Joint Education Committee

A full list of examinations boards and their addresses is given on page 295.

What is an Information System?

Data

We call raw facts and figures **data.** Facts and figures often have little meaning until they are sorted or until we calculate something from them. This sorting or calculation is called **data processing**. When data is processed, it provides **information** (see Figure 1.1).

Figure 1.1 *Processing data produces information*

Information

Information is the meaning we attach to the data. For instance, a red traffic light is a form of data. The meaning we attach to this data (i.e. STOP) is the information. Sometimes data can give rise to ambiguous information. If you are driving a car and a car travelling in the opposite direction flashes its lights at you, what does it mean? It could just mean that a friend has spotted you and is saying hello; it could also mean that there is an accident further up the road. The information that may be obtained from data depends on the way that the data is interpreted and the context in which it is used.

Data is often meaningless. For instance consider the number 250295. We could interpret this in any number of ways. For example it might be:

- your video club membership number
- the date, e.g. 25th February 1995
- the number of cars going down a certain road in a week.

The three stages of doing tasks

All tasks can be broken down into three stages: input, process and output. These are shown in Figure 1.2.

Manual information systems

We are all used to dealing with some sort of manual information system. A telephone directory is an example. There may be several hundred thousand entries, but if we know the surname and address of the person we are trying to contact, we can find the number provided that it is in the directory.

Manual information systems have many disadvantages. Let's look at an example.

Suppose you have a friend whose phone number and surname you know but whose address you need to find. You do not know their parent's initial and their surname is, unfortunately, Jones. You could find the address by taking the following steps:

1 Look up the section for Jones.
2 Start from the beginning and work through the phone numbers, looking for the area code, e.g. look for 928 and see if the rest of the number coincides.
3 Once the phone number has been found you can read off the address.

An even worse problem might be if you had a phone number of a person scribbled down on a piece of paper and you wanted to find out who you were ringing first. The telephone directory is ordered alphabetically according to surname and not in numerical order according to telephone number so to find the number would prove an immense and time-consuming task.

Figure 1.2 *The three stages of doing tasks*

Computerised information systems

Computerised information systems are much more flexible than manual ones and a lot faster. With a computerised system you could type in a phone number and, if the number was stored in the system, the name and address could be provided immediately.

Examples of computerised information systems

The Driver Vehicle Licensing Authority

The Driver Vehicle Licensing Authority (DVLA) keeps a huge collection of information concerning every driver and every vehicle in the country. Such a huge collection of data is called a **database**. Summarised details of this database are passed to the Police National Computer (PNC).

Suppose there has been a hit and run accident and a witness is able to remember only part of the registration number, e.g. _704 N__. Imagine trying to search through the thousands of car registrations having those letters or numbers in them. Even a computer can take some time doing these sorts of searches. Even worse, what would happen if we only knew that the car was a Ford Mondeo with partial registration L__ N__. This type of situation happens all the time when the police are trying to trace cars. Computerised information systems are one of the main weapons in the fight against crime.

A computerised school management system

Consider your school or college. In the secretaries' office there will be a computer containing information on all the students in the school. What are the requirements of a school information system?

Here are some of the tasks that the system would need to deal with.

1 The system must record the attendance details twice a day for all the pupils. It must be able to identify pupils who have poor attendance records so that they may be investigated.
2 It must list a pupil's personal details. This would include such things as name, address, date of birth, name of parent or guardian, daytime contact numbers and addresses, sex, religion, medical problems, form, form teacher's name, mode of travel to school, whether students stay for school dinners and so on.
3 It must be easy to produce the various lists such as lists of pupils for registration groups, teaching groups, parents' evenings and school trips.
4 It must be possible to get information easily from the system so that letters may be generated and sent to certain pupils.
5 The system must be able to cope with the administration of examination entries.
6 It must cope with all the financial aspects of running a school.
7 The system should be able to help organise a timetable, making the best use of the teachers and the rooms.

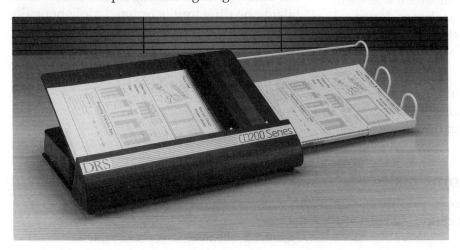

Figure 1.3 *Pupil profile forms are read automatically using an optical mark reader*

As you can see from the above list, a lot of work goes on behind the scenes in a school.

Advantages of a computerised information management system

1 You don't need lots of filing cabinets to hold all the pupils' files and other forms. A single computer can store all the information needed.
2 Terminals can be used, so that many people can access the information in different places at the same time. Whenever data is updated it is instantly available to all the people using the system.
3 There is no duplication of information. The pupils' details need only be entered once and then used for different tasks. It is possible to produce year lists, class lists, option lists etc. using the data from the pupil file.
4 The system can be used in conjunction with a wordprocessor to produce mail shots to pupils' homes.
5 Some information can be transferred to the system without using the keyboard. For instance, Figure 1.3 shows marks on a document being read by an optical mark reader.

Disadvantages of a computerised information management system

1 Everything depends on the computer system. If there is a power failure, or if the system breaks down then an alternative system will need to be used.
2 To use the system, the staff will need to be trained. When staff leave their expertise will be lost and new staff will need to be trained.
3 Security will need to be provided to protect personal pupil and staff information from prying eyes.

Figure 1.5 *A computer being used to view a pupil's personal details. Notice that it can even include a photograph*

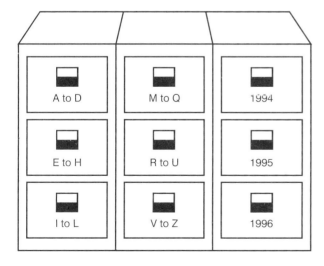

A to D	M to Q	1994
E to H	R to U	1995
I to L	V to Z	1996

Figure 1.4 *With manual systems, large numbers of filing cabinets are often needed to store records. With a computerised system, one computer could store all this information*

Pupils' personal details need only be recorded once on the system. Even a photograph can be put onto it as shown in Figure 1.5. The system is easy for everyone to use and can use the **Windows** style of menus as shown in Figure 1.6. All aspects of the school's administration can be dealt with by the system, from running the school library to recording pupils' option choices. The form shown in Figure 1.7 is used to record pupil option choices. Each option has a different barcode, which can be stuck to the form. The details can be read by using an optical character reader.

The Schools Information Management System enables the head teacher of the school to run the school as efficiently as possible for the benefit of all the pupils. Tasks that would have taken a long time now can be done quickly.

Figure 1.7 *This form is used to record pupil option details. Each option has a different barcode, which is stuck to the form. The details can be extracted using an optical mark reader or a barcode reader*

Figure 1.6 *A Windows screen from the Schools Information Management System*

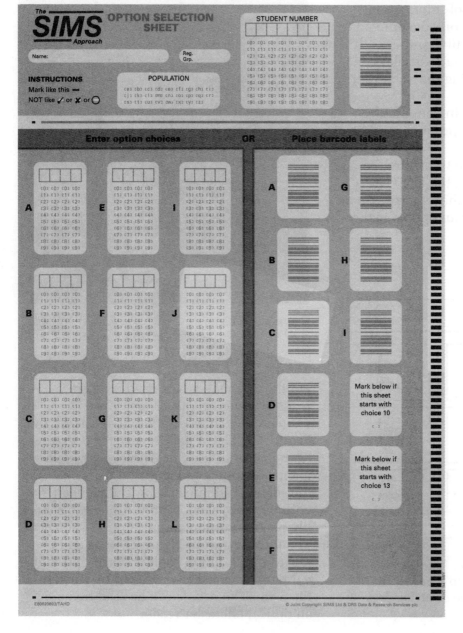

1   Write a list of manual information systems that you use in your everyday life.

Here are a few to start you off:

- Dictionary
- Library catalogue
- Mail order catalogue
- Guinness Book of Hit Singles
- Bus timetable

See how many more you can think up.

When you have finished, compare your list with your friends'.

2   You have been asked to produce a geography project on a particular country such as Iceland. You intend to do this using traditional reference books. What manual information sources would you use? Write a list.

3   Find out about the information systems (manual or computerised) used in your school office. You need to investigate each of the following:

(a)   How does the data get into the system?

If the school uses a manual system, explain how the system deals with the various tasks mentioned in the text. If a computerised system is used, how is the data entered into the system? Also, what information does the system provide?

(b)   Find out what sort of information needs to be held about each pupil, including you. Write a list of the information and explain for each one, why it is held.

INVESTIGATION

Everyone seems to be talking about CD-ROMs at the moment. CD-ROMs are able to hold huge amounts of data which previously could only be found with great difficulty in huge sets of encyclopaedias, atlases, dictionaries and other reference books. Material held on CD can provide many things that books can't. If you are interested in a particular composer, such as Mozart, you can see a picture of him, read the text and hear his music all at the same time. It is important to be able to access reference material held on a CD-ROM.

1   Find out the titles of any CD-ROMs your school or college has. If they do not have any then you will need to visit a large library. List the titles and what sort of information they contain (you can usually get this information from the piece of paper inside the sleeve). Have a look at any which seem interesting.

2   Taking a disk whose subject matter interests you, see if you can access information by:

(a)   using the main index

(b)   using the word search facility

(c)   using any sound sequences if available

(d)   using any animations (moving diagrams).

3   Select an article that contains both a photograph and some text referring to the photograph and print it out.

4   What are the main advantages of using CD-ROMs rather than using manual information systems such as books?

5   Choose a topic (it could be some work you have to do for GCSE coursework) and produce a selection of output that you could use as reference material.

The Components of an Information System

Hardware and software

There are two parts to all computer systems; the hardware and the software. Hardware is the term used for the parts of the computer that you can touch and handle. Hardware is the collective name given to all the devices that make up a computer system. Some examples of computer hardware are shown in Figure 2.1. Basically these devices may be split into:

- **input devices**, which are used to get the data into the computer
- the **central processing unit**, which is the brain of the computer
- the **backing storage**, which are the disk drives used to store data when the power is switched off
- the **output devices**, which consist of devices such as printers, VDUs etc., used to provide output such as printouts, screen displays, etc.

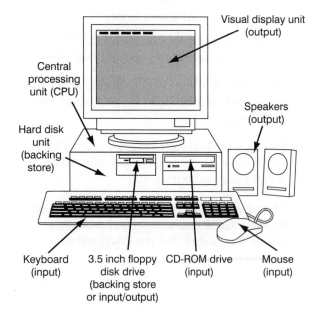

Figure 2.1 *The parts of a typical microcomputer*

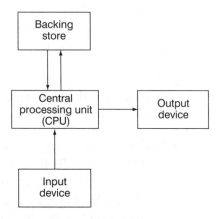

Figure 2.2 *A simple computer system*

The arrangement of these in a typical computer system is shown in Figure 2.2.

Software is the word used for the actual programs that allow the hardware to do a useful job. Without software, hardware is useless. Software is made up of a series of instructions that tell the computer what to do.

To understand the difference between hardware and software, think of a tape recorder and a blank tape. The tape recorder and the tape are the 'hardware' because we can actually pick them up. But if we recorded some music onto the tape, then the music would be the 'software'.

Why use computers?

Computers are extremely fast

A large computer used for producing weather forecasts is able to perform over one million calculations per second. This may appear to be excessive, but many millions of calculations are needed to produce a weather forecast, and forecasts need to be produced quickly. Computer systems used by the gas and electricity boards have to produce bills to be sent out every three months. Without fast and powerful computers, this would be impossible.

Computers are very accurate

We have to remember when we see stories in newspapers about computers making huge mistakes that it is the people who have programmed them or entered the data that have made the mistakes. Computers only do what they are told to do. We often use the saying 'garbage in, garbage out' or GIGO for short: what it means is that if some data is put into the computer incorrectly the computer won't realise that it is incorrect so it will give out a strange answer. If the computer is given the right information, then provided that the hardware and software are working correctly, it will always produce the right output.

Computers can keep large amounts of information in a small space

Keeping all the information we need written on paper in files is an enormous task. Once you have gone through the tedious task of making up the files and cataloguing them, you then have the problem of finding the file you want and sometimes you may have millions of them to hunt through! But if you use computerised storage you can keep millions of files in a very small space and can get the information from them in seconds. You can also have a spare copy in case of accidents – imagine having duplicate written files (Figure 2.3).

Computers can work continuously for 24 hours a day

Computers don't become ill, they don't take lunch breaks or tea breaks and they don't go on strike (Figure 2.4). Computers can easily work 24 hours per day, 365 days per year. There are many things that are probably best left to humans though (Figure 2.5).

Computers can do some jobs that would be impossible without them

Airline booking, the use of credit cards and SWITCH cards, weather forecasting and space exploration would all be impossible to perform without the use of computers.

The clerical cost of filling a three drawer filing cabinet is reckoned to be about £1500.
In addition, annual maintenance of the files would cost about £1200

Some 70% of paper filed is lost. However, the average document is copied seven times and this increases the chances of finding it again. What a waste!

Figure 2.3 *Manual filing systems can take up a lot of space and are difficult to organise*

Figure 2.4 *Computers don't have tea breaks and they don't go on strike!*

Figure 2.5 *Many things are best left to humans*

Are there any drawbacks in using computers?

Computers can replace people
There is no doubt that the use of computers has lead to unemployment.

Computers hold personal information which may be misused
It is very easy to misuse the personal information held about individuals on computers. This will be looked at more closely in Chapter 18.

Problems arise when computers cannot be used
Sometimes a computer system breaks down, so things have to be done manually or postponed until it is fixed.

Staff need to be trained
Training can be expensive and if the staff leave then new staff will need to be trained.

Processing data

Computers are used to process data. What we mean by 'process' is doing something to the data. Processing includes:

- **calculating** – for example working out how much pay an employee gets
- **sorting** – your teacher may require a class list arranged in alphabetical order
- **searching** – your head teacher may want to produce a list of all pupils who stay for school dinners
- **storing** – information may be stored on the computer instead of a using a paper based system; old letters or memos may never be needed again but it might still be worth keeping them for a few years
- **drawing** – you might use a paint package in your art lesson or a computer aided design (CAD) package in your technology lesson to design a product.

The central processing unit

The central processing unit (often known as simply the processing unit) processes the raw data and turns it into information. We need not look to deeply into how it works because, as you can imagine, it is quite complicated. If you ever need to open up the case of a microcomputer you will see that there is a series of circuit boards containing the main processor along with various memory chips. You will also find a transformer and sometimes a fan which is responsible for the hum that you get from a computer. Chips give out quite a bit of heat during operation, so the fan is used to cool them down.

There are three main elements of the central processing unit:

- the **control unit**, which is responsible for co-ordinating the input and output devices
- the **arithmetic and logic unit**, in which all the calculations and all the logical decisions are made
- the **immediate access store**, which provides immediate memory for holding data and programs.

The immediate access store (IAS) is stored on a chip or a series of chips inside the computer. Data held here can be accessed immediately, unlike data held on disk, which can take some time to load.

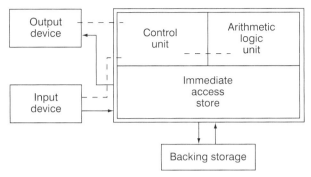

Figure 2.6 *Central processing unit with peripherals*

Figure 2.6 shows how these three main parts of a computer are arranged. In this diagram the solid lines are the data signals passing between the various sections or units. The dotted lines show the signals that are used to control the peripheral devices.

Processing units for large mainframe computers look like metal cabinets. Smaller microcomputers, as shown in Figure 2.7, come in a variety of types: desktop, mini-tower and tower.

The two types of signal

There are two kinds of signal that pass between the main processor and the other hardware. These are:

- **Control signals** – These include signals sent out by the main processor to the printer to tell it to be ready to receive some data.

- **Data signals** – These are the groups of binary digits that are used to represent characters (letters of the alphabet, numbers, punctuation marks etc.).

Types of computer

There are three types of computer: microcomputers, mainframe computers and mini computers. We will look at each of these in turn.

Microcomputers

Microcomputers are the computers that you are most likely to encounter at home or in school or college. Different types include Apples, Acorns and PCs.

Mainframe computers

A mainframe computer is a large, powerful computer which is capable of supporting large numbers of terminals (typically 500+). The larger mainframe computers are capable of carrying out 250 million instructions per second (MIPS). An instruction is the equivalent of adding two numbers together, and these machines can do that 250 million times per second. Because of their immense power they give out considerable amounts of heat, so computer rooms have to be air

Figure 2.7 A *Desktop,* **B** *mini-tower and* **C** *tower computers*

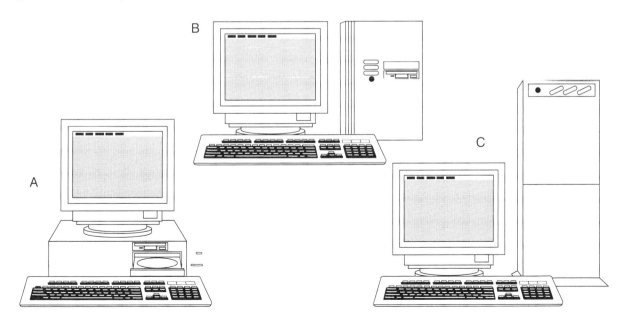

conditioned and some mainframes are water cooled.

Banks, building societies, large insurance companies, the utility companies (i.e. gas, electricity, water companies) all make use of these powerful mainframe computers.

Mini computers

Mini computers have a size, power and cost somewhere between those of microcomputers and mainframes. Because of the rapid advances in technology, it is common to find modern minicomputers which are much more powerful than some of the mainframes still in use.

Peripheral devices

Peripheral devices are devices that are outside the central processing unit but are under its control. These devices may be input devices used to get the data into the computer, such as keyboards, output devices, such as printers, and storage devices, such as disk drives.

Microprocessors

A microprocessor is a single chip that performs the functions of a central processing unit. A chip consists of millions of tiny electronic components etched on a piece of silicon. A microcomputer consists of a microprocessor, together with other chips such as memory chips.

Microprocessors are used to control devices such as washing machines, video recorders, burglar alarms and microwave ovens. In fact, it is hard to think of any electrical or electronic device that could not have a microprocessor to help control it.

Microprocessor-based devices in the home

Washing machines

Automatic washing machines have been around for a long time but their method of control is now quite different. Older control systems are electro-mechanical which means they are made up of many plastic and metal moving parts. These moving parts frequently break down and because of their complexity fewer washing programs are available.

All modern washing machines are controlled using microprocessors, so their control systems are much more reliable and cheaper to replace when they do go wrong.

Advantages of microprocessor control
1 It is more reliable because there are no moving parts in the circuits.
2 Chips are cheap, so if a unit goes wrong then the whole unit is just replaced which reduces labour costs.
3 A microprocessor controlled washing machine can typically have 24 different washing programs.
4 Energy consumption is reduced since the older systems would dry the clothes for a certain time whereas the newer ones operate only until the clothes are dry. Some machines sense the weight of the washing in the machine and adjust the water, detergent and energy usage accordingly, so are much 'greener' than the older machines.

Disadvantages of microprocessor control
1 If part of the control unit goes wrong then it is necessary to replace the whole unit and this discourages people trying to repair things cheaply themselves.
2 Many of the features microprocessor-controlled offer will never be used.
3 The instruction manuals can be very complicated and confusing.

TEST YOURSELF

Using the words in the list below, copy out and complete sentences A to H, underlining the words you have inserted. The words may be used once, more than once or not at all.

programs   GIGO   hardware   information

software   searching   quick   peripheral

backing   microprocessor

A   A computer system consists of two parts: _____ and _____.

B   Software is the name given to the _____ which enable a computer to perform a useful task.

C   A simple computer system consists of a CPU, input and output devices and some external storage called _____ storage.

D   Gas and electricity boards use computers because they are very _____ at producing bills.

E   A computer will give the right result only if you feed it the correct information to start with. This is often referred to as _____.

F   Computers are often used because they are able to hold lots of _____ in a very small space. They are also quick at _____ for this information.

G   A_____ device is the name given to a device that is outside the CPU but still under the control of it.

H   A single chip which performs the functions of a CPU is called a _____.

---

1   Tick one box for each of the items below to show whether it is hardware or software. If you get stuck use the index or the glossary at the back of the book to help.

	Hardware	Software
(a) Keyboard	☐	☐
(b) Floppy disk	☐	☐
(c) Visual Display Unit	☐	☐
(d) Mouse	☐	☐
(e) Central Processing Unit	☐	☐
(f) Wordprocessor	☐	☐
(g) Operating system	☐	☐
(h) Joystick	☐	☐
(i) Spreadsheet	☐	☐
(j) Database	☐	☐

2   (a)   Give the name of the chip that carries out the functions of a central processing unit.

(b)   If you buy a floppy disk with a computer game on it, have you bought hardware, software or both?

(c)   Give three reasons why a computer is more efficient than a human being.

3   (a)   Name two jobs that it would be impossible to perform without computers.

(b)   For the two jobs you have named, give reasons why it would be impossible to perform them manually (by hand).

4   Not all aspects of using computers are good but their good points far outweigh their bad points; otherwise we would not use them.

Write a short paragraph on any disadvantages in using computers.

THINGS TO DO

3

The 'Ins' and 'Outs' of Systems
Input and Output

The 'ins' and 'outs' of a video library

When designing any information system, you need first to consider what information you want to get out of the system. The output depends on the type of job (application). If you were considering a video library, you could decide that the following output is needed:

1 screen displays of videos out on loan and those that should be on the shelves
2 printouts containing details of members who have not returned their videos
3 letters to send to members reminding them to return their videos
4 membership lists
5 letters telling members they have to pay for videos they have failed to return (if the reminder in 3 above has had no response).

Then you need to consider what you should put into the system to get the above output. These **inputs** to the system might include:

1 membership details, such as membership number, name, address, etc.
2 details of all the videos kept, such as video number, title, category, etc.
3 details of the videos lent (these will link the membership numbers to the video numbers)
4 details of when videos are returned.

On the face of it, it looks as though you could use a visual display unit (VDU) and a printer for the output, and a keyboard for the input. This is only one solution. You should look at other alternatives so that you are able to choose the best one. You could use a barcode reader to read a barcode on the member's card and link it with the barcode on the video. This could prove more accurate and quicker than having to type in the membership and video numbers, but it may prove too expensive. You must always consider all the options and then choose the best.

If there aren't many members or too many videos, a manual card boxed system may be more cost effective than a computer system.

Input devices

Input devices are used to get data into a system. The ideal input device would be able to get data into a system as accurately as possible, in the least amount of time and preferably without human intervention. The device would also be relatively cheap. Unfortunately, no perfect input device is available and the choice is always a compromise. The fastest input devices are suitable only for a narrow range of applications. Here are some of the main input devices in use today.

Keyboard

The keyboard is the oldest and most familiar of all input devices. Keyboards are intelligent devices and contain their own chips. Basically each key acts as a switch which closes when the key is pressed. The microprocessor scans the keyboard hundreds of times a second to see if a key has been pressed; if it has, a code that depends on which key has been pressed is sent to the processing unit. The CPU translates this code into an ASCII code (the code that computers use to represent characters on the computer keyboard),which is then used by the computer program. Figure 3.1 shows a keyboard and VDU being used by police officers.

Figure 3.1 *The most common input and output devices: the VDU and keyboard are being used here by police officers*

Mouse

A mouse is an input device that translates its movements on the desktop into digital information; this is fed to the computer which in turn causes the cursor to move on the screen. Underneath the mouse is a ball which rotates as the mouse is moved on the desk, and sensors pick up this movement to move the cursor. Mice usually have one, two or three buttons, which are used to make selections on the screen.

Tracker ball

A tracker ball is like an upside down mouse. The ball is rotated by the user but this time the 'mouse' stays still. The advantage of a tracker ball compared with a conventional mouse, is that it takes up much less space, and this is why tracker balls are often seen on lap-top computers. Figure 3.3 shows a lap-top containing a tracker ball.

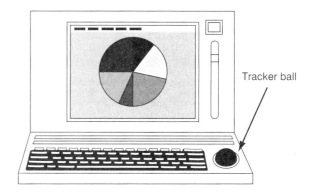

Figure 3.3 *A lap-top computer*

Joystick

A joystick is similar to a tracker ball. Whenever the stick is moved, the cursor moves in a similar direction on the screen. Joysticks are mainly used for games (Figure 3.4), but you can also see them being used in, for example, scanners in hospitals.

Figure 3.2

Figure 3.4

Light pen

A screen cursor can be moved by touching the screen with a light pen. Light pens are mainly used for design work and need special software to make them work.

Touch screen

A touch screen is a special kind of screen which is sensitive to touch. A selection is made from a menu on the screen by touching part of it. These screens are ideal for use in banks and building societies, where customers who are not used to keyboards can obtain information about the services offered. You can also see touch screens in restaurants and bars.

Graphics tablets (digitisers)

Graphics tablet are rather like electronic tracing paper and, like paper, they come in all sizes from a modest A4 size to a very large A0 size which will occupy the best part of a desk. A cursor or puck is used on a graphics tablet to trace over technical drawings put on the screen using a computer-aided-design package such as AutoCAD.

Magnetic stripe reader

You can see magnetic stripe readers at the side of computerised tills called point-of-sale terminals. Figure 3.5 shows one being used to read information contained in the magnetic stripe of a credit card.

Figure 3.5 *A magnetic stripe reader*

Barcode readers

If you think that barcodes are used only in supermarkets then you should take another look. Barcodes are used in library systems, luggage handling systems at airports and warehouse stock control systems. Barcodes systems are now at an advanced stage and readers are able to read the barcodes at distances of five metres or more. This fact has increased the number of applications.

Figure 3.6 *A bee with a barcode!*

In America, researchers have painstakingly glued barcodes to the backs of some bees (Figure 3.6). These barcodes are scanned every time the bee enters or leaves its hive thus providing valuable information about pollination.

Figure 3.7

Optical character readers and optical character recognition (OCR)

Optical character recognition (OCR) is a method of inputting text using a scanner along with special software to turn the scanned image into standard ASCII code In other words, the text is no longer treated as a picture, since each individual letter is recognised on its own and may therefore be edited using word processing software.

Figure 3.8 *Recognising some characters is not easy*

Since OCR software must be able to distinguish between an S and a 5 or a B and an 8, the original text really needs to be typed. As well as being able to recognise the different characters, optical character readers must be able to read different fonts (i.e. different patterns of letters), different type sizes and upper and lower case letters.

OCR software can also be used to scan financial documents such as company accounts directly into spreadsheets as well as to scan text directly into wordprocessors.

Magnetic ink character reader and optical character recognition (MICR)

Magnetic ink characters are the rather strange looking numbers that you see at the bottom of cheques. Figure 3.9 shows them. The characters are printed using an ink which contains iron and may be magnetised. The magnetic pattern of the numbers is read by a special reader called a magnetic ink character reader.

When a cheque is printed, the account number, branch code and cheque number are all printed in magnetic ink. When someone writes a cheque, the receiver takes it to their bank and pays it into their account. The bank then has to type the amount onto the cheque using magnetic ink before the cheque is dealt with.

Magnetic ink character recognition uses expensive equipment and is suitable only for very large scale applications. The expense of the system is an advantage in banking since it is unlikely that people would be able to build the equipment and start to print their own cheques.

Anybank	45-83-21
Anytown Branch 23 High Street Anytown	*19*
Pay	*only*
	£
	Mr J Smith
ı00063 45 83 2ı 46075598	

Figure 3.9 *A cheque showing the magnetic ink characters*

Optical mark readers and optical mark recognition (OMR)

Optical mark readers are able to sense marks made on a special form in certain places. Figure 3.10 shows a typical example of such a form used to collect details regarding student enrolments. Notice that just to collect a single letter, 26 marks have to be used.

Uses for optical mark readers include multiple choice answer sheet marking, capturing data from questionnaires and enrolment forms and the checking of football pools coupons.

15

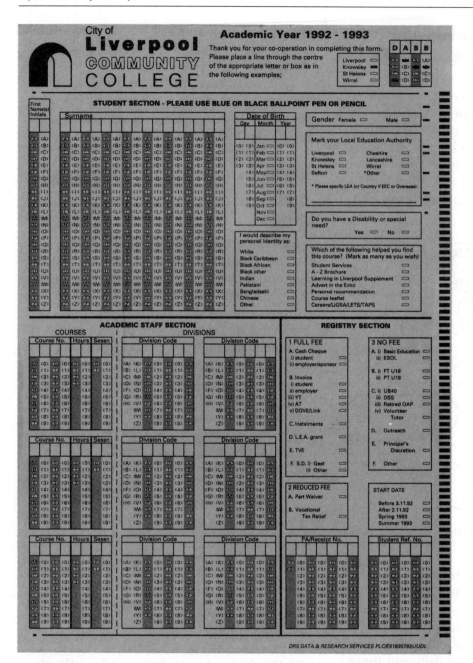

Figure 3.10 *An OMR form used by a college to collect student details for enrolment*

People who have never completed optical mark reading sheets can have problems filling them in. For instance, in a questionnaire to find out people's opinions of television programmes, the following 'variations' were obtained, despite the correct method of shading in the complete box being explained.

Just some of the variations were:

Did you enjoy the programme? YES NO

Did you enjoy the programme? YES NO

Did you enjoy the programme YES NO

Did you enjoy the programme? YES NO

Disadvantages

1 If the forms are being filled in by the general public then very clear instructions will be needed. A couple of examples should be chosen as an illustration. No matter how clear your instructions are you will find that a high proportion of forms are filled in incorrectly. The rejection rate is found to be around 30%.

2 If the forms are creased or folded then they may be rejected or foul the machine. This will add to the time needed to read the forms. Badly damaged forms will need to be rewritten or keyed in manually.

Advantages

1 The use of OMR means that details do not have to be typed in; typing could introduce errors and takes time.

2 OMR reduces the cost of inputting large volumes of data because people do not need to type the details.

3 The method is useful when results of tests are needed very quickly, e.g. with an aptitude test for a job.

Punched card

Punched cards contain holes in different positions which mean something when they are read by a reader. Before screens and keyboards were widely used, punched cards were the main method of entering data into computers. They are seldom used now but two uses still remain: the Kimball tag mentioned in the next section and the clock card which is used to record the hours a person works so that wages can be worked out.

Kimball tag

Kimball tags are the small cards with holes punched in them that you see attached to clothing in certain shops. When you buy the goods, one of the tags is removed and sent for processing to a computer centre. A card reader then reads off the information contained in the holes such as stock number, size, colour, etc. This information is then used to keep stock records and to re-order stock. Figure 3.11 shows a Kimball tag.

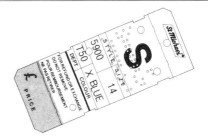

Figure 3.11 *A Kimball tag*

Voice recognition

With voice recognition you speak directly to the computer. Its use is limited at the moment, but is useful for handicapped people with limited movement.

Electronic point of sale (EPOS) terminal

EPOS terminals are the cash registers which also act as terminals to a main computer system. As well as providing customers with itemised bills, these systems also give useful management information.

Electronic fund transfer at point of sale (EFTPOS)

EFTPOS terminals are similar to EPOS terminals but with some additional features. For instance, they are able to transfer funds from your bank account directly to a store's account using a card called a debit card. A Switch card is an example of such a card. If you have a debit card you can use it instead of a cheque and it is a faster method of payment. The advantage to a store is that the money is instantly transferred into their account, whereas with cheques and credit cards there is a delay before the money reaches the store.

There are some disadvantages with such cards: they may be stolen or forged; they may also be said to encourage people to spend more money.

Video digitiser

A video digitiser is a combination of hardware and software that converts an analogue video signal into a digital signal in the computer's memory. Each frame from a video is converted, using the video digitiser and it may be played back in any required sequence. Taking a video frame and digitising it is often called image grabbing or frame grabbing.

Grabbed video images take up a lot of main memory and when stored they take up large amount of disk space. A 640 × 480 pixel VGA 24 bit colour picture takes up about 900 KB of memory and a 60 second video sequence of stored pictures will take around 1300 MB.

Video digitising is used to convert a frame from a video sequence into a picture, which can be printed in isolation in a magazine or document. Digitising is also used to make television adverts and to produce pop videos.

Scanner

Scanners are used to scan text or pictures into a computer's memory where they can then be manipulated in some way before being printed. They can be cheap hand held ones or flatbed A4 size. Both black and white and colour scanners are available.

Optical character recognition (OCR) involves scanning in the image of a page of text with a scanner and then using special software to recognise each of the characters separately, so that they may be altered, if needed, using a wordprocessor. Scanners often have OCR software included in the price.

Scanners are also used to scan in photographs and pictures for use in desktop publishing. One of the main problems you encounter when scanning in images is the amount of space they take up on the disk. A full-colour A4 image scanned at 300 dots per inch (DPI) produces a file which takes up around 25 MB of disk space. However, special software, called file compression software, can be used to reduce file sizes.

Still digital camera

If you have to take pictures like photographs which are then to be incorporated into a document, then instead of taking a photograph, developing it and then scanning

it, you can take a direct route by using a still digital camera. These cameras, the most popular of which is the Canon Ion camera, can be used to take a picture and send the digital signals directly into the Canon video grabber card which then stores them on disk.

Which input device?

Here are some situations where you have to decide which would be the best input device to use. You should give reasons for your choice:

1 Your teacher would like to keep a bank of past GCSE questions in a certain subject such as history. She does not want to have to type them all in but she may want to alter them slightly using her wordprocessor. What do you suggest?

2 A firm runs an aptitude test with multiple choice style answers for all applicants for jobs. The applicants first take the test and if they pass it they are given an interview. The whole test (usually around 50 sheets) needs to be marked quickly and accurately whilst the applicants are having a coffee break. Which input device could be used?

3 A video library would like to have a new way of recording the membership number and video numbers when a video is rented. At present the six digit number of the member and video are typed in and this causes a lot of errors. Which alternative method could they use?

4 A building society is thinking of introducing a new cheque book account. Which input method would be best for the process of cheque clearing?

Data from sensors

Sensors are used to obtain data automatically. For instance, traffic lights have a sensor which records the frequency of the traffic. A microprocessor can then alter the sequencing of the lights to improve the flow of the traffic. Burglar alarms and central heating thermostats both contain sensors. We will be looking at sensors in a later chapter.

Output devices

Output devices provide the results after processing, in a suitable form. In many cases this will be in the form of a hard copy (printout), or on a screen. With the widespread use of electronic mail, output could be in the form of an electronic message to another computer.

Visual display unit (VDU)

VDUs or monitors are almost taken for granted as output devices. They are ideal for showing the results from an enquiry where no printout is needed. For instance, if you go into a travel agency and ask if a particular holiday is available on a certain date then all you need to know is yes or no and it is not necessary to print this out.

Graphical display unit

Graphical display units are usually larger than normal VDUs and have greater resolution so that the lines on the screen don't look as though they are made up of lots of tiny dots. Graphical display units are often used in conjunction with light pens.

Laser printers

Laser printers offer both high speed and excellent print quality of text and graphics. Laser printers have toner cartridges which contain a fine powdered black plastic called toner. A laser beam is used to form an image on a rotating charged metal drum. The charged image then picks up the toner particles, which are transferred to the paper, which is also charged. Once the image has been transferred, heat and pressure are used to stick it to the paper permanently.

Figure 3.12 shows a laser printer. As you can see it looks very much like a small photocopier.

Colour laser printers are now available. Although they are expensive, they are likely to come into widespread use eventually.

Ink-jet printers

Ink-jet printers are also commonly called bubble-jet printers. The print head of an ink-jet printer consists of nozzles (usually 64). The ink flows through the appropriate nozzle, where it is heated and a bubble forms. This expands and breaks, releasing a very small ink droplet. The dots formed by each drop bursting are much smaller, and there are more of them, than in a dot-matrix printer. This means that ink-jet printers can print high quality text and graphics, almost comparable to that produced by laser printers. Also, they are silent in operation.

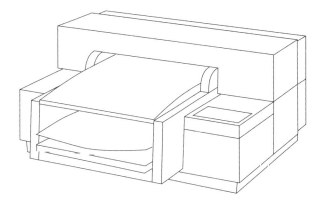

Figure 3.13 *An ink-jet printer*

Ink-jet printers are cheaper to buy than laser printers and are slightly more expensive than dot-matrix printers. They are, however, quite expensive to run, because the ink cartridges are expensive and need frequent replacement. If you do not do a large amount of printing, an ink-jet printer could be the best type to buy.

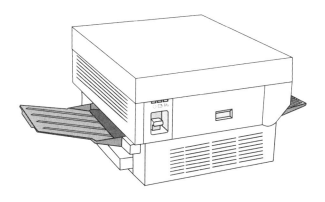

Figure 3.12 *A laser printer*

Another advantage of ink-jets is that they can print in colour. While dot-matrix printers can also print in colour, the colour produced is not as uniform as that produced by ink-jets.

Dot-matrix printers

A few years ago dot-matrix printers were by far the most popular type of printer but with the decrease in costs of laser and ink-jet printers, most people now buy one of these. Dot-matrix printers are cheap and have the lowest running costs of any printer. They use tiny pins in a rectangular arrangement or matrix, which are fired out to hit an inked ribbon, which produces a pattern of dots on the paper. The greater the number of pins, the higher the quality of the print or graphics. The most common arrangements of pins are either 9 or 24. Dot-matrix printers are able to display both text and graphics and are able to print in colour. With colour dot-matrix printers, the ribbon is split into four colours: red, yellow, black and blue, and is moved relative to the print head into position for the required colour.

Dot-matrix printers are impact printers, which can transfer print through layers of paper. This means that they are able to print multi-part stationery. So if you want to print a multi-part sheet where, for example, the white topsheet goes to the customer, the yellow goes to accounts, the blue to the stores, then you will need to use a dot-matrix printer.

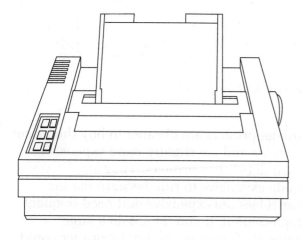

Figure 3.14 *A 24-pin dot-matrix printer*

Figure 3.15 *Printer ribbons are difficult to change and can make you look as though you've been to a fingerprinting session at the local police station*

Advantages and disadvantages of laser printers

If you look at each type of printer you can see that the laser printer is probably the best overall printer with the ink-jet printer a close second. There are some advantages and disadvantages of laser printers as we will see here.

Advantages of laser printers

1 Since they are page printers they are able to print a page at a time so this means they are very fast. The speed of a laser printer is typically about 8 ppm (pages per minute).
2 They produce high quality text and graphics. Typically laser printers print at 300 or 600 dpi (dots per inch). This improves the quality (called the resolution) of the image compared with other types of printer.
3 They are quiet in operation compared with dot-matrix printers, which are very noisy. The only sound laser printers make is the sound of the cooling fans and the paper moving.

4 Laser printers are equipped with paper trays for both the input and the output paper and this means that once the printer has been set up it does not need supervision.

Disadvantages of laser printers
1 Laser printers are more expensive than dot-matrix or ink-jet printers.
2 Consumables cost more. The toner cartridges are very expensive compared with printer ribbons or ink-jet cartridges. Toner cartridges can cost from £50 to £150, almost as much as a cheap dot-matrix printer.
3 They are quite large and can take up a lot of desk space.
4 They are quite complex, so the repair bills can be high.
5 Because they are non-impact printers, multi-part stationery cannot be used. With a dot-matrix printer, the impact can make marks on several sheets of paper at the same time. These thin sheets can then be sent to different departments within a company.
6 Laser printers are page printers, so they cannot be used with continuous stationery.

Graph plotters
Graph plotters enable accurate line diagrams to be produced on paper. They are ideal for plans, maps, line diagrams and three-dimensional drawings. Graph plotters use pens to produce images and different pens may be used containing different coloured inks. There are two types of graph plotter. The flat bed plotter is shown in Figure 3.16 and the drum plotter in Figure 3.17. The drum plotter has the advantage that very large drawings can be produced.

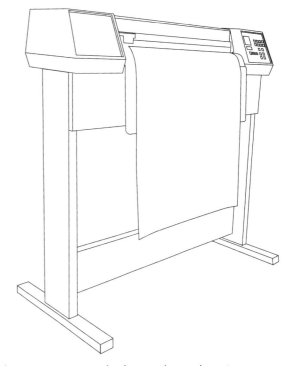

Figure 3.17 *A graph plotter (drum plotter)*

Voice output
Visually handicapped people find the spoken word from a computer invaluable. For instance, when they use special software with a wordprocessor they can hear on headphones each letter as it is typed and if they go to the start of the word then they can hear it.

Electrical signals
Sometimes the output from one computer system can simply be a series of electrical signals. This is the case if one computer is being used as a terminal and the work that is done on the terminal is sent as electrical

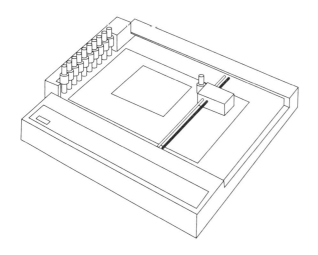

Figure 3.16 *A flat bed plotter*

signals to a main computer which is remote from the terminals.

Electrical signals can be output and used to control all kinds of devices, such as central heating systems, burglar alarms etc.

Robots

Electrical signals from a computer can be used to control a robot arm like the one shown in Figure 3.18. Robots are dealt with in Chapter 21.

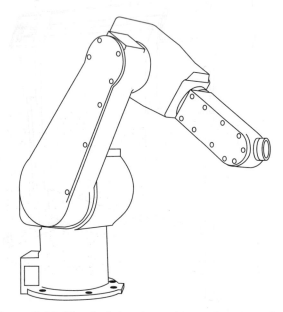

Figure 3.18 *Electrical signals can be used to control a robot arm*

TEST YOURSELF

Using the words in the list in the next column, copy out and complete sentences A to L underlining the words you have inserted. The words may be used once, more than once or not at all.

mouse   optical mark recognition   keyboard
laser   optical character reader   Kimball tags
joysticks   light pens   barcode readers   ink-jet
magnetic ink character recognition   retail

A The commonest input device, which comes with all computers is the _____.

B A _____ is used to move the pointer around the screen and to make selections.

C _____ are used primarily with games.

D _____ _____ are used with computer-aided-design packages to produce technical drawings on the screen.

E _____ _____ are used in supermarkets for recording the details of goods as they are passed over the laser scanner.

F Text may be read directly into a computer using a device called an _____ _____ _____.

G The method used by banks when inputting the details contained on cheques during the clearing process is called _____ _____ _____ _____.

H Optical mark readers are able to read the marks made on special forms. The process is called _____ _____ _____.

I The punched card was an old fashioned input device which can still be found in the form of _____ _____.

J EPOS and EFTPOS are systems that are used extensively in _____ outlets.

K The type of printer that produces the highest quality print and uses a toner cartridge is called a _____ printer.

L A cheaper printer, which squirts a jet of ink at the paper is called an _____ _____ printer.

1 A bathroom design company uses a computer to help plan new bathrooms. The company sends a salesperson out who measures up the bathroom and makes certain suggestion regarding the arrangement of the toilet, bath, basin, shower, etc. When the client is happy with the arrangement, the salesperson returns to the shop where the bathroom design is transferred to the screen. The client is then sent a three-dimensional diagram of what their bathroom will look like.

(a) Name a device, other than a keyboard, that the designer could use as an input device and say why it is suitable.

(b) A very accurate and high quality printout is needed for the installers to work from. Name an output device that could produce a high quality plan.

(c) What other tasks could the computer perform other than those already mentioned?

2 The following diagrams show a variety of input or output devices.

For each one:

(a) name it

(b) say how it is used

(c) give an application for it (e.g. you need to mention the type of job each is suited to).

3 A great many printers are now available, ranging from small slow devices to versatile fast printers. Describe various types of printer that are now in use, giving an indication of their comparative speeds and paying particular attention to:

(a) the different facilities that they provide

(b) typical applications for which they are appropriate.

(It is best to get your information for this question from recent copies of any computer magazine)

4 A friend has asked you for your advice on buying a suitable printer. Write down a list of questions that you would need to ask them, before advising them.

 INVESTIGATION

BETTERBUYS

Betterbuys is a small chain of food supermarkets. At present there are 20 shops scattered throughout Britain.

The present manual system at the checkout is as follows:

1 The customer brings their basket or trolley to the checkout.

2 The price of each item is on a ticket which is stuck onto the goods when they are placed on the shelves. The till operator keys in the price of each item, presses a key to tell the till to display the total when ready and keys in the amount of money the customer has paid. The till automatically calculates how much change should be given.

3 The stock is checked each day by a person with a stock list going around the shelves and counting the stock of each item.

Some of the problems with the existing system are:

1 Sometimes goods are brought to the till with no label on them. Looking them up takes time and angers the shoppers in the queue behind.

2 All the main competitors are now using EPOS systems, where an itemised bill is produced, which gives all the names of the goods, along with their prices.

3 Changing prices for special offers is difficult, since it is necessary to stick new price stickers over the existing labels.

4 Customers are often complaining that the supermarkets frequently run out of certain items such as bread.

Task 1

Visit a large supermarket (e.g. Tesco, Sainsbury, Asda, Safeway, etc.) which uses EPOS terminals. Produce a word processed report outlining the way in which EPOS terminals are used in the supermarket you have visited.

Task 2

Mr C Watts, the recently appointed managing director of Betterbuys, wants to know what the main advantages are in using EPOS terminals compared with the existing manual system. In a word processed document, explain what these advantages are. Are there any disadvantages to the supermarket or to the customers?

Task 3

It is eventually decided to go ahead with the EPOS system and you have been asked to produce a leaflet explaining how the system works and how it will be better for shoppers. This leaflet should be produced using wordprocessing or (better) desktop publishing software. This leaflet will be given to shoppers to help explain the new system.

INVESTIGATION

In this project you have to research stock control systems in different retail outlets. Don't restrict yourself to only food stores: all types of shops should be considered. You should aim to visit about three stores. Not all the stores you choose need to have a computerised system, since the object of the exercise is to look at all the various methods of stock control. Things you need to include are:

1 the importance the shop attaches to stock control

2 problems that each shop has with its systems

3 a survey of the various methods used

4 an explanation of how you have approached the task, along with reasons for doing it the way that you have done

5 a conclusion (i.e. a summary of what you have found out from your survey).

Your report should be typed and illustrated (you could use clip art) and you should try to obtain sample documents from the shops. Appropriate graphs could be produced, using a suitable package.

PROJECT ADVICE

How do I decide which input method to use?

Ask your teacher what devices are available at your school or college that could be used for inputting data.

If you are working to a tight budget then some input devices will be too expensive. For instance, the magnetic ink character recognition equipment used in banks costs hundreds of thousands of pounds. Keyboard input is the cheapest (all computers come with one) but you need to consider that someone will need to sit in front of a computer entering the data before the data can be used. You would need to consider the cost of this. In addition keyboard entry can introduce typing errors. If the input needs to be done quickly, then other methods should be considered.

See if your school has a barcode reader or an optical mark reader. If it has one of these see if the reader could be used as an input device for your system.

Remember that a good choice of input device is a good choice because all the other choices have been considered, but then rejected. In any documentation to your project you should say which other devices have been considered and why they have been rejected.

Sometimes you could use a combination of input methods, so a membership form could have a barcode which could be used to enter the membership number with the rest written in by hand.

Storing Data

Computers store data either in chips inside the main processor, in what is called memory (main store), or on other media such as magnetic disk, in what is called backing store.

The storage of data

The number of instructions and amount of data a computer can store in its memory is measured in **bytes**. One byte contains 8 bits (short for binary digits, 0 and 1). Computers work by using pulses of voltage which represent either 0 or 1. A low voltage pulse represents a 0 and a high voltage pulse a 1. In most cases, 8 bits are needed to store one character. So, a single character (letter, number or symbol on the keyboard) can be stored in one byte. We normally refer to storage capacities in terms of kilobytes (KB) or megabytes (MB).

1 KB = 1 kilobyte = 1024 bytes
1 MB = 1 048 576 bytes
1 GB = 1 gigabyte = 1000 MB

From this you can see that for each megabyte we could store 1 048 576 characters.

Memory (main store)

There are two types of memory or main store:

- read-only memory (ROM)
- random-access memory (RAM).

Memory (or main store) is the name given to the group of chips inside the processing unit where data is held temporarily whilst processing takes place. The data held in the memory is instantly available to the computer, unlike backing storage which has to be accessed on disk or tape. The memory

needed to run programs that use icons and graphics has increased enormously over the last few years. Even laser printers now have more memory than computers did only a few years ago (Figure 4.1).

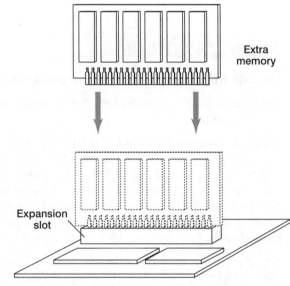

Figure 4.1 *Most computers have expansion slots for extra memory chips*

The memory is used to hold the following:

1 programs – these may be the operating system (programs which control the hardware) or applications programs (programs to do a particular task such as wordprocessing)
2 input data – this is put into the memory before processing
3 working area – this is used to store the data that is currently being processed
4 output data – this is put into the part of the store ready to be output to the printer.

Read-only memory (ROM)

ROM is held on a chip inside the processor and is used to hold data which cannot be changed by the user. Programs are stored on the ROM chips when a computer is manufactured. Usually, the data held on ROM will be the software that tells the computer how to load the operating system (called the boot program). Since data is permanently stored on ROM it will still stay stored even if the power is switched off. ROM is often referred to as non-volatile memory.

Random access memory (RAM)

RAM is again held on a chip but data in RAM is held only temporarily, which means that the data disappears when the power is switched off. For this reason, RAM is often called volatile memory. RAM is used to hold both data and programs during processing.

Magnetic media

Magnetic media storage devices include floppy disks and hard disks.

Floppy Disks

Floppy disks come in two main sizes, 3.5 inch and 5.25 inch. Although the smaller floppy disk is in a hard case the disk inside is floppy.

The smaller of the two disks actually stores more data since the data is packed closer together on the disk. Both disks store binary (a series of 0s and 1s) data as a magnetic pattern on the disk surface. The

anatomy of a 3.5 inch disk is shown in Figure 4.2. Most newer computers use the smaller disk, which has the advantages of being able to hold more data and is also less liable to damage. Both types of disks must be looked after and some things to avoid are illustrated in Figure 4.3.

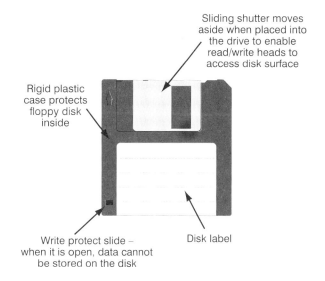

Figure 4.2 *The anatomy of a 3.5 inch floppy disk*

A typical 3.5 inch floppy disk holds 1.44 MB of data. Before data is stored on a disk, the disk needs to be formatted. This creates a magnetic map of the disk surface to enable the data to be either read from the disk or written onto the disk, quickly.

Figure 4.3 *How **not** to treat your floppy disks!*

Hard drives

Hard drives usually consist of several disks on a single spindle. Each disk surface is able to store data and this has the advantage that each surface can have its own read/write head as shown in Figure 4.4. This enables the read/write heads to operate simulta-neously, which means that the data can be transferred more quickly than by using a single larger disk. Hard disks are available in all sorts of sizes and bigger sizes are becoming available all the time. A typical personal computer will have a hard disk capacity of over 1000 MB (1 GB).

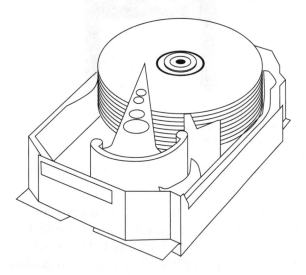

Figure 4.4 *The inside of a hard disk drive showing the arrangement of disks and read/write heads*

Magnetic tape

Large spools of tape are used by very large computer systems that need to hold huge amounts of data. They are not as common as they used to be. Tapes in cartridges as shown in Figure 4.5 are now becoming much more common. These look similar to audio cassettes, except they are larger. Their main use is for making backup (security) copies of hard disks. Backing up a hard disk is not feasible with floppy disks because of the number of disks needed and the time it would take. A 3.5 inch floppy disk can hold 1.44 MB of data and a large hard disk holds in excess of 1000 MB. A simple calculation

(1000/1.44) shows that to back up such a hard disk when it is full of data and programs you would need nearly 700 floppy disks and a large amount of time. Small tape drives are cheap and the tapes themselves are removable and cheap. Larger capacity tape drives use the same tapes but they have the ability to compress the data before it is stored.

Figure 4.5 *Data cartridges used to back up large hard disks can have capacities from 10 to 2100 MB*

Optical disks

CD-ROM drives

CD-ROM drives use the same technology as CD music disks and CD players. The data is stored on the disk digitally and a laser beam is used to read the data off the disk. Because light is used to read the disk, the data may be packed closely and the disk therefore has a huge capacity. CD-ROM drives are included in multimedia systems. Because of their huge storage capacities they are very useful for distributing software on a single disk where normally many floppy disks would be needed. CD-ROMs can be filled with clip art (pictures you can use in your documents), encyclopaedias, photographs and all sorts of reference material.

CD-ROMs are read-only disks, which means that you can read the data off the disk but not alter it or store new data.

Figure 4.6 shows the backing storage media, including a CD-ROM drive, used in a typical multimedia system. A typical CD holds around 600 MB of data.

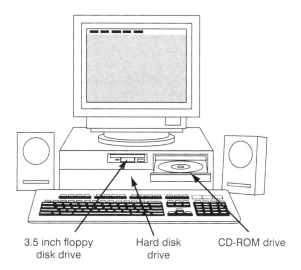

3.5 inch floppy disk drive   Hard disk drive   CD-ROM drive

Figure 4.6 *Backup storage devices for a multimedia system*

Comparison between hard disks and CD-ROMs

1 CD-ROMs are more portable than hard drives. Although you can get removable hard drives they are bulky and expensive.
2 CD-ROMs are easier to transfer from one computer to another.
3 It is faster to access material on a hard disk than on a CD-ROM.
4 Typically, CD-ROMs hold about 600 MB of data whereas hard disks can hold as much as 9000 MB on a PC.
5 The data on hard drives can be erased and new data stored on the drive. New data cannot be stored on a CD-ROM, nor can a CD-ROM be erased.

Uses for CD-ROMs

Typical uses for CD-ROM include the following.
1 New software can be supplied on a single CD-ROM, rather than on, say, 15 floppy disks. This makes the software much easier to install.
2 Encyclopaedias are now often supplied on CD-ROMs. The small amount of time it takes to search for the required

information on a CD-ROM encyclopaedia is nothing compared to the time it would take to search through many paper-based volumes.

Magneto-optical disk

Magneto-optical disks combine the technologies from both magnetic and optical drives. The operation of these disks is complex, but they can store data on the disk as well as reading it off the disk. These disks are ideal for mass storage (e.g. for very large databases) or for taking a backup copy of a hard disk.

TEST YOURSELF

Using the words in the list below, copy out and complete sentences A to I underlining the words you have inserted. The words may be used more than once.

character one byte kilobytes memory megabytes floppy CD-ROMs magnetic tape RAM ROM hard

A A bit is the smallest unit of storage and may be nought or _____.

B A group of 8 bits is called a _____.

C One byte is used to store one _____.

D Storage is usually measured in _____ or the larger unit _____.

E Data and program instructions currently being dealt with are held in _____.

F There are two types of storage: one retains data when the power is removed and is called _____; the other looses data when the power is turned off and is called _____.

G The commonest backing storage media are _____ disks and hard disks.

H Optical disks, called _____ are used in multimedia systems and can store around 600 megabytes of data.

I Because _____ disks store so much information, taking back-up copies using floppy disks takes too long and uses too many disks, so data is best transferred to _____ _____.

1 The words RAM and ROM are often used when computer memory is discussed.

  (a) What do the following abbreviations stand for?

   (i) RAM

   (ii) ROM.

  (b) What are the main differences between RAM and ROM?

  (c) Backing storage is storage outside the central processing unit. Why is backing storage needed?

2 A general practitioner's surgery contains a personal computer on which all the patients' records are stored. What type of backing storage would it be most likely to have?

3 Data may be stored by a computer either in memory (internal storage) or backing store (external storage). For each of the following, say whether they are used for internal or external storage.

   RAM   hard disk   3.5 inch floppy disk   ROM   magneto-optical drive
   CD-ROM   magnetic tape.

Software

What is software?

Software is the general name given to all the programs that can be run on computer hardware. There are two main categories of software: operating systems (systems software) and applications software.

Operating systems (systems software)

An operating system is a program that controls the hardware directly. For instance, it controls the operation of the disk drives so that you do not need to worry about how the data is stored on the disk and whether there is enough space to store further data. An operating system performs other functions such as controlling the operation of the printer. In other words, the operating system provides an interface between the user and the computer hardware. Figure 5.1 helps to explain this. Without an operating system, a computer would be useless so the first thing a computer looks for when it is switched on is the operating system. Once the operating system has been found, the computer loads it from disk.

An example of an operating system is MS-DOS (short for Microsoft Disk Operating System), which is used by most personal computers.

User interfaces

The user interface is what you see when you turn on the computer and it consists of the cursors, prompts, icons, menus, etc. which allow you to get something done by your computer. Ideally the user interface should be as easy to use as possible, so it should be obvious to someone who has never used the software before, what they have to do.

User interfaces may be:

1 command-driven
2 menu-driven

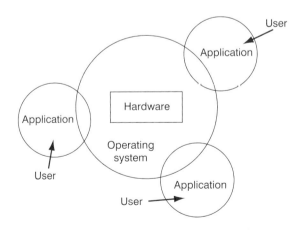

Figure 5.1 *The operating system acts as a 'shell' around the hardware. For programs to work, they need an operating system. For users to get useful work out of the computer they have to use applications programs and the operating system to communicate with the hardware*

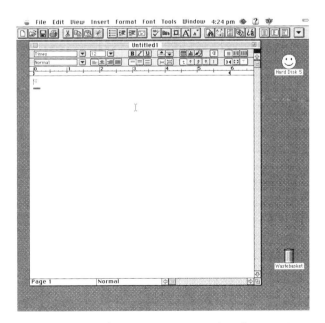

Figure 5.2 *Wordprocessing on a Macintosh computer*

3 graphical (commands referred to as a graphical user interface or GUI).

Command-driven interface

With a command-driven interface, you type in an instruction, which is usually abbreviated, in order to get something done. Command-driven user interfaces are not easy to use. If you are new to the software you have to remember many commands in order to be able to use the software quickly. Commands for different software packages are rarely the same, so people often get the commands mixed up. Some people, mainly those who are used to using them, prefer command-driven menus because they can be faster to use once you have learnt all the commands.

Menu-driven interface

This type of user interface produces a list of commands or options available within a program and the user can make a selection by using either a mouse or a keyboard. Both Microsoft Windows and Apple Macintosh programs are menu driven.

Graphical user interface

A graphical user interface, abbreviated as GUI, provides a way for the user to communicate with the computer through pictures called icons and through pull-down menus. Windows is an example of a GUI. Windows provides a common way of using programs, which makes them easier to learn. It also takes care of some common chores such as working with the printer and the disk drive.

Apple Macintosh computers were amongst the first to use a GUI (Figure 5.2).

Designing a user interface

To make a user interface as user friendly as possible it is necessary to take care when designing it and take into account the following.

- **Consistency** – each part of the software should behave in the same way as another making the program easier to learn and use.

- **Positioning of items on the screen** – icons, menus etc. should be consistent, again making software easier to learn and use.
- **Use of colour** – some colours are easier for the eye but others make things harder to see; colours should be chosen carefully.
- **Use of sound** – sound can be annoying to some people so it is best to make sound an option which a user can turn off if necessary.
- **Availability of help** – most software has on-line help which means that it is often not necessary to refer to a manual; the user simply accesses the help screen for a particular function or topic.

Utility programs

Utility programs are often provided as part of the operating system although they may be bought separately. A utility program is a program that performs a task which is often needed (e.g. a sort routine or providing a list of files).

Figure 5.3 *Some popular utility programs*
- *Norton Utilities is handy for recovering files that have been corrupted.*
- *Stacker effectively doubles the size of your hard disk capacity*
- *XTreeGold is file management software which copies groups of files quickly*

Tasks carried out by utility programs include:

- listing files on a disk
- deleting files
- copying files
- sending files to a printer
- sorting data
- repairing damaged files.

Other utility programs can be bought to supplement those supplied by the operating system. Some of these utilities, and what they do, are shown in Figure 5.3.

Translation programs

Translation programs are also part of the systems software and we will look at these in more detail later.

Applications software

Applications software is used to perform specific tasks. Three broad types of applications software are described below.

Applications packages

There are many different types of applications software, ranging from the wordprocessing packages used widely to write letters and reports, to specialist packages that are only used within one industry. Examples of applications packages are:

- wordprocessing software, such as Word and WordPerfect
- spreadsheet software, such as Lotus 1-2-3 and Excel
- database software, such as DBase.

Integrated software

Integrated software consists of a collection of application packages which share a common set of commands. Putting it simply, an integrated package may consist of a wordprocessor, spreadsheet, database and graphics package, all in one. One advantage of having such a package is that the commands are common throughout so it is easier to get used to than several different packages. Also, moving data from one program to another is easier. For instance, if you wanted to print out details of amounts outstanding from your database you could transfer the data to your wordprocessor. This would be easier to do with the integrated package than with the two separate programs.

Integrated packages tend to be much cheaper than separate packages and this is one main reason for their popularity.

There are some disadvantages. Integrated packages tend to be strong in one area and weak in others. For instance, a package may have a good database but a poor wordprocessor. If you want the best wordprocessor, database, etc. and are prepared to pay a higher price, then it is best to buy the separate packages.

Tailor made software

An organisation may write its own software or employ an outside company to write it. This tailormade software can be very expensive and is used only by companies with large computer departments, or where applications packages are not available.

General purpose packages

Much applications software is not specific to a particular type of business. For instance, a wordprocessing package can be used by any business. Some database packages such as dBase can be used to develop tailormade software. General purpose packages are very popular because their documentation (manuals, tutorials etc.) tends to be very good, the programs are well tested and they are relatively cheap.

Programming languages

A program is a set of instructions that the computer can understand. Since the computer can understand only binary code, i.e. a series of 1s and 0s, all computer languages must be eventually reduced to binary code and the way that this is done depends on the type of language being used. Humans can use different languages to communicate and computers are no different. There is a variety of computer languages and the one that is chosen for a particular job depends on the job that is being done.

Low-level languages

Low-level languages are languages that are easy for the computer to understand but more difficult for the programmer to understand. Assembly language and machine code are collectively called low-level languages.

Machine language (or machine code)

Machine language is the language directly understood by the machine. In other words, it consists of a series of 1s and 0s. All other languages must be translated into machine code before the instructions can be carried out unless the program is already written in machine code. Machine code is often machine specific, which means that one computer's machine code will not be

Figure 5.4

understood by a different type of computer. A program written in machine code needs no translation and is therefore very fast. A lot of games or simulation programs are written in machine code for this reason.

Assembly language

An assembly language is a language that uses simple instructions such as ADD, SUB and LDA and is used in preference to machine code, since it is easier for the programmer to use and to debug. Debug means removing any mistakes from the program. Once a program has been written in assembly language it then needs translating into machine code by software called an assembler before it can be understood by a computer.

High-level language

A high-level language is developed with the programmer in mind rather than the computer. Such languages have the advantage that they are not as machine dependent as machine codes or assembly language, so once a program has been written it can be used on different computers with very little alteration.

High-level language instructions are similar to English, which means that programming them is made easier. Instructions in BASIC, a high-level language include such commands as PRINT, GOTO and READ which are easy for us to understand.

Advantages of high-level languages
1 Simple instructions similar to English make high-level languages easy to understand.
2 It is easy to correct errors and test programs.
3 Programs written in high-level languages can be used on different makes of computer.

Some high-level languages have been developed with a particular problem in mind. Here are some along with their main uses.

• **COBOL** is used mainly for business data

processing because of its excellent file handling.

- **BASIC** is mainly used as a teaching language.
- **FORTRAN** is used mainly in scientific applications.
- **C++** is an increasingly popular language. It is very good for graphics and good for developing commercial software.
- **LOGO** is used primarily for teaching children about programming and using computers. Children are taught to write a series of instructions to control the movement of a 'turtle', which draws a line behind it on the screen.

Translation programs

Translation programs are part of the systems software and are used to convert the program commands into machine code. There are three types of translation programs: compilers, interpreters and assemblers.

Compilers and interpreters

Compilers and interpreters are both programs that change high-level language instructions into machine code, although the way they do this is different.

An **interpreter** takes each instruction in turn, converts it to machine code and then carries it out. It is rather like a person who cannot read French taking each word in a document in turn and then looking it up in

a dictionary, translating it and then moving on to the next word. If the document needs to be read at a later date then the same process will need to be performed.

A **compiler** is software that converts the whole of a program written in a high-level language into machine code in one go. Provided that there are no mistakes in the program, the complete program is converted to machine code. Suppose an original disk contains a program written in a high-level language (called the source code), then after compilation another disk with the program written in machine code will be produced (called the object code). Whenever the program needs to be run then the disk with the program converted to machine code is used. This is like a person translating the whole of the document from French to English in one go and then using the English version if the document needs to be read again. If a program needs to be altered at a later date, then the original source code will be altered and the program recompiled.

Assemblers

Assemblers translate assembly language instructions into machine code. This translation is easy because one instruction in assembly language usually corresponds to one machine code instruction.

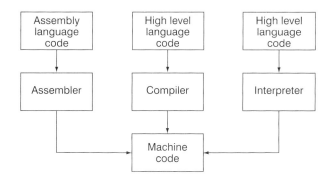

Figure 5.5 *The relationship between assemblers, compilers and interpreters*

Using the words in the list below, copy out and complete sentences A to G, underlining the words you have inserted. The words may be used more than once.

hardware   software   systems   operating
compilers   utility   assembler

A   Programs that may be run on the computer are called _____.

B   Software may be classed into two groups; _____ software and applications software.

C   Another name for the systems software is the _____ system.

D Without systems software the _____ would be useless.

E A program that performs such tasks as deleting or copying files is called a _____ program.

F Translation programs which convert high-level language instructions into machine code are of two types: interpreters or _____.

G A translation program used to convert a low-level language instruction into machine code is called an _____.

THINGS TO DO

1 Systems software can be divided into three types: the operating system, utility programs and translation programs.

(a) (i) Give the name of the system software that your computer uses.

(ii) Give two jobs performed by the operating system.

(b) Give two examples of a utility program and explain what each does.

(c) Two types of translation program are used for translating high-level languages into machine code. Explain the differences in the way that compilers and interpreters translate instructions.

(d) There is another type of program used to translate assembly language into machine code. Give the name of it.

(e) There are many high-level languages to choose from. Name two of them and for each give the type of job for which they are particularly suited.

2 This advertisement is for a computer system

```
┌─────────────────────────────────────────┐
│           MAGICIAN COMPUTER              │
│               Only £499                  │
│             Price includes:              │
│    Operating system • Utility Programs   │
│     BASIC interpreter • 'C' compiler     │
│                Assembler                 │
└─────────────────────────────────────────┘
```

(a) What does an operating system do?   (3 marks)

(b) Give two tasks that might be carried out by utility programs.   (1 mark)

(c) Interpreters and compilers both translate high-level computer programs so that the machine can use them. Describe the difference between these two types of translator.   (3 marks)

(d) The customer can also buy various applications packages. What is an applications package? Give an example of such a package, stating what it does.   (2 marks)

(SEG IS IT Spec)

3 The following is a list of types of general purpose packages:

wordprocessing   spreadsheet

database   graphics

desktop publishing.

Find out, using computer magazines to help you, which of the above categories each of the following packages falls into:

WordPerfect   dBASE

Lotus 1-2-3   Excel

CorelDraw!   Paradox

Harvard Graphics   PageMaker

4 LOGO is a computer program which may be used to control an arrow on the screen. When the arrow moves forward, it leaves a line on the screen. To control the movement of the arrow, commands are typed in. Some of the cmmands that may be used are as follows:

FORWARD distance   (in mm)

RIGHT angle   (in degrees)

LEFT angle   (in degrees)

For instance, the command FORWARD 20 would move the arrow forward 20 mm and the command RIGHT 30 would turn the arrow through an angle of 30° with the angle measured from the line drawn straight ahead from the arrow. Write down the instructions needed to draw the following shape.

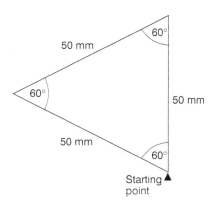

5 A DJ at the local nightclub has over a thousand CDs. Some of them are compilations (i.e. they have a variety of music on them from different artists). People often make requests for certain pieces of music and the DJ has great difficulty in finding which CD they are on. She would like to buy a small lap-top computer to hold the relevant information.

(a) She can either buy an existing package or have the software specially written.

   (i) Give two advantages of buying an existing package.

   (ii) Give two advantages of using specially written software.

(b) Given the choice, which of the two types of software would she be most likely to go for? Give reasons.

6 You have been made treasurer of your local athletics club. As the treasurer, you have to perform a variety of tasks and the members of the club have decided to buy a computer to help you. You have decided that it will be necessary to purchase the following software: wordprocessor, spreadsheet, database and graphics package.

(a) Explain what is meant by

   (i) an applications package

   (ii) an integrated package.

(b) Someone at the club has suggested that an integrated package is bought 'because it will be cheaper'. Look through recent computer magazines at the adverts for software and say whether you think they are right.

(c) Another member has suggested that 'we go along to night-school to learn how to write our own programs and therefore save the money'. It this a sensible suggestion? Give your comments.

6 *Finding the Best Hardware and Software*

Software evaluation

Suppose you are buying a piece of software, a wordprocessor for instance. How do you decide from the many available, which one to choose? One way would be to take the advice of 'experts'. You could read the reviews in computer magazines, where you can see useful comparisons between the various packages.

What do you do when you cannot find any reviews or if there is a new piece of software? One way is to see if the manufacturer can supply you with a demonstration disk with some (but not all) of the available features on it. Many of these demonstration programs are given away free with computer magazines. You should be able to get a feel for a program from such a disk.

To help you decide on a particular piece of software you could try answering the following questions:

1 Can you afford the software?
2 What features does the software provide that are more useful than features provided by similar competitive software?
3 In what areas is the software poorer than competitive software?
4 Is the price of the software justified by the benefits you are going to get when you use it?
5 Will it work on your equipment? Will you need to buy any additional hardware (e.g. more main memory) to make it work efficiently?
6 Do you have the operating system to run the software? For instance, some software needs the Windows operating system to enable it to work.
7 Is the documentation clear and easy to understand? If it isn't then you may be able to buy additional books and you will need to see what they are like.
8 If you have a network, is there a network version of the software?
9 Some software comes with a tutorial where the features of the software are explained. Help menus are usually available so it would be worth seeing what these are like.
10 Are regular upgrades (newer versions of the software) available and if so, how much will they cost?
11 Is there a help line which you can ring if you experience problems when running the software?
12 Is the software produced by a reputable company (if not then you could experience problems with bugs in the program or with viruses)?
13 If the software is a game or educational package and it uses sound, can the sound be switched off?

Deciding which computer hardware to buy

Before buying any hardware, it is necessary to look carefully at the job or problem to be solved. The software is then chosen and finally the hardware capable of running this software is chosen. It is no use buying a particular computer system and then finding out that it cannot run the software because the system is not powerful enough.

Once you have decided on a certain specification, you then have to decide which particular manufacturer to use. This decision is difficult and it is probably best to get advice from some experts. Reviews in the computer magazines compare similar machines and often give tables showing features and reliability.

It is always best to obtain the greatest amount of memory and the largest hard disk, together with the fastest processor that you can afford. New software tends to be written to exploit the capabilities of the latest machines. Expandability is very important so that a machine can have extra memory, a faster processor and more hard disk capacity added at a later stage.

Figure 6.1 *Today's computer is tomorrow's antique*

Questions to ask before you buy

1 Does the price in the advert include VAT? In most shops the price quoted will include VAT, but the prices in computer magazines usually need to have 17.5% VAT added to them.
2 Does the advertised price include all the parts you need? For instance if you were buying a printer you might expect the price to include the cable that connects the printer to your computer, but this usually has to be bought separately. Computer systems that don't include the monitor are frequently seen advertised. Sometimes, the photographs in advertisements include disk drives that are not included in the price.
3 Does the price include postage and packing charges and if not, how much are they?
4 Does the supplier guarantee delivery within a certain period? Waiting for late delivery can be very frustrating.
5 What warranty (guarantee) period is included in the price? Does the supplier repair the computer on site or do you have to return it to the supplier? This can be expensive if you have bought by mail order. Although the majority of warranties are for 12 months you can pay extra for insurance to extend the guarantee period.

Here are some important points when you are deciding on your specification.

1 Be clear about the specification that you require. For a personal computer you will need to decide on:
   (a) the type of processor – e.g. 486 DX4, Pentium, etc.
   (b) the clock speed – 66 MHz, 100 MHz, etc.
   (c) the storage capacity of the hard disk – 420 MB, 525 MB etc.
   (d) what type of monitor to use – VGA or SVGA (this choice affects the number of dots on the screen and the range of available colours). See the Glossary for a full description of VGA and SVGA.
   (e) the size of the main memory.
2 Make sure that you can expand the computer easily. Your needs may grow and your requirements may change. Remember that the computer you buy today can become rapidly out of date.
3 Although you may think that you do not need certain features try to look forward. Will you need them in the future?

1 Most people's favourite wordprocessor is the one they are most familiar with. You may have painstakingly worked your way through a manual doing all the exercises. You remember all the mistakes you have made and the difficulty of finding out how to correct them. You may even have lost work you spent ages typing in. Yes, it happens to everyone. It is therefore not surprising that we are reluctant to learn how to use a new, more up-to-date wordprocessor.

You have been asked to evaluate a wordprocessing package that you have not used before.

(a) Write a list of the features that you consider necessary. You need include only features that are not included with all wordprocessors.

(b) Look carefully at the software package. Pointing out its good and bad points, write a brief report comparing it with the wordprocessing package you are most familiar with.

2 Your teacher will give you a copy of a program which you will have not used before. Evaluate the package and write a report saying what you liked or disliked about it. Make sure you include a conclusion: is the package worth using?

3 You have been asked to evaluate a wordprocessing package for a computer column in your local newspaper. Choosing the wordprocessor that you are most familiar with, write your evaluation. The reader will want to know whether the package is worth buying. Have a look at the evaluations in the computer press and if possible try to find a review of the same package to compare it with yours. Quite often a star system is used for certain features such as ease of use, value for money, etc. Try to include this in your evaluation.

The editor has asked you to restrict your review to one hundred words. Also, she would like to see what the piece looks like as a column 30 characters or 7 cm wide.

Can you do both of these on your computer?

4 You have been asked to buy a laser printer to be used in a small office. What questions should you ask the users before you decide what make and model of printer should be chosen?

Collecting Your Data

The problems with college enrolments

Every year new students enrol on courses in colleges and each college needs to record the student details onto its computer system. Because the enrolments all happen at the same time, the main problem is with the time and the number of staff needed to enter the student details. Let's look at what details need to be recorded.

QUESTION

Write down a list of the details that a college would need to keep about each of its students. Show your list to a friend to see if you missed any items. It is a good idea to think about who is likely to use the details. Not everyone gets their fees paid for them. For example, some part-time students may have full-time jobs so they have to pay their own fees or their employers pay for them. So you need to distinguish between full- and part-time students.

Form design

In the student enrolment problem discussed above, students would have been asked to fill in a form. The students completed details that only they would know, such as names, dates of birth, addresses etc. and the college would add details such as course codes, fees, etc. The design of forms is very important, as most of the information from forms will be placed on a computer system.

We all have to fill in forms sooner or later. Some forms, if they have been carefully thought out and designed, are very good but others are appalling. Important information is left out while irrelevant information is included. Often, not enough space is left for the important information. How do we

design a good form? To do this, we should bear the following points in mind.

Have people who will be using the form been consulted?

Some users of the form should be asked about what the form should contain. Design of an important form is best not left to one person, who may forget to include something.

Headings

The title of the form should describe its use. To much information on a form will clutter its appearance.

Instructions

Instructions should be in a prominent position and should be clear. If they are not clear, then many forms will be returned with items missing or filled in incorrectly. For special types of forms, such as those used by optical mark readers like that shown in Figure 7.1, you have to remember that people may not have seen such a form before. It is therefore a good idea to include an example of the way to fill in the form on the form itself.

Layout

The layout should be simple and should follow a logical sequence. The items should be spaced out and the form should have an appropriate size.

Sections

Many forms have a part which is filled in by the subject and another part which is filled in by the person who distributed the form. Sometimes the part to be filled in by someone else says 'for official use only'. If

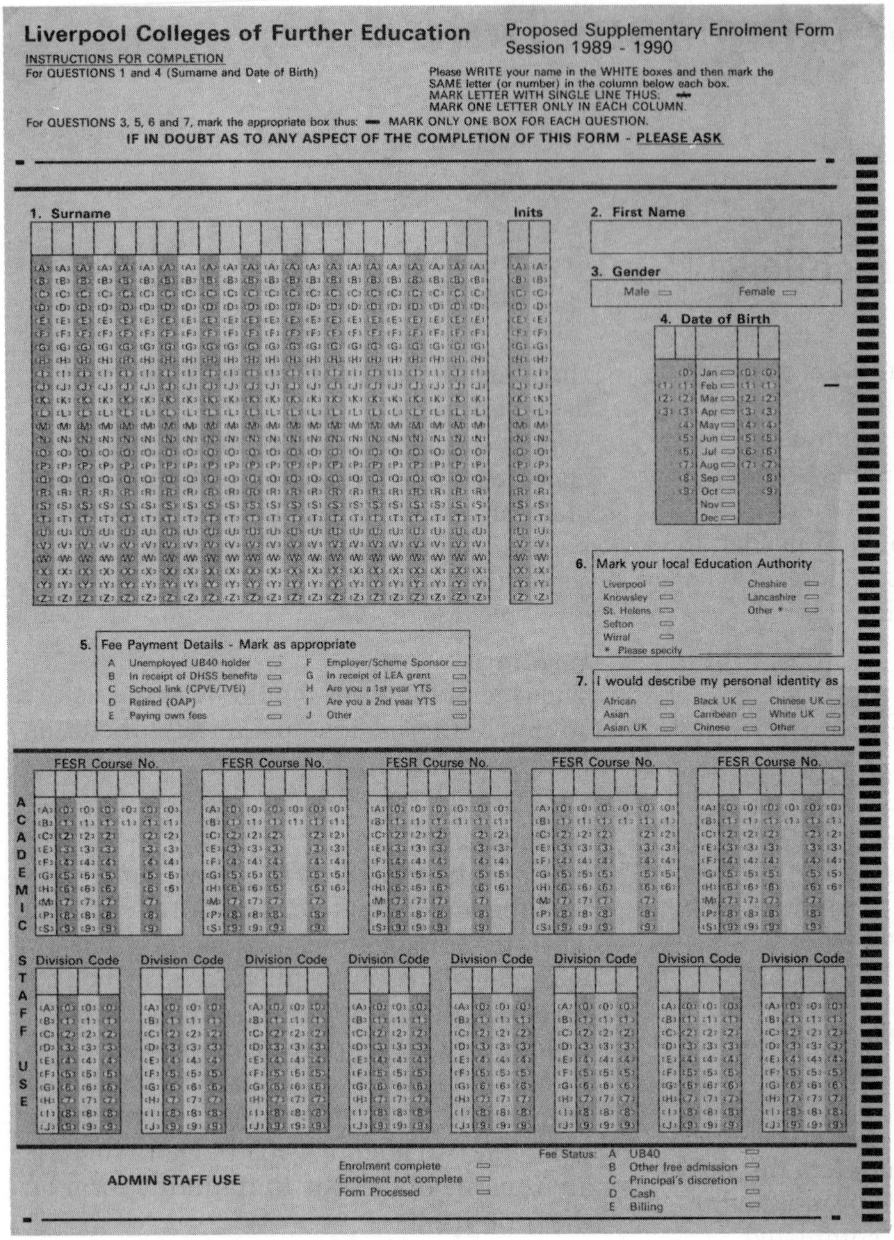

Figure 7.1 *Enrolment form to be filled in by a student writing and shading in boxes*

you design such a form, make sure that you place all the parts to be filled in by the subject together and make sure that it is clear which parts have to be completed.

Testing

It is always a good idea after you have designed a form to ask people to fill it in and then to ask them whether they found it easy to understand. Doing this will also give you an idea about whether you have left enough space for users to write in.

QUESTION

At the time of enrolment students are required to fill in an application form. Some of the form will be preprinted; part of it will be filled in by the student; and another part will be filled in by the tutor when the correct courses have been decided on. Using your answer to question 1 earlier in the chapter, design a form that could be used to hold details about the student and the courses they are following.

Coding data

In many instances codes are used to represent information, and these are useful provided we know how to interpret them. Why do we use codes? Well there are several reasons and these include the following.

1 Codes are quicker to type in, both initially and for subsequent searches.
2 Using codes reduces the sizes of the files, which in turn increases the speed of searches and any processes performed on the data.
3 Codes are often unique. For instance, if we gave each student a unique code number we could use this code number to search for a student's details. Using a surname for a search might reveal several students with the same name.

Designing codes

There are certain points to remember when designing a coding system. These are:

1 Codes should always be the same length. This is a useful check (called a validation check). If the code is too long or too short, then we know a mistake has been made.
2 Codes must be easy to use. People will not use them if they are to cumbersome.
3 Codes must not be too short. Although they are easier to type in if they are short, there is the possibility of running out of codes.

Codes may be used in a student enrolment system for the course details. When the code

INTRO TO WINDOWS(SUMMER)
HRS: 2   FEE: 45.00
Mode of Attendance 05

Figure 7.2 *Self-adhesive label containing course details. The barcode contains the code below it*

is either typed in or scanned in using a barcode reader, the computer can obtain the full details of the course, such as name of the course, hours of attendance, fee payable, etc., directly from the course file stored on disk by the computer.

Putting the details into the computer

Getting the information into a structure in which it can be processed by the computer is called **data capture**.

There are various methods that could be used and we will look at each one with its advantages and disadvantages.

Key to disk

The student enrolment form can be used as the source document and the details that it contains typed into the computer. The main problem with this is that it takes some time. Typing can also introduce many errors. This method may be used if the number of-students is small, but if, say, a college had about 8000 students then this could take too long.

QUESTION

You have been appointed to be in charge of student enrolments in a college with 5000 full-time and 6000 part-time students (11 000 altogether). All the students need to be enrolled in the first two weeks of term so that the college receives funding and the tutors can be given class lists.

(a) Using the enrolment form you have already designed, work out how many characters (letters, numbers, punctuation marks and spaces) there would be in the details supplied by the student and the tutor for an average student. Remember that you do not need to include the information that is preprinted on the form.

(b) Using the total obtained from part (a) and using the fact that a keyboard operator could input data at a rate of 50 characters per minute, find the total number of hours it would take for a single operator to key in all 11 000 student details using a keyboard.

(c) From your answer to part (b) report back to the college principal outlining the problems of using keyboard input for this number of students.

Alternative methods of data capture

The use of keyboard entry has been dismissed because of the time it takes. If more staff were to be employed then they would not be fully occupied for the rest of the year, so this method has been discounted. It would be ideal to have some way of the computer automatically reading data from the forms. Several direct input methods can be considered and these are detailed below.

Magnetic ink character recognition (MICR)

With MICR the reader would read characters written in magnetic ink. The problem here is that these characters are usually preprinted as on a cheque and only a small

amount of data is typed onto the form before processing. Because of the volume data that needs to be input, this method would be no quicker than typing the data normally. In addition, the equipment needed is very expensive so it is used only by banks for clearing cheques (Figure 7.3).

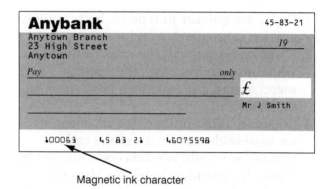

Figure 7.3 *A bank cheque*

Optical mark reading (OMR)

With OMR the student would make marks on a form similar to that shown in Figure 7.1. A machine called an optical mark reader is able to read the marks and convert them into characters in the student file. The instructions on such a form have to be made extremely clear, since many students will not have seen such a form before, although some may have come across this system with multiple choice answer sheets. One of the main problems with optical mark forms is that they have a high rejection rate (see Chapter 3). Optical mark readers are not too expensive to buy and the reading speeds are quite high although the forms are difficult to design. Nevertheless, the use of OMR is a distinct possibility for our enrolment system.

Barcode readers

Barcodes are really suitable only for preprinted information. You could not have barcode for a student's details since you would not know these in advance. Although barcodes can be printed by laser or ink-jet printers using special software (Figure 7.4), data would still have to be typed into a computer, so this would have no advantage over keying to disk. However, barcode readers are cheap and accurate. We could use them to solve part of the problem. Each course could have its own barcode so that when a student enrols, barcodes for each of their courses could be added to the form. With this method, student details such as name, address, date of birth etc. would still have to be keyed in, but for a student doing say six GCSEs, six barcodes could be used instead of all the course information being typed in.

First the bars must be related to the data that needs to be captured for each of the courses. Either an ink jet printer or a laser printer can then be used to print the barcodes. The barcodes for each course can then be read with a scanner and time in keying information can be saved.

Optical character recognition (OCR)

With OCR, the computer scans a page containing text, looks at each character in turn and compares it with characters it has previously stored. Although the reading speed is high, this method suffers from high rates of rejection and is really suitable only for reading material that has already been typed. For student enrolment the rejection rate would be high, so this method may be rejected.

The chosen method or methods

From the methods of data capture discussed, the college would decide on using either optical mark readers or on using an application form with some parts handwritten, and with sticky labels containing course information on the back. The two methods would have to be costed and it would be necessary to work out how long it would take to type the details into the computer. The college would have to bear in mind the high rejection rate with optical mark forms and the time taken to deal with rejected forms manually.

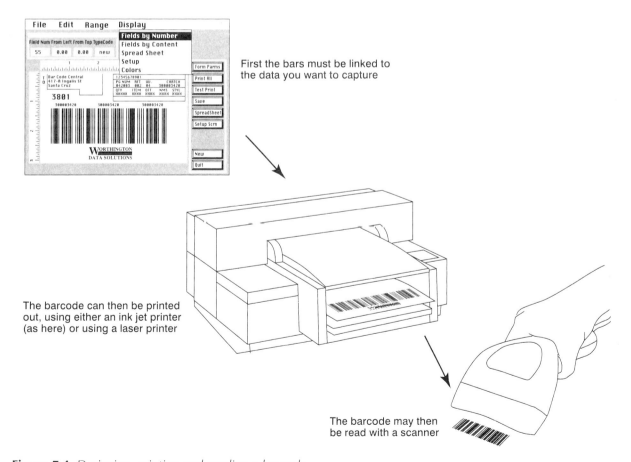

First the bars must be linked to the data you want to capture

The barcode can then be printed out, using either an ink jet printer (as here) or using a laser printer

The barcode may then be read with a scanner

Figure 7.4 *Designing, printing and reading a barcode*

Flood warning: an example of automatic data capture

Where there is low lying land near to a large river there is always a danger that, after prolonged heavy rain, the river could burst its banks and cause extensive flooding. Flooding, when it occurs, can cost insurance companies hundreds of thousands of pounds as householders put in claims for the damage caused by the water. If it is known that the river is likely to burst its banks, then remedial action may be taken to divert the water or use sand bags to build up the banks. The problem is that the river could burst its banks at any time of the day, and not just during working hours! It is not feasible for the river water level to be monitored by human staff. Instead sensors are used which are able to measure the water level. Radio links send the data from the sensors to the main computer and if there is a danger of the level rising, the emergency services can be alerted and a flood warning issued.

Automatic data capture using signals

Not all data has to be entered using a keyboard or by using special forms. Some data can be entered directly into a computer in the form of electronic signals. This data usually comes from sensors which produce a signal that depends on a physical property. For instance, components passing along a production line could break a beam of light as they pass. A sensor detects that the light is absent when each component passes and a signal is sent to a computer which enables the computer to count the components. Because a sensor receives data from the outside world it may be considered as an input device.

If local authorities wanted to know about the traffic flow along a certain road they used to employ people (usually students) to stand at the side of the road monitoring and recording the traffic flow. With the flow of traffic we now have on the roads, this would

not be feasible. Instead pressure sensors are used which record a pulse every time a vehicle passes over them. You may have seen these. They look like thick black wires running across the road and there is sometimes a box at the side of the road to house the recording system. A diagram of this arrangement is shown in Figure 7.5.

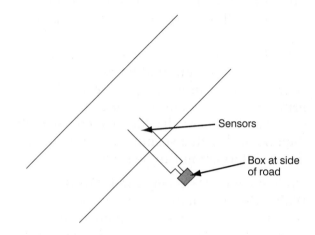

Figure 7.5 *System to monitor automatically traffic flow along a road*

Using sensors for control
Traffic light control

You may have been in a queue of traffic at the lights and thought that you would not get through before they changed to red, yet you managed to. This can happen because the lights were computer controlled. Sensors in the road detected that there was a build up of traffic on one side of the lights but not the other so they allowed the lights to stay green for longer on the side with the traffic build up. Traffic runs a lot smoother in many of our cities owing to the fact that sensors are continually monitoring the situation and relaying the data back to a central computer which can alter the sequencing of the lights.

Advantages of computer-controlled traffic lights over traditional traffic lights

1 Traditional traffic lights cannot cope with a large build-up on one side, since they have the same timed sequence regardless of the traffic flow.

2 If emergency vehicles need to take a certain route, then a computer controlled system can turn all the traffic lights along the route to green.

3 Faster flow through cities means less petrol wasted and less pollution.

4 The traffic light sequence will depend on the time of day. In the morning during the rush hour, the lights will be set to cope with the increased flow rates of traffic into a city and in the evening the pattern will be reversed.

Remote sensing

Remote sensing means sensing at a distance. The electronic signals from remote sensors can be sent through telephone wires or radio transmitters to a computer in another part of the country or even in another part of the world. Such a system is ideal for remote weather stations where temperature, pressure and wind speed can be detected at thousands of remote weather stations which send the data to a central computer.

As well as using remote sensing to detect when a river is likely to burst its banks, river authorities also use sensors to monitor the water quality in our rivers and to give a pollution alert should the quality change.

Turnaround documents

Problem

A gas board sends out bills for payment. The customers can pay the bill in various ways: they can take the bill and payment to the local gas showroom and pay, or write a cheque and put it in the post. There are other ways to pay but we will concentrate on the postal method. When a payment is made, it has to be linked to the customer and this is done using the customer reference number. Given that the reference number is 15 digits long a mistake could easily be typed in resulting in the wrong person being credited with the cheque.

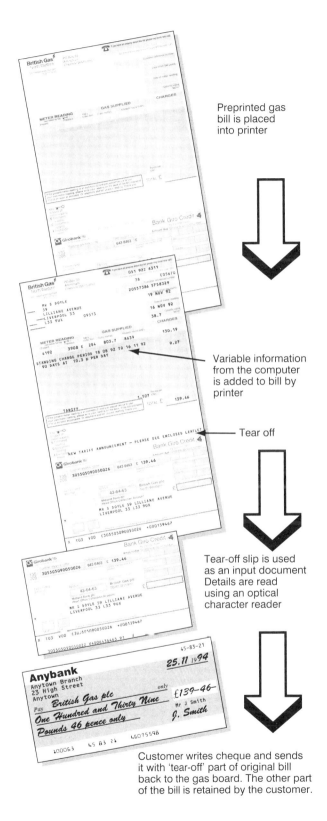

Preprinted gas bill is placed into printer

Variable information from the computer is added to bill by printer

Tear off

Tear-off slip is used as an input document Details are read using an optical character reader

Customer writes cheque and sends it with 'tear-off' part of original bill back to the gas board. The other part of the bill is retained by the customer.

Figure 7.6 *Using a turnaround document to record payment of a gas bill*

Solution

Turnaround documents are used by most companies who receive payment by post. Credit card companies, water companies and the electricity and gas boards, all use these documents.

Turnaround documents are documents produced by the computer which are subsequently used as input documents by the computer. For instance, an electricity or gas bill is such a document. These bills contain some preprinted information on them and the variable information is added by the computer such as name, address, number of units used etc. Figure 7.6 shows these processes.

The bills are sent to customers for payment. If a customer, for instance, writes a cheque to pay for electricity supply, this is sent back to the electricity board with part of the bill. This tear-off slip is used as an input document with an optical character reader. The computer then notes that the payment has been received. There has been no need to key in account or reference numbers.

TEST YOURSELF

Using the words in the list below, copy out and complete sentences A to G underlining the words you have inserted. The words may be used more than once.

MICR   key-to-disk   OMR   turnaround
sensors   data capture   laser   scanner

A Typing the details contained on a form into the computer using a keyboard and then storing the data on disk is called _____-_____-_____.

B _____ _____ is the name given to the process of getting the details into a form that can be processed by the computer.

C Banks use _____ for data capture because it is extremely quick and very difficult to forge.

D _____ involves using a form with boxes that are shaded in. Multiple choice answer sheets are an example of the use of this method.

E Barcode reading involves using a _____ _____ to read a number or code contained in the barcode.

F Data may also be captured using electric signals from _____.

G Documents which are output by the computer and are subsequently used for input into the system are called _____ documents.

THINGS TO DO

1 A motoring organisation uses a computer to work out routes for its members when they go on holiday in Britain.

The computer takes into account:
- date of travel
- type of route required (shortest, quickest, scenic, avoiding motorways)
- whether the car is towing a caravan
- the starting and finishing points
- the names of two places the route may go through.

Design a data capture form that could be sent to a member wanting to use this service.

(GCSE IS SEG HT Spec)

48

2 The form in Figure 7.7 has been poorly designed. The person who designed the form has asked you for your opinion.

(a) The purpose of the form is to capture the information so that the form can be used as a source document for keying into the computer system. Explain what is meant by

(i) data capture

(ii) source document.

(b) The form on the next page in Figure 7.8 shows the form after it has been handed to a parent for filling in. The blank parts to the form are then filled in by the headteacher. Examine the form carefully and say what is wrong with it.

(c) The head teacher has asked you to redesign the form. Redesign it paying attention to making sure that it is arranged in a logical order, that the spaces left are long enough to accommodate the information, and that there is a clearly marked section to be filled in only by the headteacher.

```
┌────────────────────────────────────────────┐
│ Application form for entry into the 6th form │
│                                              │
│  DOB_____  Pupil number_____ │
│                                              │
│  Name_____  Sex (M/F)_____    │
│                                              │
│  Address_____    │
│                                              │
│  _____     │
│                                              │
│  Postcode_____    │
│  GCSEs passed with grades                    │
│  (for 6th form applicants)_____    │
│                                              │
│  _____     │
│                                              │
│  Ethnicity_____  Religion_____    │
│                                              │
│  Home language_____     │
│                                              │
│  Mode of travel to school_____     │
│                                              │
│  Parents and contacts_____     │
│                                              │
│  _____     │
│                                              │
│  _____     │
│                                              │
│  Arrangements for lunch_____     │
│                                              │
│  _____     │
│                                              │
│  Form_____ Name of form teacher_____     │
│                                              │
│  Name and address of previous school_____   │
│                                              │
│  _____     │
│                                              │
│  Admission date_____     │
│                                              │
│  Hobbies_____     │
│                                              │
│  _____     │
│                                              │
│  Any special medical problems_____     │
│                                              │
│  _____     │
│                                              │
│  _____     │
└────────────────────────────────────────────┘
```

Figure 7.7 *A blank application form*

```
Application form for entry into the 6th form

DOB  26th March 79     Pupil number    ?

Name    Joanne Davis              Sex (M/F)____

Address    5 Cartbridge Lane,

           Crosby, Liverpool

Postcode    L23 67A
GCSEs passed with grades
(for 6th form applicants)    Mathematics (B)
English Language (C), English Literature (B), History (C),
Geography (C), Art (A), Biology (C), French (E)

Ethnicity    British        Religion    Christian

Home language    English

Mode of travel to school    School bus

Parents and contacts    Mother: Jackie Davis
5 Cartbridge Lane, Crosby, Liverpool  L23 67A


Arrangements for lunch    School Lunch


Form    ?   Name of form teacher    ?

Name and address of previous school_____
    Same school

Admission date    ?

Hobbies    Tennis, Swimming, Disco Dancing


Any special medical problems    Has Asthma.
Always needs to carry an inhaler. Has permission to
miss school games if she feels unwell.
```

Figure 7.8 *The application form after it has been completed by a parent but before the headteacher has added information*

3 The driver number on a driving licence codes the date of birth and sex of the driver in the following way:

   digits 1 to 5 – first five letters of surname

   digits 6 and 11 – year of birth

   digits 7 and 8 – month of birth (if female 50 is added)

   digits 9 and 10 – day of month of birth

   digits 12 and 13 – initials of first names or 9 if none.

(a) What information can you obtain from this coded driver number?
    KENNE409209SE9IB

(b) By referring to the driver licence code above, briefly explain the difference between data and information.

4 You are a junior systems analyst and you are working on an order processing and sales invoicing system. You have been instructed by your boss to draft the invoice/advice note which will be printed out by the computer. On this advice note will be a variety of items, along with a space,

called a data field, for the data to be inserted. You will need to decide how much space should be left for insertion of the data in each field. Your draft design should provide for the computer to print out the following data fields:

(i)   invoice address

(ii)   delivery address

(iii)   customer order number

(iv)   supplier order number

(v)   sales district code

(vi)   salesperson's code

(vii) invoice date

(viii) product code

(ix)   product description

(x)   quantity

(xi)   unit price

(xii) total price for each product

(xiii) carriage and packing charge

(xiv) invoice total.

(a) Use a full A4 page to show the design of this document and state any assumptions that you have made. For the purpose of simplicity we will ignore the VAT calculations, which would normally be present on such a form.

(b) In order to prepare a usable document, you would need to obtain further information about the 14 data fields shown above. What further information would you need?

The local newspaper has asked a record store to provide it with a list of the 10 top selling CDs each week. The record store uses only an ordinary till so there is no way of counting the sales, other than manually. To make things easier for the shop assistants, the shop manager would like to design a form which could be filled in each time a CD is sold.

(a) The manager comes up with the form shown in Figure 7.9 and has asked you for your comments.

Bearing in mind that the shop sells around 800 CDs each week, explain why you think the form would be unsuitable.

There are other problems with the form. Imagine that you are trying to record the sale of CDs using this form: can you think of any additional problems you might have? Explain these.

(b) Design an alternative form and explain how it could be used to obtain the chart.

Name of CD	Artist/Artists	Number sold

Figure 7.9 *Manager's suggested form for recording CD sales*

8 *Checking Data*

Reasons for errors

Computers can produce accurate results (e.g. payslips, bills, invoices etc.) only if the data put into them is accurate. In many systems an input document may be used and the data on this document is keyed in to the computer. In other systems, this document is input directly to the computer, thus avoiding the need for typing, which frequently introduces errors. Incorrect data can have serious or not so serious consequences! See Figure 8.1.

contained wrong information about a criminal record, that person could claim compensation.

How are errors avoided?
Verification

Let us look at a situation that we are probably all familiar with. Suppose that you go to buy goods at a catalogue-based shop such as Index or Argos. You would first look up the goods you required in the latest

Figure 8.1 *Incorrect data can have serious or not so serious consequences*

Consequences of errors

1 Customers become angry if they are sent bills that are too large and companies lose money if bills are too small.
2 Wrong decisions are made by the managers because the decisions are based on wrong information.
3 A company could be prosecuted under the Data Protection Act 1984 if the wrong information concerned a person and the consequences were that some loss was caused to that person. For instance if someone lost a job because a computer

catalogue and then fill in the order form, as shown in Figure 8.2. This order form would be taken to the point-of-sale terminal for the to operator type in the details provided on the form. This process is shown in Figure 8.3.

If you were to use an old catalogue, the catalogue number would no longer coincide with the goods required. If the operator keyed in this catalogue number then there would be two possibilities: it may no longer be a valid number or it may be the catalogue number corresponding to different goods.

CUSTOMER SELECTION FORM	**XYZ** CATALOGUE SHOP

Customer details (please fill in details in block capitals)

Name (Mr/Mrs/Miss)_____

Address _____

_____

Town _____

County_____ Postcode _____

Catalogue Number	Qty
–	
–	
–	
–	
–	
–	
–	
–	

The above details will be recorded by the XYZ Catalogue Shop for home delivery and future mailings by the XYZ Group of Companies and may be supplied to others for mailing purposes.
The above details need only be supplied in cases of home delivery.

Shop Use Only

INVOICE NUMBER ⬜⬜⬜⬜⬜⬜⬜⬜⬜ TOTAL VALUE ⬜⬜⬜⬜⬜⬜

PAYMENT METHOD	CASH 0	CHEQUE 1	VISA 2	ACCESS 3	CREDIT 4	LWD 5	XYZ 6	AMEX 7	GIFT V 8	DINERS 9

Figure 8.2 *Customer order form*

price appear on the screen and the operator would read this out to the customer who would confirm whether it was correct. A receipt would be issued. At the collection point. again the goods would be confirmed. This method of checking is called verification.

Verification also involves checking that what is on the input document is exactly the same as what is entered into the computer. Notice that this does not mean that it is correct, since the details on the form could be incorrect as in the example mentioned above.

One method of verification involves two people typing in the same data and only if the data is identical will it be accepted for further processing. The problem with this is

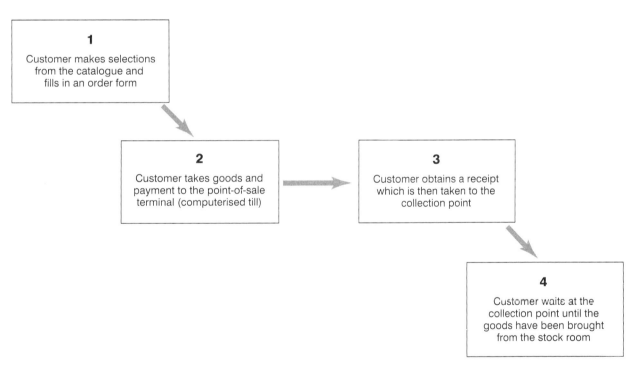

Figure 8.3 *Ordering goods at a catalogue shop*

Or, suppose the operator made a typing mistake with the catalogue number. In this case the catalogue number might not be valid or it might be a catalogue number for different goods.

In reality neither of these would cause a problem, since, once the catalogue number is keyed in, a description of the item and the

that two people need to be paid for doing the same job. Also, although it is unlikely, they may make identical errors so the mistake would go unnoticed. Another method involves carefully checking what has been typed in against what was on the original document, which is called proofreading.

Validation

Validation is the process of detecting any data that is inaccurate, incomplete or unreasonable. Validation is performed by a computer program. There are many ways that a computer can check to see whether the data is valid i.e. allowable.

Validation programs will usually perform some or all of the following types of checks.

Character type checks

Character checks make sure that the right type of characters have been entered. Such checks detect numbers where characters should have been entered and vice versa (Figure 8.4).

Figure 8.4

Range checks

Range checks are performed on numbers to make sure that they lie within a specified range. If, for instance, a program was dealing with retirement pensions and all the recipients of the pensions had to be 60 or over then, if a typist entered 18 instead of 81, a range check would detect this. However, only absurd data may be detected, so if the typist entered 69 instead of 96, then the range check would not detect this.

Hash totals

A hash total is a meaningless total. For instance, suppose we had the invoice shown in Figure 8.5. The item numbers could be added up and input separately. When the details of the invoice are keyed in, the meaningless total called the hash total is also keyed in. If the computer does not calculate this total then it means that not all the items on the invoice have been keyed in or that a mistake has occurred.

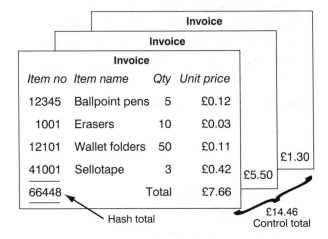

Figure 8.5 *Hash and control totals*

Control total

A control total is like a hash total except that the total has some meaning. For example the total of a batch of invoices has some meaning and could be used to check that all the invoices have been entered. Figure 8.5 shows a control total for three invoices.

Check digits

When any large number is input to a computer, either using a keyboard or using a direct input device such as a barcode reader, there is always a chance that there will be errors. These large numbers are important, since they could be product numbers in a supermarket, employee numbers for a payroll or account numbers in a bank; and it is essential that they are input correctly. For this reason an additional number is usually included, placed at the end of the original number. This additional number is called a check digit. This check digit is calculated from the other numbers.

When an account number is input the computer cuts off the last digit, which is the check digit. It then uses the rest of the numbers to recalculate the check digit, which it then compares with the removed digit. If the numbers are the same then the account number has been input correctly.

Calculating a check digit

If you look at any book, including this one, you will see a number on the back and inside the book, called the International Standard Book Number (ISBN for short). This is a unique number and is used to identify a particular book by book shops and libraries.

The computer calculates the check digit in the following way.

Suppose a book with the ISBN 0 09 172981 5 is input to a computer.

1 The computer removes the last number which is the check digit, so that it is left with

0 09 172981

2 We now have nine numbers. Working from the left hand side, the first number (i.e. 0) is multiplied by ten, the second number, also 0, is multiplied by nine, the third number, 9, is multiplied by eight and so on.

The total is then found:

$$0 \times 10 + 0 \times 9 + 9 \times 8 + 1 \times 7 + 7 \times 6 + 2 \times 5 + 9 \times 4 + 8 \times 3 + 1 \times 2 = 193$$

3 The total 193 is then divided by 11 (it is always divided by 11) and the remainder is noted. 11 divides into 193 17 times, with a remainder of 6.

4 The remainder is than taken from 11 to give the check digit:

$$11 - 6 = 5$$

which is the check digit.

5 The check digit will sometimes be 10, in which case an X is used.

This may seem quite a complicated procedure to follow, but the method has to be able to detect where digits have been swopped around. Remember that a computer can perform millions of calculations each second, so a little calculation like this is very straightforward.

Spelling checkers

Spelling checkers are used not just in word processing software. Any software where accurate text needs to be entered can have a spell checker facility.

Length checks

Sometimes a certain item of information is always of a certain length: it contains a set number of characters. A national insurance number such as YY232425A always has nine characters. If a national insurance number has more or fewer characters than this, then the length check will alert you to the fact that it has been entered incorrectly.

Types of error
Transcription errors

Transcription errors are caused by misreading or mistyping data. This may be caused by bad handwriting or confusing, for instance, the number 5 with the letter S or O with 0.

Transposition errors

Transposition errors occur when two digits or letters are swapped around. If you are typing in data at high speed you do not always look at the screen and it is very common to end up with say 'ot' instead of 'to' or 5124 instead of 5214. It is estimated that about 70% of all errors are transposition errors.

How to avoid errors

Despite all the checks that we can perform on the 'raw' data before it is accepted into a system some errors are bound to occur.

If data is entered into a system via a keyboard, then the simplest way of reducing errors is for the person who is entering the data to proof read it carefully against the original document. This simple method reduces the chances of the keyboard operator introducing new errors.

Checking for errors in a wordprocessed document

There are two different types of situation to consider:

1 The first situation is where the typist has been given a copy of a document or where a document is on an audio tape. All the typist has to do is to key in the document.
  In this situation the typist will be working at high speed (often in excess of 70 words per minute) and will be looking at the document or listening to the tape. They will not look at the keyboard and will only occasionally look at the screen. At such high speed, mistakes will not be noticed and these mistakes will not be corrected as the document is typed. Instead the typist can leave all the corrections until after the document is typed. Then the spell checking facility on their wordprocessor will be used. Secondly the typist will carefully proof read the document. Any mistakes spotted will be corrected and a copy is then printed out.

2 The second situation is where someone types a document personally. This is generally a much slower process, since the person has to think about the meaning of what is being typed. Also, such a person is likely to type more slowly than a fully trained typist. A slow typist will probably correct any typing mistakes as the text is typed. The document will still need spell checking and proof reading at the end. In some cases, an important document goes through a series of drafts. Each draft is printed out, corrected and the corrections keyed in until a final copy is obtained.

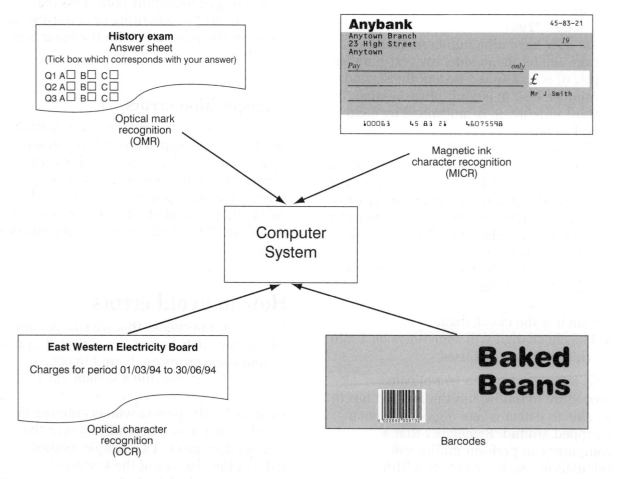

Figure 8.6 *Direct methods of data input reduce errors and are much quicker*

Automatic spell checking as you type

With newer programs like Word 6 and WordPerfect 6, errors such as 'ot' and 'teh' instead of 'to' and 'the' can be corrected automatically by the program.

Using direct input methods

To completely avoid keying in errors alternative methods of inputting the data are needed, rather than a keyboard. Some such methods include OCR (optical character recognition), OMR (optical mark recognition), MICR (magnetic ink character recognition) and barcode recognition. The input documents for these methods are shown in Figure 8.6. Although all of these methods can introduce errors, since they are so fast this leaves plenty of time for the errors to be corrected.

TEST YOURSELF

Read the chapter carefully. The following sentences are incomplete. Copy out and complete the sentences using the words in the list below.

transposition   range verification   check digit
proof reading   character type   validation
processing

A One method of _____ is to let two people type in the same data. Only if they make identical keystrokes will the data be accepted for _____.

B Another, more feasible method involves getting someone to check carefully what has been typed in. This is called _____ _____.

C _____ is performed by a computer program. Validation checks include the following; ___ _____ ____. To make sure the right type of character has been entered, _____ checks to make sure that the data lies within a certain range.

D When a large number is entered, mistakes often occur, so an extra number is added at the end which is calculated from the other numbers. This extra number is called a _____ _____.

E The commonest type of error is the _____ error which is caused by letters or numbers being typed in the wrong order.

THINGS TO DO

1 One type of error that could be made when data is typed into a computer system is a transcription error.

(a) A transcription error can be detected by a verification check. Explain how this check is carried out. (3 marks)

(b) A date can be validated as well as verified. A date is to be input in the form 25 APR 1994 (a two digit day, followed by a three letter month, followed by a four digit year). Describe the validation checks that could be carried out on dates of this form. (4 marks)

(SEG IS IT Spec)

2 The following list is a list of International Standard Book Numbers. Some of these numbers are correct and some are incorrect. Using the method shown in this chapter, check each of the following ISBNs and, showing your working out, say whether each is correct or not.

(a) 0 582 05179 6

(b) 0 582 05165 7

(c) 0 09 182438 9

3 Each of the items of data has been incorrectly typed. The following checks may be used on data:

- range check
- character type check
- check digit.

Copy and complete the following table, placing a tick if the error can be detected using the above checks and also stating which validation check is the most appropriate for the data.

Type of data	Item	Tick if error would be detected	Validation check
(a) Name	John Brwn		
(b) Sex (M or F)	N		
(c) Date of Birth (day/month/year)	310994		
(d) Examination subjects	English Physics		
(e) Exam fee paid	£2350		

SKILLS BUILDING

The following letter has been typed in using a wordprocessor. It has neither been proof read nor spell checked. Type in this document exactly as it appears here without correcting any of the errors that you spot.

> Mandy Low
> 15 Drakes Green
> Pembridge
> Herefordshire
> HR12 OBG
> 15th Jan 95
>
> Dear Sir
>
> As part of our GCSE Information Systems project we have to investagate a small busines which uses computers. We have recieved a questionare from our teacher which we would like you to fill in. I would also like to know if it would be posible for us to come to your organisation for about two hours in order to see how the computers are used. We have ot write a report on your use of computers and this will from part of our project.
>
> There are three members in my group and we have been given permission by our head teacher to attend your organisation at any time.
>
> Ihope you are able to hlep us and would be greatful of any assistance you can give.
>
> Yours faithfully
>
> Mandy Low

1 After typing in the letter exactly as it is shown, save it and then print a copy.

2 Load your document and remembering to place your cursor at the start of the page, run the spell checking facility on your wordprocessor.

3 Write down a list of the words the spell checker queried, the words that were incorrect and the words that were put in their place if applicable. You can do this in a table like this:

Words queried by spellchecker	Tick if correct cross if not	Words put in their place if incorrect

4 After the spelling has been checked, some of the words will be incorrect even though they are spelt correctly. To spot these it is necessary to read carefully through the document (called proof reading). Do this and write down the words that are incorrect and what needs to be put in their place.

5 Make all the necessary corrections on your document, save it and print a copy.

6 It is often a good idea to let someone else read a copy of your document as they might spot errors that you haven't found. Do this with a friend, make any corrections and, if necessary, print a final version.

 INVESTIGATION

You work part-time in a video rental shop which is part of a large chain of 100 shops scattered throughout the country. Each member is given a six figure membership number when they first join. The number needs to be this large because it is possible for a member to hire videos from any of the branches. The shops are having problems with members of staff keying in wrong membership numbers when hiring out videos. This has several consequences. When a membership number has been incorrectly keyed:

1 the shops have an incorrect record of who has hired the video

2 if that video is returned late, then letters are sent to the wrong member.

3 if the video is not returned at all, then the wrong member is invoiced for it.

All of this wastes time and loses customers.

The staff aren't all to blame because some customers forget their membership cards when renting but just quote their membership numbers instead.

Occasionally they may accidentally (or deliberately) quote the wrong number.

1 Figure 8.7 shows what the video membership card looks like. Would changing the design of the card help? If so, design a card using appropriate software and say why your design is better.

2 What procedures could be adopted by staff when videos are being hired out to reduce the problems mentioned above? You need to consider both verification and validation. It is best to consider various options to start with and then to chose a combination of the best ones.

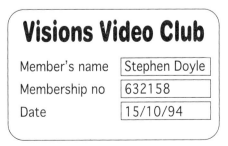

Figure 8.7 *Visions video membership card*

How Data is Stored

Databases

A database is an organised collection of information or data. Putting information into a computer database gives you far more flexibility in organising, displaying and printing that information.

The parts of a database

Files

Think of a box of filing cards like those sometimes used in libraries. A computer's equivalent of the complete box is a file. The computer's file is usually stored on a disk, which may be optical or magnetic.

Records

Within the library card box are the individual cards, each of which contains information about one book. In a computer database, the cards are known as records and most databases will display one record on the screen at a time, just as if you were browsing through the cards in a card box.

Fields

On each card will be a number of different items of information: a library card might list the title, author, publisher and ISBN (a unique number for a particular book.

Each item of information on the computer record is known as a field, and it consists of two parts: the field name and the field data. The field names are the words 'Title', 'Author' or 'Publisher'. They are the same on each record and indicate what the field data represents. Figure 9.1 shows the relationship between fields, records and files.

A card box filing system

On a card in a card box you can squeeze extra information in by writing smaller, or by writing on the back of the card. This is not possible with the computer equivalent.

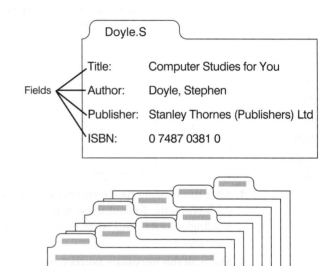

Figure 9.1 *The relationship between fields, records and files*

With a database, one of the first things you have to do is to specify the size and design of the record screen. You need to consider how you want the information to be arranged on the record and how long the data for each field will be. It is no good specifying an author field to allow up to 10 characters when you have several books by an author with a surname such as Forbes-Hamilton in the library.

You could of course go to the other extreme and specify a field length of 30 characters for names of authors. The problem here is that larger fields will take up more space on your floppy or hard disk. Another problem is that longer files take longer to process. If you have 2000 members or customers in your database, with a maximum surname length of 16 characters, then the surnames alone will 32 000 bytes on your disk. If you have allowed 30 characters for each surname, though, you have probably reserved 60 000 bytes , wasting 28 000 bytes in blank space!

As with most things, the best answer is a compromise. You should try to design your fields to cope with the largest entry you can imagine making, without reserving unnecessary disk space by over-specifying. You may find it worthwhile abbreviating the longest entries, if the overwhelming majority are shorter.

Record design

Modern databases give you freedom to design your own records. They give you an empty screen on which you can add the field names, fields and other background text such as the title. On some databases you can even put boxes around headings and even change the colour of the text.

With some databases it is very hard, or in some cases impossible, to change the structure of a record once it has been designed. So if your database is like this then you need to give a great deal of thought to the structure: it might be an idea to draw the structure out on paper first.

Some databases require you to create a different type of field for different information. You usually have to specify the type of data to go into the field. This can be:

1 numeric, which means only containing numbers. Make sure that a number does not have any starting zeros or dashes (e.g. a telephone number 0181-888-3456)
2 character, which means that numbers, letters and other symbols can be entered.
3 date, which means that the date is entered like this: 09/10/96.
4 logical, which allows Y/N (for yes/no) or T/F (for true/false).

As well as selecting the field names and the type of data to be entered some of the more sophisticated databases allow you to specify some validation checks to the field.

Figure 9.2 shows the template for the design of the database structure. The information for the first field has been filled in.

Key fields

A key field is a field that may be used to search a file. It is always useful to have one field which is unique to a particular record. For example, each pupil starting at a school will be given an admissions number. This is a number that no-one else will have and so it is unique to a particular pupil.

With the library system, the key field would be a number given to the book when

Num	Field name	Field type	Width	Dec	Index
1	ADD-PROP	Character	50		N
2	AREA				
3	TOWN				
4	POSTCODE				
5	TYPE				
6	NO-BEDS				
7	RECEIPT				
8	GARDEN				
9	GARAGE				
10	FREEHOLD				
11	PRICE				
12	DOM				
13	PROP-AGE				
14	OWNER				
15	TELEPHONE				

Figure 9.2 *Template for the design of the structure. Only the first line has been filled in*

QUESTION

Figure 9.2 shows a database structure for a database to be used by an estate agency. A database package is to be used to store the details of all the properties that the agency has on offer. Copy out the table and fill it in with appropriate field types and widths. The column headed Dec., is used to specify how many decimal places there are in the numeric field so you need to fill this in only if the field type is numeric. In the Index column you can just put N for no for all the fields.

it is bought by the library. The international standard book number would distinguish between different books: it could not be used to distinguish between copies of the same book and therefore would not be unique.

QUESTION

Databases can use any field in order to perform a search.

(a) Why should we not to use the pupil's surname as the key field?

(b) The school secretary says that there are only 1000 pupils in the school so we do not need an admission number of more than four characters. Do you agree? Explain your answer.

(c) A letter needs to be sent to a pupil who has an unreported absence from school of over a week. The teacher knows the name of the pupil but not the admissions number. What other fields could be used to perform this search?

Personnel file

Employee Number:	1473
Surname:	Doyle
Christian:	Jane
Date of birth:	15/01/54
Job title:	Systems analyst

Payroll file

Employee Number:	1473
Surname:	Doyle
Christian:	Jane
Date of birth:	15/01/54
Salary:	£22 000

Department file

Employee Number:	1473
Surname:	Doyle
Christian:	Jane
Experience:	15 years

Figure 9.3 *Data duplication with manual systems*

Manual filing systems

Figure 9.3 shows three records from three different files kept by departments in a company. As you can see, some of the data is the same on each file. This is called data duplication and is one of the main problems with manual filing systems. Data duplication means that more space is taken up by the files and more work is needed to retrieve the information.

The main problems arise in the following situations:

1 We may need to obtain information that is held on several files. Suppose we wanted to find out the names of systems analysts, with less than 16 years experience and who earn over £20 000 per year. We would need to use all three files, which are held by three different departments.

2 Also, because the data is not shared, a change in information, such as a change in surname because Jane got married, would cause three files to be updated.

3 If two people need to look at information on the same file at the same time then it would be necessary to photocopy the information, which would be time consuming and wasteful.

4 If a file is put back into the wrong place then finding it again can prove an awesome task (Figure 9.4).

Figure 9.4 *The file for Adams was in the W's!*

Computerised databases

Advantages

The main advantages of a computerised database are:

1 It is usually necessary to store the information only once, since most database software allows you to access information from several files.
2 The files can be linked together, which means that if you update one of the files, then all the other files that depend on the same information will automatically be updated. Not all databases are able to do this but those that can are called relational databases.
3 If you find that the record structure needs changing after you have put a great deal of data into the database, then this is easily done. To do this manually would be impossible.
4 Access to the information is rapid and there is less likelihood of the data becoming lost.
5 Validation checks may be made on the data as it is being entered into the database which means that there will be fewer errors in the data.

Disadvantages

The main disadvantages of a computerised database are:

1 If the computer broke down, you would not be able to access the details.
2 It is easy to copy computer files, so sensitive data should be protected by passwords.
3 Training is needed to use the system and this takes time and costs money.

File organisation

There are several methods you can use to organise files.

Serial files

With a serial file, the records do not follow each other in any particular order, so if another record needs to be added it can just be added onto the end of the file.

Sequential files

Sequential files are like serial files except that the records are held in a certain sequence. For instance you might decide to order the pupil file in admission number sequence.

Random files

Random files have to be stored on disk and, as the name suggests, they are not stored in any order on the disk surface. The disk operating system (the programs that control the storage on the disk), keeps a map of the disk surface and using this map the read/write heads can go straight to the data. In this way the data is found without the whole disk having to be read. Random access allows data stored on disk to be found extremely quickly.

Methods of accessing files

Serial access

To read a serial file, a computer has to read each record until it reaches the one required.

Sequential access

With sequential access the records are in order, so if just one record is required then the method is slow but if all the records are required then it is very fast.

Direct access

With direct access files, it is possible to go directly to a record without having to look at any other records first. You can access both sequential and random access files directly.

Types of file

There are various types of file.

Master files

A master file is the most important file since it is the most complete and up-to-date version of a file, such as a file on all the pupils in a school or a file containing all the personnel details of staff in a school. If a master file is lost or damaged and it is the only copy, the whole system will break down.

Transaction files

Transaction files are used to hold temporary data which is used to update the master file. A transaction is a piece of business, and hence the name transaction file.

Transactions can occur in any order, so it is necessary to sort a transaction file into the same order as the master file before it is used to update the master file.

Backup or security files

Backup copies are copies of files kept in case the original is damaged or lost and cannot be used. Because of the importance of the master file, backup copies of it should be taken at regular intervals in case the file is stolen, lost, damaged or corrupted. Looking after your disks will not be enough, so you should always keep backup copies of all your important data, especially project work such as IT tasks and system tasks.

The grandfather-father-son principle

There is always a slight chance that the data contained on a master file may be destroyed. It could be destroyed by an inexperienced user, a power failure, fire or even theft. For a large company, the loss of vital data could prove disastrous. But using the **grandfather-father-son principle** it is possible to recreate the master file if it is lost.

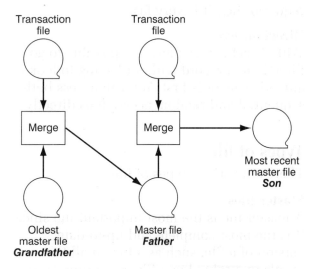

All these files are kept so that if one or more of the files are lost they can be recreated

Figure 9.5 *The grandfather-father-son principle, often used for file security*

The principle works like this. Basically, three generations of file are kept. The oldest master file is called the **grandfather** file and it is kept with its transaction file. These two files are used to produce a new master file called the **father file** which, with its transaction file, is used to create the most up-to-date file, called the **son** file. The process is repeated and the son becomes the father and the father becomes the grandfather and so on. Only three generations are needed and the other files may be re-used. Usually this system, sometimes called the ancestral file system, is used for tapes, although it could also be used for disks. Figure 9.5 summarises the principle.

QUESTION

Backup copies should always be taken at regular intervals.

(a) What is meant by a backup copy?

(b) Some programs such as databases and wordprocessors automatically take backup copies. Your friend says 'my wordprocessor takes backup copies so I don't need to worry'.

Explain what is wrong with her argument.

(c) John has a disk box in which he keeps all his disks. The box is labelled with his name, form, address and phone number. He realises that data can be lost so in his disk box he also keeps his backup copies. Is he doing all he can to keep his data safe? Explain.

Fixed and variable length fields

A fixed length field is one where the length of the field has been decided in advance. So if we decide that the field for surnames is to be 30 characters long, then even if the surname was only five characters long, like Jones, then the field would still take up 30 characters. We specify how long each field is going to be when we set up the structure of a database. Some fields, such as date or logical fields, have a length already set by

Fixed length fields

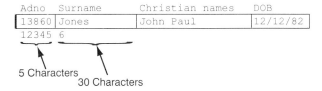

Figure 9.6 *Finding the start of a field with fixed length fields is easy*

the database we are using. If all the fields in a record are of a fixed length, then the size of the record itself will be a fixed length. For instance, if the record has the structure shown in Figure 9.6, we can calculate the length of the record as follows.

If the admission number is always five digits long, then the surname will start six characters from the start of the record and this is extremely useful when a computer is processing a file.

Variable length fields take up only as much space as the data requires. So, if a person's surname was Jones then this would take up the space occupied by five characters. Hence, with this method, there is no wasted space. With variable length records there is a special character used to separate the fields and to find a particular record the computer has to read through all the characters, counting the separators until it reaches the required record.

Variable length fields

Figure 9.7 *Variable length fields do not waste as much space but it is harder to find the fields*

Common file processes

The beauty of any computerised filing system is the ease with which sorts, searches, merges and updates may be performed. With manual filing systems these tasks are performed only with great difficulty.

File updating

File updating involves bringing a file up-to-date with any changes that have occurred since it was last updated. There are various processes that can take place during updating.

Insertions

Suppose we had a file containing the details of pupils in a school. A new pupil may have joined the school and so that pupil's details will need to be added to the file.

Deletions

A pupil could have moved to a new school so that pupil's details will need to be removed (deleted) from the file.

Amendments

A pupil has moved house so the address field needs changing. This is called amending the details.

File manipulation

The common file manipulations are sorting and merging.

Sorting

Often a field needs to be sorted into a particular order. For instance we may need a list of all the pupils in the school arranged in alphabetical order. It is also possible to sort according to several fields. So we could produce a list of all the pupils arranged in year order, with the list for each year arranged in alphabetical order.

Merging

Sometimes we want to combine the contents of two files to form a single file. The process of combining the files is called merging. If the two files to be merged are on magnetic tape, then we must sort the tapes into order before merging them. The new tape file produced will also be in order.

Merging is very useful if we want to divide the work. For instance, if a school wanted to convert its manual files for 1500 pupils, then to do this quickly, it may decide to split the work of inputting the details into the database. In effect two separate databases would be created with the same structure. These could then be merged to produce the complete database. In this way one person might type half the data and someone could else type the other half.

File interrogation

Interrogation involves getting information from a file. Fields are selected and the computer then searches through the records, finding all the records with matches on the field or fields being used for the search. A report (printout) is then produced which has either all the records found or only certain fields of those records found.

Data analysis

Some databases allow the data to be analysed in some way once it has been entered. For instance, you can produce bar charts, pie charts and line graphs using selected fields from the database. Tables can also be produced using fields from several different files.

TEST YOURSELF

Using the words in the list below, copy out and complete sentences A to J underlining the words you have inserted. The words may be used more than once.

master records   database   duplication   security
grandfather   files   fields   structure
transaction   son

A An organised collection of data is called a
_____.

B A database usually consists of many _____ which may be linked together.

C Files consist of a series of _____, each one about a certain company, person or item.

D Within each record we have _____ such as name, address, date of birth etc.

E When designing a database on a computer you have to specify the _____ of a record by telling the program what fields are needed, the type of each field and the length of each field.

F There are many problems with manual filing systems. Data _____ means that the same data is stored several times on different files.

G A _____ file is the complete, up-to-date version of a file on a certain subject.

H Master files are kept up to date with changes using a _____ file.

I Backup files are always kept for _____ reasons.

J So that a master file can be recreated if it is destroyed, the _____-father-_____ principle is used.

THINGS TO DO

1 Your are responsible for updating a file which contains details of all the members of a sports club. Copy out and label the following changes to be made at the end of one month as I, D or M according to whether they are insertions, deletions or amendments.

    Change   Type of update

(a) Change of address

(b) Resigned from the club

(c) New member

(d) Member changed her name through marriage

(e) Changed from annual member to life member

(f) Member died suddenly

(g) Previous member has re-joined

(h) Member resigned through ill health

(i) Member's telephone number has changed

(j) Member has emigrated to Australia

2 A school keeps information on each of its pupils and part of the information contained on the computer file in shown below.

Admission number	Surname	Christian name	Date of birth	Tutor initials
2312	Doyle	Stephen	19/12/84	KF
2344	Kendrick	Graham	23/06/85	PK
2367	Smith	Julie	12/09/87	HT
2380	Jones	Susan	09/01/86	BG
2381	Jackson	Joan	01/01/86	JS

(a) How many records are shown?

(b) How many fields does each record have?

(c) In all computer database systems there is a unique field.

    (i) Which is the unique field in this section of the file?

    (ii) Why is it important to have a unique field?

(d) Only part of the complete file is shown. Name two other fields that could be added to this file and give reasons for their inclusion.

You frequently need to merge (i.e. combine) the contents of two files. Type in the following letter and then save it using the name SMO1.

Grange Hill Comprehensive School
Shawfield Road
Grange Hill
London
NW10 4AA
Telephone: 0181-220-2300
Today's date

Dear Parent,

I regret to inform you that your daughter has been found smoking in school and I am concerned that you should know. Apart from the bad example that this is giving to the other children, he/she is unwise to risk attachment to a habit which is widely regarded as both anti social and damaging to health.

Yours sincerely

Mrs A Johnston (Headteacher)

The following paragraph is often incorporated into other letters when pupils have been found swearing, smoking, fighting, etc. This paragraph is referred to as DET1. Type this paragraph into your wordprocessor and save it with the filename DET1.

> I should be grateful for your support in discouraging such behaviour by reinforcing the school's punishment of a school detention on Wednesday until 5 p.m.

Julie Hill has been found smoking so the standard smoking letter is to be sent to her mother Mrs A Hill. Load in the letter SMO1 and insert the variable details such as her mother's name and Julie's as well as today's date. The headteacher decides to place Julie on school detention, so she has asked you to incorporate (i.e. merge) the detention paragraph DET1 into SMO1. You should perform this task whilst in the SMO1 letter by inserting a file and not by retyping.

Sid's Motors is a used car dealer which keeps a stock of around 300 used cars. Sid, the garage's proprietor, has decided to computerise the records held about each car.

1 Look at the adverts in your local papers or a specialist publication such as 'Autotrader' for adverts for used cars. These adverts will give you ideas about what people look for when they are buying a used car. Here are a few to start you off.

    Make: Ford

    Model: Probe

    Engine Size: 2.5 litres

    Mileage: 13 000

    etc.

Write a list of the details you need to record for each car. Put them into a suitable order, with what you consider are the most important features of the car at the top of the list.

2 Now design a form which can be filled in each time a car is added to the stock. Compare it with a friend's form to see if you have missed anything important. It is important to make sure that enough space is left for the details to be inserted.

3 Sid is pleased with your effort and has asked you if the details on the form could be put into a database.

(a) What advantages does a database have over the cards arranged in a filing cabinet?

(b) Sid often receives telephone calls asking whether he has a particular make of car. How could the database be used to help him?

Develop a suite of letters and standard paragraphs that your form teacher could use to send to parents. Ask your form teacher what kind of details should be included. Your form teacher is fairly new to computers and so will need some documentation as to how to use the system you have developed.

10

Types of Computer Operation

Life in the fast lane

John is a high flying marketing executive for a leading brand of soft drink. John works hard and has trouble fitting his schedule into 24 hours. John has to travel urgently to Frankfurt to solve a problem that the company is having with a new rival brand of cola. He needs to book on the earliest flight he can get to Frankfurt. He first tries to ring British Airways direct, but the number is engaged. He tries the German airline, Lufthansa but Lufthansa is also engaged. He thinks and then decides to drive to his local travel agent. After waiting in a queue for 20 minutes (it is January and the shop is packed with people booking their summer holidays) he gets to talk to one of the assistants.

The travel agency uses an on-line enquiry and booking service, where a terminal is connected to the main processor via a telecommunications link. A terminal is simply a VDU and keyboard or a VDU, keyboard and a processor with some backing store. The former is called a dumb terminal because it relies for its intelligence on the main processor and the latter is called a smart terminal because it has its own processor. The telecommunications link could be a telephone line or could be a microwave link or a radio link. John remembers seeing a documentary on India and he remembers it saying that British Airways deals with all bookings and enquiries from India, using a system of terminals linked internationally.

The assistant uses a terminal which has an opening screen similar to that shown in Figure 10.1. She uses the terminal to dial automatically the number of the British Airways computer. The screen changes and the terminal asks her for the travel agent's

QUESTIONS

1 Years ago the travel agent's assistant would have had to ring each airline in the same way as John and would encounter the same problems of the phone being engaged.

  (a) What advantage is there in using a terminal rather than the phone?

  (b) Explain the meaning of the term on-line.

2 As well as being able to get details on flights and holidays the travel agent can also access the Prestel system.

  (a) Explain what the main differences are between the Prestel system and the teletext system most people have on their televisions.

  (b) Explain how the Prestel system might be useful to the travel agent.

ABTA number and a password, which she types in. It then asks for the code of the outward airport and that of the arrival airport. She supplies this information. This type of system where the computer

```
          ┌─────────────────────────┐
          │   Database Directory     │
          └─────────────────────────┘
    DIR    Name                    Tel No
    1      Cosmos Holidays         639485
    2      Thomson Holidays        719385
    3      Airtours                691879
    4      British Airways         398272
    5      Kuoni Travel            818552
    6      Fastrak                 112111

    Press 1 to 6 or #
    for manual dialling

    DISCONNECTED
```

Figure 10.1 *The travel agent can dial the database by typing a number from 1 to 6 on the keyboard*

constantly asks for information which the user supplies is called an interactive system. It is like the computer conducting a conversation with the user. She then accesses the information on seats available on flights from Manchester to Frankfurt today. She tells John that there is one seat available and asks if he wants it. He says yes. The assistant takes his credit card details and hands him booking confirmation which means he only has to pick up the ticket at the office in the airport. Airline and many other booking systems, use such real-time processing.

Real-time processing

With real-time processing, when a change is made due to a transaction occurring, the system is automatically updated. So, if I booked the only available seat on a plane from Manchester to Frankfurt at a travel agents' office, then if you went to another travel agent and tried to book the same seat the computer would tell you that the plane is full. In the fast world we now live in, it is important that data is kept bang up-to-date so real-time systems have to be used.

Since in a real-time system the terminals must be connected to the computer, you can see that a real-time system must also be an on-line system.

The advantage with real-time systems is that the current situation is always being shown. At a travel agents we can find out which flights or holidays are available.

Many shop systems use real-time processing: as soon as an item is sold the system automatically deducts the item from stock so the stock file always shows the true stock position.

Real-time processing is essential for computer control. Examples of computer control include traffic lights, robots, process control (e.g. steel works and chemical processes) and flight simulators.

Doing all the processing in one go: batch processing
Problem
An electricity board wants to send out over three million electricity bills, all within a few days of each other.

Looking at the system in its simplest form we can produce the following outline:

1 When a person moves to a new house they have to go to the electricity board's office to fill in a form for the supply of electricity.
2 The details contained on the form are input via a terminal to the main computer. These details are recorded on a main file called the customer master file.
3 Every three months, the computer produces a list of customers, arranged in order of houses in a certain street for the meter reader to visit. The meter reader is given a sheet like the one shown in Figure 10.2, which is used to record the meter readings.

1420711983 Mr M. Mouse 10 Disney Drive Anytown	Customer account number	Previous reading	Present reading
	0 0 0 0 0 0 0 0 0 0	0 0 0 0 0	0 0 0 0 0
	1 1 1 1 1 1 1 1 1 1	1 1 1 1 1	1 1 1 1 1
Previous reading 12000	2 2 2 2 2 2 2 2 2 2	2 2 2 2	2 2 2 2
Expected high 20000	3 3 3 3 3 3 3 3 3 3	3 3 3 3	3 3 3 3
Expected low 14000	4 4 4 4 4 4 4 4 4 4	4 4 4 4	4 4 4 4
Present reading 14378	5 5 5 5 5 5 5 5 5 5	5 5 5 5	5 5 5 5
	6 6 6 6 6 6 6 6 6 6	6 6 6 6	6 6 6 6
	7 7 7 7 7 7 7 7 7 7	7 7 7 7	7 7 7 7
	8 8 8 8 8 8 8 8 8 8	8 8 8 8	8 8 8 8
	9 9 9 9 9 9 9 9 9 9	9 9 9 9	9 9 9 9

Figure 10.2 *A meter reading sheet with mark sense boxes. Information is coded by shading in the boxes*

4 After they have been recorded, the meter readings are then sent to the computer centre for processing.

5 First of all, the meter reading sheets are read by an optical mark reader and the details are placed on magnetic tape in what is called a transaction file.

6 This magnetic tape is then sorted into the same order as the master file to produce a new tape called the sorted transaction file. You cannot sort a tape and put it back on the same tape again, although you could do this if a disk system were used.

7 This transaction file is then processed with the master file, which is also held on tape. A new updated master file is produced along with the electricity bills to be sent out to the customers.

The production of electricity bills in this way is an example of batch processing. This is a system of collecting all the inputs together and putting them into the computer in one go or 'batch'.

Batch processing is used when a particular job needs to be done in one go rather than in a number of parts. All the relevant data is collected and put through the computer in one go. The main advantage with batch processing is that the computer operator can load the data in only one operation, no matter how many meter reading sheets there are in a batch. The programs in the computer go through the various processes and the final result is a pile of bills to be sent out to customers and an updated master file with the latest information added.

Batch processing has other uses. Preparing a company's payroll is a suitable application. Here, all the relevant information, such as hours worked, pay per hour, tax and national insurance contributions would be collected for each employee and put into the computer. Batch processing is suitable because payroll processing is usually carried out once a week or once a month.

Multitasking and multiprogramming

The processing unit works quickly, so if it is working on just one task then most of its time will be spent waiting for the slow peripheral devices to catch up. Rather than waste this valuable processing time, the processing unit can be made to process the data from several programs at once. The speed of the computer makes it appear as though it is doing two jobs at the same time, although what is happening is that the computer works on one task for a short period and then on the next. Such a system is called a multiprogramming or multitasking system.

This type of system is almost always found with large 'mainframe' computers which have many terminals connected to the central processing unit. You can also find this type of system on personal computers. Using Windows software you can print out a job at the same time as working on a different task using other software.

Transaction processing

Transaction processing takes place when needed rather than at set intervals like batch processing. Rather than wait for the data to accumulate, demand processing is usually performed on individual items of data. Suppose a monthly paid employee leaves half-way through the month. Instead of waiting for the payroll to be done at the end of the month as a batch process, the data could be input to a disk-based system and the pay worked out for the one employee.

Multi-access and timesharing

With timesharing many users can have access to the same data apparently at the same time. For instance, in the airline booking example, other travel agents could be using the same airline database at the same time. Multi-access systems give the user the impression that she is the only one

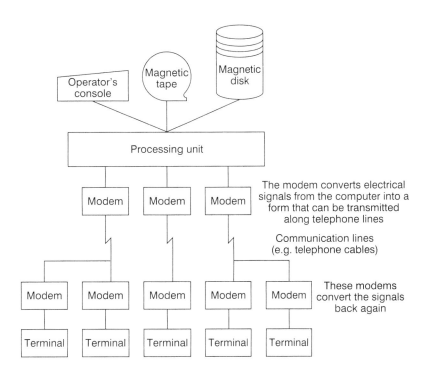

Figure 10.3

using the computer. The computer serves other people during the time she takes to press the keys (see Figures 10.3 and 10.4).

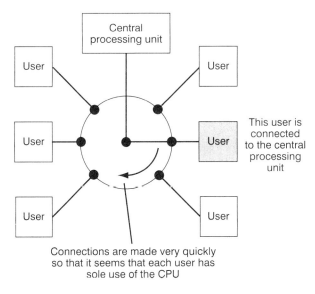

Figure 10.4

TEST YOURSELF

Using the words in the list below, copy out and complete sentences A to H, underlining the words you have inserted. The words may be used more than once.

timesharing   multi-access   on   interactive
control   real-time   batch   multiprogramming

A   If a device is _____-line it means that it is under the control of the central processing unit.

B   The type of system where the computer conducts a 'conversation' with the user, is called an _____ system.

C   The type of processing where changes are immediately acted upon and any files are immediately updated, is called a _____-_____ system.

D   _____ systems must always be real-time systems.

E   _____ processing is used where a job is all done at one time rather than in parts .

F   _____ allows the computer to work on several programs apparently at the same time.

G   A _____ system allows many terminals to access the CPU.

H   Each terminal has a certain amount of time allocated to it. This is called _____.

1 Real-time processing is being used increasingly because the information is always up-to-date. Batch processing still has advantages for doing certain types of jobs.

   (a) What types of jobs are these?

   (b) What advantages does batch processing have over real-time processing?

   (c) What is meant by the term up-to-date?

2 You go to a travel agency to book a holiday in Spain, travelling by air. The clerk makes an initial enquiry for you, using the interactive computerised enquiry system.

   (a) What input device would you expect to see on his desk?

   (b) What is meant by the term 'interactive'.

   (c) Why is an interactive system necessary for enquiries?

   You decide to make the booking.

   (d) Give seven items of data that the airline booking clerk will need before a flight can be booked for you.

   (e) The clerk gives you a booking immediately. How can he be certain that the seats will not be double booked?

   The booking will be recorded on the airline's backing store.

   (f) What type of access is necessary for booking information?

   (g) What backing storage would be most appropriate?

   (h) Give three reasons why the computerised booking system is more efficient than the previous manual one.

3 For each of the applications given below, state whether the method of processing would be real-time or batch. In each case give one reason for your choice.

   (a) A bank cash dispenser which can also give a report of the current balance in a customer's account.

   (b) An examination board system for collecting marks from examiners using mark sense forms.

   (c) A flood warning system which uses sensors to continually monitor the water level in a river.

   (d) The production of bank statements to be sent out to bank customers at the end of the month.

   (e) A supermarket POS (point-of-sale) terminal where, when an item is sold, it is automatically deducted from stock.

   (f) A central heating control system where each room can be kept at a different constant temperature.

   (g) A fast moving arcade type computer game.

Chapter 1

Data Transfer

It is common in computing to have to transfer data between different software packages and even between different computers. A few years ago you would have had great difficulty in doing this but today it is not too much of a problem.

File conversion

File conversion is an important part of computing. Suppose you are using an existing database system and your files, which have been set up over a period of 10 years, contain several thousand records. To type these in again to a new system might take several months of full-time work. If it is decided that the system needs upgrading then you need to be sure that the new database software will read the files from the old database. This is usually possible if the software is a newer version of the same software. The problem gets more difficult if the original software developer is no longer in business or if you have changed to a different database package. However, all is not lost. Most database, spreadsheet and wordprocessing files can be read by other packages, but it is always important to make sure that any new software you buy can read your old files.

ASCII files

ASCII stands for American Standard Code for Information Interchange and is a code for representing characters (letters, numbers etc.) as binary codes. All computers can store data as ASCII code and a file used to hold ASCII code is called an ASCII file.

The 8-bit binary codes used to hold the letters of the alphabet are shown in Figure 11.1

Character	ASCII code	Character	ASCII code
A	0100 0001	N	0100 1110
B	0100 0010	O	0100 1111
C	0100 0011	P	0101 0000
D	0100 0100	Q	0101 0001
E	0100 0101	R	0101 0010
F	0100 0110	S	0101 0011
G	0100 0111	T	0101 0100
H	0100 1000	U	0101 0101
I	0100 1001	V	0101 0110
J	0100 1010	W	0101 0111
K	0100 1011	X	0101 1000
L	0100 1100	Y	0101 1001
M	0100 1101	Z	0101 1010

Figure 11.1

Other ASCII codes are used for the digits 1, 2, 3, etc. and also for commas and the arithmetical signs (+, −, = etc.). Even a space has its own ASCII code 0010 0000. Thus to store the word HELLO!, the computer uses an 8-bit binary code for each character. Here is the way the word would be held in the computer's memory.

```
0100 1000  H
0100 0101  E
0100 1100  L
0100 1100  L
0100 1111  O
0010 0001  !
```

QUESTION

Show how your full name would be stored using ASCII code. Don't forget to include the ASCII code for the space between your names.

Transferring files between wordprocessors

The most common type of file transfer is between different wordprocessors. Even within large organisations people often use different wordprocessors or different versions of the same wordprocessor so it is essential that they can read each other's files. You may for instance want to send someone some notes through the post. If you send them a disk of wordprocessing files, you could save on postage costs and it will also allow the other person to edit the files. Most wordprocessors, but not all, have a file transfer facility so that, for instance, a Word file could be read by a WordPerfect wordprocessor. The only sure way to transfer text between different wordprocessors is to store every thing as ASCII files. When you transfer files of ASCII code the formatting commands (margins, tabs, etc.) and features such as underlining, bold and different fonts are all lost but the body of the text will still be there.

Comma separated variables

The World Development Database is a data file consisting of economic statistics for 129 countries. Because it is a data file you need database or spreadsheet software to be able to read the data held in the file. Nearly all database or spreadsheet software will read these files because the data is held in these files in a standard way. Statistics related to the countries are provided for several years so that you can make comparisons.

One common file format is that of comma-separated-variables or CSV for short. The CSV file format is useful because of the ease with which it is possible to transfer files. Files in this format can be read by most spreadsheets and databases.

File handling packages

Backing storage devices such as disk drives are able to store files outside the central processing unit. These files could be program files which hold the series of instructions that enable a computer to perform a useful task or they could be, for example, a file used to hold a drawing you have drawn using a paint package. Most computers now come with very large hard disk drives capable of holding well over 250 MB of data. This is a very large amount of data.

Frequently we need to perform file processes such as deleting, copying or merging files. We can do this using operating system commands or we can use a graphical user interface (GUI) such as Windows. Using either of these can be tiresome if we want to, say, delete or copy a large number of files. It is for this reason

SKILLS BUILDING

Evaluate the process of transferring a piece of text between two different wordprocessing packages. You will have to create a text file using one wordprocessing package and then transfer it to a different one. When you have done this, see if you can transfer a piece of text from one package to the other using ASCII files.

In your evaluation you should mention:

- whether the package was able to read the files directly. If it did not then explain what you had to do to make it read the files
- whether any strange characters appeared in your document and if they did, how you removed them
- whether the text kept the same margins as before and whether each line was joined up to the next
- all the problems and how you overcame them. Include a conclusion.

You will need to do the above twice: once for transferring the files from the format of the first wordprocessor to the second and the other time for transferring from one wordprocessor to the other using ASCII code.

that special software called file handling packages have been developed. These packages display the file names and enable you to mark the files you want copied or deleted. Because they can save so much time, they are very popular packages. Xtree is an example of a file handling package used with PCs.

QUESTIONS

Using the operating system or graphical user interface you are familiar with, write simple instructions that could be used by a complete novice to perform the following operations.

1 Copy a single file from a floppy disk onto another removable disk (i.e. onto another floppy disk).

2 Copy the entire contents of one floppy disk onto another floppy disk.

3 Delete a single file from a floppy disk.

4 Produce a backup copy of your work disk.

Data/file compression

Suppose you wanted to use a colour scanner to scan a photograph of yourself into your computer. Unless you are lucky enough to have plenty of spare disk space on your hard disk or one of the new magneto optical disks, which have a huge capacity, then you could run out of storage space when trying to save the photograph. One way around the problem is to use compression software to reduce the size of the picture file. Special software is able to reduce the size of files to about one quarter of their original size.

You may have heard of a zip file. Zip files are often used by magazine publishers when they include a free disk with their magazines. A zip file is one that has been compressed before being put on the disk. One disk is therefore able to hold a much greater number of files, but you need to unzip or decompress the files before they can be used.

It is also possible to double the storage capacity of the hard disk drive by using software such as Stacker or Doublespace. With this type of software, compression and decompression are carried out automatically and you use the computer as normal.

Digital and analogue computers

Data can either be analogue or digital. Digital quantities have values which jump from one to the next without any in between value. An on/off switch on a radio is a device that could be thought of as digital because there is no state between 'on' and 'off'. Some quantities can vary over a whole range of values. Temperature is an example, since it can be 10, 10.1, 10.01, 10.001°C, and so on. In fact, temperatures can be an infinite number of values. Quantities which have an infinite number of values are called analogue quantities. For analogue quantities to be processed by a digital computer they need first to be converted into digital quantities using an analogue to digital converter.

There are two types of computers: digital computers and analogue computers. Most people use digital computers since analogue computers are quite rare. Analogue computers are used mainly for the control of processes in factories and for some forms of modelling.

Digital computers like to be given their information in the form of numbers (i.e. in the form of binary digits). All information eventually has to be turned into groups of binary digits (0s and 1s).

Digital data	Analogue data
The number of cars in a car park	Temperature recorded using a mercury thermometer
Traffic light sequences	Position on a compass dial
Old fashioned watch with hands	Digital watch
Bar code	Room light dimmer switch
Data stored on a magnetic disk	Time read from a sun dial

QUESTIONS

1 Say whether the following devices would be analogue or digital.

(a) a mercury-in-glass thermometer

(b) the floor indicator on a lift

(c) a radio tuning dial

(d) the display showing the track that is being played on your CD player

(e) a speedometer on a car.

2 More and more devices which previously had analogue displays, now have digital displays. Why do you think this is?

Analogue to digital conversion (ADC) and vice versa

In chemical factories, the processes used to make chemicals are usually controlled with the help of computers. Often, a batch of chemicals must be kept at a precise temperature. The signal from a temperature sensor is usually a continually changing analogue signal and this must be converted into digital form before it can be processed by a computer. This conversion is done with an analogue-digital converter (ADC). The computer may then control the process by outputting a digital signal, through a digital-analogue converter (DAC) to an electric motor which can open or close a valve.

Modems are used to enable data to be passed from one place to another using communication links (telephone wires, optical cables, radio links, etc.).

A modem (modulator-demodulator) is used to convert the binary digits from a digital computer into an analogue signal that may be passed along ordinary telephone wires. The modem at the other end of the wire converts the analogue signal back into a digital one that the computer is able to understand.

THINGS TO DO

1 (a) Briefly describe the difference between analogue and digital data.

(b) A car fuel injection system counts revolutions to measure the engine speed and uses an electronic sensor to measure the engine temperature.

(i) Indicate why the engine speed is the digital signal.

(ii) What extra piece of equipment does the analogue temperature signal need and what does it do?

2 (a) John is writing a novel and the publisher who is going to publish the book would like to receive the final copy on disk rather than as hardcopy. John already uses a wordprocessor, so this is no problem.

(i) What are the advantages to the publisher of receiving his work on disk?

(ii) What are the advantages to John of sending his work in on disk?

(b) Before the disk is sent, the publisher asks John which wordprocessor he uses. Why is this important to them?

IT TASK

You are working with a friend on a joint project at school and have agreed to split the work between you. You will type half the work and your friend will type the other half. Since you are using the same wordprocessor, joining the files will not be a problem. Find out and then write instructions so that a complete novice could join the two files together.

System TASK

Using the Grolier *Multimedia Encyclopaedia* or another similar encyclopaedia you can copy and save tables in text format. For instance there is a table of chemical elements.

Design a system where you can take these tables from an encyclopaedia held on CD-ROM and put them into either a spreadsheet or database. Write a user guide so that a person who knows very little about computing could understand what to do. Let someone else try to copy the tables using your instructions. Can they do it? What improvements do they suggest? Incorporate the improvements into your system.

Chapter 12

Ways of Presenting Your Data

There are various ways that we can present computer output. We can present the data:

- as a screen display
- as hardcopy, i.e. as printouts on paper (text, pictures, graphs, charts)
- with multimedia presentations (sound, text, pictures, graphs and charts)
- using virtual reality
- using sound.

Hard copy

Printed information is still the main form of output from a computer system. It is used because everybody is a 'subscriber' to the system. We all have letter boxes and know the various processes involved in sending mail. Paper's universal use and acceptability makes it a very difficult system to replace. Nevertheless, there are some disadvantages with using paper. With electronic mail, messages can be created, sent and read completely on computers without having ever been printed on paper. Many people think that the mail service will never be replaced, but others think that electronic mail will soon replace it. What do you think?

Hardcopy (printouts on paper) may gradually be replaced and the reasons for this are:

1 paper is expensive to buy and to store
2 the use of paper encourages people to photocopy it so that they don't lose it
3 many bills, invoices etc. are preprinted and this is expensive
4 the use of paper is not environmentally friendly
5 moving paper around an organisation takes time.

There are, however, some advantages:

1 with a legal document, it is hard to prove that an electronic letter has been received and seen
2 everyone is able to use a paper based system
3 paper is easier to read than a computer screen
4 it is easier to flick back and forth in a paper document
5 paper can be read on the move and in circumstances where a computer might not be available.

QUESTION

Produce a diagram, using a combination of graphics and text, which could be used to describe the steps involved in producing and then posting a letter. Assume that the letter has been created on a computer and printed out using a printer.

Presentation graphics

Graphics consist of a combination of diagrams, text and charts which are used to make a visual impact when people see them. Graphics may be presented as slides, transparencies to be used with overhead projectors, paper or even as computer displays. Salespersons frequently use screens to display their products or services to potential customers. Some of them now use multimedia.

The traditional way of producing graphics was to produce brief notes about what you wanted to say and to ask a designer to draw up a series of rough designs. A graphics bureau would then transfer the designs either to paper or slides. This is labour intensive and expensive.

Now it is common for companies to do all the production themselves rather than send all of their work to graphics studios. By producing graphics within a company using computers, the company can change designs at the last minute. Presentation graphics software is now available for most computers and with this software it is possible to produce professional looking material at minimum cost.

When you are producing presentations using a computer there are some guidelines that can help make your design as effective as possible.

Guidelines

Simplicity
Simplicity is most important. There should be no more than six words per line and six lines per page/slide. Many people put in too much detail and this tends to reduce impact.

Brevity (making it brief)
Most people can only retain between three and five brief points being used in a presentation.

Language
Make sure that the language is simple. No complicated words should be used and avoid the use of jargon which might be known only to a few people.

Notes
Do not use the graphics for notes. If you are giving a presentation and you merely repeat in speech what is on the slides, then there is no point in using slides

Graphics charts
Use bar, pie and other charts to help to explain things. Try to keep to a maximum of four bars (for bar charts) and up to six slices for data in pie charts.

Fonts
Do not use too many fonts in the same slide and do not use only capital letters (called upper case). Use both upper and lower case letters.

Multimedia

'Multimedia' means the mixture of text and graphics with motion and sound, including video, audio, animation and photographs. Multimedia is interactive which means that the user can decide on different routes through the software. The images may be controlled either using a mouse or a keyboard. Multimedia is ideal for learning new things because you can control the program to work as slowly or as quickly as you like and it will not tell you off if you get things wrong. In a way, multimedia software can be an ideal teacher. Learning boring topics can be made fun using multimedia. For instance you can learn about decimal points via an adventure called Who stole the decimal point?

A multimedia system consists of an ordinary PC which has several additional devices attached to it. These extra devices typically include a CD-ROM drive, a sound board and speakers. Figure 12.1 shows the arrangement.

The PC at the centre of a multimedia system will typically have the following specification: 100 MHz Pentium with 8 MB RAM and a quadruple speed CD-ROM.

Computer aided learning (CAL)
Computers can interact with pupils to enhance the learning process. The development of multimedia has led to a huge growth in the use of computers as an educational tool in the classroom. Computer aided learning can be used to instruct pupils and then test them on what they have learnt.

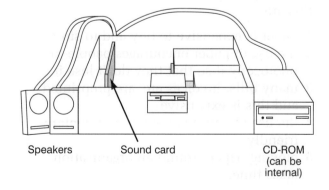

Speakers   Sound card   CD-ROM (can be internal)

Figure 12.1 *The components of a multimedia system*

Producing multimedia software

You will have seen the wonderful displays, video clips and sounds provided by multimedia software, but how are these packages written? As you can imagine, a lot of equipment is needed to produce really good software. You can prepare your own multimedia software if you have a multimedia authoring package.

Using an encyclopaedia on CD-ROM

The beauty of encyclopaedias on CD-ROM is the small amount of space that they take up. For instance the paper based Grolier Encyclopaedia consists of 21 volumes. The multimedia version occupies a single CD-ROM. It is very quick to search for references, as well. For example, to search for information on 'computers' you simply type in the word and lists of articles that mention computers are displayed on the screen. You can then use your mouse to highlight each article you want to read. If you want a printout of the article then this is easily done.

You are not just restricted to text either. You can look at video clips, with speech, of historic moments such as man's landing on the moon. You can also see animations showing how things work, such as the human heart or the internal combustion engine. Pictures are also included which may be printed out and then used to illustrate your project work.

Atlases on CD-ROM

The Software Toolworks Atlas held on CD-ROM is a multimedia atlas and is much more flexible than an atlas in a book. Really it is a combined atlas and a database on the various countries, all in one. Figure 12.2 shows some of the information you can obtain from this atlas.

Information about the countries includes:

- geography
- people
- education
- health
- government
- crime
- economy
- agriculture
- communications
- travel.

CD-ROM

Without the technology of CD-ROM, multimedia would be impossible because of the large storage capacity needed for photographs, animation and video clips. There are many useful features of CD-ROM:

1 they are easy to handle and more durable
2 they can be used for multimedia presentations
3 a single CD-ROM can hold around 600 MB of data; hundreds of floppy disks would be needed to store this same amount of data
4 they are environmentally friendly; the Friends of the Earth estimate that a single CD-ROM full of text can save up to 15 trees worth of paper
5 they can store text, sound, graphics and video.

Sound

One of the features of a multimedia system is the use of speakers. A special card called a sound card contains chips and other circuitry that enable a computer to produce high quality sound. You can then feed the sound through speakers or headphones so that you can play games, look at and hear a variety of information on CD-ROM or just listen to your favourite music on an ordinary CD. Figure 12.1 shows the components of a multimedia system.

MIDI

MIDI stands for musical instrument digital interface. Software and hardware that are designed to MIDI standards are able to send electronic messages to MIDI devices such as keyboards, musical synthesisers and drum machines. You can also use MIDI systems to control specialised devices such as theatrical lighting. An organised series of MIDI commands is called a sequence.

Suppose we connected a keyboard to a computer using a special MIDI interface. The frequency, pitch and other musical information could be converted to digital information which can be read by the computer. Music played on the keyboard can therefore be stored on the computer, and because the computer is able to produce digital signals, it can send signals back to the keyboard.

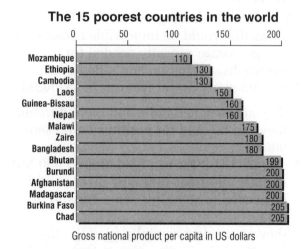

The 15 poorest countries in the world

Gross national product per capita in US dollars

Source:
THE WORLD FACTBOOK, Central Intelligence Agency,
Washington, DC, 1991

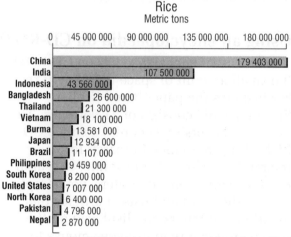

Rice
Metric tons

The 15 highest rice-producing countries in the world

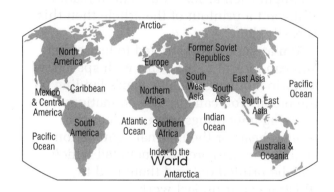

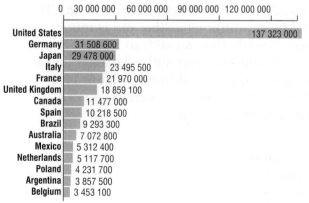

Countries with the highest number of automobiles

Automobiles in use

Figure 12.2 *Just some of the information you can find out about different countries using the Software Toolworks Atlas on CD-ROM*

Video

It is now possible to view and hear video clips on a screen. Some video clips are shown only in a small window, but with newer multimedia systems it is possible to view full-screen images.

Virtual reality

You may have seen pictures of children wearing headsets and gloves wired up to a computer and wondered what they are. This is the world of virtual reality.

A lot of research in virtual reality is directed towards military uses. Virtual reality can be used to recreate a terrain where fighting is likely to take place. To a soldier wearing a headset and gloves the battle situation can be as near to the real thing as possible.

Many other uses for virtual reality systems are being developed. One example is possible use for simulating traffic accidents for use in court. If a witness says that they saw an accident then the court can be shown exactly what the witness would have seen from a particular position on the road.

TEST YOURSELF

Using the words in the list below, copy out and complete sentences A to F, underlining the words you have inserted. The words may be used more than once.

Prestel   hard copy   electronic mail   multimedia   transparency   sound card   posted

A Output from a computer on paper is often referred to as _____ _____.

B Printouts have the advantage that they can be _____.

C The service that involves passing electronic messages from one computer to another is called _____ _____.

D Graphics may be produced using a computer and then printed out on a _____ to be viewed using an overhead projector.

E A mixture of text and, graphics with motion and sound is an example of _____.

F To use multimedia on a PC you need to insert a special circuit board called a _____ _____ in order to produce sound.

1 Friends of your family have young children and already have a computer with a large amount of memory and a large hard disk drive.

   The friends have heard about multimedia and think that it may be able to help their children with their schooling. In particular they would like to use a couple of encyclopaedias to help the children do project work.

   (a) What additional equipment would they need to add to their computer to make it able to be used for multimedia?

   (b) They do not know much about multimedia. Write a short paragraph explaining briefly what its capabilities are.

   (c) Give three features of an encyclopaedia held on CD-ROM that would help the children with their project work.

   (d) Recommend a couple of titles of encyclopaedias that might be of use to the family.

2 Presentations are often used in businesses to sell companies' products.

   (a) Explain what a presentation is.

   (b) What equipment could be used in such a presentation?

   (c) Presentation packages are available that produce slides and overhead projector transparencies. Give the name of a package that you could use for a presentation and give some idea of the features it has.

3 Output from computers can be presented in many different ways.

   (a) Software to log data in a science laboratory can present data on a screen or as hard copy. State one advantage and one disadvantage of these two methods.

   (b) In publishing systems, it is necessary to combine text and various forms of graphics.

      (i) Why is it often necessary to import graphics files into a DTP package?

      (ii) Why is it becoming increasingly easy to do this?

(NEAB/WJEC Option Q)

You have been asked by your geography teacher to produce a study about the 10 richest and the 10 poorest companies in the world. How do you define rich and poor? In our country poor may mean someone who doesn't own a video or a car, but what other indicators can be used? Some people say that the richest countries have the highest life expectancy since poorer countries cannot afford the health care that richer countries can. Using suitable software such as the World Development Database (available as a set of data files) or the Software Toolworks World Atlas (available on CD-ROM) investigate these countries and say what conclusions you can draw. You should provide a variety of graphs and use any other statistics to help you come to any conclusions.

You have been asked by the teacher responsible for health education, to produce a group presentation for first and second year senior school pupils on current health issues. Since you are working with a group you will need to select a group co-ordinator who will divide the various tasks up between the group members. You can use any computer equipment at your disposal.

Some of the issues you could look at are:

- drugs
- personal hygiene
- alcohol abuse
- sex.

After the presentation, you should jointly produce a report on the way you used IT to help with this task and the reasons for your choice of the software used.

Multimedia packages are widely used in schools for helping to teach subjects in an enjoyable way. You will probably have seen several such packages being used in different subject areas.

Choose one of the following classifications of schools

- infant
- junior
- secondary.

Evaluate a couple of multimedia packages that could be used to teach children at one of the above types of school. You should use the package yourself before evaluating it. Choose any package you like the look of.

Chapter 13

How to Describe an Information System

Describing systems

A system is a group of connected operations or things. We can describe systems in various ways. Often we can describe them in terms of inputs, processes and outputs (see Chapter 1). Figure 13.1 shows the simplest system.

Figure 13.1 *The three steps involved in the processing of data*

A diagram like this doesn't really tell us too much, so we could draw a diagram like that in Figure 13.2, which tells us a little more. Don't be afraid of drawing your own diagrams like this to describe your systems. These diagrams do their job well because everyone understands them and they help you to think about the problem as you are drawing the diagram. Don't try drawing a diagram in one go: instead try to concentrate on one aspect or part of the system. You can always draw several diagrams and then join them together to obtain an overall picture.

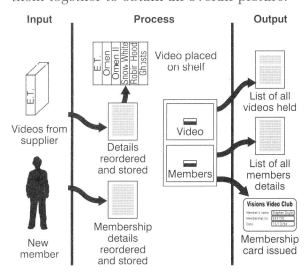

Figure 13.2 *A video library system*

Structure diagrams

Structure diagrams can be used to describe information systems. An overall task is broken down into smaller more manageable tasks. These may then be broken down further into smaller tasks. This way of describing tasks is described as the 'top down' approach.

The top down approach

Let's take a look at drawing a structure diagram for a task we are probably all familiar with: doing the weekly shopping.

First we place the overall task at the top and we write a brief description of the overall task in the box (i.e. doing the weekly shopping.) (Figure 13.3)

Figure 13.3

This task is then divided up into a series of tasks it is necessary to perform to do the main task. For instance, to do the shopping we may have to

- prepare a shopping list
- do the shopping
- put the shopping away.

So, we now have the structure shown in Figure 13.4.

Again this second set of tasks may be split up as shown in Figure 13.5.

We can now put all the stages together to produce the final structure chart as shown

Figure 13.4

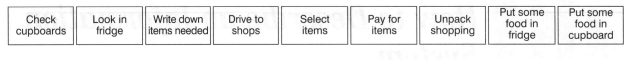

| Check cupboards | Look in fridge | Write down items needed | Drive to shops | Select items | Pay for items | Unpack shopping | Put some food in fridge | Put some food in cupboard |

We write these in the order in which they are performed ⟶

Figure 13.5

Figure 13.6 *A structure diagram for doing the weekly shopping*

in Figure 13.6. Don't worry when drawing structure diagrams, that yours looks different from other people's. They are rarely the same.

As you can see, the purpose of a structure diagram is to show the tasks in more detail as you move down. The top box is the overall view (doing the weekly shopping), and hence the term top down approach. You could carry on breaking each task down, but there comes a point where you have broken the tasks down into enough detail.

Figure 13.7 *The start of a structure diagram to make a roast dinner*

QUESTIONS

1 Pick one of the following tasks (preferably the one you are most familiar with) and draw a structure diagram for it:
   (a) renting a video from a video shop
   (b) borrowing a book from your local library
   (c) programming your video recorder to record a programme
   (d) getting ready to go for a night out
   (e) washing the dishes.

2 Draw a structure diagram for making a roast dinner with turkey, roast potatoes, carrots, sprouts and gravy. Figure 13.7 shows the top part of the diagram to start you off.

Data flow diagrams

Data flow diagrams are used to consider the data without bothering about the equipment used to store it and are used as a first step in describing a system. Four symbols are used in these diagrams and these are described below.

The box

The box is either a source of data, such as an order form from a customer, or a part of the system which uses or consumes the data, called a sink. We are not concerned with what happens to the data before it reaches the box if it is a source or what happens to it after it goes past a sink.

The sausage

The sausage is sometimes replaced by a circle on some data flow diagrams and is used to denote a process performed on the data. A process is something which is done to the data like a calculation. The process might be sorting the data or combining it with some other data. A brief description of the process should be placed inside the box.

The open rectangle

The open rectangle represents a data store. This is where the data is held. It could represent the data being held manually or on a computer. Basically, a data store is a logical collection of data. A description of the store can be placed inside the box.

The arrows

The arrows are used to show how the other symbols are connected.

Let's now draw a series of data flow diagrams for a system for a video library. The first diagram follows the data flow that takes place when a new member joins the library. To join the library it is necessary to fill in an application form and to show certain documents to provide proof of identity. If the potential member does not have this documentation, then the library manager will refuse membership. After the membership details have been checked (or

validated) a membership card is produced and given to the new member and the member's details are recorded. If the member borrows a video or if the manager wants to know whether a particular person is a member, then the details can be found. Figure 13.8 shows the data flow diagram for this part of the system.

Now we can look at the data flow diagram for a video being added to the library. This is a simple system, with the details of the video, such as name, price etc. being recorded and then stored. Figure 13.9 shows this part of the system.

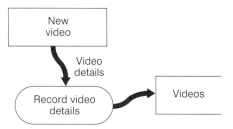

Figure 13.9 *The data flow diagram for adding a new video to the library*

Figure 13.10 shows the data flow diagram for the process of borrowing a video. Notice that the member data and video data are needed because the loans store of data will only contain the video number and the membership number. This is done to save space. By storing the video and member number together it is possible to find out a member's details and the video details if they are needed.

We could, if we wanted to get an overall view of the system, join these diagrams together but it is much easier to draw them for each part of the system and then to draw a diagram with them all joined.

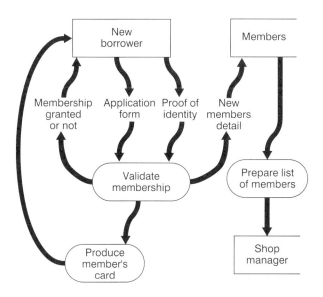

Figure 13.8 *A data flow diagram for a video library*

QUESTION

Your form teacher marks your register twice a day. Find out what happens to these attendance marks and draw a data flow diagram for the system.

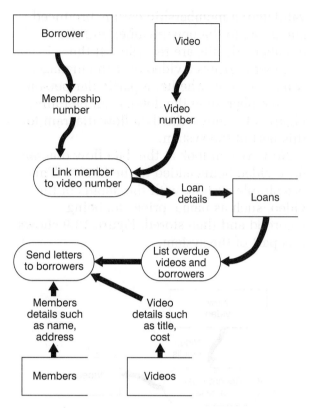

Figure 13.10 *The data flow diagram for borrowing a video*

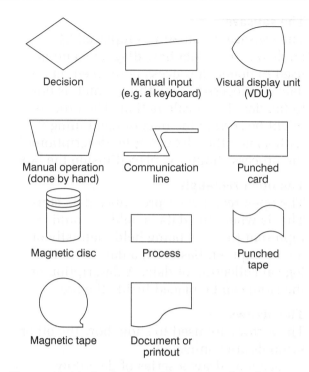

Figure 13.11 *Symbols used in systems flowcharts*

Systems flowcharts

A systems flowchart is a diagram which gives an overall view of a system. It shows the tasks that are performed on the data, such as sorting or updating and also shows the type of media (magnetic disk, tape etc.) used to hold the data. Figure 13.11 shows some of the usual symbols. The flow is always indicated by arrows. A tape will always have an arrow going into it or coming out of it, but a disk may have one in either direction or both.

For a small database system using a single computer, the system flowchart shown in Figure 13.12 is very simple.

Notice the following:

- the double arrow going between the disk drive. This shows that data can be read into the computer and written to the disk drive
- there are two ways of outputting the information, either on a VDU or as a printout (often called hardcopy).

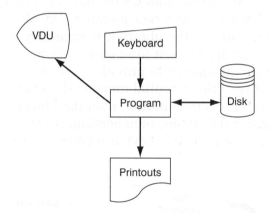

Figure 13.12 *Systems flowchart for a simple database system*

Systems flowchart for producing gas/electricity bills

The production of gas/electricity bills is an example of batch processing. Look back at Chapter 10 at the steps involved in producing an electricity bill. Electricity boards each have millions of customers, so they use large computers called mainframe computers. These usually consist of a separate processor or processors, backing storage devices such as tape or disk drives and terminals.

Figure 13.13 shows the stages involved in producing the bills. The diagram itself is fairly easy to understand. Because every customer gets a bill and there are so many customers, batch processing will be used, with magnetic tape as the storage medium. The transaction file containing all the meter readings has to be sorted into the same order as the customer master file, otherwise the processing would be very slow, because tapes would need to be wound backwards and forwards until the records matched. The bills file, also on magnetic tape, contains details of the amounts owed by the customers and this will need updating as the customers pay their bills. Figure 13.14 shows the systems flowchart for processing the bills file. Notice that there are several

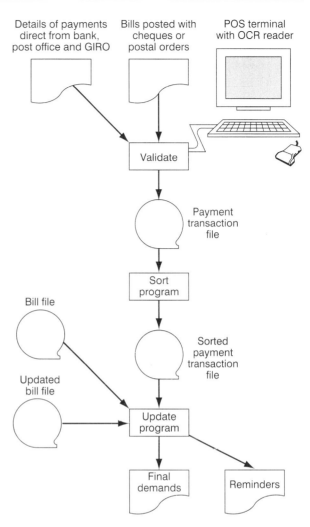

Figure 13.14 *Systems flowchart for processing the bills file*

ways of making the payments and the payments must be validated before being recorded on the transaction file. The update program is used to produce reminders and final demands to the people who haven't yet paid their bills.

Systems flowchart for a payroll system which uses batch processing

The following system is used to produce the weekly wages for a large number of staff who work in a factory.

Each employee is given a clock card at the start of each week which contains the employee's name and works number. This card is placed into a special clock which records their arrival and departure time, and

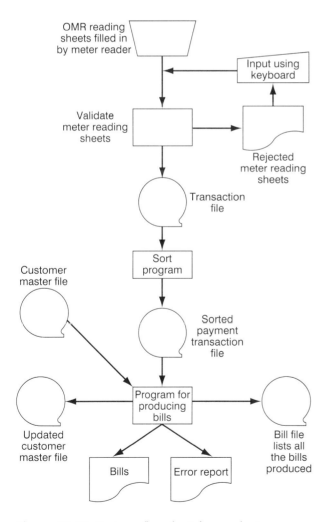

Figure 13.13 *Systems flowchart for producing gas/electricity bills*

the date. For a complete five day week, there will be 20 times recorded onto the card. The process of recording the times is called

clocking in and clocking out.

The machine punches holes into the card to record each time and these cards can be placed directly into a machine which is able to read this coded data. The data is transferred directly to a transaction file, which may be on either magnetic tape or disk. The transaction file is validated and then sorted into employee works number order. Details of incomplete clock cards (e.g. from someone who has forgotten to clock out) will be output as a list called an error report. These clock cards will need to be dealt with by a separate system. A disk file is used to hold details regarding a employee's hourly rate, tax code, taxable pay to date, etc.

The systems flowchart used to represent the above system is shown in Figure 13.15.

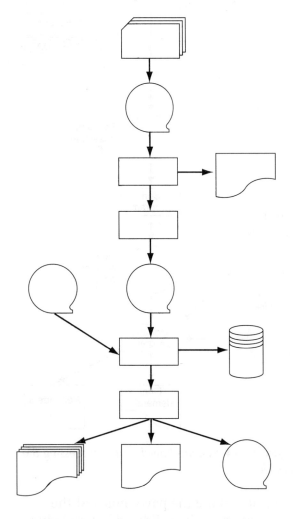

Figure 13.15 *A systems flowchart for a payroll system that uses batch processing*

QUESTION

Copy out the systems flowchart (now you can get to use your flowchart stencil!). Put each of the descriptions shown in the list below into the correct boxes in the flowchart you have drawn.

- transaction file
- wage slips
- tax tables on disk
- calculate wages
- sort program
- update master file
- updated master file
- sorted transaction file
- error report
- clock cards
- validation program
- employee master file
- error report

THINGS TO DO

1 The following system is used to update the files for payments received from customers by a small firm. Customers send their payments to the firm's offices, where the details are entered into the computer using key-to-disk. These entries form the payments transaction file. After validation, the records are output to a second disk file. Any errors are corrected and re-input. The valid fields are then sorted and used with the customer master file to produce an updated file and a list of people who still owe money.

(a) Insert the letter for the correct expression into each space in the system flowchart in Figure 13.16.

A sort payments records into customer account number order

B old customer file

C updated customer file

D error report

E error report

F validated payments transaction file

G payments transaction file

H payment records

I corrected payments records

J correct errors

K update

L sorted valid payments transaction file

M list of people who owe money

N validation

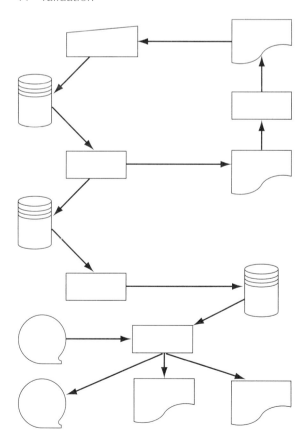

Figure 13.16 *Systems flowchart for payments update*

(b) Why is the payment transaction file sorted to customer account number order?

(c) If the customers do not send part of the bill back when they are paying, which one piece of information is needed before the payment may be processed?

(d) What name is given to the field that contains that piece of information?

(e) Three days after paying her bill, a customer received a request for payment. Why has this happened?

(f) The flowchart shows three disk files and two magnetic tape files in use. Which file will become the new son file?

(g) Which file will be the new father file?

(h) After which two stages are errors found?

(i) Name the three files which must be kept for security reasons.

2 The systems flowchart shown in Figure 13.17 shows the process of updating the master file at the DVLA (Driver and Vehicle Licensing Authority) using a transaction file.

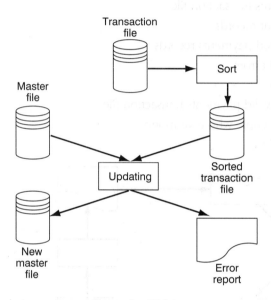

Figure 13.17 *Updating a master file at the DVLA*

(a) Explain why it is necessary to sort the transaction file.

(b) There are three different types of process which are undertaken during an update. Name these three processes.

(c) Give two examples of errors that could occur during updating and which might be included in the error report.

Chapter 14

Systems Analysis

Sounds Hard: What is it?

In this chapter we are going to find out what systems analysis is by looking at how we would perform one for a company called Harlequin Aquatics. The initial background to the company is given below.

Harlequin Aquatics

Harlequin Aquatics is a company involved in the selling of fish keeping equipment to the public. Most of the company's business comes from a catalogue which is distributed with the monthly fish keeping magazines. The customers select the items from the catalogue and either fill in the order form (Figure 14.1) at the back of the catalogue or, if they need the equipment very quickly (which is often the case), they ring up quoting their credit card number and the goods they require. The goods can be selected from the warehouse and dispatched to the customer. As well as the mail order business situated at the head office in Liverpool there are five smaller shops situated in Chester, Manchester, York, Leeds and Birmingham. These shops do not get involved in the mail order side of the business, except when they have goods which are out of stock in the main warehouse. At present all the tasks in the company are being performed manually and, although the company is very profitable, the directors realise that it has become very inefficient.

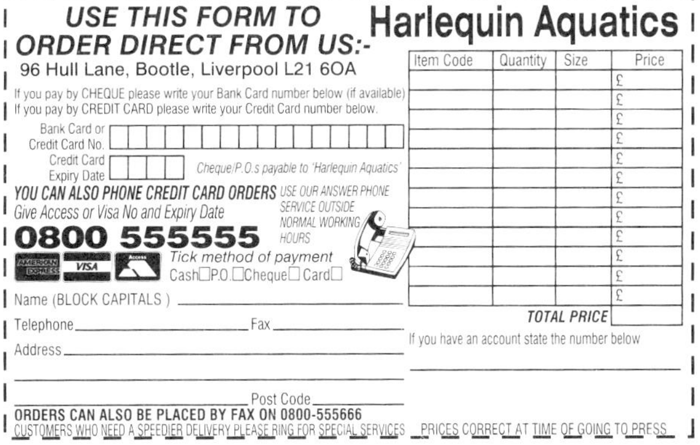
USE THIS FORM TO ORDER DIRECT FROM US:- **Harlequin Aquatics**

96 Hull Lane, Bootle, Liverpool L21 6OA

If you pay by CHEQUE please write your Bank Card number below (if available)
If you pay by CREDIT CARD please write your Credit Card number below.

Bank Card or Credit Card No.

Credit Card Expiry Date

Cheque/P.O.s payable to 'Harlequin Aquatics'

YOU CAN ALSO PHONE CREDIT CARD ORDERS
Give Access or Visa No and Expiry Date
0800 555555
USE OUR ANSWER PHONE SERVICE OUTSIDE NORMAL WORKING HOURS

Tick method of payment
Cash☐ P.O.☐ Cheque☐ Card☐

Name (BLOCK CAPITALS)

Telephone Fax

Address

Post Code

Item Code	Quantity	Size	Price
			£
			£
			£
			£
			£
			£
			£
			£
			£
			£
			£
			£
		TOTAL PRICE	

If you have an account state the number below

ORDERS CAN ALSO BE PLACED BY FAX ON 0800-555666
CUSTOMERS WHO NEED A SPEEDIER DELIVERY PLEASE RING FOR SPECIAL SERVICES   PRICES CORRECT AT TIME OF GOING TO PRESS

Figure 14.1 *An order form for Harlequin Aquatics*

At present the directors wish to streamline the most profitable part of the company situated at the head office and main distribution centre in Liverpool. At the moment there are five telesales staff who take the orders over the phone and deal with the occasional fax orders. There are also three other staff who deal with the orders through the post.

As soon as an order is received an order form is typed on a form which contains an order number. This form is in three parts: one to be sent to the warehouse, one to be sent to the accounts office and one to be sent to the customer with the goods.

The company bases its success on the fact that orders can be dealt with promptly (within 24 hours if the customer is prepared to pay for express delivery) but lately, with the volume of orders, this has become increasingly difficult to achieve. Increased competition has meant that a price war has started, with each company promising to beat each other's prices. This has meant that Harlequin Aquatics needs to be more efficient. The increase in orders has prompted the directors to look at the possibility of employing more staff, but they have now decided that they will try to deal with the greater volume of orders with the same number of staff as before. They are now looking to computerise the business and have recruited you as an outside consultant to investigate the possibilities for their business.

At present the head office of the company is located in an old converted church (used as the shop and the warehouse for the distribution of the mail-order goods) with a small new office block of three stories at the back.

In this chapter we will look at the steps involved in systems analysis. Harlequin Aquatics has not used a computer system before so the company can start a new system from scratch. The steps involved in systems analysis are:

- fact finding
- a feasibility study
- an analysis phase
- system design
- implementation
- testing
- documentation
- evaluation.

We will look at what each of the above entails.

Fact finding

Fact finding is concerned with finding about the existing system. It may be that computers are already used but not to their full extent or it may be that a manual system exists which needs computerising. In either case, we need to find out how things are done at the moment before we can suggest any improvements.

There are four main ways of finding out about existing systems, these are:

1 asking questions (interviewing people)
2 getting people to fill in carefully designed questionnaires
3 sitting with various people to observe how the job is done at the moment
4 inspecting any bits of paper, screen displays, files which are used in the present system.

The final step in fact finding is to produce a report which describes the existing system along with its shortcomings, together with some description of the output needed from the new system.

Feasibility study

The feasibility study looks at the chances of being able to solve a particular problem at a reasonable cost. The feasibility report is the

1 Have another read of the scenario on Harlequin Aquatics. You are going to carry out a systems analysis on this company.

Imagine you have just received instructions to go and investigate their present system. You have no other background information apart from the scenario.

(a) Prepare a questionnaire which you could get the company to fill in before you arrange an interview. Your questionnaire should be general to start with but then go on to ask more details later. Prepare this using suitable software.

(b) After receiving back the questionnaire you decide to arrange a visit. Write a list of questions you would ask in the light of the results of your questionnaire. Try to not ask too many questions that are simply answered yes or no but ask open ended questions such as 'can you tell me what problems you have had with the existing system?'

2 One part of the fact finding process is to collect the various pieces of paper used in the business and then examine them. Read the scenario again and decide which pieces of paper you would like to examine.

document produced at the end of the study and will give an idea of the time the project is likely to take, along with some estimation of cost. The aim of the feasibility study is to see whether it is possible to devise a system that can be implemented and that will work at reasonable cost.

The feasibility study ends when a decision whether to proceed or not with the project has been reached.

The following are usually included in a feasibility study:

1 a description of what the system is required to do (called the objectives of the system); Figure 14.2 shows some of the objectives for the Harlequin Aquatics' system
2 some preliminary design so that the costs may be estimated

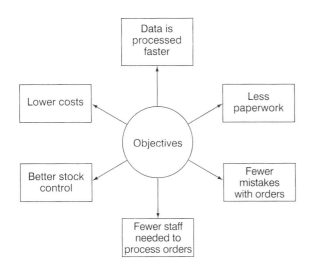

Figure 14.2 *Some of the objectives of a system for Harlequin Aquatics*

3 some alternative designs so that the most suitable one can be chosen

4 a cost/benefit analysis; this looks at the benefits and makes sure that they outweigh the costs. The costs of a system are not just the costs of the hardware and the software needed. Figure 14.3 shows some of the costs you might not have thought of

5 the conclusion, which states whether it is worth going ahead with the project and which design has been chosen.

The feasibility report

The feasibility report is a written report given to the directors of Harlequin Aquatics and is really a summary of the results of the feasibility study. Usually the report is written but it can also be given verbally in the form of a presentation.

The feasibility report should include the following:

1 a brief description of the business and any problems with the existing system

2 details of what part of the business is being looked at; for instance with Harlequin we are looking at the processing of orders

3 the objectives of the proposed system

4 a list of some of the alternative solutions considered and why these alternatives were rejected

5 the human, technical and economic factors:
 • do the staff have the expertise to cope with the new system?
 • is the technology available, i.e. can it be done?
 • is there enough money to go ahead?

6 a plan for the implementation

7 a proposed course of action (i.e. what the consultant/systems analyst suggests the company should do next).

QUESTION

Figure 14.3 shows the headings for some of the costs which Harlequin Aquatics might have to pay during the development and eventual use of the system. Write a more detailed list under the headings in Figure 14.3.

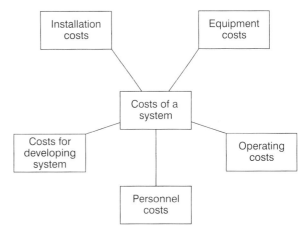

Figure 14.3 *The costs associated with an information system*

Analysis phase

The feasibility study outlines what is required from the system and in the analysis phase this study is used to design the new system. To perform the analysis, the systems analyst will need to look at the system in greater detail than for the feasibility study. When the present system is investigated, the systems analyst will find more weaknesses in it.

In the analysis phase, the charts (system flowcharts, data flow diagrams and system flowcharts) should be drawn as an aid to understanding the present system.

Included in the analysis phase are:

1 detailed objectives of the proposed system
2 facts about the parts of the old system being replaced by the new system
3 any constraints on the system: these are limitations on the solution to the problem. Many problems can be solved if the money, technical expertise and time are available. If any of these cannot be found, then they are constraints on the system
4 an update of the cost/benefit analysis based on the new information
5 an update of the plan for further development of the system.This would include such things as the responsibilities of the members of the team involved with the project and deadlines by which the stages must be completed.

System design

If the directors of the company are convinced that a new system will be worth having, work can be started designing the new system. Further investigation should be undertaken to consider what inputs, processes and outputs will be needed. Let's now consider each one in turn:

Outputs

Since the outputs from the system determine how the rest of the system operates, these are looked at first.

We need to look at each of the following areas.

1 What output is needed? For instance, we may decide that for our system we need the following:
   • an invoice (bill) which is sent out to each customer
   • a copy of the invoice to be sent to the accounts office
   • a dispatch note to be sent with the goods
   • a picking list for the storekeeper
   • a screen display so that we can find out if a particular item is in stock.

2 We then need to look at what needs to be on these documents and screens. We may be able to use the same document for different processes. In this way we could use several copies of the invoice using multipart stationery and give one to the customer, warehouse and accounts office.
3 How frequently do these documents need producing? For instance we may need a list of all the stock at the end of each day or a list of all the past customers just once a year when there is a sale on.
4 What is the volume of output? How many orders are dealt with each day? How many items are on each order? All of these determine the type of system we need to use and they also affect the input method. If lots of orders are dealt with, then alternative methods other than keying need to be looked at.

Inputs

Questions the systems analyst will need to answer are as follows.

1 Where does the data come from? In our company the orders come in a variety of ways. They are placed on an order form and posted, or they may be telephoned or faxed.
2 What data needs to be input into the system? This would include catalogue numbers, descriptions, prices, quantities, etc.
3 How much data needs to be entered and how often it needs entering? For our company, it would be useful to determine how many orders were received in a day, what was the number of items on each order and so on. To determine the sizes of files we would need to find out how many customers the company had and how many items there were in the catalogue.
4 Which input device should be chosen? This really depends on the volume of data and whether any of the data can be captured using OMR, OCR, barcoding, etc.

The systems analyst will also need to look at the design of the input screen, which should preferably match the design of the order forms.

Data preparation

Data preparation involves getting the raw data into a form that can be processed by the computer. Verification and validation are included in data preparation. Verification makes sure that, if a keyboard is being used, no typing mistakes have been made. Various validation methods can be used to trap some of the errors. Remember that validation is performed by a computer program.

Code design

We can use codes to save time typing and also save storage space. If they are to be useful codes need to be carefully designed.

File design

We need to decide how many files are needed and then to design the structure of each of the files. To understand how this is done have a look at the chapter on databases. When designing files we should make sure that we do not duplicate any of the information.

Hardware configuration

If more than one computer is used, then it makes sense to network them. Harlequin Aquatics needs a network, since paper would then not need to be transferred between the sales office and the other areas such as accounts and the warehouse. Hardware configuration also includes deciding on the type of computer, and on peripheral devices such as disk drives, printers, etc.

Software used

We first need to decide what software to use. We could hire someone to write it specially which is very expensive. Alternatively, we could use a software package. For Harlequin we would use a database package. There are many database packages available and we would need to evaluate each of these. Once the application package has been chosen we then need to look at the operating system needed in order to run it. With personal computers, the most widely used operating system is either MS DOS plus Windows, or just MS DOS on its own.

Testing the system

Before it is introduced the new system needs to be thoroughly tested. The testing of a system may be broken down into four stages.

1 The system is tested with data that contains no errors to see if it produces the correct results.

2 Known errors are now introduced into the data to see if the computer will process it. Ideally all the errors will be picked up by any validation procedures but we must remember that it is impossible for the computer to detect all types of error.

3 We now start trying to process very large amounts of data to see how the system copes with this. This is really to see if the system can cope with the extra work that might be necessary in the future.

4 Some processing is only done now and again. For instance, we might need a stock report at the end of a month so this will need to be fully tested.

5 Extreme data should be entered to make sure that the range checks included in the validation program will detect them.

If all goes well, then we move onto the next stage which is the implementation of the system.

Implementing (or introducing) the new system

How you implement a new system really depends on its size. A solution could range from a microcomputer or two, to a system that uses a number of networked PCs or even a system based on larger computers.

Systems may be introduced into an organisation in three ways and we will look at each of these in turn.

Direct implementation

With direct implementation, on a given date the users decide to start using the system. In practice, this method is only used for small computer systems since in larger ones problems reveal themselves during the first month and the result can be havoc. Usually the number of computing staff is quite small compared with the administrative staff, so if too many problems occur then they will be unable to cope.

Phased implementation

With phased implementation, each job is introduced separately rather than all jobs being introduced in one go, as with the previous method. For instance we may decide to look at the order processing first and get this running before we look at other areas of the business. One snag with this method is that it takes much longer and the benefits of the new system are delayed.

Parallel running

With parallel running, the new system is run alongside the existing system. If the new system fails, then because we still have the old system, we can use that until the problems are sorted out. Parallel running provides an ideal opportunity to compare the results from the new system with those of the old system, since both systems will be in operation at the same time. However, it does have the serious disadvantage that since each job is done twice, it means a lot

more work for users while the two systems are running in parallel. (Figure 14.4)

Documentation

Documentation is of two types: user and technical.

User documentation (or user guide)

A user guide or manual is documentation that the user can turn to for learning a new procedure or for dealing with a problem that has cropped up. The guide should cover such things as how to load the software, how to perform certain functions, how to save and how to print. It is a good idea to include examples and exercises to help the user understand the system. Since users are usually non-technical any specialist, technical language should be avoided.

The guide should detail what to do in exceptional circumstances. For instance if the system fails to read a disk or data is sent to the printer without it being switched on and the machine is locked, a user will need to know what they have to do.

As always, users have the best view of a system and so should be asked to evaluate any proposed user guide. Their comments should be incorporated into the guide. You

Figure 14.4 *Parallel running*

have probably tried to find things in manuals so you will realise just how important they are.

Technical documentation

Technical documentation is used to explain a system to a specialist, either a programmer or a systems analyst. Since these people understand computer jargon this guide does not need to be as simple as the user guide. This documentation is extremely important since it might be used by someone new to the project and there may be no-one around that was involved with the original project.

Changes always need to be made to a system at a later date so this documentation will be needed when the system is improved or upgraded.

System evaluation

After a project has been implemented it should be reviewed periodically to make sure that it is still meeting its objectives.

A good way of evaluating a solution is to ask the users of the system. They will be able to tell you if a system does what they originally wanted or if there are any improvements needed.

There are always constraints placed on the system and these might include time, money and the lack of qualified staff involved in the project. Hence the solution has some limitations placed on it. Perhaps with Harlequin Aquatics a wide area network could be used to link all the shops to the head office but the cost or lack of technically qualified people to look after it would prevent its use. Such a system could be considered in the future if Harlequin Aquatics has more money and when the staff are more familiar with computers.

TEST YOURSELF

Using the words in the list below, copy out and complete sentences A to K underlining the words you have inserted. The words may be used more than once.

output   fact find   systems analyst   parallel   documentation   analysis   trained   feasibility study   evaluated   design   feasibility report

A A _____ _____ is the person who looks at the manual system to see which parts to computerise.

B She looks at the manual system in terms of three stages: input, process and _____.

C To begin with, she will perform a ____ ____ in order to find out a variety of facts about the business.

D Going on from this, she will then perform a _____ _____ which will then look at whether an alternative system would be feasible.

E When she has completed this, she will submit a _____ _____ to the directors of the company.

F If the directors are happy with the report, they will give the go-ahead for the system and the analyst can start to _____ the system.

G Detailed systems _____ then follows where outputs, inputs, files, software etc. are all decided.

H The personnel involved with the new system will need to be _____.

I Also, _____ will need to be written.

J There are three ways that a system can be implemented: _____ running, phased implementation and direct implementation.

K After a system has been in use for some time, it needs to be _____ to make sure that the objectives of the system are still being satisfied.

1 John, the head of mathematics at a large comprehensive school, decided to take early retirement and start up[a tutorial agency matching tutors to students. He advertises nationally for both tutors and students. He does all the marketing and advertising while his wife deals with all the paperwork. The business has been a huge success but the amount of paperwork now generated is getting them both down. They are using a manual system at present but would like a new computerised system.

(a) The head of information technology at his old school suggests that they need to perform a feasibility study which will cover hardware, software, staffing and operating costs. Explain why such a study will help John and his wife select the best system.

(b) Explain the steps involved in a feasibility study.

(c) John and his wife have now performed a feasibility study and have decided to buy a Pentium computer with a 1000 MB hard disk and a tape streamer. They have also chosen a laser printer. Explain how they might go about choosing the correct supplier for this equipment.

(d) Once they have decided on a system, how should they go about getting their new system up and running?

2 British Rail use an on-line system for reserving train seats. Documentation has been written for various users of the system. For each of the users below, explain what should be in the documentation.

(a) A reservations clerk.

(b) A senior supervisor.

(c) A systems analyst, who has to maintain the system.

(SEG IT IS)

3 One stage in systems analysis is called fact finding, where the person performing the task, usually a systems analyst, will need to determine answers to a wide range of questions.

You have been asked to find out about an estate agent's system. The estate agent operates 20 agencies in a particular city and its surrounding suburbs. One of the larger shops acts as the head office.

(a) Write down at least 30 facts that you would need to find out about the estate agent's business in order to be able to advise the company on a suitable system.

(b) You are worried that you might encounter some opposition to the introduction of a new system. What can be done to ensure full co-operation from all staff?

Task 1

You have been asked by the owner of a video library to investigate its present manual system because they are thinking of computerising it. The video library only has one shop and about 1800 customers and 2000 videos. Prepare a list of questions in order to perform an initial fact find before a feasibility study.

Task 2

Harlequin Aquatics has decided to place stock details on the computer. A section of the catalogue is shown below.

(a) Look at the above section of the catalogue, which is approximately only one hundredth of the whole catalogue. Think carefully about the uses to which the stock file will be put and decide on what fields are needed. You will also need to decide on the type of field (numeric, character, date, logical, etc.). Now design the database structure for creating a stock file.

(b) A customer rings up and says 'can you let me know what internal filters you have in stock and what prices they are?' Could you answer this, bearing in mind that internal filters are just a small section in the total stock. If you can't, you will need to make some alterations in your stock file design. You could use a coding system to distinguish between the different sections.

(c) When you are happy with your structure, you can start putting the data into your database using the data in the above list and some data which you will need to supply yourself.

(d) Obtain a copy of a fish keeping magazine and have a look at some of the advertisements. Using the information from these advertisements, fill in your stock file until it contains 30 records.

(e) Give examples of reports (lists and results of searches and sorts) that you can get from your stock file.

(f) Finally evaluate your system. Does it do what you intended and what shortcomings does it have?

Internal Filters

Catalogue number	Description of item	Price
52773	Rena Filty Internal Filter	£11.99
52774	Rena 225 Internal Filter	£15.25
52775	Rena 245 Internal Filter	£22.75
52776	Rena 245S Internal Filter	£22.75
52777	Rena 325 Internal Filter	£25.99
52778	Eheim 2252-200 L.P.H.	£64.99
52779	Eheim 2248-600 L.P.H.	£45.95
52780	Eheim 2209-80 L.P.H. inc media	£26.95
52781	Eheim 2207-180 L.P.H.	£16.25
52782	Fluval 1 180 L.P.H.	£ 8.99
52783	Fluval 2 360 L.P.H.	£10.99
52784	Fluval 3 540 L.P.H.	£14.99
52785	Fluval 4 900 L.P.H.	£19.99
52786	Visijet IF 100-400 L.P.H.	£22.99
52787	Visijet IF 200-600 L.P.H.	£27.99

Part of the Harlequin Aquatics stock list

System TASK

You have been asked to build an information system for your school library from scratch. This is a substantial task and to perform it you will need to go through the various steps involved in systems analysis.

Some of the tasks you will need to perform include the following.

(a) You need to carry out a fact find of the manual system, which should include use of questionnaires and involve an interview with the library staff. Any forms, file cards and other documentation should be included in your initial report on the existing system.

You need to get an overall view of the existing library system in terms of the number of books, the number of borrowers, the number of loans per day/week, the average number of books per borrower, etc. You will need to find out how books are catalogued according to subject or author and how the reminder system for overdue books works. At the end of this analysis you should be able to identify the strengths and weaknesses of the existing system.

(b) You will need to design a system. To do this you will need to look at the objectives of the system. You will then need to look at which software, hardware and peripherals should be used. In addition you will need to design input and output screens, database structures and any printouts needed.

(c) A pilot implementation should be done to check whether the system is likely to work. Any likely training implications should be identified and finally an evaluation of the pilot should be undertaken.

(d) Some idea of the cost of the full implementation and the time scale should be given.

(e) A full-scale library system should be investigated like the one used by your local library and it should be compared and contrasted with the suggested system for your school library.

Weather Forecasting
An Application of Data Logging

Weather reporting: the old way

Figure 15.1 shows a typical school weather station. It consists of a slatted box, called a Stevenson's screen in which are held certain instruments such as thermometer, maximum and minimum thermometer, and wet and dry bulb thermometer (used to measure the amount of humidity). Outside the box are a rainfall meter, used to measure in millimetres the amount of rainfall, and an anemometer which is used to measure the wind speed. A sunshine recorder reports on the number of hours of sunshine in the day.

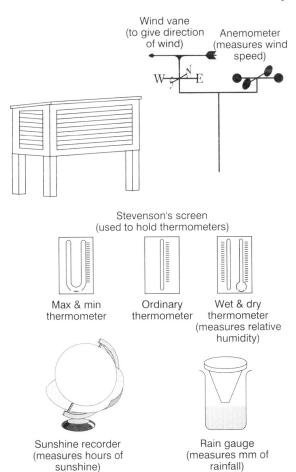

Figure 15.1 *Collecting weather data the old way: the instruments involved*

Collecting the data

The readings are taken by the pupils in the morning immediately before school starts. Two pupils take the readings and they fill in a form with the relevant data.

QUESTION

Design a form that could be used to obtain the weather data over a week. This form will eventually be used by the pupils in maths and geography lessons.

Before you design the form think about what the requirements of the form should be. It would be better if all the data for one month could be placed on a single piece of A4 paper. Are there any other requirements?

The geography teacher decides that she would like more frequent readings made. Julie and John who have to take the readings are not very keen on this idea. Although they find collecting the data interesting they don't find it *that* interesting!

Another problem is that readings are unavailable over the weekend and if both pupils are away from school on the same day, then no readings are taken for that day. Also, the equipment is not read over the summer holidays. Overall, the weather data collected is incomplete.

Problem

Ideally, the geography teacher would like the following:

1 complete records of weather data over 365 days per year (even on Christmas day!)
2 more frequent measurements made (say four times a day)
3 greater accuracy of readings (sometimes the instruments are read incorrectly).

The maths teacher who has been illustrating the use of statistics with the data would like:

1 computer printouts of weather patterns over various periods of time
2 to be able to use a computer package to draw the various graphs.

The solution

Some way is needed of recording the data at set intervals, automatically. This will solve the problems outlined above. If the equipment could transfer the data directly to a computer without necessarily being connected to the computer all of the time, then this would be another advantage. A data logging system would be an ideal choice for this system.

Data logging

A data logging system automatically collects data over a certain period of time. As well as being able to alter this time, you can also alter the frequency with which the measurements are made. Since there is no human error, the measurements will be more accurate than before.

Weather reporting

Weather reporting is an application of data logging. Data logging involves recording quantities automatically over a set period of time. For weather reporting, these quantities are illustrated in Figure 15.2.

Most data loggers do not need to be connected to a computer all the time. Instead they store the data in the logger for a period (50 hours for one particular package). It is also possible to display the data continuously, but this ties up a computer and prevents it being used for other things. Figure 15.3 shows an automatic data logging weather station with its various sensors.

The sensors

Sensors act as the input devices into the computer. Figure 15.4 shows the detailed arrangement of the components of the

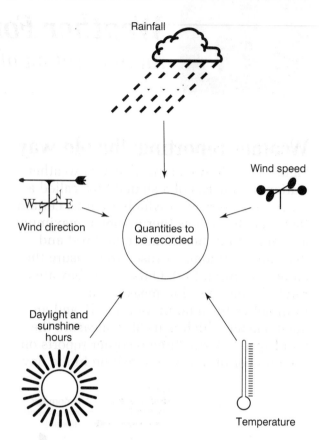

Figure 15.2 *For weather reporting, information about all of these needs to be recorded*

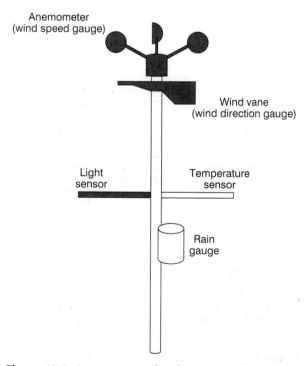

Figure 15.3 *An automatic data logging weather station*

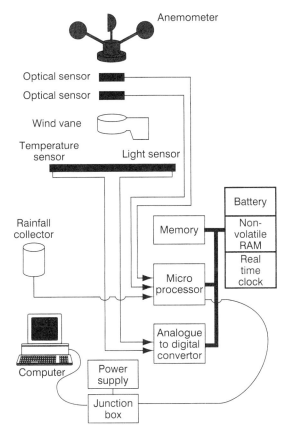

Figure 15.4 *Arrangement of the components in the Weather Reporter*

weather station. The sensors measure the following:

Temperature

The temperature sensor gives an analogue temperature signal which is converted via an analogue-to-digital converter to a digital signal, which is then stored by the microprocessor.

Wind speed

An anemometer measures wind speed by using an optical sensor to generate a binary signal each time it rotates. The wind speed is recorded in kilometres per hour.

Wind direction

The wind direction is detected on a grey code disk. As the wind vane rotates, three optical sensors read the disk and generate a three bit binary pattern. Each pattern

represents one of the eight wind directions. For instance the pattern 010 might represent north-west.

Rainfall

Rainfall is measured using a tilting bucket. As the bucket fills with water, it starts to tilt. When it is full the bucket tips the water out and brings another bucket into position ready to collect more water. An optical sensor detects the number of tips and this digital signal is passed to the microprocessor.

Daylight and sunshine hours

Sunshine is detected by a special diode. The signal from this is then passed to the microprocessor after it is converted from an analogue signal to a digital one. The digital signal is then used by the microprocessor to determine sunrise and sunset time and also to measure sunshine hours.

Additional sensors

Additional sensors that measure atmospheric pressure and relative humidity (a measure of the amount of moisture in the air) may also be connected to the system.

Analogue-to-digital conversion

All the quantities measured by the Weather Reporter are analogue quantities, because they are continuously variable and do not jump in steps from value to value. For instance, temperatures don't just jump from one degree to the next: they have many values in between each degree. Quantities which have continuous values are called analogue quantities and those that jump from one value to the next are called digital quantities.

A rainfall meter measures rainfall which in this system is an analogue quantity but the sensor itself counts the number of buckets that are filled. This is only ever 1, 2, 3 etc., so it is therefore a digital value. Digital values can be fed directly into the microprocessor or computer but analogue values need to be converted to digital values using an analogue-to-digital-converter since most (but not all) computers process only digital values.

QUESTIONS

Fill in the table shown below saying whether each physical quantity is either analogue or digital.

Physical quantity	Digital or analogue
Wind speed	
Wind direction	
Temperature	
Rainfall	

Now look at the section on the sensors used to detect these quantities and fill in the following table.

Sensor	Digital or analogue
Wind speed (optical sensor)	
Wind direction (optical sensor)	
Temperature (integrated circuit sensor)	
Rainfall (optical sensor)	

Advantages of data logging

Data logging is performed automatically without the need for a human to make the measurement. Also, because of this, the data can be collected more frequently than would be possible by doing it manually. The frequency with which the data is logged may also be varied. The electronic signals from the sensors can be relayed through communication lines (by radio or through phone wires) so the sensors can be situated anywhere in the world. Figure 15.4 shows a remote weather station as used by the Meteorological Office. Figure 15.5 shows how the weather data is presented on the screen using equipment and software such as the 'Weather Reporter'.

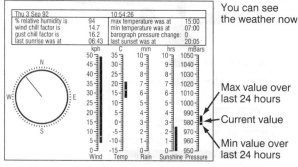

You can see the weather now

Max value over last 24 hours

Current value

Min value over last 24 hours

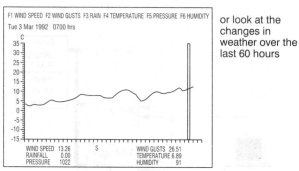

or look at the changes in weather over the last 60 hours

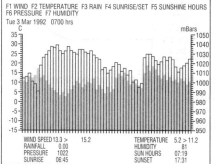

or look at the variations of two quantities over the last 58 days. (This one shows how the temperature and pressure changed each day)

Figure 15.5 *Information that can be shown on the computer screen of a fully automatic data logging weather station*

Transferring weather data to another package

It is possible to transfer weather data obtained from the 'Weather Reporter' to another package. To do this the weather data is converted to a special format which can then be loaded into a spreadsheet package such as Excel or into a database package. Transferring data out of one package is called exporting. Transferring the data into another package is called importing.

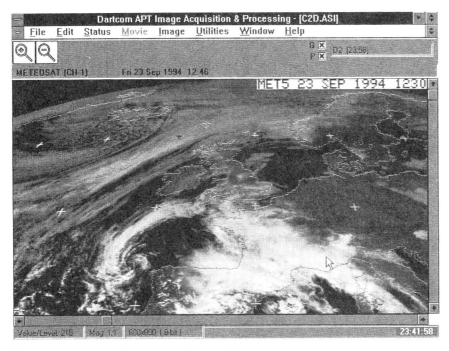

Figure 15.6 *Image from a weather satellite*

Weather satellites

By using the Weather Reporter and the images from a satellite orbiting the Earth, a more complete picture of the likely weather can be obtained. Figure 15.6 shows an image from a weather satellite.

Satellites can be placed in geostationary orbits 36 000 km above the surface of the Earth. At this height the time that a satellite takes to orbit the Earth is the same as the time that the Earth takes to complete one rotation: this is one day. Therefore the satellite stays at the same point above the surface of the Earth.

Other weather satellites, such as METEOSAT, move between the poles in complex orbits and a computer package calculates their position over the Earth.

How weather satellites produce pictures

Weather satellites transmit pictures as coded radio signals. The coded signal is picked up with a satellite dish on the Earth and decoded before being displayed on a screen. The coding ensures that only people who have paid to receive the service can use it.

Uses of satellite images

From the satellite images, we can determine the amount of cloud cover and, if we know from which direction the wind is likely to come, we can predict the weather. If infra-red (heat) images are obtained then we can see the relative temperatures of land and sea.

If still pictures are taken over a period of time and stored, then they can be played back together. This is just like animating a cartoon by joining the individual pictures up. The changing weather pattern can then be observed. You can see the way storms and hurricanes develop and move. Colours may be added to the image by the computer so that certain features stand out.

1 When the weather station is used on its own (i.e. not connected to the computer), the data from the sensors is stored in non-volatile RAM.

(a) What does the abbreviation RAM stand for?

(b) Why is it important that the RAM is non-volatile?

2 When the data is sent from the sensors to the microprocessor, the time must be sent as well. Why is this?

3 The program that controls the microprocessor is stored in ROM.

(a) What does the abbreviation ROM stand for?

(b) Why is it necessary to store the program in ROM rather than in RAM?

4 Compare and contrast the collection of weather data manually using a Stevenson's screen etc. and by using an automatic data logging system such as the Weather Reporter.

5 Manor Top is a secondary school which teaches a full range of subjects. Wherever possible the teachers at Manor Top encourage the pupils to use computers as part of their studies. Manor Top has 20 computers that the pupils can use but there are over 600 pupils. Mrs Logit, the teacher responsible for information technology, is anxious that the pupils should experience computers being used for data logging and control.

A group of senior pupils and Mrs Logit design and construct an automatic weather station. The weather station consists of such devices as a rainfall meter, a sunshine recorder, and an anemometer. Each device has to be connected directly to one of the school's computers. As it is important that the weather data is collected on a regular basis, Mrs Logit and her pupils have to write some computer programs that will run all the time.

Pupils and teachers who are involved in science, geography, the environment and statistics soon become very interested in the data that the weather station is collecting. Hence Mrs Logit is finding that she is under pressure to provide more and different data.

The computer connected to the weather station stores, in a computer file, the amount of sunshine detected each day.

(a) Name the software package that could be used to store the sunshine data.

(b) A software package is used to produce the output shown in Figure 15.7.

   (i) Name the software package.

   (ii) The chart shows two things that cannot be true. State what they are.

   (iii) Explain why, in this case, the result of the average sunshine per day must be wrong.

(c) Each day, the computer connected to the weather station stores the date and the rainfall in centimetres for that date. A database package is used to analyse the file of rainfall data.

Describe what information would be given by the following database instruction:

IF RAIN IS MORE THAN 5 THEN OUTPUT DATE

(d) Tilda Shower is a geography teacher.

Tilda wants the rainfall data to be recorded every day for a whole year. She wants the results to be printed out in the form of a booklet.

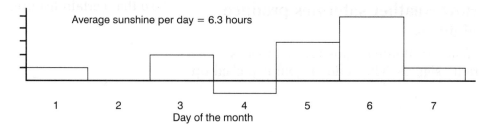

Figure 15.7

(i) Describe how this amount of data could have been collected without the aid of a computer.

(ii) Explain why, in a school, it would not have been practical to collect this amount of data without a computer.

(iii) State one advantage to Tilda's pupils of having this amount of data.

(e) The instructions below are part of a computer program which, every 30 minutes, stores the temperature that the weather station detects.

WAIT 30

DETECT TEMP

STORE TEMP

Tilda now wants the temperature to be stored every 15 minutes.

(f) Show how one of the instructions will have to be changed.

(g) (i) Explain why these three instructions by themselves would not keep on storing the temperature.

(ii) Show the extra instructions that would be needed so that the computer will store the temperature 'forever'. (You may invent your own instructions.)

(h) 50 deg. C is very very hot; –50 deg. C is very very cold. Sometimes the weather station does not work properly so silly temperature values are stored. Explain how the program could be improved to prevent the computer storing silly values for temperature.

---

1 Use a satellite receiving system capable of receiving pictures from the weather satellites NOAA and METEOSTAT. The computer could be used to add false colours to these images. To produce evidence you could either produce screen dumps to a printer or take actual photographs of the screen (ask your physics teacher how to do this).

2 Use the satellite system to produce an animated (moving) picture of

(a) cloud movements over a period of time, or

(b) temperature variation over a period of time.

Also, you could monitor the passage of a weather system over a set period.

3 Use electronic mail to transfer your data along the telephone lines to other schools and colleges in Britain. Use appropriate software to see the way the weather changes from one part of the country to another.

4 Use a weather recording system to obtain regular readings of wind speed, temperature, hours of daylight, pressure, wind direction, hours of sunshine, rainfall and humidity. Collect the data either manually, or by using data logging equipment and transfer it to the computer for processing. Display the readings in a suitable way on the computer. Can you predict the weather tomorrow from your data? Produce a 'school weather forecast' and print it out. How accurate were you?

5 Consider task 4 in conjunction with task 1 and see if this would make your weather predictions more accurate.

Design a complete weather forecasting system over a period of several weeks or months. Collect your readings either manually or by using a data logging system and transfer these to the computer for processing. Processing could include producing graphs.

Chapter 16

Transferring Data Around

A company with a communication problem

Binscope is a retail organisation that is in business to sell high quality optical equipment: terrestrial telescopes, astronomical telescopes, binoculars and microscopes. In addition to the above the company also sells books on astronomy, bird watching etc., as well as many accessories such as eyepieces, camera attachments, tripods, cases etc. It also has a small workshop where optical equipment may be repaired.

At present Binscope has seven shops: in Liverpool, Birmingham, London, Manchester, Leeds, Glasgow and Chester. The whole Binscope operation is controlled from the head office and warehouse next to the Liverpool shop. Figure 16.1 shows the Binscope 'empire'.

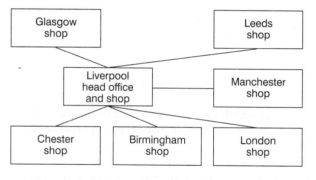

Figure 16.1 *The Binscope empire*

Much of the equipment comes from abroad and it all goes to the Liverpool warehouse where it is checked before being dispatched via carrier to the various shops.

John Bird and his wife Anne opened their first shop in Liverpool in 1989. Both of them had been teachers. The rapid expansion of the business to seven sites along with the employment of a large number of staff has caused many problems.

Many of the problems stem from the fact that the shops are scattered throughout Britain. Transfer of information between the shops and the head office causes problems and some of these are outlined here.

Problems with the existing system

1 Lists of stock are prepared by the head office and sent to each branch by fax before the shops open in the morning. The shops have to send the head office a list of what they have in stock just before they close in the evening. Since stock is continually changing throughout the day, no one really knows what the actual stock situation is.

2 To compensate for point 1, staff have to ring around the other branches to find an item that the customer wants, if it is out of stock in that particular branch. This takes time and ties up sales staff. Customers frequently get annoyed waiting while this is done and inevitably sales are lost. In addition the phone bills have been excessively large.

3 New price lists, product literature and maintenance schedules are sent by post and this takes too long.

4 Sales figures have to be telephoned to the head office at the end of each day. This is tedious, since all the shops tend to try to phone at the same time and it can take a long time to get through.

5 Orders from the manufacturers are dealt with by the head office and this makes it difficult to inform a customer in one of the branches when a particular product will be delivered without phoning the head office first.

6 The company likes to keep in touch with its customers, so it sends them a list of new products and special sales from time to time. Since each branch keeps its own

110

database, one customer who had shopped at three of the branches, receives three copies of these lists.

7   Because of the problem with stock, there are frequent delays in ordering goods from the suppliers. The company runs out of goods which are in high demand and sales are lost because customers go elsewhere.

8   Fax is used to send orders to suppliers but suppliers would like to receive payment electronically. Much of the optical equipment comes from Japan or Germany, two technically advanced countries. Companies in these countries have suggested that Binscope uses EDI but the directors of Binscope don't even know what it is.

9   John and Anne Bird frequently need information from the shops in order to manage the business effectively. This information takes time to get and this is very frustrating for them.

Binscope realises there is a problem so the directors hire a computer consultant for some advice. The consultant, who is a qualified systems analyst, will look at the present system in detail, and will identify their needs and come up with some solutions.

After looking at the business and having talks with the various staff, the consultant suggests that they need the following;

1   a stock file that is accessible to everyone
2   a faster way of sending mail and pictures (for advertising) between the head office and the shops
3   a faster ordering system between Binscope and its suppliers
4   a central file of customers that is accessible to everyone
5   a way of paying the suppliers directly using some form of fund transfer from the bank
6   as each sale is made at the various shops, the details of the transaction (piece of business) need to be sent automatically to the head office where the stock file and the customer file can be automatically

updated. Since this happens in real time it means that the stock file is continually updated and reflects the true stock position of Binscope.

QUESTIONS

1   At the moment faxes are used to transfer some of the important information between sites. Explain what is meant by faxes and how they are used. Use the glossary at the back of the book to find what a fax is if you don't already know.

2   Anne Bird has suggested that the sales figures for each shop should be transferred to a 3.5 inch floppy disk which is sent by a carrier to arrive before the start of business the next day. The stock details for the whole company can then be faxed back to the shops at around 10 a.m.

   (a)   The head office has a couple of stand-alone PCs. Explain what the term 'stand-alone' means.

   (b)   Why is it useful for the head office to receive the stock details on a floppy disk rather than by fax?

   (c)   Why do you think that the stock position is not given back to the shops on a floppy disk?

3   Put yourself in the position of one of Binscope's customers. Write a list of the problems and frustrations you might have in dealing with this company.

4   Put yourself in the position of a manufacturer of telescopes. What problems might you have in dealing with Binscope?

The solution to Binscope's problem

The consultant decides that the company needs a communications system. She suggests that all the computers should be networked so that data is easily transferred between the sites. She decides that a local area network (LAN) is used in the head office, with a wide area network (WAN) being used between the sites. Also, the company needs to consider the possibility of using electronic mail. This all sounds very complicated to Anne and John, so the consultant has made some notes to explain how the system works. Here they are.

Networks

A network is a series of computer systems that are linked together so that they are able to share computing power or storage facilities. The link may be between computers in the same building or between computers in different parts of the country or even in different parts of the world.

Binscope needs to make sure that when a network is chosen, room is left for future expansion. Who knows, in five years' time the number of shops may have doubled. For this reason the systems analyst has suggested that a dedicated file server is used. This is generally a much higher specification than the other computers, with a very large hard disk drive. All the common data such as the stock file will be held on the file server's hard disk. A dedicated file server monitors and controls the network and while it is performing this important task, it is not available to be used as a normal workstation.

Local area networks

Local area networks (LANs) are confined to a small area. Usually this small area is within a single building although it need not be confined to just a single office. Sometimes LANs spread through several buildings on the same site. Messages can be sent between the terminals and this is very useful for sending memos between offices. Figure 16.2 shows the local area network proposed for the Binscope office.

Wide area networks

Wide area networks (WANs) cover a wide geographical area. For instance, banks and building societies have their main computers situated in one place with connections made by telephone wires to all

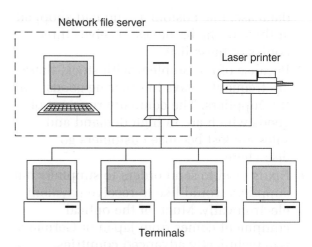

Figure 16.2 *The local area network in Binscope's head office*

the various branches. Using WANs, computers may be linked together in different countries using satellites, microwaves or telecommunication links. In practice, LANs are often connected to WANs via a special **gateway.** Using a gateway any computer system can be accessed provided that it is connected to one of the many communication systems in use.

Advantages and disadvantages of networking

Advantages
1 Expensive peripheral devices such as laser printers and scanners can be shared between users.
2 Messages can be sent between users on the same site with LANs or anywhere in the world with WANs.
3 All users can access the same files so this avoids having to duplicate information.
4 Network software can be purchased which is often cheaper than buying an individual package for each machine.

Disadvantages
1 If a WAN is used, sophisticated equipment is needed and the rental of telecommunication links makes it very expensive.
2 A loss in the ability to transmit data for even a short time can cause havoc, with tasks having to be performed manually.

Figure 16.3 *Sending messages across a local area network can be useful*

3 File security is more important with networks, especially if they are connected to the public telephone system. For instance, if a virus were to get onto a network then it could affect all the networked terminals.

4 Wiring can be expensive both to buy and to install. Wiring has to be sunk to avoid it trailing across a floor where it would be dangerous.

Modems

For Binscope's computers in the shops to communicate with the head office system, each computer in the shops will need to have a modem. (Figure 16.4)

A modem (short for **mo**dulator **dem**odulator) allows data to be passed along telephone lines from one computer to another. This device converts the digital

signals produced by the computer into analogue signals. These analogue signals are sent along a telephone line to another modem, where they are converted back into digital signals for the receiving computer.

The speed at which data is transferred is measured in bits per second (bit/s for short). The faster the modem, the quicker the data can be transferred and it is possible to get up to speeds of around 28 000 bits per second. Speed is important in terms of the cost of the transmission: the time spent connected to the phone line is directly related to the cost. If the time can be decreased, then the cost of transmission will be reduced. For example, about 10 years ago the entire contents of a 5.25 inch floppy disk could be transferred using a 300 bit/s modem in the huge time of over three hours, and costing around £125. Now, with a fast modem, the same amount of data can be transferred in four minutes at a cost of a few pence. Some modems are able to compress the data before sending it and this also reduces the transmission time.

Telecommunications

Telecommunications has been a big growth area over the last few years. More and more people are involved in working from home, and using computers and telecommunications to transmit their work to an office or to other workers in the electronic chain.

Telecommunications can be used to link up to many online databases.

BT Mailbox

Mailbox is the electronic mail service provided by British Telecom. It has about four million users. In addition to electronic mail, the system can also be used to send and receive telexes and faxes. The system is not cheap; for instance a lone user would have to pay the following charges:

- a one-off joining fee
- a connection fee paid per minute (either cheap or peak rate)

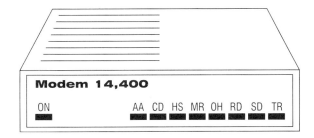

Figure 16.4 *Modem*

• a fee for each 512K block of characters sent using the system
• a fee for every 2048 characters stored by the system on the user's behalf.

CompuServe

CompuServe is a huge commercial international online service with over two million subscribers. There are 80 basic services which are free to access, although users still have to pay telecommunications charges. CompuServe offers many other services for which there is an additional charge. The system also offers a cheap method of sending electronic mail messages across the globe. Figure 16.5 shows an opening screen from CompuServe.

Just a few of the many services provided by CompuServe are:

• news from all the international press agencies throughout the world (up-to-date news as it happens)
• sports information
• financial information
• television and radio programme information
• entertainment information
• weather details
• back issues of many leading newspapers (*Guardian, Times, Daily Telegraph*, etc.). You can search them by using keywords
• thousands of magazines.

Figure 16.5 *Opening screen from CompuServe*

The Internet

The Internet can be described as a network of networks. Almost any type of information or person can be found on this network. You can access anything from a database on space science held by NASA to the touring arrangements of your favourite group. You access the Internet through information providers such as Demon or Delphi.

World Wide Web (WWW)

The World Wide Web (WWW) is a part of the Internet where graphics, sound, video and animation are used, as well as text. The word used for this mix of media is 'hypertext'. Special hypertext links are built into the World Wide Web that allow the user to move around by clicking with a mouse on words or graphics on the screen. Special software, called browser software, is needed to take full advantage of the World Wide Web. The most popular WWW software browsers are Netscape and Mosaic.

Electronic mail

Electronic mail, sometimes called e-mail, is a method of sending messages from one terminal to another via a communications link. There are various providers of electronic mail, including Internet information providers and CompuServe. Many people are confused about how electronic mail works. To communicate with electronic mail, you first have to have an e-mail address of your own and you must, of course, also know the e-mail address of the person to whom you wish to send a message. You can then write your message using e-mail software. Then you need to use your communications software and modem to connect to a service provider's mainframe computer. Once you are connected you can transmit your message.

The message is then placed in a mail box on a main computer. As soon as the person to whom you have sent the message logs onto the system they can access their mailbox and read any letters that have been sent. One of the advantages of electronic mail is that the same message can be sent to many different people at the same time simply by referring to their e-mail addresses. Obviously you cannot send mail in this way to a person who is not a subscriber to one of the electronic mail systems.

Message sending

Sending data down a communications line is not just a question of sending the streams of bits that represent each character. The problem is that each computer manufacturer has its own standards for encoding data. However, there is a standard for the connection of PCs which enables communication between all the components. This is called Open Systems Interconnection (OSI).

QUESTIONS

1 A lot of people think that when you send a message by electronic mail it automatically pops up on the screen. In fact it is stored in a mailbox on a mainframe computer.

(a) Why can't you simply send the message to the other person's computer where it could be stored on their disk drive?

(b) Many people get fed up with all the junk mail that they get in their mailboxes when they subscribe to electronic mail services.

(i) What is meant by 'junk mail'?

(ii) What feature of electronic mail makes it easier for suppliers to advertise their products and services?

2 Someone says that eventually electronic mail will replace the postal service. Do you think this is likely? Write a paragraph to support your opinion.

Protocols and handshakes

When human beings communicate with each other, we have a set of rules that we use. Although we do not think about them when we are holding a conversation, they still exist. For instance, we wait until the other person has finished talking before we say something and usually acknowledge that we have understood what has been said by nodding occasionally. In other words there is a protocol between the individuals.

We also have protocols in telecommunications. Protocols ensure that each computer behaves predictably and provides information in an understandable way. We have already come across a gateway. A gateway translates the protocols between computers so that different computers are able to communicate with each other.

Before sending data a computer performs what is called a handshake. The handshake is an exchange of signals which establishes the communication between the devices.

File compression

File compression is the process of condensing repetitive information. It is used when sending data through a telecommunications link, since the smaller the file, the cheaper the file transfer will be. File compression may be performed by software before the data is sent or by the modem itself as the data is being sent.

Electronic Data Interchange (EDI)

Many companies are using a system called electronic data exchange, which links them to their banks so that they can make immediate payments to their suppliers electronically. The old method of paying by cheques involves more expense, such as the time spent by well-paid executives to scrutinise and sign the cheques placed in front of them. However, there is one advantage of the older method – the delay in payment is often useful if there are cash flow problems and the excuse can always be made that the 'cheque is in the post'.

EDI works as follows. Companies receive invoices electronically from their suppliers asking for payment. These are checked by computer against the purchase ledger to make sure that they are correct. The computer then sends details to the bank's computer to make the payment electronically to the supplier. This would be ideal for Binscope since many of the company's suppliers are in other countries: EDI would cut down on the paperwork and problems with late payment due to the post.

Benefits to the person sending money

The person sending money benefits because:

1 no paper is needed to pay the accounts since everything is done electronically
2 the relationship with the supplier is improved, since all the invoices are paid promptly without reminders
3 future cash flow can be predicted with a greater degree of accuracy
4 bank charges are reduced.

Benefits to the person receiving money

The person receiving money benefits because:

1 they can be sure of receiving the funds and there is no waiting for a cheque to be cleared
2 the sales ledgers may be updated immediately without the use of paper
3 errors in data entry are eliminated since the data is captured electronically
4 bank charges are reduced.

TEST YOURSELF

Using the words in the list below, copy out and complete sentences A to H, underlining the words you have inserted. The words may be used more than once.

gateway   protocol   LANs   WANs   network
modems   electronic   analogue

A A group of computers linked together in order to share facilities is called a _____.

B Networks confined to a single site are called _____.

C Networks that use communication lines and are separated by a distance, are called _____.

D Computers connected together using a communications line need two _____, one at each end of the line.

E Modems convert the digital signals from a computer into _____ signals which may be passed along the telephone line.

F _____ mail allows messages to be sent from one terminal to another which may be in another part of the country or even the world.

G For computers to communicate with each other they must share the same _____.

H Different types of computer may communicate with each other provided that a _____ is used.

THINGS TO DO

1 Read the paragraph below, and then answer the questions.

In a busy local office of a large motoring insurance company there are about 10 computerised workstations, linked to each other by a LAN. The system is controlled by a powerful file-server with a 300 MB hard disk, which is accessible by all workstations. The file server also has a tapestreamer attached to it. Each workstation has its own dot-matrix printer, and there are also two laser printers linked to the network. The word processing software is capable of **mail merging**, and also has a **spell check** facility.

(a) What does **LAN** stand for?   (1 mark)

(b) Why are there both laser printers attached to the network and dot-matrix printers for each workstation?   (2 marks)

(c) (i) What does the spell check facility do?   (1 mark)

   (ii) When using the spell check facility, you can add extra words to the dictionary. Why is this important?   (2 marks)

(d) (i) What is meant by **mail merging**?   (2 marks)

   (ii) Give a relevant example of when mail-merging might be used in this insurance firm.   (2 marks)

(SEG FT IS Spec)

2 A computer retailer offers the following LAN package for five users:

- 1 × 486 Pentium file server, 16 MB RAM, with 550 MB hard disk
- 4 × 486 DX-66 SVGA colour workstations with 350 MB hard disk
- 1 × Novell Netware 3.11 network software
- 1 × Hewlett Packard Laserjet 4 laser printer
- 5 × 16 bit Ethernet cards
- 1 × 600 MB tape backup unit
- onsite installation and systems configuration
- free introductory training
- 3 years full onsite maintenance and technical support.

(a) Explain the meaning of the term LAN and explain how it differs from the other type of network called a WAN.

(b) The file server (a 486 DX-50) has a clock speed of 50 MHz whereas the workstations (486 DX-33s) have clock speeds of 33 MHz. The file server also has a larger hard disk and is most likely to have a larger amount of RAM.

    (i) Why is the clock speed an important factor when selecting a computer?

    (ii) Why do you think the file server has a higher specification than the workstations?

(c) The package includes just one laser printer. For the price of a single laser printer several dot-matrix printers could have been bought. Why do you think the laser printer solution was the one that was chosen?

Binscope would like you to design an advert for the company to be placed in a specialised magazine called *Bird Watching*. The advert is for the mail order part of the business, so only the Liverpool Head Office's address, phone and fax number need be quoted. It is February, a typically quiet month for Binscope, so they have decided to stimulate sales by offering 10% off all prices until the end of the month. The prices quoted in the advert will still be the original prices though.

Here are some of the things you will need to include in the advert. They are not in any particular order so you will have to decide the order for yourself. You can also include your own information. Remember that the purpose of the advert is to sell Binscope's equipment.

- Binscope
  67 Crosby Road East
  Crosby
  Liverpool
  L23 6TY
- Phone: 0151-211-9000   Fax: 0151-234-8976
- February Special Offer: 10% Off Everything!
- You can use your ACCESS or VISA card to order by telephone.
- Goods dispatched promptly.
- Mail order: insurance, packing and postage are free.
- Mail order service available Monday to Saturday 9 a.m. until 5 p.m.
- The friendly experts professionals recommend!

Include as many special effects, fonts and typefaces as your software allows.

Try to incorporate some diagrams or clip art into your advert. There are some diagrams on the next page that you may be able to scan in if you have access to a scanner. If not, have a look through any clip art with your graphics package and see if there are any suitable pictures. If not, don't

SKILLS BUILDING

worry. The magazine will probably charge more if there is artwork anyway. If you feel adventurous, you could try your hand at drawing some pictures yourself.

Produce a couple of drafts. Make sure that there are no spelling mistakes and show them to someone else, maybe your art teacher, for their comments.

Here are details of the equipment Binscope wants placing in the advert.

Kowa telescopes			Kowa eyepieces	
TSN 1	£349.00		20 × Wide Angle	£ 74.00
TSN 2	£349.00		25 ×/40 ×	£ 63.00
611	£316.00		20-60 ZEP	£127.00
612	£296.00		27 × Wide Angle	£109.00
TSN 3	£649.00			
TSN 4	£649.00			

Leica binoculars			Nikon binoculars	
8 × 32 BA	£649.00		Compact 8 × 23	£ 99.00
7 × 42 BA	£698.00		Compact 9 × 25	£109.00
8 × 42 BA	£718.00		Sportstar 8 × 20	£119.00
			Sportstar 8 × 30	£299.00

Nikon telescopes	
Fieldscope 2	£379.00
Fieldscope 245	£399.00

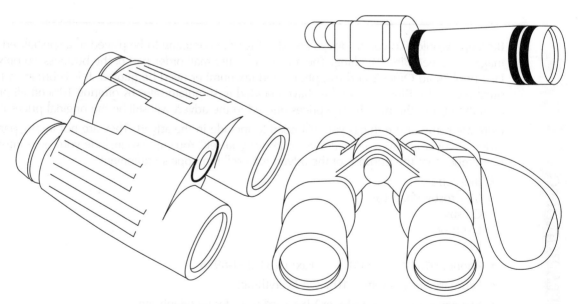

Figure 16.6 *Some optical equipment which you could scan for your Binscope advertisement*

Task 1

Use CAMPUS 2000, CompuServe, the Internet or any other electronic mail system to contact pupils or students in a school in another country. If you have any pen friends you could try contacting them or perhaps your town is twinned with another that you could contact.

Try to co-ordinate this task with your language or geography teacher. For instance, you could word process a document to be sent to a French school and for them to reply to you in English.

Remember that this task needs to be looked at from an information technology point of view and when writing it up for your IT task you should consider the following;

- a description of what you are trying to achieve
- which software you used and why it was chosen against other types of software
- the hardware needed for the system and why it was needed
- what you actually did to perform the task and your reasons for doing it in this way
- the advantages of electronic mail over telephone, letters, fax etc.
- evidence of the results you have obtained such as printouts of the electronic mail messages (both those sent and those received).

Task 2

John and Anne Bird frequently like to attend sales exhibitions of optical equipment and any other opportunity for them to show their equipment. The problem is knowing where and when there are country fairs, shows, etc. What they need is to know which online communication systems are available and whether they would be of any use to them. You have been asked to investigate.

Task 3

John and Anne Bird frequently have to travel to various cities and towns on the trains. You are employed at Binscope and have been asked how to find out travel information from the British Rail database using the Prestel system. In your documentation compare the way the computer system works compared with finding out the information using timetables and fare details available from the main stations.

Task 4

Sometimes you may need to contact someone in another part of the country by telephone. If you have their address but not their phone number then you can always contact directory enquiries or you could go to your local library and look up the telephone directory for that area. There is however a Phonebase database on Prestel which may be used for this. Using Prestel, evaluate this method of obtaining the information and compare it with traditional printed phone directories.

Chapter 17

System Security

Computer security

Computer security is concerned with taking care of the hardware, software and most importantly, the data. The cost of creating data again from scratch can far outweigh the cost of any hardware or programs lost. Loss of data can have various consequences, some of which are shown in Figure 17.1.

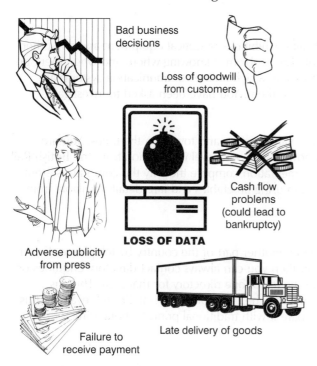

Figure 17.1 *Some of the consequences of data loss*

Physical security

Computer equipment and its data need to be protected from physical harm. Hazards could include natural ones such as fire, lightning, water damage etc., and can also include deliberate damage or theft.

Computer theft

In 1991, during the Gulf War a Wing Commander in the RAF had his laptop computer which contained the Allied plans for the war stolen from his car. Although the thief was likely to have been a petty thief, the plans for the war nevertheless had to be changed.

Although there are many ways of making sure that unauthorised people are denied access to a system through the use of keyboard locks, passwords etc., it is more difficult to prevent a thief from picking up a system and stealing it. Locks, bolts, clamps, alarmed circuits and tags are all methods of hardware protection. Although not many people would consider leaving a bicycle without a lock, people do often leave thousands of pounds worth of computer equipment unlocked and unattended.

Sometimes it is easier to improve the security around a computer system. Usually, if a building is secure, then the computer system will be secure.

Having fewer entrances to buildings, using alarms on emergency exits, using security badges and having keypad locks on all rooms will all help.

Preventing computer theft

1 A note should be made of all the serial numbers of computers and peripherals, since this may be the only way that the police can identify stolen equipment.
2 It is possible with some computers to lock the case of the computer, which prevents the computer from being turned on. This should always be done when the computer is not in use and the key should be safely stored in a secret place and not in the top drawer of the desk that the computer stands on.
3 Data should be backed up regularly and stored securely away from the computer. If the computer system is stolen then at

least the data, which would be a lot more expensive to recreate, would be safe.

4 All staff should be made aware of security and encouraged to question suspicious behaviour.

5 If an ID badge system is used, where staff and visitors have to wear a security badge which contains their photograph, name etc. then everyone from the chairman to the cleaners must wear them since this indicates to outsiders that the firm is security conscious.

Protection from fires

Fires which start in computer rooms are rare. Usually they are the result of faulty wiring or overloaded sockets. It is more likely that a fire will start in adjacent offices or in storage areas. Fireproof doors help contain fires. Smoke detectors should be used to detect fires at an early stage. Gas flooding systems are used in large computer installations and are preferred to water ones because the damage done by water is often greater than that by the fire.

Protection from dust and extremes of temperature

Air conditioning is more important for larger mainframe systems where the temperature and the humidity (amount of water in the air) must be controlled. The air must also be pure and therefore must be filtered before it enters into the room.

Software security

Viruses

Viruses are mischievous programs whose purpose is to disrupt the sensible use of computers. Many viruses do little more than display a message (usually insulting!) on the screen, but some are designed to act after a certain period of time and do such things as make the letters start to drop off the screen or even erase the entire contents of your hard disk. As their name suggests, viruses

are able to spread by 'infecting' other disks and they do this by copying themselves onto other disks which are being used by the computer. Although there are many viruses (over 2000 to date), the main problems are caused by a handful of very familiar ones with names such as: Cascade, Form, Jerusalem and Stoned. Since these viruses have been around for some time, they are well understood and easy to remove from computers by anti-virus software. Viruses are quite common, especially in situations where there is a large number of users such as in a school or a college.

Figure 17.2

Antivirus software

Antivirus software can be used to scan a computer's memory and disks to detect viruses. If any viruses are detected, then the software can be used to remove them (or to disinfect a disk, as it is often called). When choosing antivirus software, speed of checking is important. A typical antivirus program will take just under a minute to check 200 MB of files.

Avoiding viruses

1 Don't buy second-hand software unless you can scan it first.

2 Check your computer for viruses if it has been recently repaired.

3 Do not download software from bulletin boards, since this is the easiest way for the people who produce viruses to distribute their handiwork.

4 Be suspicious of all software distributed freely, such as shareware and software which comes free with magazines as these have sometimes had viruses on them.

5 Try not to use too many different computers, since this will increase the risk of passing on a virus.

6 Install anti-virus software on your machine, which checks for viruses on the hard disks every time the system is booted up and checks the floppy disks before data is taken from them.

Backing up data

Backing up data means taking a copy of the data and keeping it away from the computer in a secure place. Obviously it is no good keeping a backup copy on the same disk. The most common way to lose a file is through user error, where a person makes a

Figure 17.3

mistake with one of the commands and deletes a file or a whole series of files which they did not intend to delete. Although

there are software packages available to recover such data these should not be relied upon and there is no substitute for having a backup copy of the data in a secure place.

Rules for backing up

1 Never keep back up disks near the computer. If the computer is stolen then the thieves may take the disks as well. Never keep the disks in the drawer of a desk since this is the first place they will look.

2 If you hold a lot of data which would be very expensive to recreate, then you should invest in a fire-proof safe to protect your backups against theft and fire.

3 Keep at least one set of backup disks in a different place (i.e. at a different site).

Archiving

Archiving means placing important computer files in a safe place so that they can be found easily if needed.

Disk failure

It is important to bear in mind that all microcomputers will suffer at least one serious fault during their lifetimes. A typical hard disk unit has a mean time between failures of between 20 000 to 200 000 hours. This means that if a computer was used for 12 hours per day, 5 days per week and 52 weeks a year then you could expect its hard disk to break down once in about six years. If the computer was being used as a file server (i.e. used to control a network), then it could be switched on 24 hours per day 365 days per year, so the hard disk could fail on average every 27 months. Couple this with the chance of other components failing and you have a complete computer which is likely to break down every 14 months.

Backup copies of the programs and data on a hard disk should be taken at regular intervals. A tape streamer is usually used. This looks a little like an ordinary tape recorder. Transfer from the hard disk to the tape takes place quickly and you don't have to supervise the computer while backup is taking place. Should the hard disk become

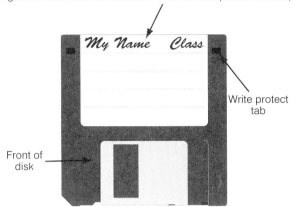

Always write where the disk should be returned if lost
(e.g. name and address of home or school or a phone number)

My Name   Class

Write protect
tab

Front of
disk

If you can see through the write protect hole
then you will only be able to read the data and not alter it.
If the hole is closed by moving the tab down you will now
be able to read and write data.

Figure 17.4 *Some of the security features on a 3.5 in disk*

damaged, then it is easy to restore files.

Figure 17.4 shows some of the security features of a 3.5 inch floppy disk.

Some systems use two hard disks in parallel with each other, which means that whatever is stored on one disk will be stored automatically on the other.

Attempted blackmail

Recruitment agencies are in business to match jobs with people, with the employer paying the agency a fee if a person is employed. The data held about the jobs on offer and the people who are looking for jobs would be valuable to a competitor.

In one case, an employee left an agency and rang up to say that he had copied a disk which he would sell to the highest bidder unless he was paid a large amount of money. The agency did not pay him mainly because the data was encoded and it was unlikely he had a decoder; the agency also thought that no other recruitment agency would pay him.

Nothing happened in this case. The blackmailer did not do anything else and the police were not contacted because of the problems with evidence, which amounted only to a single telephone call.

Protecting your files

Software can be written which does not allow access to a computer unless a password is keyed in. The password, which is never shown on the screen, should be changed regularly and should never be written down. Obvious names, such as the surname of the person using the machine, should be avoided, along with other obvious passwords such as 'access'.

Many large systems use software to limit each user's access to only those files that are needed for the performance of their particular job. So, for instance, an accounts clerk could have a password that allows access to files needed for checking invoices, whereas the accountant would have access to all the accounts files.

It is also important to try to restrict access to a computer's operating system particularly for inexperienced users. A simple command at the operating systems prompt can erase an entire hard disk. Restricted access can also be used to prevent people from copying data from the hard to the floppy disk.

Encryption

Sometimes files which contain sensitive data are encrypted (i.e. coded). If a tape or disk containing sensitive files is stolen then it would be impossible to read the data without the decoder.

Encryption is often used when important data is transmitted from one place to another. The data is coded before being sent and then decoded at the other end. Both processes are performed automatically by computers. Should the data be intercepted, then it will be impossible to understand or alter.

Project advice

Always keep backup copies of your work and don't keep your backups in the same disk box as your original disks.

If a disk becomes corrupted for whatever reason and you haven't taken a backup don't immediately throw the disk away. There are various programs that are able to recover data from corrupted disks. Norton Utilities is one such package. If you do have a corrupted disk ask your teacher to use one of these packages to look at the disk to see if it is possible to recover any of the data.

If you have accidentally deleted a file that you wanted to keep tell your teacher. Again, using special software it is possible to get the file back.

The difference between security and integrity

Data integrity

Data integrity is concerned with the 'correctness' of the data. Errors may be introduced into data in a variety of ways. They could be introduced when the person typing in the data misreads it off a source document or if a program or machine errors corrupt the data. Some types of corruption could be caused by simple typing errors. Validation and verification checks are performed on data to ensure its integrity and further information about this can be found in Chapter 8.

Data security

Data security is concerned with keeping the data safe from the various hazards that could destroy it.

TEST YOURSELF

Using the words in the list below, copy out and complete sentences A to J. Underline the words you have inserted. The words may be used once, more than once or not at all.

water   data   physical   encrypted   backup
gas   smoke   viruses   antivirus   tape   keypads
passwords

A Computer security is concerned with protecting the hardware, software and _____.

B _____ security is used to protect against theft, fire etc.

C As computers become smaller, they become more portable. To protect against theft _____ may be used on doors to prevent unauthorised access.

D Copies of data or programs kept for security purposes are called _____ copies.

E _____ copies should always be kept away from the computer since if the computer is stolen then the thieves will probably take the disks as well.

F To provide early warnings of a fire, _____ detectors are used and _____ flooding systems are used to extinguish the fire.

G Programs that are written to disrupt serious computer use mischievously are called _____.

H _____ software is used to detect viruses and to remove them.

I To copy the entire contents of a hard disk quickly a _____ streamer is used.

J Data is often _____ to prevent tampering before it is sent along communication lines.

1 It is Friday the 13th and yet another story is on the news about a computer virus which lies dormant until, on this date, it springs into life and destroys all the files.

(a) Your father doesn't understand what a virus is and how it is caught by a computer. Write a short paragraph to explain viruses.

(b) Your father uses a personal computer at work. After your comments in part (a) he starts to look worried.

What can he do to

(i) determine whether there are already viruses lurking on his computer, and

(ii) make sure that no viruses enter his system?

2 Michelle's mother is an accounts executive for a large advertising agency. She uses a personal computer at work for storing the artwork for all the agency's major customers. No backup copies are kept, since to backup a 350 MB disk full of files takes a long time and 'in any case the computer has been very reliable so far'. Michelle often brings the machine home at weekends, partly to do some extra work but mainly for the use of her son who likes to play computer games. He has just received a copy of a disk from a friend of a friend and is looking forward to playing it.

Michelle needs to be made more aware about security.

(a) Explain what a backup copy is and why it is made.

(b) Why should Michelle not rely on her machine's reliability?

(c) What security risks are introduced by bringing home the computer in her car and letting her son play games on it?

(d) Suggest a list of guidelines that Michelle should adopt regarding the security of her data.

3 Your teacher/lecturer is fed up with people not looking after their disks. Disks are constantly being left in machines after the lessons with no names on them. Some pupils are losing the data because the disks have been mishandled. Pupils have not been taking backup copies on a regular basis.

Your teacher has asked you to use a graphics package to design a poster that could be placed on the computer room wall. Using appropriate software, design and produce a suitable poster. (You may find it easier to work on paper to start with and then to do the final design using the computer).

Look through some computer supplier's catalogues at the security devices available for microcomputers. Write a brief report, using wordprocessing software, explaining how these gadgets work and how much they cost.

THINGS TO DO

 INVESTIGATION

In this project you will be given various situations which have actually happened. You need to read about them carefully and then suggest improvements that would prevent each situation from occurring again.

1. Virus attack

A firm of typesetters used computers for desktop publishing. Their software package became infected with a virus called the 'Lazy Harry' virus, which distorts the text on the screen and also causes the system to crash now and again. The company at first suspected that it was a hardware fault and its overall effect was to slow the company down and cause missed publication dates. This in turn caused financial problems. Eventually the firm discovered that the problem was a virus that had been brought into the company by the senior partner's son who had been playing games on the office PC. The work dropped by 25% and some customers were not sent invoices, which cost the company £20 000.

What strict guidelines would you lay down to make sure that this did not happen again?

2. Power failure

A minicomputer was installed in the offices of a food processing plant high up in the Pennines and in an area where lightning frequently occurred. As the lightning struck, the power supply would go off for one or two seconds, which was sufficient time for the computer system to fail. Backup copies had to be used to restore the data and sometimes this would need to be done four or five times a day.

What could be done to help this company?

3. Theft

A health authority had eight microcomputers in a busy department. The public had access to the department and the computers were visible from the street. One evening all the computers and associated equipment were stolen. The thieves gained access through the front door which had only a single Chubb lock. The theft occurred at nine o'clock at night and was witnessed by several people who thought that the department was moving to another office.

What possible security measure could this company have taken?

4. System failure

A young inexperienced computer operator was working in a computer room with a minicomputer. He switched it on early in the morning and a grating sound was heard coming from the disk drive when he loaded the operating system. He took the disk

out and placed the backup copy in the drive and tried to reload the operating system. He heard the same grating sound as before. He turned to the other drive and placed each disk in turn into it and again heard the grating sound. An engineer was called and he told the operator that both disks and drives were ruined. The problem appeared to be caused by dust on the disk.

What could the company do to prevent this happening again?

 INVESTIGATION

You have been asked to review the security of your school's or college's computer operations. Write down a list of the questions you would ask the person in charge of the computers.

Here are a few questions to start you off.

1 How often are the passwords changed?

2 Does each person using the system have the same password or are the passwords used by a group of people?

3 Does a screen turn off if a user hasn't used a terminal for a while?

4 Can a user get into the operating system?

From the answers to your questions, write down, with reasons, whether you think the security could be improved. Then make suggestions of what could be done to improve security.

18

Data and You
The Data Protection Act

Computers and privacy

The rapid explosion in the use of computers in the last ten years has benefited us in many ways. Many tasks that we now take for granted, such as the use of credit cards or airline booking, would have been impossible without them. However, there are problems. As more computers are used, more and more information about each of us is stored on computers. By linking the information gained from several computers together it is possible to build up a complete picture of a person's life. Figure 18.1 shows just some of the organisations that hold personal information about us.

Suppose that Richard goes abroad for a fortnight. Let's see how much we could find out about what he did on the holiday, if we had access to computers that stored information about him.

By linking in to travel companies' computers we could find out where he went on holiday, whether he went on his own, how long for and the dates. From the bank's computer we could find out how much money he took with him. We could find out from the travel insurance company's computer whether he had any existing illnesses before he went. If he paid by travellers' cheques or credit cards we could find out what he bought while on holiday. If he was a member of a library we could even find out which books he took with him!

This is a fairly trivial example. Let's now look at another example; this time it is a more sinister one.

Suppose we live in an undemocratic country, where there are no elections and the president is only there because he has the army to back him and people are too frightened to resist. He wants to keep control of the country, which he can do by fear. The church in the country provides the only opposition to him. All opponents are arrested and thrown in jail and the president would like to round up all the major members of the church.

Just think how computers could be useful to him. He could find out from libraries who has borrowed religious books. He could get lists of the clergy from computers. Computers can store a person's photograph. Then when an unknown person is photographed, perhaps leaving a church, the computer can identify the person. This all sounds very far-fetched but the technology exists and there are many countries ruled through force.

The reasons behind the Data Protection Act

As more and more information came to be stored on computers, much of it personal data about individuals, there became a need for some sort of control over the way that it was collected and the way it could be used. Furthermore, other countries in the EC had laws governing the ways data could be used, so to be able to trade with these countries, Britain had to introduce laws to protect people from the misuse of data about them.

The Data Protection Act was made law in 1984 and applies only to the processing of data by computer; other laws cover manual, paper-based systems. What we mean by processing is the collection, storage and distribution of information. The Data Protection Act applies only to personal data about living individuals.

The act places obligations on those people who record and use personal data; these people are called data users in the act. Data users must be open about their use of the data by telling the Data Protection Registrar (the person who enforces the act) that they

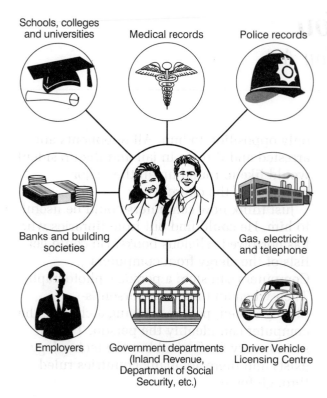

Schools, colleges and universities

Medical records

Police records

Banks and building societies

Gas, electricity and telephone

Employers

Government departments (Inland Revenue, Department of Social Security, etc.)

Driver Vehicle Licensing Centre

Figure 18.1 *Some of the organisations that hold personal information about us*

are collecting personal data and how they intend to use it. They must also follow a set of eight principles, called the Data Protection Principles.

Why electronically stored information is easier to misuse than information kept in conventional form

1 Cross referencing

It is easy to using a computer to link the data from different systems.

2 Danger of hacking

If the system uses communication links then there is a risk of people gaining unauthorised access (called hacking) and looking at or changing confidential information.

3 Making alterations

If alterations have been made to data on paper then these can usually be seen. With a computer, there is no such evidence.

4 Faster access to data

It is much quicker to gain access to electronically held data and copy or print it out than it is to search through and photocopy manually held files.

The Data Protection Principles

The principles state that:

1 The information to be contained in personal data shall be obtained and personal data should be processed, fairly and lawfully.

2 Personal data shall be held only for one or more specified and lawful purposes.

3 Personal data held for any purpose or purposes shall not be disclosed in any matter incompatible with that purpose or purposes.

4 Personal data held for any purpose or purposes shall be adequate, relevant and not excessive in relation to that purpose or those purposes.

5 Personal data shall be accurate and, where necessary, kept up to date.

6 Personal data held for any purpose or purposes shall not be kept for longer than is necessary for that purpose or purposes.

7 An individual shall be entitled:
   (a) at reasonable intervals and without undue delay or expense
      (i) to be informed by any data user whether he holds personal data to which that individual is the subject
      (ii) to have access to any such data held by a data user; and
   (b) where appropriate, to have such data corrected or erased.

8 Appropriate security measures shall be taken against unauthorised access to, or alteration, disclosure or destruction of, personal data and against accidental loss or destruction of personal data.

Data subjects and data users

Everyone, whether we like it or not is a 'data subject', because organisations and

QUESTIONS

1 The Data Protection Principles outlined above are very wordy and need to be translated into everyday language. Use a dictionary if you need to. Explain what the following words mean:

lawfully   specified   purposes   disclosed   incompatible   adequate   relevant   excessive   undue   appropriate   unauthorised

2 Now write a set of summarised data protection principles, in your own words and without using any of the words in the list above.

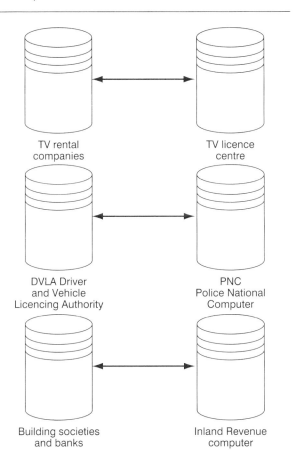

Figure 18.2 *Some database linkings which exist*

companies, called 'data users', hold personal details about us on their computer systems. The worrying thing about this is that, because of the power of and the ease of communication between computers, this data can be transferred from one computer to another at the press of a button. This

means that data collected by one computer user can be transferred to other users, who can use the information for completely different purposes.

There are many examples where data collected for one purpose is used for another and some of these are shown in Figure 18.2. For example, if you rent a television, then your details will be automatically passed to the TV licence centre. The Driver and Vehicle Licensing Centre is linked to the Police National Computer. Banks and building societies automatically notify the Inland Revenue if a person receives over a certain amount of interest in a year. The transfer of personal data between computers does have some advantages. For example, without the rapid transfer of records the capture and conviction of criminals would be made more difficult.

However, there are dangers. Suppose your record gets mixed up with someone else's

Figure 18.3 *There must be some mistake?*

record or that incorrect data is entered into your record? This could have various results: you could be refused credit or benefits or even a job. In certain cases it could result in you being arrested. Figures 18.3 and 18.4 tell you more about who has computer records about you and the possible consequences of the information being incorrect.

The Data Protection Act gives us the right to see our personal data kept on a computer and to get it corrected if it is wrong. It also gives us the right to complain to the Data Protection Registrar if we don't like the way the data is collected or the way that it is used.

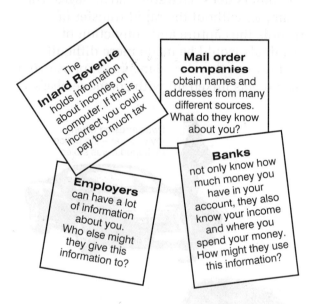

Figure 18.4 *Who knows all about you?*

How does a data user register?

If a data user holds personal data on a computer and does not fall into one of the categories covered by the exemptions, then the user must register their use. To do this a registration form is filled in. This may be obtained from any main post office. The form is filled in with the following:

- details of the personal data held
- the purposes to which this data is put
- how the data was originally obtained
- the people to whom the information may be passed

- any different countries where the data may be transferred.

There is a fee for registration, which is currently £70.

Figure 18.5 shows a flowchart which may be used to find out whether a person or organisation needs to register.

What happens if an organisation doesn't register?

If an organisation does not register its use of personal data or it provides false information to the registrar, then the organisation may be fined up to £5000 in the magistrates court or an unlimited fine in the high court.

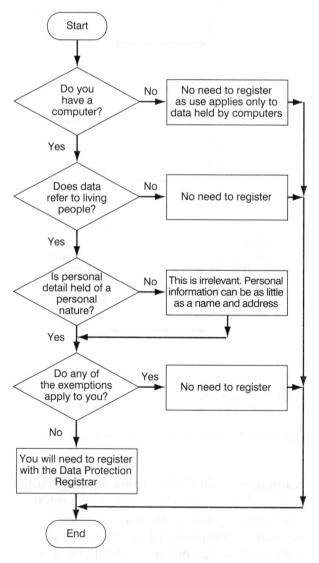

Figure 18.5 *A flowchart which could be used to find out if registration is necessary*

Is compensation payable?

If a person suffers damage because the data held about them is inaccurate or if the data is unlawfully passed to someone else, then that person may be able to claim compensation. The amount of the money to be paid is decided by the courts on the basis of the severity of the damage done.

Are there any exemptions?

Not everyone has to register their use of personal data, so, if you hold your address book or your Christmas card list on your home computer, you can sleep at night.

The following use of personal data is exempt. In other words, you do not need to register your use of personal data if your use falls into any of the following categories:

1 when the data held is being used only in connection with personal, family or household affairs, or for recreational use
2 where the data is being used only for preparing the text of documents
3 where the data is being used only for the calculation of wages and pensions or for the production of accounts
4 where the data is used for the distribution of articles or information (e.g. unsolicited mail (i.e. mail that advertises goods or services that you have not asked for)
5 where the data is held by a sports club or a recreational club which is not a limited company.

Your rights as a data subject

You have the right to see any details about you held on computer. To see the details, you need to send a letter like the one shown in Figure 18.6 to the organisation concerned.

The organisation has to respond to your request and may send a form for further details about you to aid identification or it may send the data in the form of a letter or a computer printout. An organisation is able to make a small charge of up to £10 for providing the information.

You do not, however, have the right to see all the information held about you. You may be denied the information if it is being used

QUESTION

Would you need to register the following uses of personal data? For each one say whether or not it is exempt, and why.

(a) A series of letters regarding lateness or absenteeism written by your form teacher and kept on her personal computer at home.
(b) A record of the wages paid to you held at a shop where you work on Saturdays.
(c) A file containing all the customer details for a small video rental shop.
(d) The file containing personal details about you kept on the school's computer by the school secretary.
(e) Your medical file held by your doctor at her surgery.
(f) Details of members on cards held in a filing cabinet kept by your local youth club.
(g) References for when you leave school or college which have been typed on a wordprocessor.

The Date

Dear Sir,

I wish to make an application under section 21 of the Data Protection Act 1984. Please supply me with any information which you hold about me to which I am entitled or confirm that none is held.

If you require further information from me or a fee, please let me know as soon as possible.

If you do not normally handle these requests for your organisation, please pass this letter to your Data Protection Officer or other appropriate official.

Yours faithfully,

Figure 18.6 *A letter to the Data Protection Registrar*

for any of the following purposes:

- the prevention or detection of crime
- catching or prosecuting offenders
- collecting taxes or duty (e.g. VAT)
- medical or social workers' reports in some instances.

Credit reference agencies

When people apply for a loan or a credit card, how can the companies that lend the money be sure that they will be paid back? The answer is that they can never be sure so what they do is to look back at the people's past credit records. If they have missed payments or have had goods taken back (repossessed) then they are more likely to be bad credit risks and are likely to be refused credit. There is a problem with this. How do companies know about people who may have had their previous loans with other companies? The answer is that all companies who give loans give details of bad payers to organisations called credit reference agencies and it is these agencies to which they refer if they want to find out about a person's credit worthiness.

Since it is very easy to change your name but less easy to change your address, credit reference agencies use an address rather than a person's name as the identifier. This means that people may be refused credit simply because they live at the same address as someone who is a bad payer. You can even be classed as a bad credit risk if

Figure 18.7

you move to an address where a bad payer had lived.

You may think that the passage of this information would be illegal under the Data Protection Act. However there is another act which allows it called the Consumer Credit Act 1974.

THINGS TO DO

1 Banks use information technology to handle information about customers and their accounts.

(a) List four items of information about customers and their accounts.

It is possible for a bank to use this personal information for purposes of which the customer would not approve.

(b) Describe such a potential use of the customer's personal data.

(c) Explain why this is easier when the data is stored electronically than when it is just stored on paper.

(d) Describe the possible effects of inaccuracies in the customer's data.

(RSA IT Short Course Sample Question)

2 When a baby is born, its record is immediately put on to the hospital's computer. After a week or so, the birth will be registered on the register of Births, Marriages and Deaths. This data will then be passed to the Office of Populations Census and Surveys (an extra person has been added to the population). The baby's details are also sent to the Department of Health and Social Security. As the baby grows up, more and more organisations store information on computer about it.

(a) Write down the names of four organisations which hold personal information about a 16 year old.

(b) Write down the names of five organisations which could hold information about you when you reach the age of 18 that they are unlikely to hold at 16.

3 Computerised information about individual people is held in separate databases by a wide range of organisations.
  (a) Name two organisations that might hold computer records about a teenager who has just applied for a job.
  (b) Many people are worried about the misuse of computer data. Outline four principles that you would lay down to reassure people that there would be no misuse of the information held about them.

4 The Data Protection Act applies only to computerised records and not to manual ones. A large holder of personal data could transfer all its computer files to manual ones. Is this likely? Explain your answer.

5 (a) Mary has been feeling ill so she goes along to her doctor who examines her and says there is nothing wrong with her. She thinks the doctor is hiding something so she asks to see her medical records held on computer. Is it likely that she will be allowed access?
  (b) John has committed a robbery. Later he is arrested by the police and released without charge. As time goes by he thinks he may have got away with it. He applies to see the records held about him on the Police National Computer. Will his request be granted?

6 A doctor is thinking of storing her patients' records on a computer system. She is however very worried about the confidentiality of the information and the problem of unauthorised access. Explain the various methods that could be used to ensure that the data remains confidential.

7 Part of the application form to be filled in by all potential XYZ Ltd employees is shown in Figure 18.8. If an applicant is successful then the information on the form is transferred to a database held on a personal computer in the personnel office.

Application Form for XYZ Ltd

Name_____ Height _____ Weight _____

Address _____

_____

Tel No: _____

Date of birth _____

National Insurance Number

Married (Y/N) _____ If so, how long for? _____

Religion _____

No of chidren _____

If applicable, ages of children _____

Bank Account Number _____

Are you a union member? _____

If answer to above is Y, give name of union _____

Outstanding value of mortgage and other loans _____

Do you travel to work by public transport? _____

Have you visited your doctor in the last 12 months? ____

If so, what for? _____

Have you ever been refused credit? _____

Figure 18.8 *Application form for XYZ Ltd*

(a) Write down a list of any of the questions in the application form on the previous page which you feel infringe on your privacy. Explain why you would not like the company to know these details.

(b) Choose three of the more personal questions in the application form and for each one explain what use the answer would be to the company.

8 The following questions concern the security of files held on computer. For each one of the following situations write a short paragraph explaining what could have been done to prevent the breach of security.

You may need to look back at the previous chapter on security.

(a) Mrs Jones, a cleaner, is cleaning the personnel office and notices that her best friend's personnel record is displayed on a screen. There is no-one around, so she presses the printscreen button and obtains a printout which she then takes.

(b) Sid the sneak thief goes into his doctor's surgery to order a prescription. He notices a personal computer on the desk and since there is no-one around, he unplugs it, picks it up and carries it to his car.

(c) Dianne wishes to gain access to her manager's computer. She is leaving the company soon and since she is going to work for a competitor it would be useful to obtain a list of the names, addresses and value of the orders for all the customers. She switches on his computer and it springs into life. However, a message is displayed asking for a password to be entered. Not one to be put off, Dianne looks around and finds a piece of paper attached to the back of the monitor with a single word written on it. She tries it and it works. She now gains access.

(d) John would like a reference for a job. John applied for a job a couple of months ago which he did not get. He suspects he may have got a bad reference from his boss. He would like to see the reference which he knows is on his manager's personal computer. John goes into his manager's office and turns the power on and nothing happens. He notices that a key is needed. He tries the top drawer of the desk and finds the key. He starts up the computer and has a look at his reference.

INVESTIGATION

For this project you will need to obtain detailed information on the Data Protection Act 1984. You can get this information from the Data Protection Registrar in the form of a student pack. This is free from:

The Data Protection Registrar

Wycliffe House

Water Lane

Wilmslow

Cheshire

SK9 5AF

Tel (01625) 535777   Fax (01625) 524510

The information contained in the chapter is not sufficient to enable you perform the following task to a high standard. It is therefore necessary for you to do a certain amount of research before you start this project.

Perfect Partner Dating Agency

You have just been appointed as the computer manager for the Perfect Partner Dating Agency which has been formed by the merger of three smaller agencies. You are in complete charge of the computer facilities and it will be up to you to run your department as you see fit.

Nearly all the clients (the people who are looking for partners) were enrolled with the smaller agencies before the merger. These clients had their details recorded on cards held in filing cabinets. At present there are approximately 6000 clients on the books but with a recently planned advertising campaign in most of the daily newspapers, the new agency hopes to double this number in about six months.

About 40% of business comes from adverts in magazines, where people fill in and send to the agency forms with their names and addresses. As soon as the agency receives the forms it intends to key people's names and addresses into a database. This enables the agency to send letters using the mail merge facilities of a wordprocessor. In doing this, the agency hopes to convert a greater number of enquiries into sales.

Each potential client is given a detailed application form which they are expected to fill in 'truthfully'. This form covers their own likes, dislikes and physical attributes, along with the qualities they would like to see in their 'perfect partner'. When the forms are sent back, the details are then typed into a database. For each client, this database uses a program which searches for clients of the opposite sex with as many of the desired qualities as possible who preferably live in the client's area.

As well as being used for the above task, the computer will also be used for working out the staff wages each month. At present there are 47 staff employed in the head office, but, in addition to these, there are various agents who advertise in local papers, take the enquiries by telephone and then inform head office about potential new clients. These agents are paid by the numbers of enquiries they obtain, with a bonus for each person that signs up with the agency. There are 80 local agents and their pay is processed by the computer.

In addition, the company intends to keep records of the personnel files of all its staff on the computer.

Read over the scenario several times before looking at what you have to do. All your solutions to the following tasks need to apply to this scenario.

1   The directors of the company, who have had little exposure to computers apart from having to type a few private letters now and again on the wordprocessor, have just heard about the Data Protection Act. They have asked you to produce a brief report outlining what the main purposes of the Act are, why it was introduced, and how it could apply to the type of business they are running.

2   The directors would now like to know if any of the following files stored on the computer would be exempt from the Data Protection Act:
    *   the client database (it contains all the clients' information)
    *   the name and address enquiry database (for sending mailshots)
    *   the payroll file for staff and agents
    *   the personnel file for staff and agents.

Write a memo (a brief note) to your managing director explaining which of the above files are exempt and why they are exempt.

3   Realising that it is necessary for the company to register its various uses, the directors have decided that you, as the computer manager, should be responsible for this process. Explain what steps need to be taken in order to register.

4   One of the directors is very sceptical about all this. She feels that this is just another example of government interference in the running of businesses. She has asked you what you think. You are in favour of the act.

    Produce a brief written argument in favour of the act giving examples of how the act can help ordinary individuals in their lives.

5   The same director is still sceptical and wants to know, 'What if we don't register'? Write down the various possibilities.

6   The eighth data protection principle states 'personal data should be surrounded by proper security'. With reference to your company outline the various security techniques that could be used to prevent data from falling into the wrong hands.

 INVESTIGATION

Read the following passage on the lifestyle database.

The lifestyle database

You have just been out to buy a copy of your favourite monthly magazine. When you get it home a small booklet drops out which promises a free entry to a prize draw for £5000 if you take the time to fill it in a questionnaire and send it off. There are questions such as how much you earn, how often you go on holiday, whether you donate to charity, how often you order goods through the post, down to which particular make of soap you use. There are six pages covering about 100 questions which you start to fill in. In filling in the questionnaire, you are giving the company a complete profile of your lifestyle. So who wants to know this information? Well, almost any company involved in selling goods or services. For instance, suppose a particular charity is launching a postal appeal, it can send out letters to people who said in the survey that they donate to charities and who hold a credit card. In doing this they are targeting a group of people who are more likely to respond. This is only one of the many ways that such a database could be used.

Task 1

You have decided to make your own 'lifestyle database'. Your first task is to make up a series of questions to find out when people are likely to buy goods or services. Design an attractive questionnaire using suitable software (you could use wordprocessing, DTP, graphics or even spreadsheet software).

Task 2

Get all the members of your class to fill in a questionnaire. Look at the answers they have given to your questions and then decide how this information might be used to market goods and services. Write a short description on how the information could be used to market goods and services.

Chapter 19

Computers and the Law

Computer crime

With the growth of information systems there has been an increase in computer crime. There has been a move away from cash transactions, so the amount of cash held by companies is a lot smaller than it used to be. Many more employees are now paid by cheque or by direct payment into their bank accounts. The opportunity for the criminal to steal cash is limited. However, the ease with which transactions now take place, has opened a whole new area of credit card fraud.

Credit card use

There are many types of card in use: credit, debit and cash cards. Debit cards are used as an alternative to cheques. When goods are bought using a debit card, the money is immediately transferred from the shopper's account to the store's account. Cash cards are used to obtain cash from a cash dispenser.

Credit cards, as the name suggests, enable people to obtain instant credit either against goods bought or for cash from a cash dispenser. Obtaining credit for goods involves the retailer filling in a docket either manually or by using the till and then asking the customer to sign the docket. If the card signature and the signature on the docket are the same then the customer is given the goods and the retailer sends the docket to the credit card company, where the transaction is recorded and the retailer is paid. The cardholder receives a statement at the end of each month which outlines:

- the balance at the start of the month
- the interest payable on this outstanding balance
- the amounts and details of any transactions that have taken place during the month
- the balance owing at the end of the month.

The cardholder is then able to make the decision on how much of the balance he

Figure 19.1 *Using a credit card*

wishes to pay off provided that it is greater than the minimum payment specified by the credit card company. The whole of this process is summarised in Figure 19.1.

It is now very common for there to be no documentation at the time of purchase, since so many goods and services are bought by phone with credit cards or debit cards.

Electronic fund transfer (EFT)

The system for obtaining cash from a cash dispenser using a credit card is more secure, since a number called the PIN, the personal identification number, has to be keyed before access to the machine is allowed. Cash machines are sometimes called automated teller machines (ATMs). The PIN is known only to the cardholder, so the card on its own cannot be used to obtain cash from a dispenser. When the PIN is entered at the keypad, the dispenser compares the PIN entered with the number contained in the magnetic strip on the back of the card. This method provides a higher level of security than when a credit card is used to buy goods, since signatures are so easily forged.

Figure 19.2 shows the reverse of a cash card and the magnetic stripe where the PIN is stored.

More and more payments are being made with payment cards. They are rather like cheques in the sense that the money comes directly from the holder's accounts, but payment cards have the advantage that they are quicker to use, since EFTPOS (electronic fund transfer at point of sale) terminals write slips out for users to sign. When a cardholder's signature is confirmed, the money for the goods is immediately transferred from the cardholder's bank account to the retailer's bank account. Again, because signature verification is used, the system is open to abuse if a card is stolen. A Switch card is one example of a payment card.

Credit card fraud

In 1992 there were around 80 million cards in circulation in Britain and of these an average of 5000 were stolen each day, with the total resulting fraud estimated to cost about £165 million per year. It is not surprising that ways of reducing this fraud have been looked into.

One way around the problem is to authorise each transaction as it occurs by checking via the phone or a special terminal whether the card has been stolen. Another way is to make people key in their PIN at the checkout when making purchases using credit or payment cards.

Biometric testing may also be performed, whereby the user places an index finger into a machine which compares the fingerprint with one previously recorded. Another method looks at the way a person writes a signature by concentrating on the timing, the rhythm and the invisible pen movements. Figure 19.3 shows a fingerprint being checked.

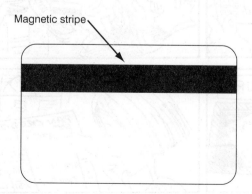

Figure 19.2 *The PIN number is stored in the magnetic stripe*

Figure 19.3 *Biometric testing is an important weapon to protect against credit card fraud*

Electronic fraud

Electronic fraud is the use of computers or communication systems to commit fraud for financial gain. The main problem with this crime compared with traditional crimes is that the criminals tend to be quite intelligent and technically competent and therefore they make considerable efforts to prevent discovery. They frequently see weaknesses in systems and set out to exploit them.

Electronic fraud often involves setting up false suppliers, who send invoices to a real company for payment. When payments are made to these fictitious suppliers the money is stolen. Great efforts are then taken to make sure that the real company's accounting system will still balance. Firms try to get around this type of fraud by making sure that several people are responsible for dealing with invoices so that to commit a fraud would need the co-operation of several members of staff.

Careful recruitment of staff and making sure that no single member of staff carries out the whole process can help reduce fraud. Some companies keep swapping staff around different departments to avoid these problems.

Phantom withdrawals

There has been a lot of discussion in the press regarding 'phantom withdrawals'. This is money which has been debited (taken out) mysteriously using an ATM without the person who owns the card, using it. This withdrawal of money usually only reveals itself when the customer checks their monthly statement. Although the courts have taken phantom withdrawals seriously, allowing groups of individuals jointly to take action for the return of their money, the banks have remained adamant that this cannot happen. In many cases, the banks say, the money has been removed by someone in the user's household who has borrowed a user's card and found the PIN number. The banks further support their case by saying

Figure 19.4 *Phantom withdrawals are on the increase*

that nearly all 'phantom withdrawals' take place near to the card holder's home.

Barclays Bank has introduced a pilot scheme where a pinhole camera secretly concealed near the screen of the cash dispenser, takes a picture of the person withdrawing the cash. This picture is digitally compressed and stored on disk along with the details of the withdrawal, such as date, time, branch and account details. These cameras may further be used to photograph vandals who try to vandalise these machines, when sensors inside the machine are activated.

Smart cards

A smart card is a plastic card which contains its own built-in microchip, which performs two security functions. First it carries the holder's identification data and secondly it verifies this data against the PIN code that the cardholder enters at a card-reading terminal. In addition to this, the smart card can also hold details of the holder's credit limit and carry a record of the transactions made within those limits.

The main objection to the use of the smart card has been one of cost since many ATMs and POS terminals would need converting to be able to read smart cards. Also, it has been found that smart cards used to decode the TV signals transmitted by BSkyB have been successfully counterfeited. Nevertheless, smart cards are used extensively in banking systems in many European countries.

Software piracy

Software piracy involves the illegal copying of computer software which is estimated to cost the software developers around £3000 million per year. In 1992 it was estimated that about 66% of the software used in Europe was illegal.

If a company has developed its own software rather than used off-the-shelf software then it will have spent a lot of time and money on its development. Large programs are usually written by a team, with each person writing a particular section or module. The number of man hours taken to write the programs can be large. Suppose five programmers are working on a project and it takes each programmer 200 hours each then the total number of man hours worked on the project would be $5 \times 200 = 1000$ man hours. The programs for the Police National Computer have been estimated to have taken around 2000 man years to write and test.

The Copyright, Designs and Patents Act, 1989

The Copyright, Designs and Patents Act makes it a criminal offence to be caught copying or stealing software.

Under the act it is an offence to copy or distribute software or any manuals which come with it without permission or a licence from the copyright owner, who is normally the software developer.

It is also an offence to run purchased software covered by copyright on two or more machines at the same time, unless the licence specifically allows it.

The act makes it illegal for an organisation to encourage, allow, compel or pressure its employees to make or distribute copies of illegal software for use by the organisation.

The Computer Misuse Act, 1990

With the widespread use of computer and communication systems, problems started to arise about the misuse of systems. The problems centred on a variety of uses that were not covered by existing laws. Several cases went to court but the courts were unable to convict because older laws did not cover these misuses. One particular case involved a schoolboy using his computer at home with a modem to hack into the Duke of Edinburgh's electronic mailbox and read his correspondence. Other schoolboy hackers were able to get through to stockbrokers, hospitals, oil companies and even the Atomic Energy Authority's computer systems.

The courts were reluctant to use the theft laws, which weren't intended to cover these situations, and advised Parliament that it would need to make new specific laws. This gave rise to the Computer Misuse Act, 1990.

Figure 19.5 *Hacking is illegal*

The Computer Misuse Act, 1990 covers a variety of misuses which were not covered by existing laws. It deals with the following:

- deliberately planting viruses into a computer system to cause damage to program files and data
- using computer time to carry out unauthorised work, such as using a firm's computer to run a friend's payroll
- copying computer programs illegally (i.e. software piracy)
- hacking into someone's system with a view to seeing the information or altering it
- using a computer for various frauds. People have been known to put fictitious employees on a payroll program and use false bank accounts opened in the name of the these employees to steal money.

Enforcing the act

The maximum penalty for unauthorised access to a computer system is six months imprisonment and a £2000 fine. For the other offences there is a maximum of five years' imprisonment and an unlimited fine.

TEST YOURSELF

Using the words in the list below, copy out and complete sentences A to H, underlining the words you have inserted. The words may be used once, more than once or not at all.

credit card   hack   hacking   piracy   theft   PIN   phantom   misuse   patents   smart

A The largest growth area of computer crime is that of _____ _____ fraud.

B Mysterious withdrawal of money from a person's account is often referred to as a _____ withdrawal.

C Cards which look a bit like a cash or credit card but which contain a microchip, are called ——- cards.

D The number coded in the magnetic strip on the back of a credit or cash card is called a _____.

E Illegal copying of software is called software _____.

F Copying of software is an offence under the Copyright, Designs and _____ Act of 1989.

G The Computer _____ Act of 1990 makes it an offence to _____ into a computer system.

H _____ means gaining access to private data using communication systems.

THINGS TO DO

1 You are in charge of a small computer network with six terminals located in different offices, but in the same building. You have been worried about the threat from viruses and some of your staff have been putting their own programs onto the computer (particularly games which they play when you are out of the office!). You have decided to put up a notice which is to be placed near to each terminal listing a set of rules that must be obeyed when using the company computers.

Using suitable software of your choice (e.g. graphics, wordprocessing, DTP) design a suitable, hardhitting notice to discourage such practices.

2 It is often said that, if software piracy could be eliminated, then so could most of the problems with viruses.

Using what you have learnt about software piracy and viruses, explain the above statement.

3 (a) Mary buys a copy of a popular wordprocessing package called WordPerfect which she intends to use on her computer at work and on her home computer. She copies it onto each hard disk. Is she breaking the law?

(b) John buys a copy of a graphics package called Harvard Graphics which he copies onto the hard disk of his computer. He puts away the program on the floppy disks in a safe place. Is he breaking the law?

(c) Paul has bought a new computer game which he shows to his friend. His friend asks him to 'make him a copy'. Is he allowed by law to do this?

(d) Sophie is approached by her boss who tells her that she will have to learn a new desktop publishing package in order to produce new company price lists. Her boss says that she needs to install the package on the computer and to photocopy the manual because her friend wants it back. Should Sophie do this? Write a short but polite memo explaining to her boss why she will not do it.

INVESTIGATION

Obtain some recent crime figures over a suitable period (about 10 years). Your local library should be able to help you get these. You could choose to do a study based on your local area or a national one.

Your task will be to present these figures in an attractive and easy to understand way and it will be up to you to choose your method of presentation. Here is some help to start you off.

1 Use spreadsheet or wordprocessing software to present these figures in the form of a table. After you have done this, write a short explanation on why you have chosen one type of software over the other.

2 Using appropriate software (explain your choice), plot suitable graphs to illustrate the trends in crime over the years you have chosen.

3 If your software allows this, incorporate your tables and graphs into a document entitled 'A study of crime', along with your explanations for questions 1 and 2 and the conclusions you have drawn from your graphs.

4 Can you make any predictions for the future from your figures? Include these predictions in your final document.

Extension

Extend your project by comparing your local crime statistics with national ones.

Chapter 20

The Social Effects of Information Systems

Social and economic effects of IT

Before the industrial revolution nearly everyone worked in agriculture. Communication was by word of mouth or paper. When the industrial revolution came, life became more complicated. People started to work in factories and the factories needed offices to deal with administration. The amount of paperwork needed to trade started to increase. As time went on, technology was used to develop machines such as the typewriter, telephone and telex machines and eventually, the computer (Figure 20.1).

We are now in an 'information age' and our society is very dependent on information storage and communication. Many are now using some form of information technology to help them.

Figure 20.1

Is information technology a good thing?

Some arguments for and against IT are given below. You may agree or disagree with these. Where you disagree, explain you arguments.

Arguments in favour

1 The jobs replaced by computers are the rather mundane ones. People are free to do more interesting tasks.
2 Higher productivity enables people to work fewer hours and yet have the same standard of living. A greater amount of leisure time will improve people's quality of life.
3 Other countries make use of IT. If we did not, our goods and services would become uncompetitive and there would be even more unemployment.
4 There are many tasks that would be impossible without the use of IT. Air-traffic control, credit cards, space travel and medical research are just some examples.
5 New jobs are being created by the introduction of information technology e.g. programming, network managing etc.

Arguments against

1 Life without IT is slower and less stressful.
2 Computers are cheaper than people so if a job can be done by a computer then it will be, leading to even higher unemployment.
3 The new jobs being created by the use of IT are only for highly skilled and qualified people.
4 The people who did the boring repetitive jobs now done by computers no longer have a job.
5 The storage of personal data held on computer has eroded people's privacy.

6 The gap will be widened between those countries able to afford the new technologies and those that can't.

Changing employment patterns

With the introduction of computer controlled technology employment patterns have changes considerably. Changes include the following.

1 Many of the manual tasks such as assembly work and paintspraying in factories are now being performed by robots.

2 Many industrial processes operate 24 hours a day and are continually being monitored and controlled by computers.

3 There are fewer paper-based systems in offices. Some jobs such as filing clerks no longer exist. New jobs involving computers have been created.

4 More and more people work from home, with the advantage of no travelling and the freedom of being able to live in any part of the country (or the world for that matter).

5 Computers are sometimes used to monitor the performance of their users. For instance, in supermarkets they can tell the management about the number of customers dealt with per hour or how many items are passed through the scanner in a day. Order entry clerks and airline booking clerks can have their work similarly monitored.

Identity cards move a step closer

Driving licences are now to be in credit card format and have a photograph of the driver on them like the one shown in Figure 20.2. Eventually the government would like to add a microchip to these cards, thus making the card into a 'smart card'. Stored on the chip will be details of any endorsements for motoring offences, whether the driver was

Figure 20.2 *The proposed 'smart' driving licence*

willing to donate organs and health details such as allergies. These cards might also store national insurance details, which would enable health details to be located.

Many people are worried about this card, since they see it as an identity card under the disguise of a driving licence. Some people argue that an identity card would help fight crime and Britain is the only European country not to have one.

Figure 20.3

144

Environmentally friendly computers

Green computers (not the colour!) are computers that have been built considering the needs of the environment. For instance, they use less electricity than ordinary computers. One way that they do this is that they power down the monitor and disk drives if the computer has been inactive for a certain period of time. It is claimed that by the end of the century computers will account for 10% of the world's power supply.

Laser printers, however, are not very environmentally friendly; they churn out a nasty gas called ozone (it's only useful in the upper layers of the atmosphere), they use a lot of power and produce used cartridges which need to be disposed of. All types of printers use a lot of power and in addition destroy forests with all the paper they use. If less paper were used it would help conserve the rainforests. This is one of the ideas behind the development of paperless offices.

Computer game addiction

Some children are addicted to computer games, sometimes playing them for more than 30 hours per week. Many experts are worried that this solitary activity is affecting the social and educational development of addicted children. Many computer games do not mimic reality and often involve simulated violence. Other people are worried that many children are becoming 'couch potatoes', are not involved in any physical activity and do not interact very well with adults or people their own age.

The shape of things to come

The merger of three technologies: the silicon chip, fibre optics and satellite communication (Figure 20. 4) has led to the concept of the information superhighway. This is a global network of computers capable of moving huge amounts of information via satellite and cable. This digital revolution is likely to change all our lives considerably. By pressing a key at any time of the day you will be able to get information in a suitable form on demand anywhere in the world. The information is not restricted to business: community information and learning data will be provided.

At the moment your television set is restricted to a few channels (more if you are lucky enough to have satellite or cable). In the near future your television will be the gateway to a fibre optic network. This will bring hundreds of channels, video on demand, home shopping, home banking and access to millions of data banks. Trips to the library to find out information for a GCSE project will be a thing of the past. You will be able to get to the information you want quickly and in the comfort of your own home.

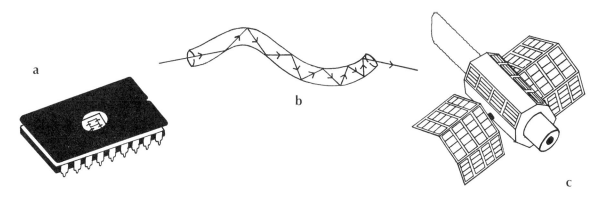

a

b

c

Figure 20.4 *The three main technologies of the information superhighway are:*
    a *silicon chips*   **b** *fibre optic cables*   **c** *satellites*

Environmental, ethical, moral and social issues raised by information technology.

Environmental issues

Reduced energy consumption

Computers now control many of the heating systems in offices and factories so it is possible for only the rooms that are being used to be heated. This can save huge amounts of energy.

Reduced wastage in industrial processes

There are many process control systems used in our factories and because these are more accurate, there is less wastage, thus saving valuable resources. For example, Chapter 25 describes how H P Bulmer, the cider maker, uses computers to control the fermentation process. Ruined batches of cider caused by human error are now a thing of the past.

Saving trees

The use of the electronic office and EDI has led to paper being almost eliminated in many offices and this means that fewer trees need to be felled, so not only are the trees saved but the energy that went into the making of the paper is also saved.

Reducing car pollution

Teleworking (working at home using information technology) means that some people no longer have to travel to the office to work. This reduces petrol consumption and car pollution.

Ethical, moral and social issues

Software theft

It could be said that the use of personal computers has made many users into thieves. How many people could honestly say that all the software on their hard disks has been purchased by them? As you can see from the Copyright, Designs and Patents Act, 1989, it is a criminal offence to copy or steal software.

Hacking

Hacking means gaining illegal access to someone else's computer system. Many people see this type of thing as a challenge and not as an illegal activity.

Privacy

Many people see the Data Protection Act as inadequate, since in 1984, when the act was made law, there weren't anything like the number of personal computers and communications networks that there are today. Some people are totally unaware of the act and think that it only applies to large companies or organisations.

Job losses

Is it right to develop new systems in the knowledge that staff will inevitably be made redundant? Should we put shareholders' dividends and profits before people? These are difficult questions and ones which need to be addressed Everyone has their own opinion on this. What is yours?

Social and ethical considerations for the Internet

The Internet provides access to a variety of information on every topic and this information comes from many different countries throughout the world. One problem with the Internet is that all the information is freely available once a user is connected. There are news areas of the Internet which contain large amounts of illegal pornographic material. Material that is illegal in some countries may be perfectly legal in others. Governments have the problem of finding a way of allowing users to gain access to the Internet but not to any illegal areas. If access to such material is restricted on one part of the Internet then a user can simply move to another area to find a way to access the material.

There is a problem in restricting access. The Internet is a global system and it is difficult to make laws to control it by single countries. Another problem with restriction is that it could lead governments to begin attempts to censor, legislate and regulate the

Internet for political, cultural and religious reasons. Civil liberty groups are naturally concerned about this aspect of control.

Social considerations for a cashless society

A future without any form of cash is unlikely but over the last ten years the use of cash for making payments has reduced considerably. We will now look at the advantages and disadvantage of a cashless society.

Advantages

1 It is far more convenient not to have to use cash. Mortgage and loan repayments, gas, electricity and phone bills are paid automatically so you don't need to remember to pay them.
2 You no longer need to take large sums of money out of the building society or bank to pay for expensive items: the risk of being robbed is reduced.
3 You don't have to queue at the bank, building society or cash machine to get the money out.
4 Credit cards allow people to buy goods and then decide whether to pay for them at the end of the month or obtain them on credit, paying a proportion each month.

Disadvantages

1 Credit is normally given only to people who are working and have a steady source of income, so certain people won't be able to get it.
2 It is possible for people to spend more than they can really afford so they can easily get into debt.
3 More information is kept about individuals. Inevitably some of this will be incorrect and lead to people wrongly being refused cash or credit cards.
4 It is harder for people to keep track of how much they have spent, since statements are usually sent only once a month, although statements can usually be obtained more frequently if they are requested.

Crime prevention and detection
Crime prevention
IT can be used to help prevent crime and the systems employed include the following.

1 Speed camera systems and camera systems which detect cars jumping red lights deter people from offending.
2 Computer controlled camera systems deter violent crime in many city centres.
3 Tagging of offenders means that they are less likely to commit crimes whilst on bail.
4 Tagging systems on bikes, cars and other property reduces the chances of them being stolen.
5 Computer controlled house security systems deter some burglars.

Crime detection
IT can be used to catch criminals and some of the ways it can do this are as follows.:

1 The Police National Computer (PNC) is used to hold details of all crimes committed and criminals.
2 The National Criminal Intelligence System is a computer system used to piece together information about individual criminals and their illegal activities. The computer can interact with data supplied by Interpol, the PNC, Customs and Excise, the Inland Revenue, and the bank and building society computers. This system is used to gather material on organised crimes such as drug smuggling.
3 DNA profiling and fingerprinting systems enable valuable, and often conclusive, evidence to be collected.
4 Police headquarters computers for each police force are used in the day-to-day administration of all the usual police work.

Problems with the Police National Computer (PNC)
1 There is a risk that illegal access to the PNC could allow people outside the police force to gain information.
2 There are worries that the running of the PNC will be passed over to a private

company. The PNC contains criminal records, details of wanted or dangerous people, disqualified drivers, stolen cars and guns and also the records of 30 million motorists. Some files indicate that a person is HIV positive. In addition to all this there are details of 70 000 people of 'long-term interest' held. The concern is that a private company running the PNC would not be trusted as much as the police and people could be reluctant to pass information to the PNC.

3 Information on the PNC might be incorrect and this could stop someone getting a job or could even result in a person being wrongly arrested for a crime.

INVESTIGATION

You are to produce two reports on the connection between the number of doctors in various parts of the world and the deaths of young babies. One is for a popular newspaper, and the other is for a serious environmental magazine.

Use the World Development Database to find out which countries have high and low numbers of people per doctor and which have high and low proportions of infant deaths. Use graphs to provide further evidence for a connection between the numbers of doctors and the deaths of babies.

Use suitable software to produce the draft of a newspaper article, which should not contain any graphs. Write 100 words, making your findings as dramatic as you can.

Choose software which can combine your lists and graphs with the article. Adapt your article to suit the more serious magazine style, extend it to 300 words and incorporate appropriate lists and graphs to illustrate your points.

(The World Development Database software is available from The Computer Project, Centre for World Development Education, 1 Catton Street, London WC1R 4AB)

(RSA IS GCSE Intermediate Tier Coursework)

1 It has been suggested that motorists might be charged for their use of roads by having a system which identifies each car. When a car passes over a sensor in the road a central computer will record that car's entry into a charge zone. One of the side-effects of this is that a record could be kept of every car's movements. Discuss some of the social implications of such a system, giving reasons why certain groups of people may be for or against the system.   (8 marks)

(SEG NT HT Spec)

2 It was mentioned in this chapter that many people would like to see the introduction of an identity card which everyone would be required to carry. Write a short paragraph explaining, and giving your reasons, whether or not you are in favour of the introduction of this card.

3 Information technology has replaced or changed many jobs.
  (a) Give the names of **two** types of job that have been replaced by IT.
  (b) Some jobs have changed their nature due to the introduction of IT. Name **two** jobs where this has happened.
  (c) With the creation of the information superhighway some jobs are in danger of being lost. Name **two** of these jobs.

4 The advertisement in Figure 20.5 appeared in newspapers during the early days of computing when many businesses were being computerised for the first time. Naturally, many people felt that their jobs could be in jeopardy and the aim of this advertisement was to explain how, in the long term, the use of computers would benefit mankind.
  (a) The list shows some of the negative aspects of computerisation. For each item in the list try to present a positive aspect. For instance, someone may say that the use of a wordprocessor de-skills the job of a typist. The positive aspect to this might be that,

Figure 20.5

because the wordprocessor is easy to use, everyone can produce high quality, accurately typed documents.

(i) Computers lead to unemployment and are therefore a bad thing.

(ii) Some computers are able to report on the number of keystrokes made per hour (particularly in supermarket point-of-sale terminals), so computers can make the employees slaves to their machines.

(iii) People need to be retrained, sometimes against their will.

(iv) There might be a reduction in the amount of overtime available.

(v) All the information held about people invades privacy.

(vi) Computers can be very impersonal.

(b) Write a report outlining some of the advantages of the use of information technology. Try to contrast the way jobs were done before the introduction of the new technology with the way they are done now.

Chapter 21

Controlling Things

Figure 21.1

When people think of computers they usually think of them being used in offices for administrative purposes. There are other things that computer can do: they can be used to control things. In this chapter we will look at how computers can be used to control devices.

Robots

We have all seen robots in science fiction films. The robots usually can talk, walk, reason with humans and occasionally go berserk (Figure 21.1). The robots in these films are far removed from the robots being used in our factories.

Robots are used in factories because they can reduce labour costs and improve the quality of the finished products. A robot may be defined in the following way:

An industrial robot is a reprogrammable, multi-functional manipulator designed to move material, parts, tools or specialised devices through various programmed motions for the performance of a variety of tasks.

This explains why an industrial robot being used in a factory to make motor cars can be called a robot, whereas a washing machine would not be considered as one.

Figure 21.2

An industrial robot can be used in different ways: it could be used to spray paint or for welding body panels. Although it has different programs, a washing machine is restricted to washing clothes.

An industrial robot may be considered to consist of three parts.

1 The **manipulator** – This is the moving part which in Figure 21.3 resembles a moving arm on a stand. Various tools can be placed in the 'hand' of the arm.
2 The **power supply** – For robots that need a lot of strength this will be a compressor which will work the hydraulic system. For lightweight robots which use stepper motors (motors which can be turned through a set angle) the power supply would be the electrical supply.
3 The **controlling computer** – A computer is a very low current device, so it needs a device called an interface in order to protect it from the much higher currents needed for motors and solenoids when they are connected to it. These interfaces also allow analogue to digital, and digital to analogue conversion.

Robots and humans in partnership

At the Toyota plant in Derbyshire, robots check the cars to a very high accuracy. Within a minute of the body shell of the car appearing on the production line, two robots measure it from end to end to an accuracy of 0.1 mm. However, further down the production line the paint work is checked by a human. The robots do the jobs that are too monotonous, strenuous and time consuming for a human. So why can't a robot check the paint work? The reason is it would take too long and a robot wouldn't be able to spot imperfections as well as the human eye.

Robots on the move

When robots start to move from place to place, there are several problems to solve.

1 How are robots able to navigate themselves?

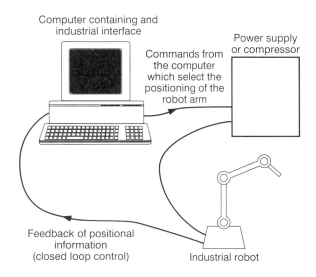

Figure 21.3 *A robot arm being controlled by a microcomputer*

2 How do robots avoid colliding with each other and with other objects?
3 How is the power provided?

How to solve these problems

To allow robots to navigate themselves, tracks are provided which are set into the floor and the robots follow these. This type of system is used in factories, where movable robots are used to move materials around the production line and also in warehouses where robotic fork lift trucks move goods. The robots also keep a record of the distance they have travelled and the

Figure 21.4 *When developing robots, some practical difficulties have to be solved*

Figure 21.5

angles they have turned through so that they always know their exact position.

What would happen if a person stood in the way of one of these moving robots or another robot dropped something in its way? On each robot there is an ultrasonic detector which emits a beam of infra red radiation. If anything gets in the way of the beam, the robot just stops.

Power is usually provided by batteries. When the batteries need recharging, the robot automatically goes to a place where it is recharged.

Computers in control
Using sensors

Sensors are used to detect various physical quantities, such as temperature, pressure, sound, light etc. The sensors are connected to a computer through an interface and with special software, the physical quantities can be displayed in a variety of ways on a computer screen.

Figure 21.6 shows a selection of sensors. Let's now look at each one together with examples of how they can be used.

Mercury tilt switch

If a device is tilted or moved then a blob of mercury in a tilt switch touches the contacts and completes a circuit. Such a switch could be used in a pinball machine to detect whether someone is tilting the machine. It

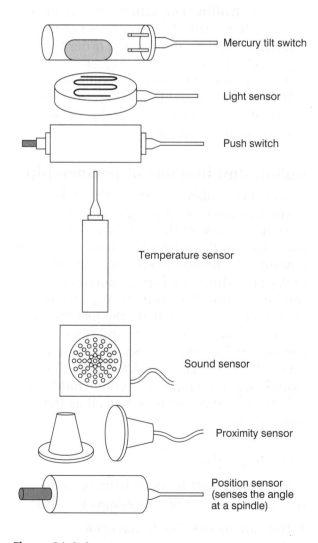

Figure 21.6 *Input sensors*

could also be used as an alarm in a vending machine.

Light sensor
A light sensor has many uses. For instance it could be used to detect low light levels so that street lighting could be turned on. It could also be used to detect the light reflected from a barcode.

Push switch
You might find a push switch being used to turn the interior light on inside a car when the door is opened. You could also use one for detecting when a fridge door was opened, so that the light could be switched on.

Temperature sensor
One of the most common sensors is a temperature sensor. These are used, for example, in central heating systems to keep the temperature of a house constant.

Sound sensor
Environmental health officers could use sound sensors to record the level of sound coming from shops, clubs, houses, etc. where loud music is being played.

Proximity sensor
A proximity sensor is made in two halves. If the halves are moved away from each other then a signal is activated. You often see these sensors on windows, so that if the window is opened the two halves of the sensor are separated and an alarm is activated.

Position sensor
A position sensor senses the angle of a spindle. It could be used to feed back the position of a robot arm.

pH sensor
A pH sensor is used to find out how basic or acidic a solution is.

Humidity sensor
A humidity sensor is used to determine the amount of moisture present (either in the air or in soil).

QUESTION

Give the name of, with reasons, the sensor you would use to:

(a) detect the temperature of the air inside a greenhouse

(b) find out whether a pinball machine has been tilted by a player

(c) detect whether a refrigerator door has been opened

(d) measure the loudness of the music coming from a boutique

(e) determine if a cup of tea has cooled sufficiently to enable a person to drink it

(f) determine whether a solution is acidic or basic

(g) measure the water content of the air in an art gallery

(h) determine whether a pot plant needs watering

(i) find out if a box on a conveyor belt has passed a certain point

(j) determine whether the street lights should be switched on

Interfaces: what are they and why are they needed?

An interface is the name given to the hardware and associated software needed to compensate for the difference in operating characteristics (e.g. speeds, codes, etc.) of the peripheral units and the computer. Figure 21.7 shows an interface used to connect sensors to the computer. Up to a maximum of four sensors can be linked to the interface box which is then connected to the computer. The software is then loaded and the computer knows which sensors it has connected to it.

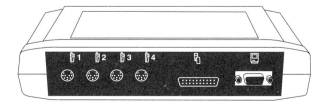

Figure 21.7 *The interface connects the sensors to the computer*

Buffers

The speed of data transfer of a device connected to a computer may be different to that of the computer. Usually a special store area, called a buffer, is used to hold data temporarily to compensate for the difference in speeds.

Actuators

Actuators are hardware devices, such as motors, which react according to signals given to them by computers. An actuator motor would, for example, be used to open a window in a greenhouse when it gets too hot.

Stepper motor

A stepper motor, as the name suggests, is a motor which turns in a series of small steps. Stepper motors generally look fatter than ordinary motors and have several wires coming out of them.

Figure 21.8 shows the positions of a typical stepper motor. The rotor can be turned through a certain angle from, say, position 1,1 to 2,2 and so on. Pulses sent from the computer instruct the motor to turn through the required angle. Stepper motors can also be sped up or slowed down and can also be operated in forward or reverse direction. To connect a stepper motor to a computer, we use a buffer. Stepper motors are used in robot arms.

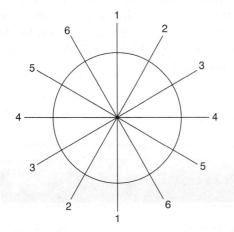

Figure 21.8 *Positions of a stepper motor*

Using sensors in hospitals

The medical condition of a patient in an intensive care unit can be continually monitored using sensors connected to the patient. Respiration, blood pressure, temperature and electrical activity of the heart and pulse can all be measured by the sensors. A computer is used to monitor the results from the sensors continually and if the patient's condition becomes suddenly worse then an alarm can be sounded so that the medical staff can be alerted.

QUESTIONS

1 What advantages are there in using computers to monitor the condition of seriously ill patients?
2 Are there any disadvantages?

Open-loop control

Suppose we wanted to move the arm of the robot through a certain angle. To do this we would need to supply a set number of pulses to a stepper motor to tell it to move through a certain angle. With open-loop control, the computer assumes that once the command has been given the arm will move to the new position. If, for instance, there is something blocking the path of the arm then the computer will assume that it has reached its required position and will carry on as normal. Some sensors are needed that are able to sense the actual position of the robot and feed this information back to the computer. With open-loop control, the output does not affect the input.

Closed-loop control and feedback

In closed-loop control sensors are used to monitor the actual position of the arm continually and to relay the position back to the computer. If the robot arm is found not to be in its correct position, then remedial action will be taken until it is in the correct position. Here, the output from the system directly affects the input. Such a system is said to employ feedback.

Computer disk drives make use of feedback. For instance, if you tell a computer to look for a file on a floppy disk and there is no disk in the disk drive then a sensor will detect this and send a signal back to the computer. The computer will then display an appropriate message on the screen. Because this happens instantly, we can say that this is real-time control.

Process control

Computers are used throughout manufacturing industry for the control of many industrial processes. They are able to monitor and control a process automatically. Like robots, they also make use of feedback.

Process control is also used in nuclear power stations, oil refineries and in the chemical industry. Various sensors are used to relay electronic signals back to computers. Such sensors include devices that measure temperatures, pressures, liquid flow rates, etc. Because these systems operate in real time they are able to respond instantly to variations in these quantities and make slight adjustments to the controls. The advantages of computer control include the following:

1 Computers are able to respond instantly to changes in conditions.
2 Fewer staff are needed, so costs are reduced, making the final product cheaper.
3 The system can keep working 24 hours per day, 365 days a year.
4 Some processes are dangerous. Keeping people away from these processes can help prevent accidents.
5 It is easy for a manufacturer to change a product by reprogramming a computer.

The disadvantages of computer control are as follows.

1 Fewer people are needed to do a job, so this leads to unemployment.
2 Computers tend to be expensive to introduce initially.

Computers on the farm

A cow may be considered to be a mobile chemical plant which needs expert control if it is to function in the way that a farmer wants. Once a cow has been identified to a computer, the computer can keep a complete history of the cow, such as her milk yield, calving, etc. At each stage of her life she will need a different quantity of feed. The computer can be used to work out the mix of feedstuffs to produce the results needed. For instance, when the animal is in calf it will need more food.

Many dairy farms are now computerised. Each cow carries a special device around its neck which emits a radio signal when the cow enters the milking parlour. The signal identifies a particular cow to a computer. The computer can then record her milk yield and give her the right amount of feed whilst she is being milked. The computer is also used to record the total amount of milk collected for all the cows, keep track of the amount sold and also do the farm's accounts.

Pseudo-code

Pseudo-code is useful for writing instructions in ordinary English before these are translated into a language that the computer can understand. With pseudo-code you can express the logical flow of a program in ordinary words. Many control languages use a language similar to pseudo-code.

Using pseudo code you start at the highest level by writing a list of the tasks that the program must perform. You can then refine the program by making it more structured. Let's now look at a task you should be familiar with: washing the dishes.

The first level could be a simple description of the task such as:

wash the dishes

This could then be broken down into the sub-tasks like this:

collect dishes
take to the sink
add small amount of washing-up liquid
wash dishes
put on drainer to dry
dry hands
dry dishes with a cloth
put dishes away

Each of these sub-tasks could be broken down even further. For instance, 'fill sink' could be broken down in the following way:

put in plug
turn on hot tap
turn off hot tap
if water too hot
turn on cold tap
turn off cold tap
ENDIF

If you look at the above list carefully you will see that it probably doesn't represent the way you would actually fill the sink. For example, there is nothing that tells you when you should turn off the hot or cold taps. Also it does not cover the situation where the sink is about to overflow. We need to refine this program to take into account these situations. Here is the final attempt:

IF water in sink
pull out plug
wait for water to drain away
ENDIF
put in plug
turn hot tap half on
turn cold tap half on
DO UNTIL water is deep enough
IF water too hot
turn down hot tap
turn up cold tap
ENDIF
IF water too cold
turn down cold tap
turn up hot tap
ENDIF
ENDO

Even the above could be broken down further, but it is in sufficient detail as a general program. However, if a robot were to

be washing the dishes it would need to have a lot more information. For instance the part of the above program for turning on the hot tap could be broken down into the following:

move arm to position above hot tap
lower hand until it touches tap
get hold of tap
turn tap anti-clockwise
rotate tap for half a turn
release tap
move arm away from tap

Breaking a large complex task down into its smaller more manageable tasks is called the top-down approach. We used the same approach when we drew structure diagrams in Chapter 13.

Computers in greenhouses

For successful growing of plants it is necessary to give them the correct environment and to keep this environment constant. In particular, the temperature and humidity (the amount of moisture) in the air must be kept constant. Sensors are used to record the humidity; signals from these sensors are sent to a computer. If the humidity falls then the computer will operate a motor to close any open windows and then switch on a pump for a certain period, which will spray water as a fine mist inside the greenhouse. An increase in humidity (i.e. too much moisture in the air) will cause the windows to open to assist in ventilation and drying out the air.

The temperature may be controlled in the following way. If the greenhouse gets too hot, the windows are opened. If it gets too cold, then the windows are closed and a heater is switched on. With such careful control of conditions, the plants grow much faster.

The inputs and outputs of the system are as follows:

Inputs
Humidity – analogue signal
Temperature – analogue signal.

Outputs

Windows – digital signal (either open or closed)
Heater – digital signal (either on or off)
Pump for water spray – digital signal (either on or off).

In practice, the control could be much more complicated than this. For example, we could have windows which opened by small amounts depending on the temperature and the humidity.

QUESTION

The greenhouse in Figure 21.9 is used to grow delicate plants and must be kept at a constant temperature of 24–28°C throughout the year. If it gets too hot, the glass panel is opened by a motor. If it gets too cold, the glass panel is closed.

You now have to write some pseudo-code which will do the following:

- start with the window closed
- wait for the temperature to rise above 28°C
- produce a sound (e.g. a buzz) and then open the window to allow the cooler air in
- wait for the temperature to fall below 24°C
- produce a sound (e.g. a buzz) and close the window.

It is decided that this system would be incapable of maintaining the temperature in the winter, so a heater needs to be included. Decide on the series of steps that the system would take and write a new piece of pseudo-code for the control program.

Figure 21.9

Computers and safety of cars

Many new cars are fitted with a braking system called ABS, which stands for antilock brake system. ABS uses sensors to detect the rotational speed of each wheel when the brakes are applied. The speed of each wheel is relayed to the computer. If the wheels start to lock, the computer sends a signal which eases the pressure on the brakes at each wheel. This prevents the wheels from locking and sliding out of control. Using ABS, a driver is able to control the car more safely during braking.

Data logging

Data is often collected automatically over a period of time and then processed at a later date. You may have seen pressure sensors which look like thick wires placed across the road to record the volume of traffic passing. If you follow these sensors they lead to a black box which is usually padlocked to a lampost to prevent it from being stolen. This box, called a data logger, records data about the volume of traffic passing. The alternative way of recording this data would be to use humans to do it manually. This is clearly expensive and not the most exciting of jobs.

There are two main types of data loggers: those which need to be connected to the computer all the time and those which don't.

Data loggers with permanent computer connections
These data loggers take readings and then send them to the computer via a wire or an electronic signal. The computer can either process the readings at once to produce a graph or store them on disk for processing at a later date. These data loggers are ideal for experiments in the laboratory but suitable ones for use in the field are too expensive for schools to use.

Data loggers with temporary computer connections
These data loggers are ideal for monitoring environmental conditions over a period of time in the field. As with all data loggers,

the time intervals (the time between each reading) and the period over which the logging takes place can be varied.

The readings are stored by the data logger and the stored readings can be loaded into the computer at a later date where they can be processed and displayed. Because they are used in remote places, these data loggers need their own power supply.

Data logging has many advantages:

1 it can be performed 24 hours per day, 365 days per year if necessary
2 it is possible for processing to be carried out immediately if the data logger can send the data in the form of a radio signal to the main computer.

QUESTION

You have been concerned about the road where you live being used by lorries, vans and cars as a short cut to avoid a busy junction. You have persuaded local residents to sign a petition which has been sent to your local council.

The council has said that it will monitor the situation and place a data logger on the road for two weeks.

(a) Explain what a data logger is.

(b) To monitor the flow of traffic you got together with the other residents to stand at the side of the road and to count the number of certain types of vehicles travelling along the road between 10 and 11 in the morning.

  (i) What advantages does the data logger have over your manual method?

  (ii) What methods of display could be used to present the data from the data logger?

THINGS TO DO

1 (a) A computer program is used to control a robot, which is moving and stacking boxes in a warehouse. The program uses commands to control its movements

FORWARD steps
BACK steps
RIGHT angle
LEFT angle
UP steps
DOWN steps

Figure 21.10

For example,
FORWARD 50 moves the robot forward
50 steps in a straight line.
RIGHT 45 turns the robot 45° to the right.
UP 2 raises the forks 2 steps.

The robot is found to be dropping the boxes in the wrong place.

Give two different mistakes in the program that could be causing this.

(b) Following a nasty accident, the robot has to be adapted to stop if it meets an unexpected obstacle in its path. What changes would need to be made to the robot design?

(NEAB/WJEC 1993)

2 The heating of water in a tank is under the control of a microprocessor. Cold water enters the tank via valve 1. It is heated to a set temperature and leaves the tank via valve 2.

(a) Describe how feedback could be used in the system.

(b) (i) Where should an analogue-to-digital converter be placed in the system? Draw your answer on the diagram.

(ii) Why is an analogue-to-digital converter necessary?

(MEG 1993)

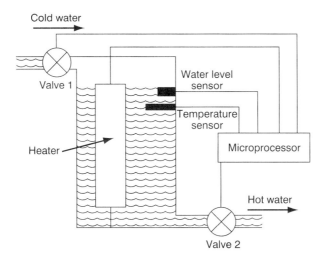

Cold water

Valve 1

Water level sensor

Temperature sensor

Heater

Microprocessor

Hot water

Valve 2

Figure 21.11

3 (a) A washing machine is designed to wash, rinse and spin for predetermined times regardless of whether the washing is clean or not. Is this an open-loop or closed-loop control system?

(b) A central heating system is continually monitoring the temperature of a room. If it is too cold, the heating is switched on. When the room gets too hot the system switches the heater off. Is this open-loop or closed-loop control?

(c) Traffic lights may either use closed-loop or open-loop control. Using traffic lights as an example, explain the difference between open-loop and closed-loop control.

4 Computer systems are now being used in hospitals as part of life-support systems.

(a) Blood pressure is a human physical response suitable for monitoring by computer. Suggest two others.

(b) Give three reasons why computers are used in life-support systems.

(c) Give three tasks for which human medical staff are more suitable than computers.

5 A robot is used to retrieve fuel rods from a nuclear reactor. To get the rod labelled X, the following instructions could be given:

FORWARD 3

TURN RIGHT

FORWARD 1

TAKE

(a) The robot has an instruction (INPUT var) that allows numbers to be input into variables, which can then be used instead of the numbers indicated above. Write a program so that it will allow any rod to be retrieved. Make sure you clearly identify the use of your variables   (4 marks)

(b) Why would a robot be used for this job?   (2 marks)

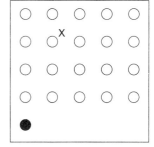

Figure 21.12

(SEG NC IT Spec)

6 A car park entrance is controlled by a microprocessor.

When a car approaches the barrier a ticket is produced, which the driver takes. The barrier then opens, and the light changes from red to green. When the car has passed, the light changes to red and the barrier comes down.

(a) Describe a suitable sensor for detecting the approaching car. (2 marks)

(b) List the steps involved in carrying out this process, using suitable instructions. (4 marks)

(c) What information needs to be on the ticket? (2 marks)

(d) Give two ways in which this can be encoded in machine readable form. (2 marks)

(SEG NC IT Spec)

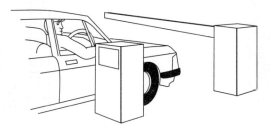

Figure 21.13

7 The table shows a number of different situations. Fill in the boxes to show the time intervals between logging and the overall period of logging.

(NEAB/WJEC Option Q)

Situation	Sensor	Time interval	Period of logging
Collecting data on seasonal temperature variations for weather records	Heat		
Collecting data about the temperature change which takes place when ice is added to a beaker of water	Heat		

8 The greenhouse shown in the diagram must be kept at a temperature between 24°C and 28°C throughout the year. It has been decided to use a computer controlled system. Produce an outline design for the system which is required.

(NEAB/WJEC Spec Option R)

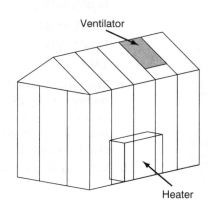

Ventilator

Heater

Figure 21.14

9 A diagram of a refrigerator is shown in Figure 21.15.

(a) What quantity does the sensor measure?

(b) A refrigerator makes use of feedback. Explain what feedback means and say why it is necessary to have it in the refrigerator.

(c) A control program is stored on the chip. Write down a series of instructions which will help keep the refrigerator at a constant temperature.

(d) When the door of the refrigerator is opened a light comes on. Examine your fridge at home and see if you can find out how this sensor works.

(e) Insurance companies pay out large sums of money each year to people who have ruined food by leaving the door slightly open. Design a system which could help prevent this problem.

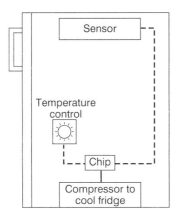

Figure 21.15 *Refrigerator*

You are to connect a heat sensor and a buzzer to the computer through a buffer box. Use appropriate external devices, together with safe interfacing equipment and suitable software to write a sequence of instructions which will sound an alarm when a temperature is reached at which butter melts.

Replace the alarm device with appropriate equipment to record the temperature over a period of time, and load suitable software. Find out the total amount of time for which the butter was melting.

Connect suitable equipment to drive a small fan, and amend the original sequence which sounded the alarm so that the fan will start when the butter starts melting and stop again when it drops enough for the butter to solidify.

(RSA Spec)

22 Computers and your Health

The problems

There are many health problems that can occur when you are working with computers for long periods. Repetitive strain injury (RSI), backache, eyestrain, headaches and skin rashes are conditions which can occur. By using various devices, correct posture and good working practices, these conditions can be prevented. Figure 22.1 shows some things you ought to pay attention to when working with VDUs.

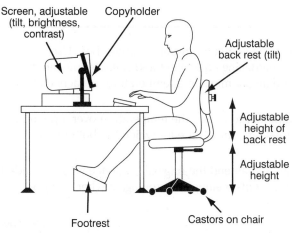

Figure 22.1 *What you need to work efficiently at a computer*

Repetitive strain injury (RSI)

RSI is caused by the joints in the fingers constantly being pounded by typing at high speed. RSI causes pain in the joints and can cause long term disability. Good keyboard design, a well positioned keyboard, a good typing technique and frequent breaks can help prevent RSI from occurring. You can also buy wrist guards which ease fatigue when you are using keyboards for long periods.

Eyestrain

In a study of VDU operators, it was found that nearly 70% suffered some form of eye problem such as eyestrain, irritated eyes or blurred vision. However eyestrain is fairly common in other types of close work. One way of avoiding eyestrain is to look at a distant object now and again (ask your physics or biology teacher to explain why this helps). Regular computer users should have regular eye checks.

Reproductive hazards

There have been some stories in the newspapers regarding abnormal births in pregnant women who have been using VDUs for long periods. VDUs, like a lot of other electrical appliances, give out radiation when they are working. Most of this radiation is given out from the back and the sides of the VDUs. A large amount of research has been done on this and at the moment there is little evidence that VDUs do any damage.

Figure 22.2 *There are lots of scare stories concerning radiation from VDUs. There is no real evidence though, so you needn't worry*

Figure 22.3

Protecting the workforce

Because of the various health problems that can occur with incorrect computer use there is now a law which requires employers to provide the following:

- **Inspections** – Desks, chairs, computers, etc. should be inspected to make sure that they reach the required standard.
- **Training** – Employees should have training on health and safety matters.
- **Job design** – The job should be designed so that the worker has periodic breaks or changes of activity when using computers.
- **Eye tests** – For computer users there should be regular free eye tests, with glasses provided if necessary, at the employer's expense.

The law also lays down some minimum requirements for computer systems and furniture. All new furniture and equipment bought must meet these standards:

- **Display screens** – These must have a stable picture with no flicker. Brightness, contrast, tilt and swivel must be easily adjustable. There must be no reflection off the screen.

- **Keyboard** – This must be separate from the screen and tiltable. Keyboards should be easy to use and the surface should be matt to avoid glare. There must be sufficient space for people to change position.
- **Desks** – Desks must be large enough to accommodate the computer and any paperwork and must not reflect too much light. An adjustable document holder should be provided so as to avoid uncomfortable head movements.
- **Chair** – This must be adjustable and comfortable, and allow easy freedom of movement. A foot rest must be available on request.
- **Lights** – There must be no glare or reflections on the computer screen. Windows must have adjustable coverings.
- **Noise** – This should not be loud enough to distract attention and disturb speech.
- **Software** – This must be easy to use and appropriate to the user's needs and experience.
- **Other matters** – Heat, humidity and radiation emissions must be kept at adequate levels.

Things to consider when designing an office

1 Single pendant lamps (like the ones you have in your house) should be avoided since they produce glare on the screen. Instead, fluorescent tubes with diffusers (plastic covers) which spread out the light, should be used.
2 Carpets made of man-made fibre should be avoided. These cause static electricity which can destroy data stored on magnetic disks.
3 Windows should have adjustable blinds on them to avoid sunlight producing glare on the screen.
4 Cables should not be left trailing across the floor.
5 Ample sockets should be fitted so that it is not necessary to use multiple sockets, which could be dangerous.

Figure 22.4

1 The cartoon in Figure 22.4 shows all sorts of poor working practices and bad equipment. How many can you spot? Write a list and say what needs to be done to put them right.

2 There are various products for sale in computer catalogues which are aimed at the 'computer safety market'. Look at these catalogues and write a brief report stating what devices are available and how much they cost.

3 You have been asked to look at the equipment and the working conditions in your school or college's computer rooms. Some of the things you should look at are:

   • whether sockets have too many plugs in them
   • whether carpets are made of man-made fibre
   • whether document holders are provided
   • whether there are adjustable blinds on the windows
   • whether wires trail across the floor.

   (a) Your task is to complete this list of things to look for. After you have completed your list design a suitable document which may be filled in when you look around the room. This document should be wordprocessed.

   (b) Look around the computer room and fill in the document.

   (c) Prepare a report which gives a summary of what you have found, making any recommendations where necessary.

 INVESTIGATION

Sue, Grabbitt and Runn is a partnership of solicitors. The original partners are now retiring and new partners have come into the business. The new partners wish to get rid of the firm's old fashioned image and would like to improve efficiency. They would like to make the main office open plan. Each of the five partners in the firm has to have his or her own office, since the firm's clients would like privacy when discussing personal matters. The accounting system is to be computerised and all the letters and forms, both sent out and received, are to be recorded on the system. The use of a local area network (LAN) will enable both office staff and the solicitors to view client information via their own terminal.

There are various problems with the existing office:

   • the office chairs do not have castors and are non-adjustable
   • the carpet is made of nylon and staff frequently complain of getting electric shocks
   • the main lighting is from single lights hanging from the ceiling. This causes uneven illumination
   • the partners have curtains on their windows which frequently have to be closed because of the sunlight coming in
   • each partner has a highly polished oak desk: staff in the open plan office have shiny, Formica desks

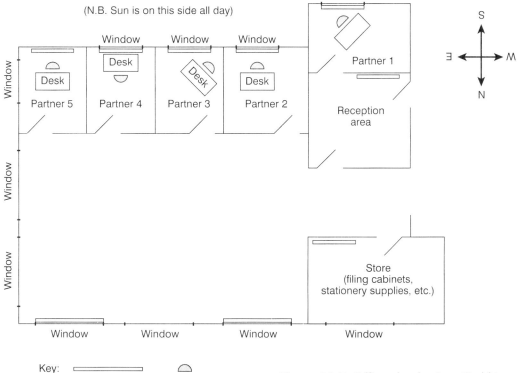

Figure 22.5 *Office plan for Sue, Grabbitt and Runn*

- the three computers in use at the moment, have keyboards and VDUs in one unit.

You have been asked to help plan the installation of the new information system. Figure 22.5 shows the layout of the office at the moment. You do not need to get involved in the actual dimensions of the office since this would make the project far too complicated.

1 Prepare a report, using wordprocessing software, making some preliminary recommendations concerning new office furniture and equipment. Your report should identify the factors to be considered when deciding the location and layout of the various terminals in the main office.

2 Obtain, from equipment and office furniture suppliers, prices for the equipment you have suggested and detail your costs using an appropriate software package.

3 The partners prefer to have their desks in the positions marked on the plan but you think that, with the introduction of the terminals, some of these positions are unsuitable. Write short memos to the partners concerned explaining why the positions of their desks should be changed.

For the whole of the office, design your best possible layout. A diagram should be drawn, either by hand or using a suitable software package, showing the positions of the main pieces of equipment, desks,

etc. Also include a report outlining the reasons behind your proposed arrangement.

Staffing and equipment information

Staffing

5 partners   1 solicitor

2 trainee solicitors

1 office manager (in charge of administrative/secretarial staff)

1 senior secretary   2 junior secretaries

1 general/filing clerk   1 receptionist.

Equipment

5 terminals (1 for each partner)

1 terminal for the solicitor

2 terminals for the trainee solicitors

1 terminal for the office manager

All the secretarial staff have terminals, which they mainly use for wordprocessing. Staff without terminals still have a desk.

2 laser printers (connected to the network)

1 document scanner (used to scan documents into the system)

1 fax machine   1 photocopier

1 drinks machine   1 typewriter.

Chapter 23

The Electronic Office

The paper chase

Processing insurance claims

Claims occur when, for instance, a car is crashed and the money is claimed for its repair. Here are the steps that used to be taken by an insurance company when it was processing claims:

1 The post is opened.
2 The appropriate file is found in the series of filing cabinets.
3 The files are taken to the person who is handling the case.
4 The person who is handling the case writes letters concerning the case.
5 Letters are sent to the typist for typing.
6 Typed letters are received back by the person handling the case.
7 Letters are signed and posted, and copies of the letters are placed back in the file.
8 The files are sent back to the filing clerk for filing.

The above system of 'paper chasing' would take several days and another problem was, if a customer rang, then it was difficult to locate a file. This all resulted in slower claims and high administration costs. These costs meant that the company had to charge more for their insurance and this caused loss of business to other insurance companies, who were more efficient and therefore cheaper.

The company therefore decided to try to remove paper from the office and to do as many as possible of the tasks electronically. In other words the company decided to move over to an electronic office.

When the electronic office was introduced, everything was stored on the system. All correspondence, including diagrams of scenes of accidents and photographs could be scanned into the system. All paper correspondence and photographs are destroyed quickly (usually after about seven days). When the claims staff arrive at work they now log into the system and it gives them a list of jobs which need action. The system provides a complete history of the claim, including brief details of any telephone calls made.

Advantages of the new system

1 The clerks do not need to leave their desks, since all the information relating to a particular claim is available from the computers on their desks.
2 Claims are handled much more efficiently, which in turn means more satisfied customers.
3 Paper costs have been cut and photocopying costs are much lower, since it is no longer necessary to keep a copy of every letter sent out.
4 The costs of phone calls have decreased: it is no longer necessary to call people back because files needed to be 'hunted down'.

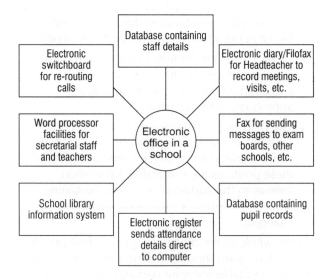

Figure 23.1 *Electronic office in a school*

QUESTION

Figure 23.1 shows just some of the components of an electronic office that are present in a particular school. Your school may be more or less electronic than this.

Investigate the electronic 'systems' in your school and produce a diagram, similar to the one in Figure 23.1, to illustrate your findings. You can produce your design by hand or use suitable software.

Equipment and facilities in an electronic office

Fax

A fax machine is rather like a long distance photocopier, where you put the document into the fax machine at one end and a copy comes out of a fax machine at the other end. The original is first scanned with a beam of light and then converted into electronic signals that can be passed along the telephone lines. The copy is printed out at the other end on the recipient's machine.

Faxes are particularly useful, since drawings can be transferred. Also, because a fax is really a picture of the document, letters or contracts which include a signature may be sent and this is useful to lawyers.

Problems with fax machines

To keep costs down, the scanner used to scan a document in a fax machine has a low resolution which means that the image is nothing like as sharp as the original. Couple this with the fact that the printers are often poor and you can get a very poor quality and distorted copy. However this is changing as the printers used in fax machines change over to ink-jet or laser technology. Also, people like to store faxes, but they take up space and are untidy since they are all different sizes.

Electronic mail (e-mail)

With electronic mail (or e-mail), data or messages can be sent electronically via the telephone network or other data networks and via a central computer. Electronic mail has advantages of speed and economy (there is no need for stamps, envelopes etc.) With electronic mail both sender and recipient can store the letters or documents on disk for future reference.

Electronic mail is used extensively by companies that have networks for their internal mail. The wider use of electronic mail is hindered because not everyone has the facilities.

Figure 23.2

QUESTIONS

1 How would the following make use of a fax machine? For each one say how the fax machine would be useful:

(a) a solicitor

(b) an accountant

(c) an architect

(d) an engineer.

2 A document can also be sent using electronic mail. A solicitor needs to send a copy of a contract which has been signed by a client to a building society. It is important that the client's signature is on the copy. What problem is there in using electronic mail?

167

Document image processing

It is very difficult to make an office completely paperless, mainly because customers don't always have access to the new technology. Because of this many documents still come into companies from outside on paper. Traditionally, this paperwork was held in large banks of filing cabinets. Now, these paper documents can be converted into electronic form by scanning them. A scanner digitises documents and makes it possible for them to be stored on either magnetic or optical disk. These documents may then be stored alongside text which has been keyed in or entered in other ways. Since the documents are stored as images rather than as text it is not possible to edit them. In some ways they may be considered to be like photocopies stored on disk.

Document image processing is used by most large companies. It has the advantages that the information may be retrieved rapidly and many people can access documents at the same time. In addition once a document has been scanned in, it may be disposed of, so storage needs are reduced.

Electronic data interchange (EDI)

EDI is the method by which different companies' computers automatically exchange data. Large food retailers such as Tesco use this method. When Tesco stores are running low on a certain item such as baked beans, an order is automatically issued and sent electronically to the supplier's computer where it is dealt with. Payment for the goods is made electronically from the retailer to the supplier via their bank accounts. This all happens without any paperwork.

Viewdata

Viewdata is any system that provides information through a telephone network to a terminal or television screen. Viewdata is different from teletext because it is interactive: You can send information as well as receive it.

The viewdata service provided by BT is called Prestel. Prestel can be considered as a large collection of databases. To use Prestel, you need to subscribe to the system. You pay for the time you are connected to the computer and some of the information providers also charge for the pages you view.

Figure 23.3 shows the different ways in which the signals arrive for teletext and Prestel.

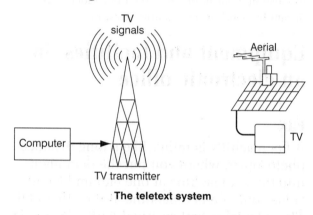

The teletext system

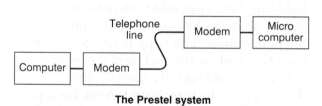

The Prestel system

Figure 23.3 *The different ways that signals arrive for Teletext and Prestel*

Differences between Prestel and Viewdata

Teletext	*Prestel*
Provided by the television companies	Provided by BT
Transmitted at the same time as TV pictures	Sent via telephone cables
Special TV needed	Telephone, modem and computer or terminal are needed
Non-interactive	Interactive
Cheap	Expensive
Limited number of pages	Huge amount of information on all subjects

Teleconferencing

Teleconferencing is set to take off in a big way. Soon we will be able to conduct conversations with people in different parts of the country or even the world using a telephone, a computer system and video camera. With such a system it is possible to conduct meetings with several people in different locations without leaving your home or office. Figure 23.4 shows the system. Notice the small video camera on the top of the VDU.

Figure 23.4 *Teleconferencing system*

The savings to be made with teleconferencing are great. Suppose a company wanted to hold a sales meeting in London for all its sales staff who normally operate from home. Even if the meeting were to take only two hours, many staff could still take the best part of a day to get to London. Some staff from Scotland might have to stay in a hotel. The travel expenses, hotel costs and the loss of business whilst the sales staff were not out selling would all have to be met by the company.

With teleconferencing, all the participants could hear and see the other people taking part in their own homes. Minutes of the meeting, notes and charts could be passed to each person electronically.

Telecommuting

As our cities become more congested and polluted, people will start to look at alternative ways of working. Consider the insurance company we looked at earlier. In this company everything was done electronically. Using networks it would be possible for a worker at home to access all this information. Many companies are considering allowing staff to work at home.

There has been much concern in the press concerning the general move for many people from employed status to self-employment or contract work. From a company's point of view, the increasing use of IT is providing more and more rapid changes, making competition more intense and producing pressure to reduce the workforce. From an employee's point of view, the reducing cost and increasing power of telecommunications, computer equipment and software are making self employment a more viable option.

There are some disadvantages in teleconferencing and telecommuting:

- while computer hardware is cheaper than it was, it is still expensive
- telecommunication costs are high
- people like personal contact.

QUESTION

You have been asked by the insurance company we looked at earlier to work from home. The company will install and pay for all the necessary equipment in your home.

(a) What advantages might there be in your being able to work from home rather than travel into a central office each day?

(b) Are there any disadvantages of working from home? Explain what they are.

(c) There are also some advantages to the insurance company of this way of working. What are they?

A paperless online hospital

A 260 bed hospital in Clydebank has implemented a complete clinical information system. The system covers everything from the ordering of drugs to the reporting of test results. Paper systems have been completely eliminated.

All patient information is available online from terminals scattered throughout the hospital. Doctors and nurses can gain access to patient records in any part of the hospital at any time of the day. There is no longer any need to wait for X-rays, prescription records or test results, since these are available online. Also, patient records can be transferred to any hospital in the world provided that the hospitals have compatible equipment. The system can even alert the doctor if she prescribes a drug to which a patient is known to be allergic.

TEST YOURSELF

Using the words in the list below, copy out and complete sentences A to G, underlining the words you have inserted. The words may be used more than once.

document   fax   electronic   interchange   data teleconferencing   viewdata   telecommuting telephone

A An office which keeps paperwork to a minimum is called a paperless or _____ office.

B A machine which is a bit like a long distance photocopier is called a _____.

C _____ image processing involves using a scanner to scan the documents into the system so that the original paperwork may be disposed of.

D Electronic ____ _____ uses computers automatically to issue orders and pay for them.

E _____ enables conferences to be organised without the people involved, leaving their homes or offices.

F The _____ service uses the _____ system whereas teletext is a television signal sent at the same time as the TV programmes.

G Staying at home and working using computers and telecommunications equipment is called _____.

THINGS TO DO

1 Draw a diagram of a paper-based office and include on your diagram the usual areas such as:
   - photocopier and print room (containing a photocopier and a duplicating machine)
   - filing room (containing filing cabinets and a microfilm reader)
   - typing area (containing manual typewriters)
   - accounts area (containing typewriters and calculators)
   - post room (containing addressing machines, postage meter, sorting racks for incoming mail, telex and telephone switchboard).

2 Now draw a diagram of the office after it has been converted into an electronic office.

3 With the introduction of electronic offices, some people's jobs will change, while others may even disappear. With reference to the following list, say how each job might change and state which, if any, of the jobs will remain the same.
   - filing clerk
   - copy typist
   - shorthand typist
   - secretary

- post-room clerk
- manager
- accounts clerk.

4 Explain the differences and similarities between the following information systems: teletext and Prestel

5 An ordinary telephone which has no special features can be used only to dial numbers and receive incoming calls. Investigate the latest phones and explain the features that are now available.

6 There has been a great increase in the use of systems involving communication between computers.
Describe a system which makes use of a communication network.

(NEAB/WJEC Spec Option Q)

Evaluating a database

You have been asked to evaluate a remote database of your choice, available on Prestel, and to compare the system with the corresponding manual method of finding out the same information.

You could try:

- the British Rail database which contains information about fares and times of trains
- The Phonebase database, which is a database of all the information contained in the phonebook (remember that the phonebook you regularly use applies only to a small area of the country).

Setting up a bulletin board

A bulletin board is an area of a viewdata service where one user can leave messages which are available to all other users.

Set up a bulletin board using Prestel or one of the other services.

Chapter

24

Simulations
Almost as Good as the Real Thing

Figure 24.1 *Computer modelling*

Modelling

Suppose you are the Chancellor of the Exchequer for a moment (Figure 24.2). Your job will be to control the economy as best you can. You will have to make decisions about what to do. For instance, you can alter interest rates, the amount of taxes people pay, how much the government spends on education, benefits, the NHS etc. Changes in any of these will affect the economy. One false move could plunge the country into a recession and make life miserable for millions of people.

Before making any decisions, the chancellor needs to ask 'what would happen if I did this?' For instance, if a minimum national wage were to be enforced (i.e. no one could be paid below a certain amount) what would the result be? Would it reduce poverty or would it lead to mass unemployment?

A computer simulation can be used to provide an answer to these sorts of

questions. We can create on the computer a 'pretend' economy and then take certain courses of action and then see what the results are. Doing this, we can see the effect of any disastrous decisions on our artificial economy rather than have to suffer the consequences on our own economy.

This all sounds simple. If this works, why do we have such high unemployment? Well, we could produce a model of the economy in many different ways. Different models use different equations. For instance the model used by the UK Treasury has about 1300 equations. As you can see, there is plenty of room for error here.

In this example we have used the words model and simulation. There is a difference in the meanings of these words. A model consists of a set of equations which describes the behaviour of a process or object. In a computer model we use the computer to solve these equations so that

Figure 24.2

we can carry out a simulation. An equation for part of the economic model might be

unemployment = people able to work
 – people working

A simulation involves feeding values into the model to see how the model behaves.

3-D modelling

3-D models are often set up by architects and design engineers to see what a finished building or product will look like before it is built or produced. For instance Tesco, the food retailer, uses CAD (computer aided design) and 3-D models to produce three-dimensional views of stores and can show the effects of varying light sources, intensity of colour and different finishes of materials. Tesco also uses 3-D modelling to look at the way to blend a new store into an existing main street. 3-D models are also use to plan the outside of stores.

Modelling inflation

Suppose you are planing for the future and would like some money for when you stop working. In other words you need a pension. A pension is a sum of money you get each week when you retire from work. Everyone has to think about this sooner or later, but how much might you need? Suppose you are earning £275 per week now, what will you be earning just before you retire? The answer is, you just don't know. However, if you are arranging a pension, you need to have an idea of how much you are going to need.

So you need a model. Let's design a model to determine how much a 23-year-old person who earned £275 per week in 1995 would be earning in 2036, the year before they were due to retire.

There are various constraints to our model.

1 No-one knows what the percentage rate of inflation will be over the next 40 years. We could look at the past rates of inflation over, say, the last 20 years (you should be able to get these figures from the library or your economics teacher) and use an average value, or you could use another value.

2 To make things simpler, we have to assume that the person doesn't get promoted and his wage increases only in line with inflation. When you have got used to the model you might try increasing the wage at some point in the future.

3 Our worker's wages may rise faster than the rate of inflation. Some occupations have done well over the last 20 years and others have fallen behind (particularly those in the public sector such as teachers, nurses and civil servants). Is it possible to take these factors into account?

QUESTION

(a) The first five years can be calculated manually, assuming that the inflation stays at a constant rate of 5% per year. Before you attempt this, we will look at how we would do this for the first couple of years.

We will fill in a table with these column headings:

End of year   Wage

To work out how £275 would need to change in order to keep pace with inflation we would perform the following calculations. We find 5% of 275 in the following way:

$$5/100 \times 275 = £13.75$$

This is the amount by which the weekly wage would need to grow. Hence,

new weekly wage
at the end of year 1 $= 275 + 13.75$
                        $= £288.75$

We can add these to the table like this:

End of year	Wage
1	£288.75

We then repeat the process using this new wage:

5% of £288.75 $= 5/100 \times 288.75$
                 $= £14.44$

Hence,

weekly wage
at the end of year 2 $= 288.75 + 14.44$
                        $= £303.19$

You can start to build up the table like this:

End of year	Wage
1	£288.75
2	£303.19

You now have to complete the table for the first five years by repeating the processes outlined above. Good mathematicians will be able to do these calculations using a faster method than that shown above. If you want to know more, ask your mathematics teacher.

(b) Obviously, for this type of repetitive calculation, a spreadsheet would be ideal. Prepare a model using a spreadsheet and find out how much the person would need to earn in 2036 to just keep pace with inflation.

(c) Try to refine your model so that it reflects reality better. For instance, collect some inflation figures and see if 5% seems about right.

Managing BT engineers

Models are used to imitate real situations. BT, the telecommunications company, has developed software that can be used to model the job of a manager of a group of engineers. When you use this software, you are the manager and have to manage your staff to the best of your abilities. (The Priority Educational Software can be purchased from BT Education)

You are an engineering manager and have to allocate the faults to be repaired. As a manager you need to bear in mind the following before allocating the jobs:

- people skills – to minimise work time
- location – to minimise travel time
- priorities – to cope with emergencies.

Sometimes the above are in conflict: you could have an engineer who is near to a particular job but doesn't have the skills to repair the fault quickly. A good manager gives the right jobs to the right people and plans each day carefully.

At the end of the week you can obtain statistics on the number of jobs your staff have completed and the number of hours worked. By comparing your results with someone else's you can determine who is the better manager. You can also save these statistics and import them into your spreadsheet package, where you can perform further analysis on them.

Using the model supplied you can also investigate issues such as:

- whether, given a fixed budget, a wage increase can be afforded
- the costs of dealing with different types of fault
- preparing a report on the effect of losing a manager
- writing an appraisal report on each employee, outlining the average time spent on different jobs and showing how these compare to the average for the engineering team as a whole.

As you can see, managing people is not simply telling them what to do!

Games

Many computer games are simulations. For instance, when you play a football game on your computer you are simulating a real game. Some games, such as Themepark, simulate running a business in an exciting way. With Themepark you have to build rides that will attract the public. The more entertaining your rides are, then the more people will come to your themepark.

You can have simulations without using a computer. Monopoly is one example of many.

Flight simulators are very popular on home computers, so if you fancy landing a jet on an aircraft carrier, then you can buy a package to realise your dreams. These simulations either run in non-real time where things happen slower than they would do in real life or in real time where things happen at the real speed. Although visually they resemble the real thing, only a genuine flight simulator gives the movements and feel of actually flying the aircraft.

Model Builder

Model Builder is a very useful software package available from the address at the back of the book. You can use Paint (a Windows drawing and painting package) to design illustrations for the model. You then have to decide where to place the blocks, which are like spreadsheet cells. These blocks can contain numbers, text, pictures, graphs or actions (formulae). Like spreadsheet cells, these blocks react when they are sent messages from other blocks. Graphs are easily drawn from the results of the model.

As with a spreadsheet, you can produce a rough model and then refine it to give a better resemblance of the real thing.

With the Model Builder package you can develop and evaluate your own models or use the models that have already been set up to simulate a real life situation. Figure 24.3 shows a screen display from Model Builder of a model showing how nutrients are recycled through a woodland ecosystem.

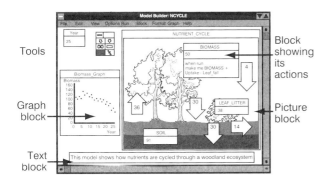

Figure 24.3 *Model of the nutrient cycle in a woodland*

Models you can make include:

- population growth
- supply and demand
- chemical reactions
- nutrient cycle
- nitrogen cycle
- carbon cycle
- growth of algae in a pond.

Expert systems

Expert systems are programs that mimic the intelligence of a human expert in a specific field of knowledge. For instance an expert system could be set up to give medical advice. The computer is given a base of knowledge from the expert and then given the rules for processing the information. The idea is that the computer asks questions similar to those the expert would ask and then it comes to a similar conclusion.

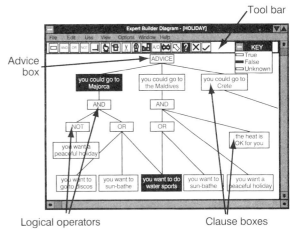

Figure 24.4 *Model to provide advice about holiday destinations*

Expert Builder

Expert Builder is another package that enables you to construct logical diagrams of your knowledge. This software helps you to understand a problem more clearly and consolidate this knowledge. Figure 24.4 shows a screen from Expert Builder. Here, this model is being used to provide help about holiday destinations. As with Model Builder, you can add diagrams like the one shown in Figure 24.5 to provide explanations.

Energy Expert

Energy Expert is a software package consisting of four modules, covering advice, heating, forecast and comfort.

- The 'Advice' module investigates how to save energy by using insulation etc. A screen is shown in Figure 24.6.

Advice being offered after exploring the model

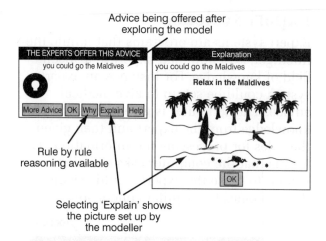

Rule by rule reasoning available

Selecting 'Explain' shows the picture set up by the modeller

Figure 24.5 *You can add diagrams using Expert Builder*

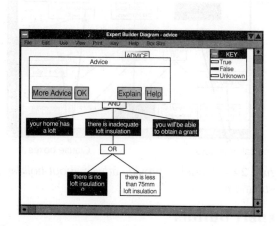

Figure 24.6 *Advice on how to save energy*

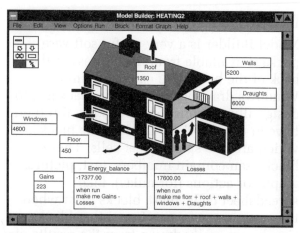

Figure 24.7 *Heat losses in a typical house*

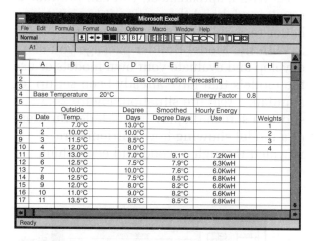

Figure 24.8 *Using a spreadsheet to compare the links between outside temperature and domestic demand for heating*

- The 'Heating' module is used to explore the heat losses in a typical house and how these can be reduced using certain features when the house is built. Heat losses and gains can be calculated using a spreadsheet and these can then be displayed graphically. Figure 24.7 shows the model.
- The 'Forecast' model is used to compare the links between outside temperature and domestic demand for heating. Figure 24.8 shows a typical screen.
- The 'Comfort' model looks at the way the human body regulates its temperature. It looks at biological concepts such as cell respiration, human temperature regulation and homeostasis (Figure 24.9).

Figure 24.9 *Looking at why one person can feel hot while another can feel cold, even in the same room*

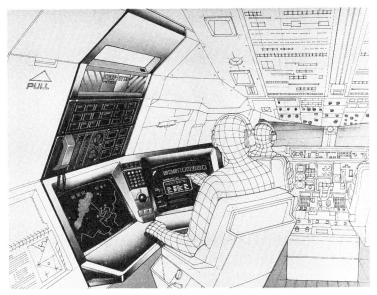

Figure 24.10 *Inside a flight simulator*

Simulations

When most people think of simulators they think of flight simulators, but there are other types of simulations. Simulations are useful, for example, in experiments that would be too difficult, too dangerous or too costly to carry out.

Examples of simulations include:

• experiments in chemistry
• nuclear physics experiments
• airline training
• queues at petrol filling stations
• traffic light systems
• queues at supermarket checkouts.

When new bridges or buildings are being designed by engineers, we can simulate the construction of a bridge by using the computer to calculate the stresses at various points and discover the safest construction without having to build it first. Simulations are usually performed to avoid the expense or danger of making mistakes.

Flight simulators

Airlines find it very expensive to tie up aircraft for the training of pilots, so they use simulators instead. In addition, all manner of dangerous flying conditions, some of which the pilot would never be likely to experience, can be simulated. A landing simulation with ice on the runway, thick fog

Figure 24.11 *Flight simulator viewed from the outside*

and with only one of the of the four engines working would really test the pilot's ability.

Flight simulators like the one shown in Figure 24.10 enable pilots to experience turbulence, snowstorms, thunderstorms, fog and airpockets as well as landing at different airports throughout the world, without leaving the ground.

If you look at Figure 24.11 you can see that a flight simulator is a windowless capsule that looks like a spacecraft. The hydraulically controlled struts (i.e. the legs) can propel the machine in six directions, simulating the pitch and roll of a real plane. In helicopter simulators a vibrating pilot's seat is used to add reality; and in fighter plane simulators the seat has air pumped into it to simulate the 'g' forces when the pilot performs tight turns.

The scene out of the 'windows' is as realistic as the behaviour of the plane. When a particular airport is chosen the scene looks identical to the surroundings of that particular airport.

An example IT task
A predator/prey model

Suppose that we wanted to protect the vegetables in a greenhouse against attack by greenfly. We could either use pesticides, or use an organic, natural method by introducing a predator of the greenfly, namely the ladybird. To find out the optimum number of ladybirds to introduce, we have to understand something about the how the predator (the ladybird) and the prey (the greenfly) reproduce. With no control over their numbers, the greenfly would multiply at an alarming rate and eventually would destroy all of the crop. On the other hand, it is hard to eliminate all the greenfly and, if we did this, the ladybirds would all starve to death. The optimum state is when the population of the greenfly has reached equilibrium, where the numbers of greenfly are constant. When this occurs the ladybirds will have enough to eat and the damage to the crop will be minimal.

When setting up this model you will need to decide on the inputs to the system.

What are the inputs?
We can divide the inputs into two:

- inputs for the predators (i.e. the ladybirds)
- inputs for the prey (i.e. the greenfly)

The inputs for the predators will be:

- the number of ladybirds at the start of the year

- the breeding rate (factor by which they increase each month)
- the number of greenfly each ladybird eats each month.

The inputs for the prey will be:

- the number of greenfly at the start of the year
- the breeding rate (factor by which they increase each month).

We now need to design a spreadsheet model. We will use three columns:

Start of Month	Number of ladybirds	Number of greenfly

Let us first look at the situation for the first month, January. The situation will be as follows:

Start of Month	Number of ladybirds	Number of greenfly
JAN	10	100

At the start of February the following will happen. The number of ladybirds will increase by a factor of 1.5, so there will now be 15 of them. The greenfly will breed, increasing their population by a factor of 4, making their number 400. However, during January some of them will be eaten. If we assume that the 10 ladybirds at the start eat 30 greenfly in the month, then 300 greenfly would be eaten making a total of 100. So, at the start of February, we will have 15 ladybirds and 100 greenfly, as shown in the table:

Start of Month	Number of ladybirds	Number of greenfly
JAN	10	100
FEB	15	100

QUESTION

You have been asked to extend this model for the whole of the 12 months. Do this using a spreadsheet and make sure that you link the cells using formulae.

Problems with the model

The above model is too simple. It does not take account of the following areas.

1 The breeding rates of the ladybirds and the greenfly won't stay the same throughout the year. The rates will probably increase in the warmer months. We really need to alter the breeding rates for the summer months and make them different than the winter months.
2 If there is not enough food for the ladybirds to eat, then they will die.

3 We also need to incorporate a death rate for the ladybirds into our model. To make it simpler, you could assume that the greenfly will remain alive provided that they do not get eaten by the ladybirds.

QUESTION

Produce a revised model taking the above into account.

THINGS TO DO

1 Write down **one** reason why computerised simulation is better than using a manual simulation for each of the following situations:
   (a) a simulation to find out how many checkouts will be needed at a new supermarket
   (b) an experiment to find out the best temperature for carrying out a chemical process.

2 You can use spreadsheet software to make a computer model.
   (a) Give an example of an investigation for which you would use a spreadsheet package to make a computer model.
   (b) Describe how you would set up the model on the spreadsheet.
   (c) Explain why you would use the computer model instead of creating the real thing.

(MEG, 1993)

3 (a) Give one advantage of using a computer model to study the relationship between hunting animals and their prey.
   (b) Give two reasons why your teacher may prefer to use a simulation rather than a school trip to an African jungle.
   (c) What software package would you use to display the data collected.

(MEG 1993)

4 Flight simulators are used to train airline pilots.
   (a) Describe what a flight simulator is.
   (b) What advantages are there is using such a flight simulator rather than using a real aircraft?

5 A local council wants to know if it should re-design a road junction. It has three options – leave it as it is, put in a set of traffic lights, or construct a roundabout.
   (a) Explain how a computer model could be useful to the council.   (3 marks)
   (b) What data would be required for the model?   (3 marks)
   (c) For each item of data above, describe how the council could collect the data.   (3 marks)
   (d) What other variables might be used in the model?   (2 marks)

(SEG q4 HT Spec Question)

1 A certain type of bacteria increases its numbers at the rate of 20% per hour. If there are 100 bacteria at the start of the day produce a model showing how the population will have grown over each hour in the day.

2 This task is suitable only for students taking level R mathematics at GCSE.

The iterative formula for finding the cube root of a number N is given by

$$a_{n+1} = 1/3 \, (2a_n + N/a_n^2)$$

Produce a spreadsheet where you can put in a number N, and the computer simulates the iterative process and comes up with the answer correct to five decimal places. Test your model using the following numbers: 27, 50, 1480 and 3600.

Some ideas for models and simulations

1 Explain the effect of pollution on a river system.

2 Collect data from a science experiment and then use the data from the results to find the relationship between the variables.

3 Look at the heat supply and the heat loss from a house.

IT TASK

The depreciation of cars

You have been asked by a car dealer to produce a model of the depreciation of cars. You will need to consider the following when building or refining your model.

- Is the depreciation the same for each year or do cars depreciate more in the early years?
- Do some cars depreciate more than others? How can this be built into the model?
- You could try comparing the values in your model with values obtained from a car price guide which you can obtain from any newsagents.
- You could produce a series of graphs showing how the price varies over a number of years.

Finally, produce a report on your model/simulation.

Dangerous situations

Simulations are often performed using computers where the real situation would be too costly or dangerous to perform any other way. Investigate such situations and produce a brief report outlining your findings.

Bulmers
A case study

HP Bulmer Ltd (cider makers)

HP Bulmer is a medium sized British company based in Hereford and has been involved in the making of cider for over 100 years. Cider is an alcoholic drink made by fermenting apples and it has enjoyed an upturn in popularity over recent years, with an increased consumption of 8% in 1994. The company produces the brands Woodpecker, Strongbow and Scrumpy Jack, amongst others (Figure 25.1). There are around 1000 employees and approximately 500 of these use computers. About 400 use personal computers (PCs) in the course of their work.

Bulmers information systems

As with a lot of companies, it is common to see old information systems being replaced by modern systems.

The older computer equipment is being rapidly replaced by Unix equipment. Unix is an operating system used primarily in multi-user computing where a lot of terminals are used. The advantage of Unix over other operating systems is that it can be used with a variety of different computer hardware. In the past, if you bought one make of computer hardware then you generally had to stick with the same company when upgrading the system. This tended to make systems expensive both to buy and to maintain. There is a very large number of application programs available to Unix users and this is another of its advantages.

One problem with the old system was that there was more than one customer file used by different departments. This meant that analysing sales was difficult because the results were different depending on which version of the customer file was used.

Figure 25.1 *Three of the top ciders in Britain's bars – Strongbow, Scrumpy Jack and Woodpecker*

The new system

The largest system used by Bulmer is the Distribution Management System. This system manages the distribution of the bottles, cans and kegs (the aluminium barrels) to the customer, telesales and credit control (making sure the company is paid for the cider).

There are other systems. For instance, there is a system that deals with giving important financial information and is able to track the bartop equipment which is installed in many pubs up and down the country. Other systems are involved in pricing, and customer and product information.

The keg information system

Bulmer sells draught cider in tens of thousands of pubs, wine bars and restaurants throughout the UK. The keg technicians are responsible for installing and repairing the equipment needed to dispense the draught cider at the bar. This equipment includes the pump you see on the top of the bar, the cooler unit and all the pipework which goes to the aluminium barrel, called a keg.

When something goes wrong with the equipment or a new customer needs equipment installing, a telephone call is made to the head office where the scheduling is organised. The schedules for each of the 30 technicians scattered throughout the UK are transferred overnight via telephone lines to each technician's hand held terminal.

During the day, the technicians record the jobs they have done using their hand-held terminals and this information is relayed back over the telephone lines to Bulmer's head office where the central computer files are updated. Using this system, the technicians are able to deal with more calls in a day and the people involved in co-ordinating this activity can be engaged in other tasks. A future development might be that technicians will be given portable modems in their cars so that the files can be updated in real time. If any problems crop up in the course of the day, then the

technicians can be alerted. If a particular technician is near where the problem is, then that technical may be able to squeeze in an extra visit.

Personal computers

All the company's PCs are networked in a local area network (LAN). Each terminal can therefore be used for sending electronic mail. Electronic mail is also used to send mail to a subsidiary company in Australia and is now being used with some of the company's major customers.

Electronic data interchange

Many of Bulmer's larger customers operate electronic data interchange (EDI), where orders and invoices are sent and received electronically, thus eliminating the need for paperwork.

EDI works by connecting personal computers via a modem to a carrier called Tradanet. In this way Bulmer can deal with all its main suppliers such as the bottle manufacturers and its main customers such as Tesco electronically.

Process control by computers

The cider making process at Bulmer's world famous Hereford cider mill has almost jumped a century. The traditional methods of the nineteenth century, which had changed little since Percy Bulmer founded the business in 1887, have been replaced by the latest computer controlled technology. Cider maker Jonathan Blair now has a computer screen to assist in the art of cider making (see Figure 25.2).

In 1994 the company invested £20 million in a brand new cider making plant, giving it the most modern cider making plant in the world. All the processes such as fermentation, microfiltration (to remove the yeast and make the cider clear) and the movement of the cider around the plant, are controlled by computer. Figure 25.3 shows a cider production worker checking the flow of cider on the computer. Figures 25.4 and 25.5

Figure 25.2 *Cider maker Jonathan Blair now has a computer screen to assist the art of cider making*

Figure 25.3 *A cider production worker checking the flow of cider on the computer*

show the inside of the fermentation hall and the view of the 50 foot high fermentation vessels from the outside. Overlooking the hall is a control room where a single person can run several processes using computers.

So that the changeover to the new equipment went as smoothly as possible, the staff took part in 'hands on' simulation courses. Here they could use computers to

Figure 25.4 *Inside the fermentation hall*

simulate control of the new system. Any mistakes did not matter, whereas if they happened with the actual equipment mistakes could ruin a 50 000 gallon batch of cider.

The use of this equipment allows Bulmer to produce a consistent high quality product at a lower cost.

Figure 25.5 *A view of the 50 foot high fermentation vessels from the outside*

Computers in the laboratory

To make sure that the cider is of the highest quality, frequent tests are performed on it. The laboratory systems record the results of the tests and action can be taken if necessary. Although it is possible for the computer controlled equipment to measure the alcohol quantity (Figure 25.6) etc. the real flavour of the cider can only be appreciated by a human taster (Figure 25.7). For this reason Bulmer still uses a panel of tasters whose job it is to taste the cider (and spit it out, unfortunately). As you can imagine, this is a difficult job but someone's got to do it!

Figure 25.6 *Computer control enables the strength of the cider to be continually monitored*

Using computers to help with presentations

At Bulmer, presentations have to be given regularly to the city, potential customers and to the company's own staff. Because of the costs involved in sending presentation material to outside agencies the company is now able to produce the material itself. Bulmer has a graphics presentation unit with scanning equipment, a special printer capable of printing acetate slides in colour and a large 37 inch VDU to display the work. A graphics analyst is employed, whose job it is to run the unit. This person checks the work that comes in from other departments to make sure that it is of a high standard before it is printed. The cost of sending the material to an outside agency was around £200 000 per year; doing the task within the company has reduced the cost to about £70 000 per year.

Possible new developments

One new development that is currently being pursued is to equip the sales staff who visit new customers with portable PCs so that they are able perform account planning using spreadsheets and so that they can record details of contacts and arrangements for follow-up calls. Already, they are using multimedia packages for customer presentations.

Figure 25.7 *Some jobs, such as cider tasting, are best left to humans*

1 (a) Bulmer uses an operating system called Unix.

  (i) Name two other operating systems.

  (ii) Give three functions of an operating system.

 (b) Large companies frequently upgrade their systems. Explain what this means.

2 PCs are connected together to form a local area network (LAN).

 Give three advantages of using a network rather than using stand-alone machines.

3 Bulmer uses EDI (electronic data interchange).

 Explain what advantages there are to:

 (a) Bulmer

 (b) the company's customers

 in using this system.

4 As well as using computers for administrative tasks, Bulmer also uses computers for controlling the processes involved in the making of cider.

 (a) Explain what advantages there are in using computerised process control rather than doing the tasks manually.

 (b) Before the new process control equipment was introduced, staff were sent on a course which involved computer simulation.

  (i) Explain what simulation is.

  (ii) What is the advantage of using simulation rather than actual equipment?

5 Bulmer is now giving presentations using multimedia and uses portable PCs for graphics presentations.

 (a) What is multimedia and how does it differ from a presentation on an ordinary computer system?

 (b) In what ways do you think multimedia would be useful in promoting the company's products or image.

6 Bulmer can be considered to be an environmentally friendly company. After reading this chapter, what evidence is there to suggest this?

7 What do you think are the benefits and drawbacks of the new system? How has the nature of the work changed over the years?

1 The data below shows the volume share of the premium cider market. Premium cider is the more expensive, higher strength bottled cider. The percentages shown below refer to the years 1992 and 1993.

Name of brand	Year	
	92	93
Merrydown	38.0%	28.8%
Diamond White	29.7%	22.8%
Scrumpy Jack	6.8%	9.5%
K	6.2%	8.3%
Strongbow Super	3.6%	6.8%
Red Rock	5.0%	4.5%
Electric White	0.8%	3.7%
Blackthorn Super	2.2%	2.4%
1727	0.1%	2.1%
Others	7.6%	11.1%

(a) Using spreadsheet or graphics software, produce a side by side bar chart so that the market information in the above table can be compared.

(b) From the bar chart you have produced, write a brief report on the brands that have done well and those that have suffered.

2 To produce new brands that will appeal to the new drinker, Bulmer has to do market research. The company has to find out what characteristics a typical cider drinker has. The table below shows a profile of today's cider drinker.

	All adults	Strongbow drinkers	Regular lager drinkers
Regularly read			
The Times/FT/ Guardian/Independent	9%	13%	9%
Agree that:			
"I like to try new drinks"	27%	44%	39%
"I like to stand out in a crowd"	12%	19%	15%
Drink:			
Brandy	29%	36%	32%
Port	22%	32%	24%
Malt Whisky	21%	30%	27%

Also important is a profile of the type of outlet (e.g. pub, wine bar, etc.). You have been asked to prepare a questionnaire that the Bulmer representatives or technicians can fill in when then visit a new establishment. They need to find out if it is a typical old fashioned 'boozer' full of older men drinking pints of bitter or mild, or a new trendy place for younger people drinking newer bottled premium beers and cider. You should include boxes to be shaded in so that the forms can be read using an optical mark reader.

3 When people buy cider from retailers such as Tesco, Asda, Sainsbury, etc., they are able to buy it in a variety of different sizes and packaging. For instance they can buy cans and bottles of

different sizes. To see which are the most popular packages and volumes bought, the following data has been collected.

	1989	1992	1993
Cans	5.9%	12.0%	15.6%
1/1.5 litre	30.4%	23.6%	20.8%
2.0 litre	47.4%	43.5%	41.5%
3.0 litre	5.3%	9.9%	11.1%
Other	11.1%	11.1%	11.1%

Using graphical or spreadsheet software, produce a pie chart, for each year to show the above data.

By looking at each one, say what trends you can spot. Produce a brief report using wordprocessing software and, if you can, try to incorporate the charts you have created into your wordprocessed document.

4 The following recipe is for Cider Mulled Punch.

Ingredients
2 small eating apples
6 cloves
10 cm (4 in) cinnamon stick
10 ml (2 level teaspoons) ground ginger
50 g (2 oz) soft brown sugar
1 small orange
1 bottle Strongbow cider

Method
(a) Remove the cores from the apples and 2.5 cm (1 in) width of skin from around the tops.
(b) Stick two cloves into the sides of each apple and then bake in a moderate oven at 180°C, 350°F, gas mark 4 for 20 minutes.
(c) Meanwhile, put the other two cloves, the cinnamon stick (broken into four pieces), ginger, sugar and water into a medium sized pan.
(d) Heat the pan slowly until the sugar dissolves, bring the mixture to the boil and simmer it for 5 minutes.
(e) Cut the orange into thin slices. Remove the pan from the heat, immediately add the orange and leave it to stand.
(f) When the apples are cooked, transfer them to a punch bowl and break up the flesh without removing it from the skin.
(g) Strain the spiced water into the punch bowl. Pour in hot (but not boiling) cider and serve at once.

This recipe looks rather dull the way it is presented here. Try to make it more appealing by using DTP, graphics or wordprocessing software. Can you incorporate any graphics or clip art to brighten it up? See what you can do.

5 Figure 25.8 shows a table which has been drawn and then typed. Your task is to produce a copy on your wordprocessor. Not all wordprocessors have the facility to produce tables so you

will need to check with your teacher. If your wordprocessor is unable to do tables then see if you can do it using spreadsheet software.

```
STRONGBOW        COMMENTS
Appearance:      Clear, straw-coloured, lightly sparkling.
Aroma:           Slightly fruity with a bittersweet apple character.
Flavour:         A medium dry, fruity, full-bodied cider with a clean
                 slightly astringent aftertaste.


WOODPECKER
Appearance:      Clear, amber-coloured, lightly sparkling.
Aroma:           Sweet and fruity with a slight toffee-apple note.
Flavour:         Clean and sweet with a fruity cider apple character.


ORIGINAL
Appearance:      Clear, pale amber, lightly sparkling.
Aroma:           Fruity dessert apples.
Flavour:         Sweet, dessert apple cider.


SPECIAL RESERVE
Appearance:      Clear, amber, lightly sparkling.
Aroma:           Alcoholic, fruity dessert apples.
Flavour:         Clean, slightly sweet and alcoholic with a full body and
                 slightly sharp culinary apple character.
```

Figure 25.8

Chapter 26

Computer Applications

Information technology: helping to solve crime

Crime has become very sophisticated and, as a result, harder to detect. To handle this, the police have very sophisticated methods of crime detection at their disposal. Information is the key word in crime detection and this information must be accurate and obtained quickly.

The Police National Computer (PNC)

The Police National Computer (PNC) now provides rapid access, day and night , to information of national as well as local significance, to all the police forces in England, Scotland and Wales. This large mainframe computer is linked to terminals in police stations throughout the country. Since there are a large number of terminals linked to the main computer there is a complex switching mechanism and this allows each terminal to obtain information from the main computer in as short a time as possible. Some police vehicles are equipped with terminals which are used to access the PNC directly.

The information held on the PNC is separated into indexes with each index dealing with a particular subject. Some of these indexes are cross-referenced. Here are some further details on each of the main indexes.

Stolen and suspect vehicle index

Every day hundreds of vehicles are stolen. Some are taken only for joy rides and are recovered by the police fairly quickly, while others are stolen permanently and are re-sold or stripped down for their parts. Many stolen cars are used in other crimes or are involved in accidents.

As soon as an owner reports that a car is missing, information such as the registration number, make, model and colour are keyed into the PNC at one of the many terminals. Once this information has been obtained, it is transmitted via radio to policemen in patrol cars, who are then on the lookout for the vehicle.

As well as holding the obvious details about the car, the index also holds chassis and engine numbers, since many cars will have their identities concealed by the use of false plates or by being sprayed a different colour.

There is a partial registration number facility, so if only part of the registration is known, then a list of cars can be produced fitting the bill. This is very useful if the car is used for a robbery or if it has been involved in a hit and run accident and witnesses can only partially remember the number or type of vehicle.

Vehicle owner index

The information for this index comes from the DVLA (Driver Vehicle and Licensing Authority) at Swansea. The index contains all the names and addresses of the registered keepers of vehicles, together with descriptions of the vehicles.

If the registration number is known, then the owner can be contacted if the car is stolen and he/she is not aware of the theft. Again, if the number is only partially known, the vehicle can still be traced.

It is possible for the stolen and suspect vehicles index and the vehicle owner index to be searched together, using the registration number as the search key.

Names indexes

The police have records in these indexes of people who fall into any of the following categories:

1 persons convicted of serious offences
2 persons wanted or sought by the police for various reasons
3 persons missing or found
4 disqualified drivers.

As soon as the police receive details about any person who falls into one or more of the above categories, they can obtain information from the PNC.

The computer can assist the police by informing them if a suspected person is likely to be armed or dangerous. It is also possible for the computer to search all the files simultaneously to find out everything known about a particular person.

Computerised fingerprint index
Fingerprinting is the science of using the patterns of ridges on our fingertips for identification purposes and it was one of the earliest forms of scientific evidence accepted by courts of law.

Fingerprints obtained from objects at the scene of a crime are taken and then compared with the suspect's fingerprints. Although fingerprints cannot always prove that a suspect committed a crime they do prove that they were at the scene of the crime at some time. Fingerprints used to be compared manually but now many police forces are use a computerised system designed to store and match the prints.

Broadcast system
Other than indexes, the PNC is also used to help the police in other ways. The broadcast system allows one police force to send urgent information to other police forces. If a car is stolen and used in a serious crime, then all the police forces along, say, a certain stretch of motorway can be alerted. Ports and airports can also be alerted using this system, to stop criminals escaping to another country.

Other computers used by the police
As well as being able to access the Police National Computer, all police forces have their own computer systems situated at their headquarters for help with administration

and also to help in solving major crimes. One system called MIRIAM (Major Incident Room Index and Action Management) is used to store information from enquiries about serious crimes so that senior officers can decide how to go about their investigation. Figure 26.1 shows how MIRIAM co-ordinates all the information.

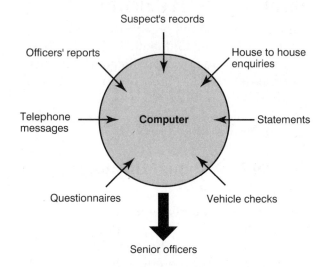

Figure 26.1 *How MIRIAM sorts out all the information from a large scale enquiry, so the senior officers can make decisions about how to solve the crime*

Electronic tagging

Bike tagging
Over one in every three new bicycles sold are bought to replace stolen machines and this costs insurance companies millions of pounds per year. A new security system has been developed which consists of brightly coloured warning stickers to deter thieves in the first place and one or more small tags, only about the size of a grain of rice which are secretly hidden on part of the bike. The police are able to locate the tags using a special device and then read the owner's details.

The police have some doubts about the value of the scheme since it would be difficult from a legal point of view to stop cyclists to check if the cycle they are riding has been stolen.

Tagging of offenders

Offenders can be tagged when released early from prison so that their whereabouts are known and this makes them less likely to re-offend.

DNA profiling

DNA is a large complicated molecule which is often called the double helix of life, because of its shape and the fact that it is found in every living thing. There are certain characteristics of DNA which make it unique for each person. So one person's DNA is slightly different to another's and it is this fact that makes it useful to the forensic scientist whose job it is to help solve crimes.

If the DNA from a sample and a suspect are found to be the same then you can be fairly sure that the sample belonged to the suspect (there is a one in a million chance that a sample with the same DNA as the suspect's has come from a different person).

There is now a national database containing the DNA profiles of criminals. The database, kept in Birmingham, is expected to contain the details of samples from 135 000 burglary, serious and sex crime suspects. Eventually the police are hoping to widen the system so that it holds details of all offenders. The police and politicians are hoping that this will improve the justice system, save time and money and increase conviction rates.

The system will use samples from mouth swabs or hair strands; these will be processed and a DNA profile built up of the suspect. Samples from the scene of a crime are obtained and their DNA profile is built up. By using a computer to make comparisons the police can see if the suspect is likely to have committed the crime. As well as leading to conviction, DNA profiling can also be used to clear a suspect.

Using 3D modelling to help to solve crimes

In many murder cases the body is found months or even years after the crime was committed. Frequently there is only a skeleton left, so identification of the victim is made very difficult. It is often necessary to produce a picture of what the person might have looked like using the skull as a frame. In the past this was done by an artist working with a Plasticene model. Now, detailed measurements of the skull are input to a computer and the computer comes up with a three-dimensional model of the likely face belonging to the skull. The advantage of the new system is that the face can be modelled quickly and costs are reduced.

Electronic security cameras

Electronic security cameras have helped cut down violent crime and robberies in many of our city centres. Sometimes these cameras are visible and act as a deterrent, whereas others are hidden and are used during police surveillance. Although most people feel safer in city centres with the use of these cameras, some people feel that they are an infringement of privacy. Cameras are also used for traffic control at busy junctions and on motorways.

Figure 26.2 *The police often use hidden cameras*

Information technology in the supermarket
Tesco : a case study

Tesco is the largest food retailer in Britain. Tesco used to have many small shops on every high street, but the company has been concentrating on the development of the huge units we see today called superstores. Each superstore stocks over 14 000 food lines alone and has a sales area of over 25 000 square feet.

The laser scanning system (bar code reading system)

Tesco was one of the first high street companies to use a bar code reader which now is called a laser scanner.

The objectives of the scanning system are to improve the service to customers and to increase company productivity and profits. Figure 26.3 shows the scanning system used to scan in a bar code.

The scanning system uses a laser beam to read the bar code on the goods. The bars contain the same information as the numeric code at the bottom of the bar code without the likely inaccuracies of typing the number in. As the bar code is passed across the scanner this number is read and the prices and description of the goods are obtained from the computer, the sale registered and an itemised receipt produced.

Figure 26.3 *Using a bar code reader in the desk of a point of sale terminal*

Benefits of the system to the customers

There are numerous benefits to customers and these include the following.

1 With the old system, prices were entered into the cash register manually. With the scanning system this is done automatically, which eliminates typing errors, so accurate pricing is assured.
2 The scanning till is estimated to be 15% more efficient, so customers will spend less time waiting to be served.
3 Produce such as loose tomatoes are weighed at the checkout so customers no longer have to queue twice; once at the pricing point and again at the checkout.
4 Customers can have their cheques and credit card vouchers automatically printed.
5 Customers using a debit card such as Switch can withdraw £50 in cash from any checkout.
6 More promotions may be offered, such as buy two and get one free (multisaver).
7 An itemised receipt is produced. This receipt will often include detailed information about what has been bought.

Benefits of the system to the company

Some benefits are easily quantified but others are more difficult.

1 Checkout accuracy is improved. There are no longer any operator errors and fraud is limited, since in the past it was possible to key in a lower price and pocket the money.
2 Throughput is faster and more efficient. There is, on average a 15% saving in time to register the goods in a shopping trolley.
3 Customer service can be improved. New services such as Clubcard, multi-savers, etc., ensure customer loyalty.
4 Productivity is increased. There is no need to price each individual article, as in the past. Prices are included on the edges of the shelves next to the articles. Weighing and pricing at the checkouts eliminates the need for separate pricing points.
5 Sales information from the checkout is used to create the orders for stock replacement.

6 Stock levels can be reduced. More efficient stock control means less money tied up in stock and less likelihood of running out of certain items on the sales floor.

7 Wastage is also reduced. Perishable goods such as fresh meat and salads can be ordered accurately using the sales information obtained from the checkout.

8 Promotional analysis and sales analysis are improved. Scanning data can be used to assess the effectiveness of special promotions and can provide important information about the sales of certain goods.

The bar-coding system

Figure 26.4 below shows a bar code from a tin of Heinz baked beans. The number at the bottom is called the European Article Number (EAN); a number is allocated to all product manufacturers by the Article Number Association. The system works as follows:

- the first two digits represent the country where the goods are produced
- the next five digits identify the suppliers of the goods
- the following five numbers identify the product
- the final number is a check digit and is used to check that the other 12 numbers have been entered correctly.

EFTPOS and the use of debit cards

EFTPOS stands for electronic funds transfer at point of sale and is the method used by Tesco to transfer money from customers' credit card companies or debit cards directly to the Tesco bank account. A debit card is rather like a cheque, since the money comes straight out of the bank account. However, there is no limit to the amount you can spend using one of these cards, provided that you have the money in your account. This is in contrast to cheques where there is a limit, usually £50 or £100, to the value of the cheque that you can write.

Using checkout information for planning bakery production

Sales information from checkouts is used by in-store bakeries to plan the production for the same day for the next week. This reduces wastage and means stores are less likely to run out of bread.

Sales based ordering

Sales based ordering is the automatic re-ordering of goods from the warehouse using the sales information from the checkouts. If, for example, 200 tins of baked beans are sold from a certain store in one day, then 200 tins will be automatically re-ordered and delivered to the store the

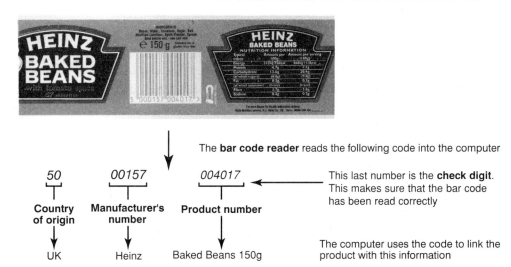

Figure 26.4 *How a computer uses a bar code*

following day from one of the Tesco distribution centres.

The large articulated vehicles you see are specially constructed: they have compartments which can be kept at different temperatures, so, for instance, chilled food, frozen food and other types of food which do not need cooling may be carried in the same vehicle.

Stock control

All ordering is performed by computer. There are fast electronic communication lines between the shops, the distribution centres and the head office. There are also direct links to the major suppliers, which means that orders can go straight through to production lines. One advantage of this is that stock arrives just in time before sale so it is always fresh. Another advantage of this system is that money does not need to be tied up in stock and can be used for more productive purposes.

Electronic shelf labelling

Tesco is developing a system with liquid crystal shelf labels containing the price, description and ordering information about goods. The label is operated from the computer using radio signals and this avoids human error, where a price change on the computer is not transferred to the shelf. This means that changing a price on the computer database and shelf can be done at the same time so the price stored and that on the shelf will always be the same.

Electronic data interchange (EDI)

Electronic data interchange is a method of speeding up the transfer of orders to suppliers. Using EDI eliminates the need for paperwork, since the ordering is done by data being transferred between the supplier's computer and Tesco's computer. This system is less expensive and faster than sending the orders by phone, post or fax and cuts out errors, such as lost or wrongly printed orders. Tesco can send information to suppliers regarding sales

forecasts and information about stock levels so that they may plan their production appropriately.

Once an electronic order has been placed, the electronic invoice is generated automatically by the supplier's computer. This is sent back and checked by the Tesco computer before payment is made.

Tesco: The hardware

We have looked at the systems in use by Tesco. As you can imagine, the computers to run these types of operation are some of the most sophisticated and powerful computers in the world.

The mainframe computers are situated in two computer centres and each is capable of running the company's systems on its own. The computers are capable of delivering 216 MIPS (million instructions per second) and are the fastest commercial computers in the world.

Since computers are so vital to Tesco's operations, there are backup procedures in place so that even if one of the computer centres were completely destroyed, the other would be able to re-establish the vital systems within 48 hours. The backup procedures are tested each year so that staff know exactly what to do if a disaster were to occur.

Designing store layouts using CAD

It is no longer necessary to use drawing boards for planning new stores and re-designing existing ones. Instead, computer aided design is used (CAD) and this has reduced the time taken to plan new stores. A databank holds designs and plans from many stores and these may be adapted for new stores. CAD is also able to show three dimensional views of the stores; and colours, lighting and different finishes of material can be altered simply with a mouse.

When a new store is to be placed in an existing high street, photographs of the existing shops in the street can be used in conjunction with CAD to see what the street will look like with the Tesco front in place.

CAD is also used to design warehouse layouts, the roads and the surrounding areas around the distribution centres. This is important since the company needs to make sure that there is ample room for the large articulated vehicles to turn round.

Warehouse systems

Computers are used in the warehouse to monitor complex stock control procedures and make the best use of space, time and labour. Like all areas of retailing, better operating methods need to be found to ensure Tesco's continued success. As with all the other systems, paperwork has been eliminated wherever possible, so the thick binders containing stock items are replaced by computer terminals. In fact, these terminals can be found mounted on fork lift trucks; they give the operators information regarding the movement of the pallets so that they may be moved quickly and efficiently. If some stock goes out of the warehouse then a slot is available for the new stock arriving and notification of this is obtained from the terminal. Efficient use of the available space means that the trucks have to travel shorter distances and the whole process is therefore faster.

The computer system also monitors where each fork lift truck is situated in the warehouse so that a particular job can be given to the fork lift truck best able to complete it in the least amount of time.

Electronic mail

Tesco, like a lot of forward looking companies, has realised the benefits of using electronic mail. With conventional methods of communication there are a variety of problems, such as lost post, unanswered telephones, engaged fax machines, people not at their desks, etc. To try to contact someone urgently during office hours can be more difficult than you think. Electronic mail eliminates many of these problems.

The store system used by Tesco uses a series of standard forms, so memos, letters, reports, etc. all have a set format. Some of the advantages to Tesco in using electronic mail are as follows.

1 The recipient does not need to be there when the message is sent; he or she can receive mail at any terminal connected to the system. Compare this with a telephone call where someone needs to be available to answer the call.
2 People can be sure that the messages are received.
3 It is possible to send mail to a department or a group of people. Anyone in the company can send mail to a whole department without knowing anyone in the department by name.
4 The electronic mail system is used as a company information and notice board. Members of staff can find out about the latest job vacancies and appointments, and look at the latest share price.
5 Electronic mail can be sent to the major suppliers, thus speeding up orders etc.

Information technology in the music industry
Sound recording

Sound recording involves detecting sound and then storing it somehow in analogue or digital code on either tape or disk so that it can be played back at a later date. During playback, the coded data on the storage medium is recovered, amplified and fed to loudspeakers to create a copy of the original sound.

Synthesisers

In a modern recording studio, the sound waves are picked up by microphones which convert the sound signals into electrical signals. The signals from each microphone may be combined together using a device called a mixer to give the final recording.

In many pop recordings, the electrical signals which correspond to the desired sounds or notes are generated directly using a device called a synthesiser. These signals can be combined with signals produced from conventional instruments and recorded.

Recording studios

Many rock groups do not just turn up and play a piece of music for it to be recorded. Instead they like to experiment with the music and try many different approaches. Often the vocals or rhythm patterns are on the first track of a 24-track tape. Different instruments, such as drums, pianos, guitars, keyboard synthesisers are added one at a time to the other tracks. Certain qualities of the music from each track can be altered separately, such as volume, echo and, reverberation. Then all the tracks can be mixed together. Because the music is recorded onto tape, this process can take a long time.

The use of computers in recording studios has considerably speeded up the recording process. Modern studios use tapeless recording, with the music initially stored digitally in the random access memory (RAM) of the computer. For permanent storage, the music can be stored on the computer's hard disk. Because the music is initially stored in RAM it provides immediate access should it need to be altered. Sounds can be added or removed very easily.

Sound sampling

Sound sampling is performed when a sound is taken into the computer system. For instance, a microphone can be used to take 'a sample' of a certain sound such as the bark of a dog. The computer stores the sampled sound as a digitally coded signal which can be altered if necessary and replayed when needed.

IT and the TV/video industry

Computer generated graphics

Computer generated graphics are images designed by graphic artists that are used for logos, commercials and new inserts during television or video transmissions. The artists use systems similar to a painting package produced for microcomputers. Some of the more sophisticated graphics systems allow artists to produce 3-dimensional images.

Special effects

Sometimes when watching the television you see images manipulated in some way to produce special effects. These may be produced with digital video signals since each pixel (dot of light) on the screen can be moved individually. Using a computer with special software it is possible to change the shape of a picture to, say, a circle or hexagon. You can also zoom into the image, rotate it and even manipulate several different images on the screen at the same time.

Animation

In the past, to produce animation, it was necessary to draw a series of diagrams, with each one differing slightly as the movement proceeds. A picture is taken of each diagram, called a frame, and then the series of frames is played back. This process is tediously slow and requires whole teams of artists, so the final piece of animation or cartoon is very expensive.

The individual frame can be created using graphics software. A start frame and an end frame are produced, then the software produces the animation between these two frames automatically. The computer has to be told about the rate at which the intermediate images are to be produced. Because the number of frames is often quite large, powerful computers with large hard disk capacities are used for this type of work.

Information technology and medicine

All hospitals make use of information technology and, because of the diverse nature of the work that hospitals do, the computer has many quite different uses.

Organ transplants

Computers are very good at looking at and comparing lists. When a person dies and their organs such as heart, kidneys etc. are donated, the computer can be used to match

Figure 26.5

and identify a patient to receive them. This needs to be done extremely quickly and is why computers are essential (Figure 26.5).

Computers are used to diagnose many illnesses (Figure 26.6). Often the information is fed directly into the computer from machines attached to the patient, such as electrocardiographs, which measure the heartbeat, and body scanners.

Computers can be used to locate tumours at an early stage when, by other means, they cannot be easily and surely detected. Body scanners send rays into the human body (Figure 26.7) and the rays are picked up by a

Figure 26.6 *Computer diagnosis!*

detector. Signals from the detector are analysed by the computer and are converted to a digital form which can then be displayed as a picture on a television screen (Figure 26.8). On the screen the tumour appears as a dark patch.

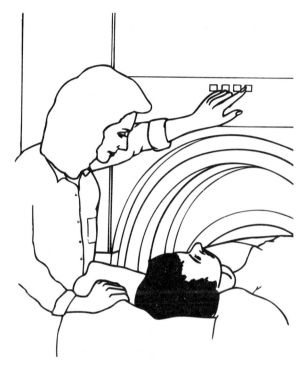

Figure 26.7 *Using a body scanner with computer diagnosis*

Intensive care

In intensive care units, computers are used to monitor instruments which record important data about the patient. If the data moves outside certain limits, an alarm is sounded, so that immediate medical help can be brought.

The measurements constantly taken by the computer might include blood pressure, pulse rate, heart waveshape from an ECG, respiration rate and volume, and electrical signals from the brain. Previously, these measurements needed to be taken so regularly that a nurse was needed for each patient. Now, many more patients can be looked after by one nurse.

Computers are also used to monitor vital data during surgery in the operating theatre.

Keeping patients records

Computers can be used to provide a complete, accurate, up-to-date and readily available source of information about patients' health. Records of patients are usually kept for the duration of their lives so, in the past, a large amount of space was taken up by paperwork. There were also problems in locating a particular patient's file – especially if, say, the patient moved about the country a great deal.

Most hospitals now store patients' records on magnetic tapes or disks. The information can be found immediately by the computer. There are terminals at certain places in the hospital. The doctors or nurses can find details of a particular patient very quickly.

Inpatients' records are probably best kept on magnetic disk. This method allows quicker access because it is a random access storage medium. These records will be needed much more often than the outpatient records. Outpatient records contain a large quantity of information that may only be used, say, a couple of times in a patient's lifetime. So these records can be stored on magnetic tape which has slower access time.

New data can be added to the patient's records by keying this into the computer via a terminal. Thus the patient's record can be kept up-to-date with the latest information about his or her condition or circumstances.

Doctors and nurses used to spend about 30 per cent of their time processing information in files, but now this has been vastly reduced because of the introduction of computers.

One problem with using a computer in this way is that very confidential information is kept about the patient. Obviously, many patients would not like this information to be seen by just anyone. One way round this problem is to introduce a code or password which the user needs to type into the computer before he or she can gain access to the patients' files. Another way, used in some of the extremely complicated systems, is to only allow the terminals a certain amount of necessary information for different users. So, a nurse could obtain some information, and a doctor would be able to get further details.

Information technology and banking

Banks were one of the first business organisations to use computers and this experience has meant that they have always been at the forefront of any new technology. Banks make use of a variety of systems and many of these have already been encountered. If you need any information on the following aspects of banking, then you should refer to the index. To help you locate this information, here is a list of topics that have been covered elsewhere in the book.

MICR (magnetic ink character recognition)
EFTPOS (electronic funds transfer at point of sale)
EDI (electronic data interchange)
Credit card use
EFT (electronic fund transfer)
Credit card fraud
Smart cards

Figure 26.8 *Information from the body scanner is used, here, to build up a picture of the human brain, in sections. Any tumours can thus be precisely located*

Some aspects of banking which have not been covered elsewhere are detailed below.

Cheque clearing

Suppose Jane wants to buy a portable colour television from Comet Electrics and pay by cheque. Jane banks with Lloyds and Comet Electrics banks with Barclays. the Figure here and on the next page shows what happens to the cheque from when it is given to Comet Electrics to when the money is subtracted (debited) from Jane's account and added (credited) to Comet Electrics' account. This process is called **cheque clearing** and, because of the huge number of cheques cleared each day, computers are used for nearly all of the process.

1 *Jane writes out a cheque for £240.00 made payable to Comet Electrics.*

2 *Comet Electrics pay the cheque into their Barclays branch.*

3 *Barclays Bank types in the amount of the cheque in magnetic ink characters so that it can be read at the clearing house using MICR.*

4 *All cheques, including this one, are sent to a bank in London called a* **clearing house.** *Here, all the cheques are sorted into bank sorting code numbers.*

5 *The details of all the transactions (items of business) are sent on magnetic disk to the Bank of England from the clearing house. The Bank of England transfers the £240 from Lloyds Bank to Barclays Bank.*

6 *The cheque is sent from the clearing house to Jane's branch of Lloyds Bank, identified by a sorting code number, where the amount is deducted from her account.*

7 *Barclays Bank receives notification that the cheque has been cleared and credits Comet Electrics' account with £240.*

8 *The whole process of cheque clearing takes a minimum of three days.*

Figure 26.9

Bankers' Automated Clearing Services (BACS)

Bankers' Automated Clearing Services Ltd was set up by the larger banks to deal with standing orders and direct debit payments. It is situated in Edgware, north-west of London, on the spot where the old De Havilland aircraft factory stood and where Amy Johnson's famous aeroplane was built in the late 1920s.

As well as processing transactions that take place in this country, BACS also houses the Swift computer for the UK which deals with international payments.

The BACS service is used to pay two-thirds of all monthly salaries directly into employees' accounts. It is also used to pay regular bills and payments such as pensions, local authority rates, mortgages, loan repayments etc.

The BACS computers keep a diary of all the payments to be made. These payments are made and are transferred between the banks on magnetic tape. The fact that not many people have heard of BACS shows the system's reliability and success.

Chapter 27

Advice on Coursework

Coursework is the main element in GCSE Information Systems and can be worth up to 60% of the total marks. You must identify a problem, then analyse it. You then need to design solutions and to evaluate them. Then you need to refine your solutions to make them better. Problem solving skills are important in doing this coursework. This means that the examiners want to make sure that you have approached a problem correctly. Therefore, as well as solving a problem, you have to provide evidence that you have gone about the task in the right way. You need also to test your solution to make sure that it works. You must fully document your solution, which means that you have to write about it and provide evidence along the way. 'Evidence all the way' should be your motto when doing coursework. Unless you have written about it or produced other evidence such as printouts or even photographs, then the examiner will not know that you have done the work.

Some or all of the five strands must be covered by the coursework and all five have to be covered in the theoretical work for the examination. They are:

- communicating information
- handling information
- modelling
- measurement and control
- applications and effects.

What software can I use?

The minimum list of software you should have experience of is:

- wordprocessor
- database
- spreadsheet
- desktop publishing
- programming language (e.g. BASIC or LOGO)
- data logging or control software
- simple modelling/simulation software.

You may also need to know about the following:

- hypermedia software (another name for multimedia software)
- graphics
- statistical software
- drawing and painting software.

You can use other software in addition to the types above but always make sure that the software you are using is the most suitable software for performing the task.

Hints and tips

1 Plan your work beforehand and make sure that you have or can obtain the software and hardware necessary for the task.
2 Choose your coursework carefully (if you have a choice) and don't be too ambitious. Discuss it with your teacher to make sure that it is not too difficult.
3 Wordprocess or desktop publish your work. Since you are following an IS/IT

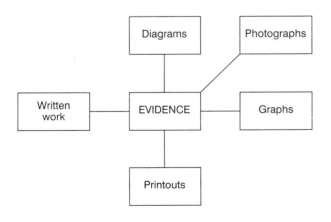

Figure 27.1 *Evidence all the way*

course, you should make use of all the latest technology.

4 To save time, type your work directly into the wordprocessor without writing it out first. If you need to make changes, such as insert text, delete text or shuffle material around, then this is easily done.

5 Always include all your work, even the parts that didn't work. The work provides evidence of your solution and must be included to maximise your marks. Remember that a good solution to a problem is a good solution partly because of the all the bad solutions that have been rejected.

6 Make the front cover look attractive but do not spend too much time on it.

7 Include diagrams wherever possible. They brighten up the page and by using them you can cut down on the number of words used. Diagrams you should use, if appropriate, include systems flowcharts, structure diagrams etc.

8 Always keep backup copies of your work held on disk and do not keep the backup copy with the original. It is a good idea to get a photocopy of any text.

How much do I write?

Remember that it is quality, not quantity, that the examiners are looking for. Some examination boards stipulate a maximum number of pages for each piece of coursework and you should check with your teacher whether your exam board is one of them. Usually the number of pages excludes computer output. Do not think that because a friend's project is much thicker than yours, that it will be better.

Use diagrams wherever you can to help describe the project and do not include anything that is not relevant.

Can my teacher help me?

Your teacher might be able to give you some ideas for projects. Her or she will know your abilities and will give you advice on the suitability of your project choices.

No one other than your teacher should help you. You will be asked to sign a form to say that the work is your own.

Note – Your teacher/lecturer will be keeping an eye on your coursework as it progresses and will know the level of your abilities. If someone helps you, then this will be cheating and your teacher will be able to tell.

Do you get marks for your English?

All GCSE subjects, and IT and IS are no exception, have 5% of the marks allocated for grammar, spelling and punctuation.

When you are doing the coursework you can use the facilities offered by most wordprocessors and some DTP and graphics packages to check the spelling. Some advanced wordprocessors will even check your grammar for you.

Don't forget that if you use these useful tools, they are not substitutes for careful proof reading. It is a good idea to get someone else to proof read your work for any obvious mistakes.

What is entailed in the coursework?

The coursework really depends on the examination board and the syllabus you are following. It is always a good idea to get a copy of the syllabus so that you know exactly what you have to do. Your teacher may be able to supply you with a syllabus or you can buy one by asking for a price list of syllabuses and past papers from the examination boards, whose addresses are at the back of this book.

IT tasks and Systems tasks

In this book we have divided the coursework into two types: **IT tasks** and **Systems tasks**. So what is the difference between them? Well, just using a particular package to do a certain task and then explaining how you did it (i.e. documenting the solution) would be an IT task. Developing a whole system, including the various stages such as identifying, analysing, using/implementing and evaluating will involve a great deal more work and is called a Systems task.

Some examination boards call the coursework either **Resource tasks** or **Capability tasks**. Resource tasks are rather like IT tasks, since they look at how you can apply a narrow range of knowledge and skills. Capability tasks involve a lot more work and are the same as Systems tasks.

Chapter 31, the chapter on databases, includes a section called 'Creating an information system using a database'. This section tells you what information you need to include when developing an information system. Much of this is applicable to other types of information systems which do not use databases.

Example coursework briefs

Here are some coursework ideas from the various GCSE examination boards.

A doctor needs to be able to obtain lists of patients who have certain attributes, e.g. patients who are mothers. Identify some other simple information needs that a doctor would have.

What advantage would there be for the doctor in using IT for this task? State what software you would use to set up a system which would be able to provide this information for the doctor.

Identify the data which the doctor would need to be able to obtain the information specified. Design a form for new patients to fill in to give this information. Test it on your friends and family, and change it if necessary.

Set up an information system which would handle the doctor's requirements. Test the working of the system under a variety of conditions.

Write a technical report which describes the hardware and software used, show how reports would be produced, how files would be structured, and how it would deal with changes to patients' conditions, as well as the arrival of new patients. A system flowchart should be provided.

Produce a non-technical guide for the system which explains how to produce the required reports and keep the files up-to-date.

Write an evaluation of the system which explains and justifies the choice of software, identifies limitations and makes suggestions for improvement.

Identify other needs for information that a doctor would have, and explain how your system could be extended to meet these needs.

(RSA NC HT or IT)

MEG resource tasks

1 Design and produce a leaflet giving information about (selected) lunchtime activities within a school for new year 7 pupils. Include at least one illustration from a graphics package or imaging package.

2 Using a sourcebook such as Philips Geographical Digest or the UN Yearbook, create a database of 30 countries: include information on population and wealth indicators such as GNP, TV, telephone or car ownership; health indicators such as birth rate, death rate, infant mortality, life expectancy, calories eaten daily, to a maximum of 12 different fields. Search and sort the database and display the information gathered in a variety of ways (tabular or graphical) to draw conclusions about the relationship between wealth and health of different populations. At least five different conclusions should be attempted. Comment on the validity of the conclusions.

3 Model the growth of bacteria against time with additional variables such as food supply and temperature.

4 Design an environmental control system for a greenhouse to monitor some or all of the following: temperature, humidity, light.

MEG capability task

Carry out a survey of shops and/or amenities in your local area. Collect suitable data and produce information for use by the following groups of people:

(a) residents of the area

(b) tourists visiting the area

(c) the manager of the shop/amenity listed

(d) the local council.

One or two samples of work suitable for each group of people are required. The samples should cover a wide variety of output.

Asthma, a disease which makes it difficult to breathe, is on the increase. A simple survey of the people in your class will reveal just how many people suffer from it. There are many different drugs on the market to help the sufferer, and the doctor has the difficult choice of deciding which one would be best for the patient. One way of deciding this is to use a device called a peak flow meter.

A peak flow meter is used to find out how good someone's breathing is. The patient blows into the mouthpiece, a marker moves along the barrel and a reading is obtained. The higher the reading, then the better the person's breathing. Usually three readings are taken and the highest reading is the one that is recorded.

Readings are taken using the meter twice per day, once before the patient gets up and once before they go to bed. The doctor gives the patient medicines to take and, using the peak flow meter, the doctor can see which one works best. The best medicine will give the highest peak flow readings.

(a) Design a form to be used by a patient to record the peak flow readings over a 21 day period. The readings are taken twice a day (three readings each time) and the highest of the three readings is the one that is recorded.

(b) A patient has been using a peak flow meter and has obtained the readings on the next page.

Using graph/spreadsheet software, plot this graph. Write a suitable title for the graph and label both the x and y axes.

You should be able to spot the following from your graph:

• when the patient had a very bad cold

• when the patient was transferred to the new medicine which improved her condition.

(c) The company that makes the peak flow meter has heard of data logging and would like to investigate a system whereby the meter could log the data over a 14 day period, store it and then be able to feed it into the doctor's personal computer so that the graph is obtained automatically.

Investigate this idea. Some of the things you should look at include;

• what sensors to use

• what additional equipment might be needed

• whether it would be too expensive.

Produce a feasibility report with your findings.

Readings from a peak flow meter

Date	a.m. reading	p.m. reading
22/6	390	560
23/6	260	560
24/6	380	520
25/6	250	550
26/6	270	550
27/6	400	580
28/6	320	560
29/6	410	550
30/6	300	350
1/7	300	400
2/7	400	570
3/7	430	550
4/7	440	570
5/7	480	580
6/7	480	560
7/7	450	540
8/7	460	550
9/7	470	560
10/7	460	570
11/7	450	560
12/7	450	570

History
Handling information

You have been asked to investigate the date of the First World War and the reasons that it started. You must use technology to find the answers, e.g. encyclopaedias on CD-ROMs.

Science
Measurement and control

A lady called Joanne likes hot coffee. Just before she adds the milk, the phone rings. Should Joanne add the milk before or after the phone call? Assume that the phone call lasts 5 minutes.

Home economics
Information handling

Obtain nutritional information from the backs of packaged foods. Each person in the group could be responsible for collecting and collating the data from a particular group of foods, so one person could collect the data relating, for example, to different makes of baked beans.

You will need to decide as a group how you are going to store the data using database software. Having decided this, enter all your group's data onto the database you have designed.

Using your database, do the following tasks.

1 Compare foods of the same type across the various brands. Are there any marked differences?

2 A person has been instructed by the doctor that they must eat a high fibre diet. Produce a list of the foods in order of the amount of fibre that they contain.

3 Do foods with a high fat content also have a large number of calories? Investigate this.

You are to produce two reports on the connection between the number of doctors in various parts of the world and the deaths of young babies. One is for a popular newspaper, and the other is for a serious environmental magazine.

Use the World Development Database to find out which countries have high and low numbers of people per doctor, and which have high and low proportions of infant deaths. Use graphs to provide further evidence for a connection between the number of doctors and the deaths of babies.

Use suitable software to produce the draft of a newspaper article, which will not contain any graphs. Write 100 words, making your findings as dramatic as you can.

Choose software which can combine your lists and graphs with the article. Adapt your article to suit the more serious magazine style, extend it to 300 words and incorporate appropriate lists and graphs to illustrate your points.

(RSA NC IT)

Chapter 28

Wordprocessing and Wordprocessing Exercises

Wordprocessors are the most popular type of computer software in use. For many people a wordprocessor is the only software they use. It is hard to think of a single job where some use for wordprocessing could not be found.

Many people now type their own documents directly into a computer rather than give them to a typist to type. This saves time, if people can type quickly. Because the text is stored in memory once it is typed, people can alter their text before finally saving and printing (Figure 28.1).

Now, even printing letters is becoming out-of-date because electronic mail is often used to send wordprocessed documents in electronic form from one place to another. There is no need for an envelope or a stamp and the recipient may store the letter on disk for future reference, thus saving valuable storage space.

Hardware and software for wordprocessing

The most common hardware arrangement is:

- a microcomputer
- a high quality printer (a laser or ink-jet printer)
- a mouse (necessary if the wordprocessor uses Windows or the Macintosh operating system)
- a keyboard.

Apart from the operating system, the only software needed is a wordprocessing package. This can be a separate package which just does wordprocessing or part of an integrated package, where the wordprocessing is only one part of the complete package.

Notes prepared beforehand   Thoughts, ideas keyed directly in

Figure 28.1 *Typing your thoughts directly into the wordprocessor saves time, but its not quite as easy as working from notes*

The advantages of wordprocessing

Wordprocessing has several advantages compared with typing.

1 Much more professional results can be obtained by everyone and not just those who are experienced typists, because typing mistakes are easily altered on the screen before printing out.

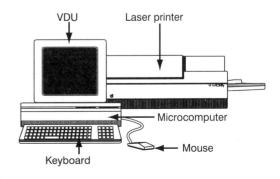

Figure 28.2 *A typical wordprocessing system*

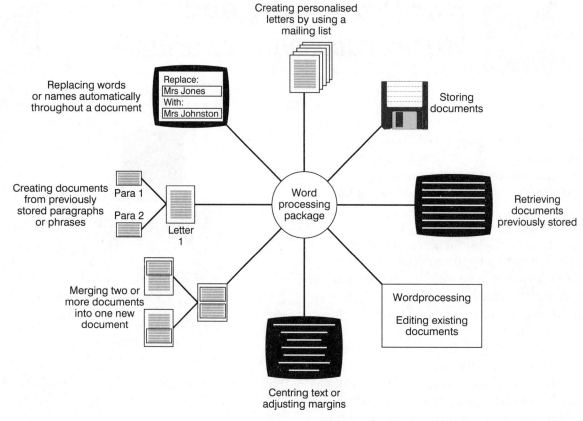

Figure 28.3 *Some of the features you might find in a typical wordprocessing package*

2 Fewer resources are used, provided that material is carefully proofread on the screen before finally printing. Since we can edit and correct mistakes before printing, this reduces the amount of paper we need to use. Most large companies now send all their internal letters and memos using electronic mail. The widespread use of electronic mail will help to conserve our valuable resources.

3 More people are able to produce their own documents rather than pass them to someone else to type. This can save both time and money.

4 More wordprocessors are becoming like simple desktop publishing packages. These extra facilities enable people to produce notices, posters, tickets, etc. with very little training.

What can you do with wordprocessing software?

Wordprocessing software is software that is able to store, edit and manipulate text. All wordprocessing software will allow you to enter text then edit and rearrange it before storing it and printing it out. Some wordprocessors are 'WYSIWYG' which means 'what you see is what you get'. This means that you are able to see on the screen exactly what the page will look like when it is printed out.

Most wordprocessors allow you to change the fonts (type styles and sizes). Figure 28.3 shows some of the many features you might find in a typical wordprocessing package. Some of the more advanced features you will find are listed on the next page.

Spell checkers

Nearly all wordprocessors have a dictionary against which the words in a document can be compared to check their spelling. Most allow you to add words to the dictionary which is useful if you use special terms in subjects such as law or medicine. It is important to note that spell checking a document will not remove all the errors. For instance, if you intended to type 'the' and typed 'he' instead, then the spell checker will not detect this since 'he' as a word is spelt correctly. After using a spell checker it is still necessary to proof read a document.

Thesaurus

A thesaurus is useful for creative writing (perhaps for English GCSE coursework). It allows you to highlight a word in a document and the computer lists words with similar meanings (called synonyms) (Figure 28.4).

Mail merge

Mail merging involves combining a list of, say, names and addresses, with a typed letter, so that a series of similar letters is produced, each addressed to a different person. The list is either created using the wordprocessor or by importing data from a database of names and addresses. The letter is typed, using the wordprocessor, with blanks where the data from the list is to be inserted.

Indexing

Indexing allows you to highlight words that you would like to use in an index. The wordprocessor keeps a record of the words, and creates an index when instructed to.

Macros

Macros allow you automatically to produce a sequence of keystrokes so that, for example, you can just press one key or a combination of keys and have your name and address printed at the top of the page. You can also insert dates just by pressing a couple of keys. Macros are very useful for things that need to be done repetitively.

Grammar checkers

Some of the more sophisticated wordprocessors have a feature called a grammar checker. These are useful if your English is not so good. If the wordprocessor you use does not have this facility, then you can buy a separate grammar checking package to use with it. Figure 28.5 shows a grammar checker being used. Because of the complexities of the English language, grammar checkers do have their limitations. As yet they find only a few faults and do tend to provide an incorrect analysis of the grammar of writing. You need to exercise care when using them.

Figure 28.4

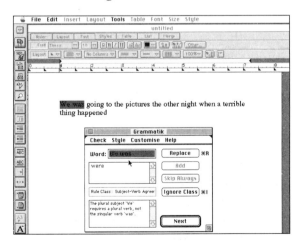

Figure 28.5 *The text above contains a grammatical error. The grammar checker on this wordprocessor is able to find it and suggest how it could be corrected*

QUESTION

Find out how to do each of the following tasks using your wordprocessor. Write down for future reference how you would perform each task.

(a) how to load the wordprocessing software

(b) how to edit a document

(c) how to alter the margins

(d) how to do special text effects such as

- bold type
- underlining
- italics

(e) how to centre text

(f) how to insert a line

(g) how to produce a temporary indent

(h) how to save text

(i) how to load previously saved work

(j) how to move blocks of text around (called block moves or cut and paste)

(k) how to print a document.

Choosing a wordprocessing package

Ideally, you should choose the software you want to run and then choose hardware to suit that software. However, since many people are using existing hardware, their choice of wordprocessing package may, to some extent, be dictated by the hardware.

Most people's favourite wordprocessor is the one they are used to, but there are many new and useful features in the newer packages to tempt you. How do you decide which one to use? You may like to ask yourself the following questions to help you decide.

(a) If you are a fast typist then you would look for a wordprocessor that could keep up with your typing speed. Some of the Windows wordprocessors can be slow, so a DOS based package might be better.

(b) If you would like to do simple desktop publishing, then many of the Windows, Macintosh or Windows 95 based wordprocessors would be suitable. Many of them have some of the features you used to find only in DTP packages.

(c) If you need to send out a number of letters to lots of different people, it would be best to go for a wordprocessor with a mail merge facility. Mail merging allows you to create standard letters and link them to a database of names and addresses so that you can make it appear that the letters are all tailor made.

(d) If you use a variety of wordproccessors, then you need to check if it is possible to transfer the files between the different packages. With some it is easy, but with others you may find that one wordprocessor is unable to read files from a different wordprocessor.

QUESTION

This question concerns the more advanced features of wordprocessors.

Find out how to do each of the following using your wordprocessor and write down for future reference how you would perform each task.

(a) how to spellcheck a document

(b) how to use the thesaurus

(c) how to use the search and replace facility

(d) how to use macros

(e) how to use mail merging.

Learning to type

As you will probably discover, being able to type quickly is a very important skill when working with computers. No matter how fast the computer hardware or software is, if you cannot type very quickly this will slow you down. For this reason it is best to use a typing tutor to teach yourself to touch type. A typing tutor is a software package which makes learning to type fun. Ask your teacher if the school or college has one and practise regularly. It will certainly help you with project work (or with any work that needs typing).

TEST YOURSELF

Using the words in the list below, copy out and complete sentences A to F, underlining the words you have inserted. The words may be used more than once.

wordprocessor   DTP   high   electronic mail
grammar   spellchecker

A The most commonly used piece of software is the _____ .

B With a wordprocessor, you can type in a letter and then send it directly to another part of the country or even the world, using _____
_____ .

C One of the main advantages of wordprocessing is that an inexperienced typist is able to produce ____ quality documents.

D Many wordprocessors now contain features you would normally find only in ___ packages.

E The most useful advanced feature on the wordprocessor is the _____ , which is used to check the spelling of an entire document after it has been typed.

F The more advanced wordprocessors have _____ checkers where you can check that the structure of the English is correct.

THINGS TO DO

1 (a) What does a wordprocessor consist of?

(b) As a document is being typed, where is it stored?

(c) Why is it always advisable to save your document before printing it and not the other way round?

(d) The minutes of a meeting have been typed on a wordprocessor and stored on a disk. The draft copy shows one mistake. In the middle of a long paragraph, the word 'the' has been typed in twice. Describe briefly how the operator would correct the minutes.

2 A friend of yours has never used a wordprocessor before. Explain to her what advantages wordprocessors have over conventional typewriters. Give at least four advantages.

3 You have just loaded the 'Quickword', wordprocessor and the menu shown in Figure 28.6 appears on the screen. You want to retrieve a previously saved document, make a couple of alterations and finally produce a printout. Write down the order in which the commands should be used.

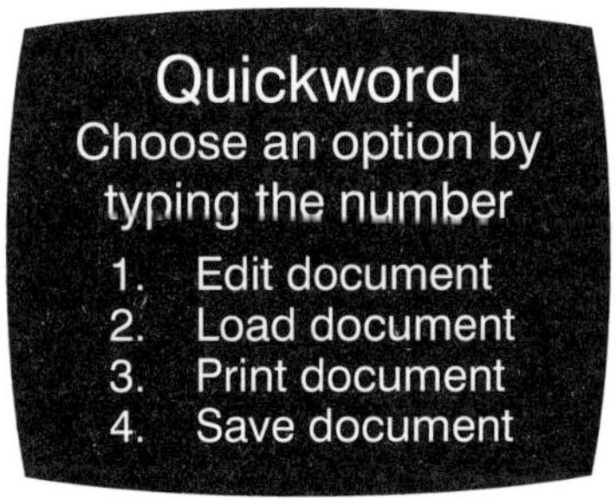

Quickword
Choose an option by
typing the number
1. Edit document
2. Load document
3. Print document
4. Save document

Figure 28.6

Task 1

Load your wordprocessing software and type in the following text making sure that you do not press the return or enter key at the end of a line unless you want to leave blank lines between paragraphs.

When you first start to use the wordprocessor you may find it hard to think up what you are going to say and have to write it down first. This does destroy the point of the wordprocessor (i.e. it is supposed to save time). Try to type your work directly in and remember that the beauty of the wordprocessor is its ability to let you change things around.

Also, beginners often correct their mistakes as they go along whereas high speed typists will probably not know they have made the mistake until they carefully read through their document (proof read) afterwards.

(a) Proof read the above document and correct any errors that you spot.

(b) Save your document.

(c) Print the document.

Task 2

Here is a Christmas menu. As it is presented it does not look very interesting. You have been asked to improve the presentation but not the content using your wordprocessor. You could try centring each line and use different sized text and fonts for the headings. Do you have any Christmas clip art that you could include?

```
Christmas Fayre
MENU
Freshly Made Soup of the Day
or
Egg Mayonnaise with Tuna
or
Prawn Cocktail (£1 Extra)

Roasted Lincolnshire Turkey with chestnut stuffing,
cranberry sauce, chipolata sausage and bacon, three fresh
vegetables, roast potatoes and gravy.

Christmas Pudding
or
Sweets from our trolley

Freshly Percolated Coffee with mint wafers

£9.95


(Available All Through December)
```

Task 3

Type the following letter into your wordprocessor.

```
Dear Mrs Hanley

This is just the chance you have been waiting for. You have been
specially selected to enter our prize draw. Just imagine the difference
our £100 000 first prize would make to your lifestyle. Or if you don't win
the first prize, imagine the envy of your neighbours when a brand new
Nissan 200 SX sports car appears on the Hanley drive.
```

```
All you have to do Mrs Hanley, to enter our new competition is to
purchase a copy of 'Your rights as a consumer'. This useful book looks at
all matters related to consumer problems and deals with such things as
your rights when taking goods back, problems with credit, how do deal
with shoddy home repairs. In fact nearly every problem you could
encounter is mentioned in this invaluable book.

All you have to do Mrs Hanley is return the enclosed entry form. You do
not need to send any money. The book will be sent to you together with
the invoice for £19.95. If you do not wish to purchase the book, simply
return the postage paid package within 14 days and you will still be
entered for our prize draw. If you reply within 7 days then you could win
a cash bonus of £10 000. Can you afford not to reply, Mrs Hanley?
```

1 Proof read the document by carefully comparing it with the original. If there are any errors, correct them.

2 Save, and the print a copy of the document.

3 Highlight 'Your rights as a consumer' using bold print.

4 Underline 'You do not need to send any money'.

5 Search for and then replace all occurrences of 'Mrs Hanley' by 'Mrs Ho' (n.b. you must use the wordprocessor's search and replace facility to do this).

6 Search for and then replace all occurrences of £100 000 with £50 000.

7 Start a new paragraph for the sentence starting 'If you reply within 7 days ...' by leaving a blank line.

8 Save the revised document.

9 Print the final document.

Task 4

You have been asked to produce a slip to explain a special deal that a company which manufactures calculators has given your school. The slip is to be photocopied and one is to be given to each pupil in the school (there are 1600 pupils in the school). Because the school wants to save paper and photocopying charges, it would like to copy this document three times, if possible, onto an A4 page.

Type in the following text:

```
S P E C I A L    O F F E R
Here is a very special offer to all our pupils. We have managed to
negotiate a special price on a CASIO 6543 Scientific Calculator which we
recommend to all our pupils. This calculator is the cheapest on the
market at only £9.99 and has all the features of calculators costing
twice as much.

It is easy to get a calculator. Just fill in the form and return it with
payment (cash or cheque payable to Green Hill PTA) to the school
secretary, who will supply your son/daughter with the calculator.

Name................................     Form...............

Number of calculators you wish to buy .............

Signature of parent/guardian...............................
```

(a) Try to make this advert as appealing as you can by the use of bold type, italics, underlining and different fonts.

(b) Copy this document to see if it will fit on an A4 page, three times.

(c) When you are happy with it, save and print the page.

Task 5

Load your wordprocessor and type in the following document.

Curriculum vitae

A curriculum vitae is used to tell people about yourself and what you have done with your life so far. By reading this, another person is able to get an impression of you by the personal details and experience you have put down. CVs are normally attached to a letter of application for a job. A CV should include what your achievements have been to date and an outline of your qualifications (or exams taken if you are still awaiting the results). A CV is very important so you need to take time to produce a good one.

It is best to produce a list of the things you need to include and then produce a first draft. Ask another person to read through it. Your English teacher may check it for spelling mistakes and grammatical errors. You should then produce the final version.

Make sure that you leave plenty of space between the various items and make sure that it is no longer than about two sides of A4 size paper.

Make sure that you include such things as qualifications, what interested you at school, any work experience, any positions of authority you have held, details of hobbies and sports played. Remember, the purpose of the CV is to sell yourself.

(a) Type in the above document exactly as it appears above.

(b) Proof read the document by looking at it carefully on the screen and checking that it compares exactly with what was written above.

(c) Save your file using a suitable name.

(d) Print out a copy of the file.

Task 6

In task 5 you typed in a passage about CVs. Now you are going to design one of your own. Imagine that you are applying for a college place or a job and have been asked to supply a CV. Produce your CV using wordprocessing software.

Task 7

Your maths teacher would like you to investigate how to type equations into the wordprocessor. He would like to be able to use the wordprocessor to produce a worksheet on Pythagoras's Theorem. As well as the equations, he would like you to investigate the possibility of including labelled diagrams of triangles in the worksheet. He has handed you the following hand written sample of part of the worksheet.

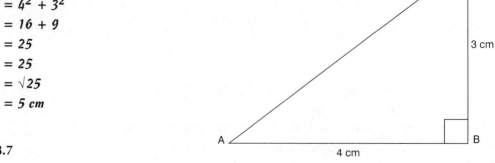

Using Pythagoras's Theorem

$$AC^2 = AB^2 + BC^2$$
$$AC^2 = 4^2 + 3^2$$
$$AC^2 = 16 + 9$$
$$AC^2 = 25$$
$$AC^2 = 25$$
$$AC = \sqrt{25}$$
$$= 5 \ cm$$

Figure 28.7

214

Design and produce a worksheet which could be used by the mathematics teacher to teach Pythagoras's Theorem. Your worksheet should look appealing and not too cluttered. Try to import labelled diagrams of the triangles into the document.

The mathematics teacher shows your efforts to the chemistry teacher, who is very impressed. She would now like you to find out about doing similar worksheets containing chemical equations. Although she is familiar with the simple functions of the wordprocessor, she has no idea how to import diagrams or how to produce the equations. She has asked you to produce a guide for her, along with a couple of examples of what can be done.

The chemistry teacher supplies you with the following equation as an example of a typical chemical equation.

$$H_2SO_4 + 2NaOH = Na_2SO_4 + 2H_2O$$

Task 8

Using the tabular features of your wordprocessor, produce a copy of your school or college timetable.

Task 9

Investigate the mail merge facility on your wordprocessor.

Chapter

29

Spreadsheets and Spreadsheet Exercises

What is a spreadsheet?

Spreadsheets are much easier to use than to explain. A spreadsheet consists of a grid of cells into which may be placed text, numbers or formulae. Spreadsheets are useful for 'what if' calculations. If you change the contents of one cell, then all those cells whose contents depend on it will change as well.

Rows, columns and cells

Figure 29.1 shows a spreadsheet grid with its horizontal rows and vertical columns.

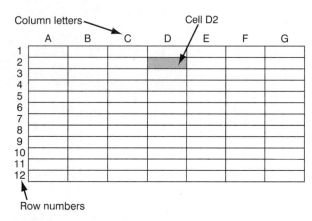

Figure 29.1 *Spreadsheet grid*

Figure 29.1 shows only part of a spreadsheet. Spreadsheets are frequently very large and only a small part of the sheet can be viewed on the screen at any one time. It is rather like looking at the sheet through a movable window as in Figure 29.2.

Spreadsheets are made up of cells, each of which has its own address. For instance the intersection of column D with row 4 will give a cell with the address D4.

All spreadsheets can total columns or rows of numbers. To do this, you type formula into the cell where you want the

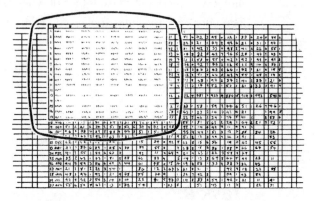

Figure 29.2 *Looking at a spreadsheet through a 'window'*

total to be displayed. This formula must state which is the first cell in the series that is to be added up and which is the last.

What can you put into a cell?

You can put in:

1 words (titles, row headings, column headings, etc.)
2 numbers (ordinary numbers, currency, dates, etc.)
3 formulae (used to perform calculations with the numbers).

Entering data correctly

There are two common mistakes that people make when using spreadsheets.

1 Entering numbers as text

When people first start using spreadsheets, they like to be able to centre the data when they type it in. They soon find that they can do this by pressing the space bar several times before they type in the data. If a number is typed in after the space bar has been pressed then the number will be treated like text and it will be impossible to use this number in calculations. Most spreadsheets have a function which will move the cell contents to the right, left or centre. It is best to get all the data typed in and then change the position of the data in the cells.

2 Referring a formula to its own cell

Suppose we wanted to add up the data in the cells c1 to c7 and put the total in c8. If we typed in @sum(c1:c8) then we are using the cell where the formula is, which is not allowed. Instead we need to type

@sum(c1:c7).

Here is a sample spreadsheet

	A	B	C	D	E
1	Expenses				
2	Phone	152·80			
3	Electricity	262·40			
4	Gas	189·00			
5	Stationery	76·00			
6	Postage	101·00			
7	Car expenses	896·00			
8	Total				

To calculate the total and put it into cell b8 we could move the cursor to this cell and then type in a formula like this

+b2+b3+b4+b5+b6+b7.

This is tedious especially if we had to find the total of 100 cells so there is a quicker command @sum(b2:b7) which adds up all the cells from b2 to b7 inclusive. These formulae may not work with your particular spreadsheet. Unfortunately not all spreadsheets are the same so you will need to ask your teacher how to enter formulae if the above does not work.

If we changed the electricity cost from 262·40 to 362·40, then as soon as we entered it, the spreadsheet would automatically recalculate the new total.

One of the most useful features of a spreadsheet is that cells can be copied. They can be copied absolutely or relatively.

When a cell is copied absolutely, the same number is copied. For instance suppose you had a spreadsheet showing expenses and on

this there was a column to show a rent of £180 per month. Rather than type in the same amount 12 times for the whole year you could just enter it once and use the copy facility to copy this amount into the other cells. Absolute copying does not alter a formula in any way to compensate for the different cell positions.

When a formula in a cell is copied relatively, the spreadsheet takes into account the new cell positions and adjusts the formula.

Tips for building a spreadsheet

1 Start with a title saying what the spreadsheet does. Also include the date.
2 Fill in the column and row headings.
3 Fill in the data, leaving blanks where the results of calculations need to go.
4 Fill in the formulas and copy them where necessary.

QUESTIONS

1 Find out how each of the following is done using your spreadsheet and write down for future reference how you perform each task:
   (a) how to edit a cell
   (b) how to insert a row or column (this is useful if you forget to put one in)
   (c) how to widen a column (the column width is usually set at nine characters but you can set it to another value)
   (d) how to position the text or numbers in each cell; for instance you may wish to centre the contents of a group of cells
   (e) how to enter a formula
   (f) how to copy a cell; cells may be copied absolutely or relatively
   (g) how to load a spreadsheet (it must have been previously saved)
   (h) how to underline, make bold and italicise text (some spreadsheets do not have this facility)
   (i) how to save a spreadsheet
   (j) how to print out a spreadsheet; you can

either print part of a spreadsheet by specifying a certain range or you can print out the whole sheet.

2 This question is about writing formulas for your particular spreadsheet. Not all spreadsheets use the same commands and you have to construct formulas differently for some spreadsheets. Your teacher will tell you how you should construct a formula.

Write down the formula you would put in a cell to do the following:

(a) add cells B3, d7 and e11 together

(b) multiply cells b3 and c3 together

(c) subtract cell d3 from cell c3

(d) find 5% of cell d4

(e) divide cell a2 by cell b4

(f) find 17.5% of cell a4

(g) add all the cells from cell a5 to f5 inclusive

(h) find the average of cells from a3 to g3 inclusive

(l) add cells a3 and b3, and then divide this total by cell e5.

Printing spreadsheets

Spreadsheets can be quite large so there can be problems printing them out. Usually we want to fit the sheet across the width of the page. The better spreadsheet packages are

Figure 29.3 *Printing a worksheet in landscape mode (below) and in portrait mode (right)*

able to do this by adjusting the size of the type. It is also possible to use condensed print.

Printing may be done in either portrait or landscape formats as shown in Figure 29.3.

Graphs

All spreadsheets enable you to produce graphs like the ones shown in Figure 29.4.

Business decisions

Julie, the sales manager of a company can use a spreadsheet to help make business decisions. She sets up a spreadsheet which includes all the income (money coming into the business) and costs or expenditure (money going out of the business). A series of formulae is used to total the figures and work out the profit (profit = total income – total expenses). The company could, on the basis of the profit, decide to employ more salespersons. The cost of employing them will be an expense and these will need to be added to the expenses. The profits will now go down because the expenses are greater. What happens to the sales though? Having more people selling the goods should increase the sales and therefore the income,

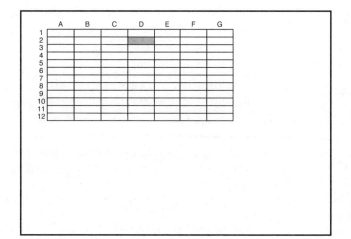

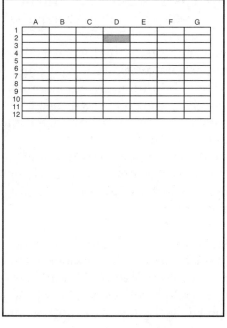

Half-yearly Sales

Month	Sales
Jan	1250
Feb	3400
Mar	980
Apr	1200
May	3178
June	4329

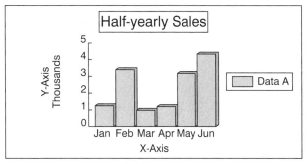

3-D bar chart

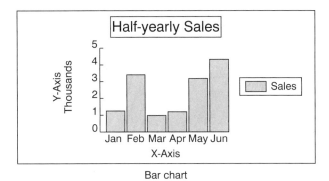

Bar chart

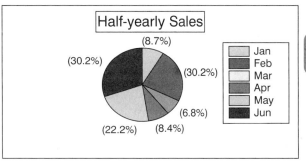

Pie chart

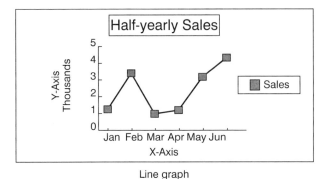

Line graph

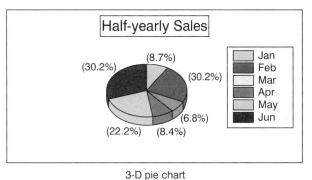

3-D pie chart

Figure 29.4 *All these graphs are produced from this simple table of half-yearly sales figures*

but by how much? Julie reckons that the extra sales staff should increase the income by about 10%, so she adjusts the spreadsheet and the profit alters. The spreadsheet shows is that it is worth employing the extra staff, assuming that Julie's assumption about the increase in income is correct.

Spreadsheets are used in all types of businesses to provide information on which to base decisions. They are the second most used piece of software (wordprocessing is the most widely used).

QUESTION

Market gardener spreadsheet

John Hughes is unemployed and would like to start his own business. Having recently completed a course in horticulture, he decides to set up as a market gardener. His uncle owns a large garage and next to this is a field which his uncle also owns. He agrees to rent the field to John at a rent of £80 per month. John decides that he will grow a variety of vegetables on the land, which he will sell to customers who come into his uncle's garage.

219

John realises that his first year's trading will be tough and he needs to make sure that he has enough money coming in each month to pay his overheads. To make sure of this he sits down and writes a list of all his income and likely expenditure.

1 Figure 29.5 shows the data you have to type in. Make sure that you include the title of the spreadsheet along with the date. Then type in the information on the sheet accurately, leaving blank spaces for the missing data.

2 Put in a formula in the column for April to work out the total income. Add this column up manually to check that your formula is correct. Now use the copy command to copy this formula relatively so that all the totals for the months are filled in.

3 Using a suitable formula, find the total expenditure for each of the months.

4 Calculate the profit, using a formula to subtract the total expenditure from the total income.

5 We will now look at the cumulative total for the profit. This represents the money that John would have left at the end of each month. He would need this money to continue trading. Remember that his trade will be seasonal, so he will need some money to tide him over the slack periods.

The cumulative total for April will be zero, as this is his first month of trading, so there will be no profit from the previous month to carry forward. All subsequent months need to have the last month's profit/loss added to the cumulative total.

Using a formula, work out the cumulative profit/loss for April and then copy this formula for the other months to give you your final spreadsheet. Figure 29.6 shows the completed spreadsheet.

Finding the maximum volume of a box made from a sheet of metal

Varipack is a company that makes metal boxes from sheet metal for various customers.

An open box (i.e. one without a lid) is to be made out of a rectangular sheet of metal by cutting out squares of metal from each corner, bending the sides up and then welding the joins. Figure 29.7 shows how this is done.

If we had a sheet of metal 50 cm by 30 cm and cut out squares of 5 cm from each

Figure 29.5 *Blank 'Market Gardener' template*

1995 to 1996	CASH FLOW ANALYSIS FOR J HUGHES MARKET GARDENER											
INCOME	APR	MAY	JUN	JUL	AUG	SEP	OCT	NOV	DEC	JAN	FEB	MAR
Sales	245.31	303.58	458.31	683.92	647.84	609.72	648.67	560.98	758.42	858.90	680.40	416.84
Rent Allowance	120.00	120.00	120.00	120.00	120.00	120.00	120.00	120.00	120.00	120.00	120.00	120.00
Grant	115.00	115.00	115.00	115.00	115.00	115.00	115.00	115.00	115.00	115.00	115.00	115.00
Total Income												
EXPENDITURE												
Rent	80.00	80.00	80.00	80.00	80.00	85.00	85.00	85.00	85.00	85.00	85.00	85.00
Heating	40.00	12.00	0.00	0.00	0.00	0.00	0.00	0.00	0.00	48.28	84.30	126.00
Fertilisers	240.00	0.00	0.00	0.00	0.00	286.30	15.00	0.00	86.00	12.00	25.62	12.80
Lighting	8.62	4.84	3.22	3.41	4.84	5.26	6.00	7.84	26.80	25.60	17.23	14.00
Petrol	12.00	13.00	10.54	8.21	7.54	14.80	28.50	12.90	16.40	14.85	13.23	12.56
Loan	54.84	54.84	54.84	54.84	54.84	54.84	54.84	54.84	54.84	54.84	54.84	54.84
Seeds	40.00	15.00	2.50	1.80	0.00	0.00	12.00	1.80	4.40	1.85	0.00	0.00
Gro-bags	32.00	10.80	0.00	0.00	0.00	0.00	0.00	0.00	0.00	2.64	15.70	0.00
Compost	85.00	0.00	0.00	0.00	0.00	0.00	0.00	0.00	0.00	18.50	20.00	45.00
Van hire	18.00	18.00	18.00	18.00	18.00	18.00	18.00	18.00	18.00	18.00	18.00	18.00
Equipment	12.00	125.00	0.00	0.00	0.00	0.00	0.00	0.00	0.00	0.00	0.00	0.00
Seed trays	14.00	5.00	0.00	0.00	0.00	0.00	0.00	0.00	0.00	0.00	0.00	0.00
Boxes	25.00	0.00	0.00	0.00	0.00	0.00	0.00	0.00	0.00	27.00	0.00	1.80
Wages	120.00	120.00	120.00	120.00	120.00	120.00	120.00	120.00	120.00	120.00	120.00	120.00
TOTAL EXPENDITURE												
PROFIT/LOSS												
CUMULATIVE PROFIT/LOSS												

1995 to 1996				CASH FLOW A[NALYSIS]							
INCOME	APR	MAY	JUN	JUL						FEB	MAR
Sales	245.31	303.58	458.31	683.92	64?					680.40	416.84
Rent Allowance	120.00	120.00	120.00	120.00	120					120.00	120.00
Grant	115.00	115.00	115.00	115.00	115					115.00	115.00
Total Income	480.31	538.58	693.31	918.92	882					915.40	651.84
EXPENDITURE											
Rent	80.00	80.00	80.00	80.00	80.					85.00	85.00
Heating	40.00	12.00	0.00	0.00	0.				46.28	84.30	126.00
Fertilisers	240.00	0.00	0.00	0.00	0.			0.00	86.00	12.00	25.62	12.80
Lighting	8.62	4.84	3.22	3.41	4.84	5.26	6.00	7.84	26.80	25.60	17.23	14.00
Petrol	12.00	13.00	10.54	8.21	7.54	14.80	28.50	12.90	16.40	14.85	13.23	12.56
Loan	54.84	54.84	54.84	54.84	54.84	54.84	54.84	54.84	54.84	54.84	54.84	54.84
Seeds	40.00	15.00	2.50	1.80	0.00	0.00	12.00	1.80	4.40	1.85	0.00	0.00
Gro-bags	32.00	10.80	0.00	0.00	0.00	0.00	0.00	0.00	0.00	2.64	15.70	0.00
Compost	85.00	0.00	0.00	0.00	0.00	0.00	0.00	0.00	0.00	18.50	20.00	45.00
Van hire	18.00	18.00	18.00	18.00	18.00	18.00	18.00	18.00	18.00	18.00	18.00	18.00
Equipment	12.00	125.00	0.00	0.00	0.00	0.00	0.00	0.00	0.00	0.00	0.00	0.00
Seed trays	14.00	5.00	0.00	0.00	0.00	0.00	0.00	0.00	0.00	0.00	0.00	0.00
Boxes	25.00	0.00	0.00	0.00	0.00	0.00	0.00	0.00	0.00	27.00	0.00	1.80
Wages	120.00	120.00	120.00	120.00	120.00	120.00	120.00	120.00	120.00	120.00	120.00	120.00
TOTAL EXPENDITURE	781.46	45848	289.10	286.26	285.22	584.20	339.34	300.38	411.44	428.56	453.92	490.00
PROFIT/LOSS	-301.15	80.10	404.21	632.66	597.62	260.552	544.33	495.60	581.98	665.34	461.48	161.84
CUMULATIVE PROFIT/LOSS	0.00	-221.05	484.31	1036.87	1230.28	858.14	804.85	1039.93	1077.58	1247.32	1126.82	623.32

Figure 29.6 *The completed worksheet. Check that yours is the same as this*

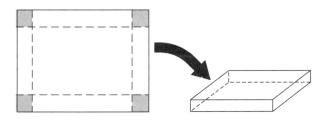

Figure 29.7 *Cutting out squares from each corner and then folding along the dotted lines makes the box*

corner we can work out the length, width and height of the box in the following way.

The length of the box will be $50 - 2 \times 5 = 40$ cm, the width will be $30 - 2 \times 5 = 20$ cm and the height of the box is the same as the corner size, i.e. 5 cm.

The volume of this box is calculated using the formula

volume $=$ length $\times$ width $\times$ height

so

volume $= 40 \times 20 \times 5 = 4000$ cm^3

There are many different sized boxes that could be made out of this sheet of metal.

Varipack wants to know what size corners to cut out, so as to make the volume of the resulting box as large as possible.

To do this we can use a spreadsheet with the following formulae;

length of box $= 30 - 2 \times$ corner size
width of box $= 20 - 2 \times$ corner size
height of box $=$ corner size

To start off, we can produce a spreadsheet using corner sizes from 1 cm to 10 cm in

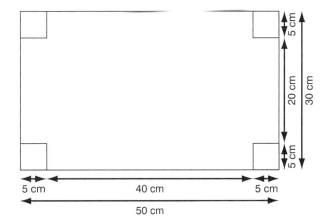

Figure 29.8 *Working out the dimensions of the box from the corner size*

	A	B	C	D	E	F
1	Spreadsheet 1 to determine the rough corner size to give the maximum volume.					
2						
3						
4	Corner Size	Length of box	Width of box	Volume of box		
5	1	28	18	504		
6	2	26	16	832		
7	3	24	4	1008		
8	4	22	12	1056		
9	5	20	10	1000		
10	6	18	8	864		
11	7	16	6	672		
12	8	14	4	448		
13	9	12	2	216		
14	10	10	0	0		
15						
16	Spreadsheet 2 to determine a more accurate corner size to give the maximum volume					
17						
18	Corner Size	Length of box	Width of box	Volume of box		
19	3.50	23.00	13.00	1046.50		
20	3.60	22.80	12.80	1050.62		
21	3.70	22.60	12.60	1053.61		
22	3.80	22.40	12.40	1055.49		
23	3.90	22.20	12.20	1056.28		
24	4.00	22.00	12.00	1056.00		
25	4.10	21.80	11.80	1054.68		
26	4.20	21.60	11.60	1052.35		
27	4.30	21.40	11.40	1049.03		
28	4.40	21.20	11.20	1044.74		
29	4.50	21.00	11.00	1039.50		

Figure 29.9 *Using a spreadsheet to work out the corner size to give the maximum volume*

steps of 1 cm. We cannot have a corner size greater than 10 cm, since this would make the width of this box zero.

From this first spreadsheet, we see that the maximum volume occurs when the corner size is 4 cm. We need to set up a spreadsheet to get a more accurate value for the corner size. We will now investigate from 3.5 cm to 4.5 cm in steps of 0.1 cm (i.e. 1 mm).

We now find that the corner size to give us the maximum volume is 3.9 cm. If we wanted we could investigate either side of this figure to get an even more accurate value. You may like to do this. Also, try using the graph plotting facility to plot the volume on the y-axis and the corner size on the x-axis for the three spreadsheets.

Documenting your spreadsheet

Frequently, the person who has to use a spreadsheet is not the same person who created it, so it is important always to document any spreadsheets you produce. You may decide to use a spreadsheet to solve a problem for your project and you will have to fully document it. The minimum documentation should include:

1 a printout of the final spreadsheet, showing the data
2 a printout of the spreadsheet with the formulas in each cell displayed
3 a user guide to the spreadsheet. The origins of the data (i.e. where it comes from) and how to produce the output (printouts, graphs, etc.) should be mentioned
4 any handwritten annotations (these are little notes) on the printouts explaining how the spreadsheet works.

THINGS TO DO

1 The spreadsheet below shows data on agriculture in the British Isles.
   (a) Which cell would you use to put the total Agricultural Area?   (1 mark)
   (b) What formula would you put in that cell?   (2 marks)

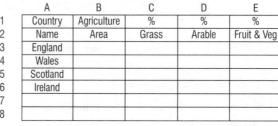

	A	B	C	D	E
1	Country	Agriculture	%	%	%
2	Name	Area	Grass	Arable	Fruit & Veg
3	England				
4	Wales				
5	Scotland				
6	Ireland				
7					
8					

Figure 29.10

(c) The spreadsheet has the ability to produce the following types of graph:

Bar   Line   Pie   Scatter

Which one would be most suitable for showing:

(i)   the proportions of grass, arable and fruit & veg for England?

(ii) to compare the agricultural areas for the four countries?   (2 marks)

(d) If you want to add similar data for other countries where could you find that data?
(1 mark)

(SEG FT Spec)

2 A spreadsheet is being used in a small machine knitting shop to keep records of income and expenditure every quarter.

		Estimate for year	Total to date	Jan to March Estimate	Jan to March Actual	April to June Estimate	April to June Actual	July to Sept Estimate	July to Sept Actual	Oct to Dec Estimate	Oct to Dec Actual
1											
2											
3	INCOME										
4											
5	Knitting Machines	21,000	9,490	6,000	6,135	4,000	3,355	4,800		6,200 **Y**	
6	Yarn	10,400	5,109	2,000	1,940	2,800	3,169	2,500		3,100	
7	Accessories	5,200	2,361	1,200	1,107	1,200	1,254	1,200		1,600	
8	Repairs	5,300	2,114	1,100	987	1,200	1,127	1,500		1,500	
9											
10	TOTAL INCOME	41,900	19,074	10,300	10,169	9,200	8,905	10,00		12,400	
11											
12											
13	EXPENSES										
14											
15	Knitting Machines	12,000	5,950	3,000	2,895	3,000	3,055	3,000		3,000	
16	Yarn	6,500	2,530	1,000	750	2,000	1,780	2,000		1,500	
17	Accessories	3,200	1,726	800	950	800	776	800		800	
18	Staff Costs	14,700	6,700	3,500	3,250	3,500	3,450	3,700		4,000	
19	Rent & Rates	3,120	1,630	780	780	780	850	780		780	
20	Office Costs	700	210	150	127	150	83	150		250	
21	Miscellaneous	800	239	200	77	200	162	200		200	
22											
23	Total Expenses	41,020	18,985 **Z**	9,430	8,829	10,430	10,156	10,630		10,530	
24											
25											
26	GROSS PROFIT	890	89	870	1,340	-1,230	-1,251	-630		1,870	

Figure 29.11

The cell **Y** is in row 5 and column 10, which can be written as r5c10. Similarly cell **Z** is written as r23c3 and this cell has a formula in it to calculate the total expenses to date. This formula adds up the items in column 3 from row 15 to row 21, which can be written SUM(r15c3:r21c3).

(a) In which cell is there a formula to calculate the total income to date?

(b) What is the formula in that cell?

(c) (i)   Which cell will have to be changed in order to show that the office costs for the April to June quarter are in fact £88?

(ii) Which other cells will be changed?

(d) The company decides to expand and sell sewing machines as well. They wish to see as a separate item the income from selling sewing machines, and the expenditure on them. Explain clearly all the changes that will need to be made to the spreadsheet to do this job.

(e) Give **one** other example of a job that could be made easier by the use of a spreadsheet (**not** to do with income and expenditure).

(SEG HT Spec)

3 Jane and David have set up in business making bird tables. They make two types: 'Cottage' and 'Mansion'. The wood for 'Cottage' costs £8.80 and for 'Mansion' £11.80. The costs of fittings (screws, nails, etc.) for each are £1.20. The 'Cottage' model takes 2.6 hours to make whilst the 'Mansion' takes 3.1 hours to make. Jane and David would like to pay themselves £5 per hour. They hope to sell 20 of each type at a profit of 30%. Find out, using a spreadsheet, how much they should sell each model for.

4 Sometimes spreadsheets are used for things that don't include calculations. For instance it is possible to show the lines that make up the columns and rows and this can be useful if you want to draw tables. Some wordprocessing packages can be used to do this but sometimes it is easier to use a spreadsheet.

Using a spreadsheet, produce a copy of your school timetable and print it out. Evaluate the use of the spreadsheet for this task, stating the problems and limitations you encountered.

5 Investigate a variety of spreadsheet packages and, using the spreadsheet's matrix to help you, design a page that a magazine reader could use to compare the various features.

6 A friend of yours says, 'spreadsheets are a waste of money because they can't do anything that you cannot do with a pen, paper and calculator'.

(a) Can you think of any functions included in spreadsheets packages which would take a long time using the manual method? Write them down.

(b) Give as many advantages of the use of spreadsheets as you can think of.

Task 1

1 Load your spreadsheet package.

2 Enter the following data into the spreadsheet. You may need to widen the column for the package names.

SKILLS BUILDING

	A	B	C	D	E	F	G
1	Monthly sales of software for a computer shop						
2	Package	Net Price	VAT	Total Price	Number Sold	Total	
3	PageMaker	394			4		
4	Clipper	292			3		
5	Symphony	385			1		
6	Info Publisher	145			12		
7	AutoSketch	61			3		
8	Floorplan	129			2		
9	AutoCAD	373			10		
10	DBase 5	245			28		
11	Lotus 1-2-3	247			52		
12	CorelDraw!	415			27		
13	WordPerfect	214			58		
14	Wordstar	227			42		
15	Grammatik	33			12		
16	Excel	219			28		
17	Visual Basic	193			15		
18	Paradox	275			41		
19							
20							
21							
22							
23							

Figure 29.12

3 To work out the VAT at 17.5%, we can use a formula in cell c3. To calculate 17.5% of the net price we can use the formula VAT = net price × 17.5/100. To enter the formula into the spreadsheet at cell c3 we have to adapt the formula to read: +b3*17.5/100. When the formula is entered, the VAT is put automatically into the cell. The next formula is placed in cell c4 and would be +b4*17.5/100. In fact it would be very tedious to do this all the way down the column, so there is a way of copying the original formula, taking into account the slight change in cell positions. This is called replicating (or copying) a formula relatively. Find out how to do this for your spreadsheet package and complete the column.

4 We now need to add the VAT to the net price to give the total price. The formula +b3+c3 is placed in cell d3. This formula is then copied relatively down the column.

5 To work out the total amount, we multiply the total price by the number of items sold. Do this by placing the correct formula in cell f3 and copy this formula relatively down the column.

6 Save your spreadsheet, calling it MSALES.

7 Print your spreadsheet, trying to get all of it on a single page if you can.

Task 2

Last year Jordan Kung kept a record of his finances using a spreadsheet package. Figure 29.13 shows what his spreadsheet looked like at the end of the year.

	A	B	C	D	E	F	G	H	I	J
1	Month	Wage	Rent	Elect	Gas	Phone	Food	Car	Clothes	Hols
2	Jan	850	120	134.76			129.34	138.12	86.21	30
3	Feb	850	120			45.23	135.98	125.34	23.78	30
4	March	856	120		189.23		78.21	128	12.98	25
5	Apr	857	120				200.76	134	48.99	45
6	May	912	120	287.02			100.23	187.98	201.99	70
7	June	908	120			23.39	78.34	143.98	100.23	100
8	July	945	120		103.67		176.19	125.9	10.99	100
9	Aug	965	120				123.53	145.65	34.99	80
10	Sept	965	120	120.98			123.76	154.65	76.45	30
11	Oct	1000	120			56.99	109.01	200.07	230.12	10
12	Nov	987	120		100.05		165.45	167.95	201.76	10
13	Dec	1200	120				250.45	140.98	300.34	10

Figure 29.13

1 Start off with the heading 'Jordan Kung's income and expenses for the last year'. Type in the data exactly as it appears in Figure 29.13.

2 In the next empty column, insert the heading 'Expenses'. Expenses are the total amount of money that Jordan is spending each month. In this column total the January expenses on the January row.

3 Replicate this formula relatively down the column for February to December.

4 Using a formula, deduct the expenses for January from the wages for January and put this in the next empty column, under the column heading 'Balance'. This is the amount of money he had left.

5 Replicate this formula down the column for February to December.

6 Calculate the total income, expenditure and balance for the whole year. Put these in a suitable position on the spreadsheet.

7 Save your spreadsheet using a suitable filename.

8 Print your spreadsheet.

Task 3

The table shown in Figure 29.14 shows the number of calories you burn up when you do certain activities.

1 Enter this table into a spreadsheet (you will need to widen some of the columns).

2 Design a form to give to your friends to record the time spent doing the various activities during the day.

3 Design a method by which the spreadsheet could be used to work out the calories burnt by each of your friends per day.

4 Explain carefully, using printouts where appropriate, how you solved this problem. Mention any things you tried before you arrived at the final solution to this problem and explain why you discounted them.

Activity	Men	Women
Moderate cycling	256	192
Hard cycling	660	507
Domestic work	200	153
Ironing	160	120
Rowing	800	600
Moderate running	592	444
Hard running	900	692
Squash	600	461
Moderate swimming	300	200
Hard swimming	640	480
Tennis	448	336
Moderate walking	224	168

Figure 29.14 *Number of calories burnt when you do certain activities*

Chapter 30 *Desktop Publishing*

With the aid of desktop publishing software, people can produce high quality documents without having to go to a typesetter. This can save time and money.

Desktop publishing (DTP) can be used to produce pages that combine text and graphics (photographs and line drawings) for books, magazines, posters and leaflets. Different typefaces, or fonts can be used to add interest, and diagrams can be added, with the text flowing around them. Photographs can be scanned in and their size can be adjusted so that they fit in a particular position on a page. The only real limit is your own imagination.

Figure 30.1 shows examples of a poster and a brochure that have been produced using DTP. Figure 30.2 shows the types of document you can use desktop publishing for.

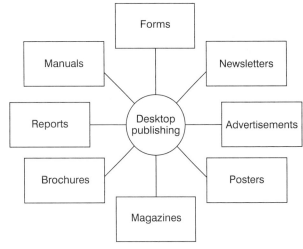

Figure 30.2 *Some of the documents you can produce using DTP*

Equipment needed
The computer
To work effectively with DTP packages you need a computer with a high specification, ideally with the largest amount of RAM (random access memory) and the highest capacity hard disk that can be afforded. DTP files consisting of text and pictures take up a lot of disk space. Ideally, either an IBM PC compatible or an Apple Macintosh computer is used.

A mouse
The mouse is one of the most important tools in desktop publishing. The mouse is moved around on the desk and it transmits the movement of your hand and fingers to the computer. Buttons on the mouse are pressed in order to make selections.

Desktop publishing software.
There is a variety of software available. If you require only simple features, then you may be able to buy a wordprocessing

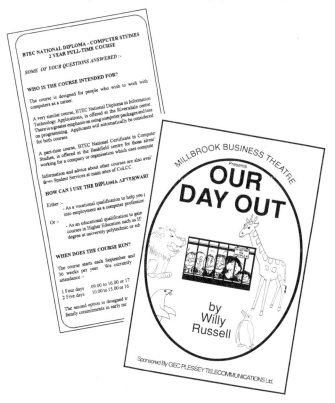

Figure 30.1 *Just two examples of DTP documents*

package which contains them. The more features you require, the more likely you are to need to buy specialist desktop publishing software.

The visual display unit

The monitor should be the largest that you can afford (usually larger than 14 inch which is the standard size) in order to avoid eyestrain. You often have to work with two pages on the screen at once, so the text can be quite small and difficult to read.

The printer

Either an ink-jet printer (cheaper) or a laser printer could be used to output DTP documents. A dot-matrix printer is unsuitable, because any black areas in the page vary in blackness when printed out, and dot matrix printers usually take a long time to print graphics pages.

The scanner

If you want to incorporate your own photographs or hand drawings into your documents, then you will need to use a scanner to scan them in. There are two types of optical scanner: for ordinary DTP use the cheaper hand-held scanner is shown in Figure 30.3 and the more expensive but better flat-bed scanner is shown in Figure 30.4. If you are using the scanner only now and again then the hand-held one would be best, although they do take some getting used to, since you have to move such a scanner across the photo or drawing at constant speed.

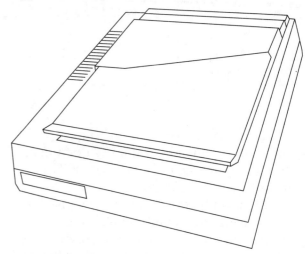

Figure 30.4 *The flat-bed scanner is easier to use but is more expensive*

Some features of desktop publishing

Figure 30.5 shows some of the features of DTP.

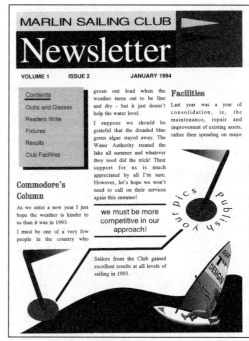

Figure 30.5 *Some of the features of DTP*

Columns

In wordprocessors you work in pages, but in DTP you will need to be able to work in both pages and columns. A look at a newspaper or magazine will show you how common the column format is.

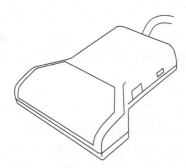

Figure 30.3 *A hand-held scanner*

Frame layout

Many DTP packages use a frame based system of layout. Here, text and graphics are placed in boxes called frames, which can be moved and repositioned around the pages. Some software, including one of the most popular packages, PageMaker, are, however, not frame based.

Embedded graphics

It is possible to place drawings and pictures in position and then to flow the text around them, as shown in Figure 30.6.

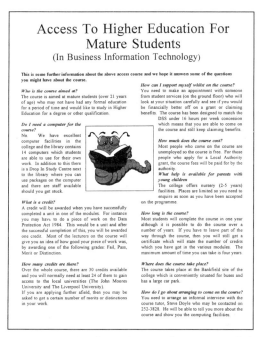

Figure 30.6 *Notice how the text flows around the diagram in this newsletter*

Templates

Templates are used to record certain properties of a document such as its page size, margins, headers (the space at the top) and footers (the space at the bottom). Templates usually also include styles and any standard text that will be included in all documents to be based on them.

Style sheets

Style sheets are used to help make the main text, headings and subheadings consistent. When you are choosing the fonts and type sizes for a DTP document, you can highlight each paragraph or heading in turn and select the typeface and size. However, if a document is to be consistent it is better and faster to set up style sheets and then to apply styles to the text.

Scaleable fonts

There are many fonts available in DTP packages and sometimes it is difficult to choose which one to use. It really depends on the type of document you are designing. Some fonts would not be used for business type documents but could be ideal for invitations to an 18th birthday party. A huge range of sizes is usually available for each font, varying from the very small to the very large. Font sizes are measured in points. One point is 1/72 of an inch.

Advantages of desktop publishing

Here are just a few of the many advantages of DTP, for preparing books, magazines, posters and leaflets, compared with word processing.

1 You have much more control over the way the text is laid out compared with an ordinary wordprocessor especially over the formatting and arrangement of text.
2 DTP can be used to bring lots of different files together on the same document.
3 DTP may be used to produce the output in a certain way so that the material can be professionally printed, if required. This is usually done if you want the pamphlet, leaflet etc. to be in colour. If your work is going to be output professionally, then you will need to make sure that you use one of the major DTP packages such as Quark Xpress or PageMaker.

When to use a DTP package

Modern packages are so full of features that it is difficult to choose software. Wordprocessors have some DTP facilities, and some graphics packages can be used to produce simple posters and leaflets. For a simple poster, like the one shown in Figure 30.7, you will probably find that a graphics package is the easiest one to use.

Figure 30.7 *Poster designed using a graphics package*

As far as your coursework is concerned, you need to decide which type of package to use. You have to give reasons why you choose a type of software for a particular job (e.g. why you might choose a DTP rather than a wordprocessing or graphics package). The reason could simply be that the task couldn't be performed with the other two or it could be that you found the DTP package was better suited to the job.

DTP acts as an integrator because with this software you can bring many different files together into the same document. You can bring in text from a wordprocessor, graphics from a painting or drawing package, images from a scanner, frames from a video grabber and stills from a camera. Figure 30.8 illustrates this.

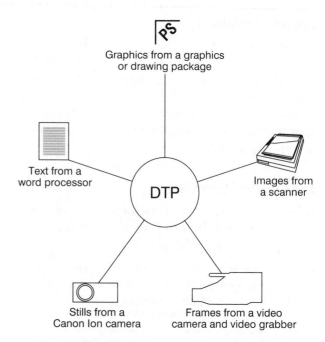

Figure 30.8 *DTP acts as an integrator, bringing lots of different files together*

Basic techniques used in DTP

Here is a list of some of the basic techniques used in desktop publishing.

Page set up

The first step in preparing a DTP document is often to specify the size of the pages and whether they are to be in portrait or landscape format (see Figure 30.9). The second step in setting up the page is to decide on the number of columns.

The column guides make the text word-wrap to the columns automatically. It is

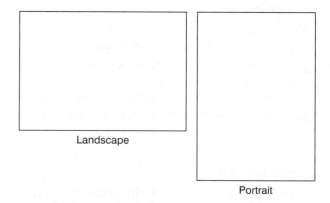

Figure 30.9 *Pages arranged in landscape and portrait formats*

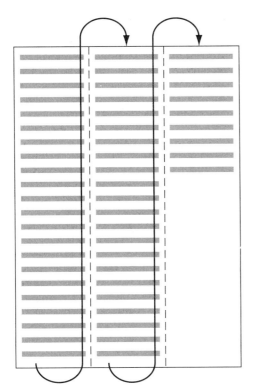

Figure 30.10 *Snaking using three newspaper-style columns*

rather like wordprocessing in a single column. Figure 30.10 shows snaking, where, once one column is filled, the text automatically flows to the top of the next column.

Typing text

Most DTP packages allow you to type text directly into them, but you may find it easier to use a wordprocessor to do your typing and then import the files into the DTP package. Wordprocessors tend to have more facilities such as spell checkers and thesauruses and they are often quicker to type into.

Placing text

When you import text you can decide in which of the columns the text should be placed.

Placing graphics

When you import graphics you need to decide on the graphics you will be using and their position on the page. It is possible to place a blank area around a drawing or photograph so that the text cannot flow too close to the drawing or photograph.

Sizing and cropping graphics

Cropping means removing part of a picture by cutting off and discarding the part that is not needed. For instance, in a photograph of a group of people scanned in with a scanner, you might want to include only one of the people. You could crop the picture and leave just the required part. This part could then be resized to fit the space available.

Drawing lines and boxes

You can make your text stand out more by placing it in a box. Sometimes it is possible to choose different designs for the box and to have, for instance, shading around the box.

Glossary of terms used in desktop publishing

Bold text   Text in heavy type.
Bullet   A symbol placed before a paragraph in a list to make the paragraph stand out.
Clip art   A library of artwork you can choose to put into your documents.
Clipboard   A temporary storage place for text, frames or pictures which have been cut or copied.
Crop   Selecting part of the image and removing the rest.
Cut   Removing an area containing text or a picture and placing it on the clipboard.
Font   A complete set of characters of the same design, style and point size.
Frame   A rectangular box in which you can place text, pictures or graphics.
Header   The line of text included at the top of every page.
Import   To load text or pictures created by a different package.
Italics   Text that slants to the right; the characters are a different shape.
Justified   Text that is aligned with the right and left margins.

Kerning The process of adjusting the spacing between the characters.

Leader This is usually a row of dots to guide the reader across the page in, for example, a table of contents.

Paste The process of inserting the contents of the clipboard into a document.

Template The master page and paragraph styles for a given document.

TIFF A special file format used for images.

WYSIWYG Stands for 'what you see is what you get'. You see on the screen exactly what will be printed out.

THINGS TO DO

1 (a) With DTP packages, text can be imported from a wordprocessing package.

    (i) What does the abbreviation DTP stand for?

    (ii) Explain, in simple terms, what the above sentence means.

  (b) Pupils in your school are going to produce a school newsletter which will be produced using desktop publishing.

    (i) Give three items of hardware which they might use apart from the computer (i.e. apart from the CPU, keyboard, VDU and mouse).

    (ii) Give reasons for your choices in (b)(i).

2 Why is it important to use a large VDU if you are working on DTP packages all the time?

3 Describe fully the features which would be desirable in a desktop publishing package for it to be used to prepare a high quality school prospectus. State clearly why each of the features is necessary.

(NEAB/WJEC Spec Option R)

4 In order to advertise the Xmas fayre, the secretary created the poster in Figure 30.11 using her wordprocessor:

XMAS FAYRE

Come and
visit
Santa

At
Middlebrige School

Sat. December 2nd 1995
2.00 p.m. start

Figure 30.11

XMAS FAYRE

Come and
visit
Santa!

At
Middlebrige School
Sat. December 4th 1993
2.00p.m. start

Figure 30.12

To improve the appearance of this poster, it was decided to use a desktop publishing package and the resulting poster is shown in Figure 30.12.

  (a) Describe the changes to the poster which have been made by using the desktop publishing package.

  (b) Explain how you could have created such a poster using your desktop publishing package.

(NEAB/WJEC Spec Option Q)

5 Figure 30.13 shows an advertisement for a Canon Ion camera. The advert itself was produced using desktop publishing software. Read the advertisement carefully and then answer the following questions.

Figure 30.13 *Advertisement for a Canon Ion camera*

(a) The Canon Ion camera looks like an ordinary camera but uses a disk rather than a film.

  (i) What main advantage does the Ion camera have over a conventional camera?

  (ii) What disadvantages might it have?

(b) This camera is used by some schools to take photographs. The photographs are then imported into a desktop publishing package.

  (i) Give an example of a situation where you might want a photograph rather than a drawing in a document.

  (ii) A school buys a camera to take a picture of each pupil in the school and then imports the photos into the pupil database. Why might it be useful for the school to have a photograph of each pupil in its database?

(c) Now look at the Canon Ion advert from the DTP point of view.

  (i) How many different fonts have been used in the advertisement?

  (ii) How many boxes have been used?

  (iii) At the top of the page there is a photograph of the Ion camera. When it was on the screen it was a lot clearer than when it is printed out. Why is this?

Importing text into a DTP package

Here is a piece of text which you should type in exactly as it appears here.

```
Basically a DTP package in its simplest form, allows you to deal with
graphics and text at the same time. Usually, a DTP package has some
wordprocessing and graphics facilities but they are never as comprehensive
as the facilities in the separate packages. Some DTP packages may contain
a spell checker. This is very useful to make sure that you don't produce
posters with spelling mistakes that everyone else spots except you.
```

A feature of a DTP package is its ability to import text from a wordprocessing package. Using your DTP package import the text you have just typed into your wordprocessor.

Choosing the right font

Selecting the right font is very important in DTP work. For each of the following, choose a suitable font and then use your DTP package to type the relevant sentence in the font you have chosen:

- an invitation to a party
- a poster for a disco to be held in your school hall
- an advertisement for a new restaurant or pub
- a menu for a wedding
- an advertisement for a new car
- an invitation to a mediaeval night at a local castle.

DTP skills

Here is a series of tasks you could have to carry out when doing project work in IT, IS or other subjects:

- select pictures or photographs from a CD-ROM and place them in separate files
- type in the text to go with the artwork on your wordprocessor
- load the pictures into your DTP package and adjust them if necessary
- load the text from the wordprocessor and make it flow around the artwork.

Try to do the above tasks using the software and hardware you have available.

Take a look at a leaflet or poster. Look at it from the DTP point of view (choose one that is not too complicated).

- How many different fonts have been used and why have they been selected?
- How many sizes of type have been used?
- Does the text flow around any diagrams or photographs?
- Has any clip art been used?

Your company is a rapidly expanding mail-order company that sells aquarium equipment from adverts placed in specialist fish keeping magazines. You have been asked to investigate desktop publishing for your company and produce a report on its value.

In your report you should include the following along with any other material you think is important:

- what DTP is (is it hardware or software or a combination of the two)
- the minimum equipment for running DTP
- any additional equipment which might be useful, e.g. scanners

- how DTP is different from a sophisticated wordprocessing package such as WordPerfect
- what an average DTP package can do
- what packages are available, how much do they cost, which one you think is the best and why.

Your local police station wishes to crack down on crime. It wishes to draw people's attention to crime prevention. The police have asked you to produce some fact sheets and posters with hard-hitting messages on crime prevention. To help you with this you could try to get hold of crime statistics and incorporate these into your material.

The information technology co-ordinator in your school has been asked by the headteacher to run an 'Introduction To Computers' course on a Tuesday evening. The course is to start on Tuesday 12th September between 6 p.m. and 9 p.m. and will run for 30 weeks. The cost of the course is £75.

The course is practically based and covers:

- wordprocessing
- databases
- spreadsheets
- graphics
- desktop publishing.

You have been asked to produce a desktop-published leaflet that can be placed in local libraries, supermarkets, etc. advertising the course.

All the essential course information needs to be included and it is decided that a map showing where the school is should also be included.

Chapter 31

Database Coursework

Before looking at this coursework chapter it would be a good idea to refresh you memory on the contents of Chapter 9 'How Data Is Stored'. In this chapter some of the database concepts and terms are explained. In particular you should understand the terms file, record and field and you should be able to design a record.

Creating a database

Before creating a database, you first have to give some thought to its structure. To help you, here is a list of steps which should be taken.

1   Decide on which fields you need and write them down as a list. Then put your list into order of importance, with the most important field at the top (n.b. the most important field is usually the key field).
2   Give each field a suitable fieldname. The fieldnames do not have to be the same as in step 1 and you will probably want to abbreviate the longer ones. Make sure that, when you are describing your system, you mention what the various abbreviations mean. Also, try not to make the fieldnames too long, since they will have to be typed in when you are performing searches.
3   Decide on the field types. This is whether they are numeric, character, date or logical fields.
4   Decide on the field lengths. A sample of the data you are going to put into the database will reveal how many characters long each field needs to be.

Sometimes you will need several databases. For instance, for a system to be used in a video library, there would be three:

- a member database to hold all the members' details such as name, address, etc.
- a video database, to hold details of the videos kept by the library, such as title, price, etc.
- a rental database to hold the details of the rentals, such as the video number, member's number and date borrowed.

We will now look at a problem and see how we can design a database to provide a solution to the problem.

The problem

Widgets Ltd is a small manufacturing company employing around 40 staff. The company has its head office in Chester and this is where most of the administration work is done. At the head office there is a personnel department which keeps information on all the staff. At the moment, although other departments make use of computers, the personnel department still keeps manual records of all staff in a series of filing cabinets.

There are various problems with the manual system and these are:

- files can take a long time to find, especially if someone has put them back in the wrong place
- to answer questions such as 'How many women do we employ under 20 years old?' would involve looking at every file and then calculating everyone's age from their date of birth; doing this could take a long time
- files need to be kept about ex-employees in case they want a reference in the future. The filing cabinets are taking up more and more space.

Research

A questionnaire has been sent to all the members of the personnel department asking them about the sort of information that they frequently need to know about the employees.

Interviews with the staff who will be using the system and the results of a questionnaire filled in by staff revealed that the following information was necessary for each member of staff:

- surname
- forename
- title
- first line of address
- second line of address
- third line of address
- postcode
- home phone number
- date of birth
- date the member of staff started with the company
- job department the staff member is in (i.e. production, sales, accounts, etc.)
- job grade (each job is given a grade from 1 to 5: grade 1 is the highest level of responsibility)
- job salary (how much each staff member earns per year before deductions)
- job hours (how many hours per week each staff member is contracted to work)
- days off work sick so far this year
- National Insurance Number
- holidays total (the number of days holiday entitled to)
- holidays taken (number of days taken this year).

We now need to decide on the field names that we are going to use for the above and the type of data that will be in each field (i.e. numeric, character (sometimes called text,) etc.) and also the number of characters or numbers in each field.

QUESTION

What would be the best way of determining the width of the fields for the above data?

After careful examination of the manual records to make sure that the field lengths are adequate and the type of field is correct, the following structure was developed.

Num	Field Name	Field Type	Width	Dec
1	EMPLOYEE_NO	Character	4	0
2	SURNAME	Character	30	
3	FORENAME	Character	20	
4	TITLE	Character	4	
5	ADD1	Character	30	
6	ADD2	Character	30	
7	ADD3	Character	30	
8	PCODE	Character	9	
9	HPHONE	Character	13	
10	DOB	Date	6	
11	START_DATE	Date	6	
12	JOB_DEPT	Character	10	
13	JOB_GRADE	Numeric	10	
14	JOB_SALARY	Numeric	8	2
15	JOB_HOURS	Numeric	2	0
16	DAYS_SICK	Numeric	3	1
17	NAT_INS_NO	Character	1	5
18	HOLS_TOTAL	Numeric	2	1
19	HOLS_TAKEN	Numeric	2	1

Figure 31.1 *Database structure*

At this stage it is not too important to get the structure exactly right since, in our example, a database program is being used where it is possible to go back and change the structure even after data has been entered. Ask you teacher if you can do this with the database software you are using.

TASK

1 Load your database program.
2 Create a new database, calling it Person.
3 Set up the structure set out in the table in Figure 31.1.
4 Save your structure.
5 Print a copy of your structure.

Putting data into the database

Once the structure has been set up, the data may be put into the database. This usually involves typing the data into the database using the keyboard but this isn't the only method. If the equipment is available, you could scan data in.

Widget PLC has decided to type the data in. A list of some of the employees is in Figure 31.2.

N.B.: You need to decide on the format of the data you are going to type in. It is probably best to use capital letters for the start of a word and then small letters for the rest of the word.

TASK

Produce a list of all the records in the database and verify them by checking that they are identical to the list in Figure 31.2. Make the corrections if necessary.

EMPLOYEE_NO	0001	0002	0003
SURNAME	Gregson	Dawkins	Prescott
FORENAME	Margaret	Steven	Simon
TITLE	Miss	Mr	Dr
ADD1	12 Wood Lane	3 River Road	The Verlands
ADD2	West Derby	Aintree	Warren Road
ADD3	Liverpool	Liverpool	Liverpool
PCODE	L13 8BQ	L9 4HG	L23 3ED
HPHONE	0151-252-3542	0151-525-0999	0151-924-0008
DOB	12/12/41	01/03/46	01/07/54
START_DATE	01/03/61	03/09/87	05/05/82
JOB_DEPT	Production	Sales	Production
JOB_GRADE	2	3	1
JOB_SALARY	14800	12300	28500
JOB_HOURS	35	35	35
DAYS_SICK	0	03	07
NAT_INS_NO	YY432512D	YY346523E	FX208974R
HOLS_TOTAL	28	28	30
HOLS_TAKEN	09	07	21

EMPLOYEE_NO	0004	0005	0006
SURNAME	McGinley	Ahmed	Johnston
FORENAME	Stuart	John	Mark
TITLE	Mr	Mr	Mr
ADD1	3 Robin Close	12 Moor Lane	5 Forrest Court
ADD2	West Derby	Waterloo	Crosby
ADD3	Liverpool	Liverpool	Liverpool
PCODE	L13 9MM	L22 6RT	L23 5RR
HPHONE	0151-252-6875	0151-928-8732	0151-924-7865
DOB	12/04/65	12/05/70	01/02/69
START_DATE	07/01/82	12/11/94	10/12/75
JOB_DEPT	Production	Sales	Accounts
JOB_GRADE	5	3	4
JOB_SALARY	4800	6700	7100
JOB_HOURS	40	40	40
DAYS_SICK	14	21	05
NAT_INS_NO	SD453623G	GH346512Y	HJ901834K
HOLS_TOTAL	28	28	28
HOLS_TAKEN	05	10	26

EMPLOYEE_NO	0007	0008	0009
SURNAME	Hughes	Sumner	George
FORENAME	Julie	Suzanne	Julie
TITLE	Mrs	Miss	Mrs
ADD1	5 Orchard Hey	2 Ocean View	The Coach House
ADD2	Maghull		Blundellsands Hesketh Bank
ADD3	Liverpool	Liverpool	Southport
PCODE	L31 8AF	L23 8TT	PR8 9YT
HPHONE	0151-520-8100	0151-931-6534	01704-12776
DOB	03/07/50	26/10/69	07/01/65
START_DATE	09/10/66	03/06/87	02/08/78
JOB_DEPT	Admin	Admin	Accounts
JOB_GRADE	2	5	1
JOB_SALARY	14500	6300	20500
JOB_HOURS	35	40	35
DAYS_SICK	01	0	08
NAT_INS_NO	YY872322P	TT765323U	FF983203P
HOLS_TOTAL	35	28	35
HOLS_TAKEN	20	06	23

EMPLOYEE_NO	0010	0011	0012
SURNAME	Murphy	Davies	Jones
FORENAME	Sean	Paul	Samantha
TITLE	Mr	Mr	Miss
ADD1	12 Bewley Road	12 King Street	54 Moor Drive
ADD2	Kirkby	Wavertree	Hesketh Bank
ADD3	Liverpool	Liverpool	Southport
PCODE	L13 7YY	L17 8UU	PR5 9YU
HPHONE	0151-531-9089	0151-342-7765	01704-34223
DOB	01/02/55	30/12/53	25/02/40
START_DATE	09/03/88	23/11/70	23/05/66
JOB_DEPT	Sales	Production	Sales
JOB_GRADE	3	4	1
JOB_SALARY	12300	18000	28900
JOB_HOURS	30	35	35
DAYS_SICK	12	09	0
NAT_INS_NO	WW769000T	RR600004T	YY454672K
HOLS_TOTAL	28	35	35
HOLS_TAKEN	10	21	24

EMPLOYEE_NO	0013	0014	0015
SURNAME	Flynn	Jones	Jones
FORENAME	James	Debbie	Julie
TITLE	Mr	Ms	Miss
ADD1	2 Copy Lane	5 Bellair Ave	5 Bellair Ave
ADD2	Maghull	Aintree	Aintree
ADD3	Liverpool	Liverpool	Liverpool
PCODE	L31 9KJ	L9 7HH	L9 7HH
HPHONE	0151-531-0009	0151-534-4566	0151-534-4566
DOB	12/11/50	27/09/70	30/01/73
START_DATE	09/12/69	12/12/94	03/04/90
JOB_DEPT	Production	Marketing	Admin
JOB_GRADE	2	2	3
JOB_SALARY	19000	21000	14500
JOB_HOURS	40	35	35
DAYS_SICK	12	03	08
NAT_INS_NO	TT231276F	RT900078Y	RO679797G
HOLS_TOTAL	28	35	28
HOLS_TAKEN	13	28	14

Figure 31.2 *Part A*

FIELD						
EMPLOYEE_NO	0016	0017	0018	0025	0026	0027
SURNAME	Dewer	Stephenson	Ho	Sinnot	Jones	Rowlands
FORENAME	Alison	Carl	Michael	Jackie	Gareth	Julie
TITLE	Miss	Mr	Mr	Mrs	Mr	Miss
ADD1	5 Cobley Court	4 Moor Drive	6 Pit Street	23 Osbert Road	2 Firs Close	3 Blandford Road
ADD2	Wavertree	Crosby	Everton	Blundellsands	Formby	Ainsdale
ADD3	Liverpool	Liverpool	Liverpool	Liverpool	Liverpool	Southport
PCODE	L24 6FT	L23 6HH	L12 6TT	L23 8GY	L34 5TR	PR4 5DS
HPHONE	0151-675-8900	0151-924-5565	0151-253-9000	0151-924-7322	01704-98899	01704-11223
DOB	03/11/67	01/08/40	30/09/48	01/11/37	27/08/48	30/09/49
START_DATE	01/05/81	04/09/89	23/08/76	12/02/79	12/12/71	12/12/71
JOB_DEPT	Sales	Admin	Accounts	Production	Sales	Admin
JOB_GRADE	5	4	5	2	4	2
JOB_SALARY	3400	5200	2800	4700	14500	17000
JOB_HOURS	25	25	15	15	40	35
DAYS_SICK	02	02	03	0	07	10
NAT_INS_NO	YY909076G	HH897678R	GG878789U	TH435200T	YY767678R	FT090976R
HOLS_TOTAL	20	20	15	12	35	35
HOLS_TAKEN	17	08	07	03	12	10

FIELD						
EMPLOYEE_NO	0019	0020	0021	0028	0029	0030
SURNAME	Johnston	Stuart	John	Doyle	Doyle	Smith
FORENAME	Mark	South	Jones	Norma	Ruth	Tony
TITLE	Mr	Mr	Mr	Mrs	Miss	Mr
ADD1	5 Hart Street	5 Fir Crescent	4 South Road	5 Trevor Drive	5 Trevor Drive	4 Bridge Road
ADD2	Formby	Southport	Waterloo	Crosby	Crosby	Waterloo
ADD3	Merseyside	Merseyside	Liverpool	Liverpool	Liverpool	Liverpool
PCODE	L45 8MM	L34 5TT	L22 6GG	L23 6GT	L23 6GT	L22 6GG
HPHONE	01704-45464	01704-67738	0151-928-0088	0151-924-8989	0151-924-8989	0151-924-8767
DOB	31/01/45	09/01/43	03/05/75	02/05/52	03/10/70	01/02/47
START_DATE	02/09/69	02/09/69	01/02/94	03/01/71	18/09/87	05/05/94
JOB_DEPT	Production	Production	Sales	Sales	Production	Admin
JOB_GRADE	2	2	5	5	3	5
JOB_SALARY	18700	19000	3900	5900	6500	7800
JOB_HOURS	35	35	27	25	30	30
DAYS_SICK	10	09	10	0	0	9
NAT_INS_NO	WW352920R	YY875658T	HJ870020G	GG902323R	HJ880213F	DE562376S
HOLS_TOTAL	28	28	28	15	25	35
HOLS_TAKEN	14	09	10	10	12	13

FIELD						
EMPLOYEE_NO	0022	0023	0024	0031	0032	0033
SURNAME	Wong	Owens	Hughes	Snell	Peat	Farley
FORENAME	Christine	Susan	Stephen	Peter	Fred	John
TITLE	Miss	Mrs	Mr	Mr	Mr	Mr
ADD1	23a Devon Close	54 Wood Street	5 Rotten Row	2 The Close	5 Geraints Way	2 Channel View
ADD2	Walton	Aintree	Southport	Seaforth	Waterloo	Thornton
ADD3	Liverpool	Liverpool	Merseyside	Liverpool	Liverpool	Liverpool
PCODE	L14 6TR	L9 8HY	L65 6YY	L21 5RR	L22 6RD	L18 5FF
HPHONE	0151-525-3123	0151-523-0099	01704-78222	0151-931-2121	0151-928-0078	0151-924-7923
DOB	12/07/69	25/09/39	15/09/36	19/03/49	13/12/40	01/04/67
START_DATE	03/06/89	09/06/88	07/07/69	17/04/71	15/05/72	12/12/94
JOB_DEPT	Sales	Marketing	Accounts	Production	Marketing	Production
JOB_GRADE	3	1	1	2	2	2
JOB_SALARY	15000	29000	38000	16000	14800	16300
JOB_HOURS	35	35	28	40	35	40
DAYS_SICK	09	01	08	03	09	10
NAT_INS_NO	GS676799K	WW780367F	GG566658L	RR234237T	QQ545454Y	TG090988T
HOLS_TOTAL	35	35	40	35	35	35
HOLS_TAKEN	23	30	12	12	21	18

Figure 31.2 *Part B*

EMPLOYEE_NO	0034	0035	0036	EMPLOYEE_NO	0037	0038	0039
SURNAME	Jackson	Low	Crowther	SURNAME	Jenkins	Pauling	Smith
FORENAME	Roy	Jane	Louise	FORENAME	Sheila	Jenny	Carol
TITLE	Mr	Mrs	Ms	TITLE	Mrs	Mrs	Ms
ADD1	3 Crane Street	5 Hart Street	45 Park Lane	ADD1	2 Cobham Road	3 Belham Road	32 The Byway
ADD2	Wavertree	Seaforth	Kirkby	ADD2	West Derby	Thornton	Crosby
ADD3	Liverpool	Liverpool	Liverpool	ADD3	Liverpool	Liverpool	Liverpool
PCODE	L13 5FD	L21 5RE	L31 4AS	PCODE	L13 8HU	L23 6TH	L23 4FR
HPHONE				HPHONE	0151-252-3409	0151-924-6512	0151-924-0071
DOB	12/12/54	16/01/65	12/09/76	DOB	30/09/50	27/02/51	29/04/61
START_DATE	15/01/95	17/01/95	08/05/95	START_DATE	12/10/71	13/12/75	10/02/93
JOB_DEPT	Production	Sales	Admin	JOB_DEPT	Personnel	Marketing	Production
JOB_GRADE	3	4	4	JOB_GRADE	1	2	1
JOB_SALARY	12300	8900	9550	JOB_SALARY	20500	17500	23000
JOB_HOURS	35	35	35	JOB_HOURS	35	35	35
DAYS_SICK	0	0	03	DAYS_SICK	4	0	0
NAT_INS_NO	YY354323C	CC676741V	FR566643D	NAT_INS_NO	FF342345R	HK090945R	JH890148F
HOLS_TOTAL	28	35	28	HOLS_TOTAL	28	28	28
HOLS_TAKEN	12	05	00	HOLS_TAKEN	28	15	28

Figure 31.2 *Part C*

Data verification

Data verification is a pre-input check to make sure that what is on a form is exactly what goes into the database. For the personnel database, it is a question of proof reading each record on the screen to check that it is exactly the same as what is on the form.

Data validation

Validation checks are checks that the database performs to make sure that the data is allowable. Databases will not allow you to put letters into a field which you have specified as numeric. Validation is performed by the actual database software.

QUESTION

A person tries to type a number into a field that has been specified as a character field. Will the computer accept it?

Using the database
Queries

Performing a query is sometimes referred to as searching or interrogating a database. Basically this involves extracting information from the database. For instance, you could make a request of the database to list the details of all personnel over a certain age.

Suppose we don't want a list of every field in the database but only wanted a list of surnames and addresses, we could issue a command such as:

LIST SURNAME, ADD1, ADD2, ADD3, PCODE

Notice the list of the required fields after the LIST command.

TASKS

Write commands that would enable you to list the following fields (n.b. if your database commands are different, then use them):

1 a list of surnames, job departments and salaries for all employees
2 a list of surnames, their holiday totals and their holidays taken
3 a list of all employees' surnames, forenames and home telephone numbers.

Using search conditions

You may not want all the specified fields for each person to be listed. For example, you may just need the details on people in a certain department.

Suppose you wanted the surnames and salaries of the personnel in the production department. We could use a command similar to this;

LIST SURNAME, JOB_SALARY FOR
JOB_DEPT = "Production"

Or, you might want to list the employee
number, surname and job department for all
employees earning over £15 000. You could
use a command like this;

LIST EMPLOYEE_NO, SURNAME,
JOB_DEPT FOR JOB_SALARY > 15000

Note that > is the symbol meaning greater
than.

TASKS

Write commands to perform the following searches
and check that they work by producing a printout
from the personnel database:

(a) the employee number, surname and
department of staff working under 20 hours

(b) the names and addresses of all staff in the sales
department

(c) the names and addresses of all the male
employees (note you will need to think about
how to do this)

(d) the surname, job department and grade of all
the staff who have taken no time off sick

(e) the names, job departments and dates of birth
of all staff who joined the company after 1/1/86.

Combining conditions

You can combine conditions using AND, OR
and NOT. If you wanted to search the database
for members of the production department
who earned over £20 000 you could issue a
command similar to the following:

LIST SURNAME, JOB_SALARY,
NAT_INS_NO FOR JOB_DEPT
="Production".AND. JOB_SALARY
>20000

If you wanted a list including people in the
production department earning £20 000
exactly you would replace the last part
>20000 by =20000.

Notice also that JOB_SALARY is a
numeric field and you do not put inverted
commas around the number. Inverted commas
are placed only around character fields.

Adding new records to the database

Following expansion of the company, three
new employees have been taken on. Add
information about these to the database (n.b.
this process of adding records to an existing
database is called appending the database).

EMPLOYEE_NO	0037	0038	0039
SURNAME	Kent	Marshall	Hall
FORENAME	Colin	John	Peter
TITLE	Mr	Mr	Mr
ADD1	3 Hall Road	10 The Close	5 Bows Lane
ADD2	Seaforth	Thornton	Crosby
ADD3	Liverpool	Liverpool	Liverpool
PCODE	L20 9YU	L23 6RT	L23 5FD
HPHONE	0151-928-0087	0151-924-4546	0151-924-8976
DOB	30/09/49	20/10/43	21/09/57
START_DATE	10/03/78	11/12/45	12/12/56
JOB_DEPT	Production	Admin	Personnel
JOB_GRADE	5	4	5
JOB_SALARY	9000	11000	8500
JOB_HOURS	40	35	35
DAYS_SICK	0	0	0
NAT_INS_NO	FR232355H	GF802023F	HJ651023L
HOLS_TOTAL	28	28	28
HOLS_TAKEN	0	0	0

Deleting records

Julie Hughes and Steven Dawkins have left
the company so their records need removing
from the database. Perform this task and
then explain how you did it.

Amending the database

Following the annual review of staff
performance, the following staff have been
promoted:

• Suzanne Sumner is now grade 3 and has a
new salary of £8500
• Sean Murphy is now grade 2 and has a
new salary of £14 700
• Margaret Gregson is now grade 1 and has
a new salary of £17 800.

Also, the following amendments need to be
made to staff records:

• Miss Margaret Gregson now becomes Mrs
Margaret Hewitt
• John Ahmed has moved to the following
address: 15 Forefield Road, Aintree,
Liverpool, L9 7ET Phone 0151-546-2111.

It is the end of the month, so the holiday

and days off sick records need amending. The following people have been sick or taken days off.

	Holidays taken this month	Days off sick this month
Sean Murphy	1	2
Margaret Gregson	5	
Simon Prescott	7	
Mark Johnston	2	
Stuart McGinley	1	3

Make all of the above amendments to your database.

QUESTION

How can the personnel department be sure that the personnel records are up-to-date?

Sorting and indexing

Sorting

Suppose we want to sort the personnel database into alphabetical order according to SURNAME. We could use the SORT command. With the SORT command a new file is produced which has the same contents as the original file but in a different order. Using the SORT command is quick but has the disadvantage that a new file is produced which takes up as much disk space as the original. Performing several sorts using a large database could mean that you could run out of disk space.

Using SORT you can usually sort on only one field. To sort a file into alphabetical order according to SURNAME you can use a command similar to this:

SORT ON SURNAME TO S1

N.B. SURNAME is the field we are sorting and S1 is the file name we are giving to the new sorted database.

Indexing

Each record in a database is given a record number by the computer. This is not the same as the EMPLOYEE_NO. The record

TASKS

Using the personnel database do the following:

1 Sort the file into alphabetical order according to SURNAME. Produce a printout showing the fields SURNAME and EMPLOYEE_NO to check that the sort has taken place.

2 Sort the file according to JOB_SALARY, with the personnel earning the most money at the start of the file (n.b. it is possible to sort in ascending or descending order; in this case it will be in descending order).

number is used to produce an index. Let's look at the first five records of the file.

Record number	SURNAME	FORENAME
1	Gregson	Margaret
2	Dawkins	Steven
3	Prescott	Simon
4	McGinley	Stuart
5	Ahmed	John

If these were to be placed in alphabetical order according to SURNAME the record numbers would need to be in the order 5, 2, 1, 4, 3. These record numbers are contained in an index and when displaying or printing out the list the computer uses this index to put things in the correct order. Indexing has the advantage that it does not eat up disk space, since only the index and the original database need storing.

Not all databases have an index facility. Check with you teacher so see if yours has.

You can index on a main, primary field and then have another secondary index. So you could have employees in departmental order and then in alphabetical order of surname within each department.

TASK

Produce a list of personnel in alphabetical order according to surname:

(a) using a SORT

(b) using an INDEX, if your database can do this.

Forms and screens

Forms, or screen designs as they are often called, are used to allow the user to type data into the system. You can design boxes on the screen where the user can type in the data.

Reports

Reports are summaries of the data held on a database. They have a date and title, and contain neat columns of data. Reports are usually printed on paper.

Labels

Some databases allow you to print names and addresses from your database on self-adhesive labels to be used for mail shots. Some systems also allow the production of barcodes from the data in the database.

Comma separated variables

The file shown below, consisting of names and addresses, has been typed into a wordprocessor. Each of the items of data enclosed between quotes and separated by commas can be transferred directly to a database and the items correspond to the fields in the database. We can therefore export the data from the wordprocessor and import it into the database.

> "Stephen","Doyle","12 Bancroft
> Rd","Crosby","Liverpool","L23 4ER"
> "Norma","Prescott","3 Forest
> Rd","Formby","Merseyside","L31 OBQ"
> "Jim","Jones","3 Foregarden
> Ave","Waterloo","Liverpool","L22 4RR"
> "Frank","Moor","123 Edge
> Lane","Prescott","Merseyside","L13 5SE"

Comma separated variables, sometimes called comma delimited variables are often used for merging data from a database into the gaps in a standard letter. This is called a mail merge.

If you are using an integrated package (i.e. one with a database, spreadsheet and wordprocessor all in one) then you will find the transfer of the data between the modules a lot easier.

Creating an information system using a database

The problem

To create an information system we must start with a problem to be solved. It may be that there is a manual system that needs replacing or it may be that an existing computer system is inadequate and needs improvement. For either of these, the processes involved in the design and implementation of a system are the same. It is very important to make a careful choice of the problem to be solved. If it is too ambitious then it will be hard to satisfy the assessment objectives and if it is too simple then all the objectives will probably not be met.

Always choose a topic that interests you or something you can find information about easily. Use friends or relatives to come up with problems they might encounter in their jobs. Often, the better projects are real projects that have been developed for an actual problem.

Make sure that the school or college has the equipment available to enable you to perform your project and that you will have enough time to complete it.

Initially you will be asked for a statement of the problem. Before stating what the problem is, it is best to write a short passage on the background of the organisation involved.

Research

If you are basing your project around an actual company or organisation, then you will need to find out about what it does and how it is done. The best way to do this is to produce a questionnaire (wordprocessed of course) and send it to your contact in the organisation concerned. When you get this back read it carefully and write down a list of interview questions which come to light from the questionnaire.

Try to arrange to see the potential users of your system.

Description of the existing system

1 The existing system

A description of the existing system along with its strengths and weaknesses should be included. Any manual documents should be copied and diagrams should be drawn to illustrate the flow of paperwork for the administrative procedures.

2 User requirements

The users will be more familiar with the problem to be solved than you will be, so it is important to ask them about the input, output and processing. Since you will be regarded as being more knowledgeable about what is technically possible, you should be able to make suggestions.

3 Constraints

The usual constraints of time and money always apply. Too much time may be needed to develop the new system or project. The user will need to be convinced that the benefits of the new system outweigh the costs of its introduction. For instance, the large volume of data that would need to be keyed in might prohibit the use of a large database. Alternative input methods such as barcoding and OCR could be looked into as an alternative to keying in.

4 The social implications of a new system

An appreciation of the effect of the new system on the work force should be considered. Many employees will be naturally sceptical about a new system. You will need to have some answers to their fears.

System design

An alternative system (alternative to the original) should be developed, bearing in mind the constraints, that will do as many of the things suggested by the user and yourself. Sometimes, there may be several ways of solving the problem. Bear in mind that the best solution to a particular problem isn't always the one that is chosen and that the choice is nearly always a compromise.

When designing your system you need to mention the following.

- Explain how the proposed system works, using diagrams rather than text wherever possible. The diagrams should include system flowcharts and structure diagrams.
- Hardware and software requirements should be outlined with reasons for their choice.
- Show how features have been designed. For instance, with a database you would need to mention how you arrived at the structure or with a spreadsheet you would mention how the format you have adopted was arrived at.
- Input and output need to be considered. Here you should look at the most appropriate form for the input and output. Methods of data capture can be included, along with the reasons for their choice.
- Information is needed about the choice of storage media along with justification.

Implementation

You need to give information about the implementation of a system, including:

- the method of implementation along with the reason for its choice (e.g. step-by-step, parallel running, etc.)
- how existing files are to be changed to the new file format, including how data will be keyed in (or the use of alternative methods such as OCR)
- how the new hardware and software are to be installed
- how the people who will be using the new system will be trained
- how the new system will be maintained – what needs to be done and how often in order to keep the system up-to-date
- the social effects of the implementation of your system.

Documenting the system

Two levels of documentation are needed: one for the user and the other for the technical specialists.

User documentation

This should include:

- input and output formats

- sample runs to show the output
- error messages and what to do when things go wrong (e.g. data is sent to the printer without it being switched on)
- brief limitations of the system.

Technical documentation

This should include:

- the purpose of the system
- the requirements of the system
- the input and output formats
- the method of solution
- the further development potential (how the system could be improved or any extras which could be added on).

Working in teams

People involved in setting up information systems frequently have to work in teams. Why is this? Some of the reasons are given below.

1 The task might be too large for one person to perform in a reasonable amount of time.
2 Some members in the team will have expertise in a particular area. When you form a team you need to find your team members' strengths and weaknesses and allocate the tasks accordingly.
3 Teams are able to discuss the solution to the problem and 'bounce' ideas off each other. As the old saying goes 'two heads are better than one'.

QUESTIONS

1 This question concerns the problems that might be encountered when people are working in teams. You have been asked by your teacher to develop a database system in a team with four members.

What do you think the disadvantages would be if:

(a) the teacher picked the members of the group
(b) the teacher let you pick the members of your own group.

Which of the above situations, (a) or (b), are you more likely to find in real life when working as a group?

2 If you had to develop an information system from scratch working in a team of three, what would your particular strengths and weaknesses be?

3 Debbie, an information technology manager says 'It's no use having a computerised database unless it is properly maintained.'

(a) What does she mean by properly maintained?
(b) What sort of tasks would be involved in maintaining the database?

4 In the 'personnel' database, we did not record a person's age but instead recorded their date of birth (DOB). Why isn't the age included?

5 Take a look at your parents' car insurance details to see what details are held.

Suppose a mistake was made by someone in the insurance company's office while keying the information in. What could be the consequences of such an error?

1 Jane, who is a dentist, would like to install a computer system in order to provide information regarding her patient's teeth; their appointments; their treatment and how much their treatment costs.

She decides to buy a 486 PC with a 500 MB hard disk and a laser printer.

(a) What type of application software should she buy? Give reasons for your choice or choices.

(b) Describe how the system could be used to handle the information for the various uses she has. Also mention the output she could expect from such a system.

(c) What advantages are there is using an off-the-shelf application package rather than a tailor-made programmed package? What disadvantages might there be?

(d) Give a possible advantage of the new system to each of the following groups of people:
• receptionists
• nurses
• dentists
• patients.

(e) What possible disadvantage might there be in using the new system?

2 A company of estate agents, with a main branch in one town and several branches in nearby towns, is planning to change from an manual system to a computerised one.

(a) The company plans to set up a computer file with details of houses that are for sale. This file will store the name of the owner, the address, the phone number and type for each house. Suggest **four** other fields that might be included on the file.

(b) Explain why some of the data in the fields in this file is stored in coded form.

(c) The file will store details of several thousand houses. People interested in buying any house should be able to obtain a print-out of the details by simply calling in at a branch of the company. What type of store would be needed for the file? Give **two** reasons for your choice.

(d) Some of the fields in this file are of fixed length, others are of variable length.
(i) Give **one** advantage of using fixed length fields.
(ii) Give **one** disadvantage of using fixed length fields.

(e) Describe the hardware the company will need to install in each of its branches and in the main office for the new computerised system.

(NEAB/WJEC Spec Option Q)

3 A company sells general hardware. It stores details of stock in a database.

For each item the database stores the following:
Stock_no
Description
Location_code (aisle number)
Supplier_code
Reorder_quantity
Minimum_stock_level
Current_stock_level
Lead_time (days)
Date_of_last_delivery

(a) The database can be accessed using a special query language,
e.g. List Stock_no,Description,FOR Current_stock_level less than 50.

Write down a query command which would print out the description, for all the items that the company has more than 100 of in stock, with a Lead_time of less than 14 days.

(b) The company cannot function without the database. Which backup procedures should be used for the database files?

(c) The database file is very large. What method can be used to minimise storage requirements when archive copies are made?

(d) To be able to produce orders to be sent to suppliers, an additional database file is issued.

(i) What file would this be?

(ii) What type of information would it contain?

(iii) Copy and fill in the table below to show the structure of this file.

Field name	Field type	Size

(e) Describe, using any suitable method, the way in which the two files would be used to produce orders for all items where the current_stock-level is below the Minimum_stock-level.

(NEAB/WJEC Spec Option Q)

4 A video-film club hires films to members. The club uses separate database files to store details about:

films;

members;

films hired.

The table below shows **part** of the **FILMS** database file.

Film number	Film name	Film category	Rating	Hire charge
0123	Mermaids	Comedy	15	£2.00
0124	JFK	Drama	15	£2.50
0254	Star Wars	Adventure	U	£1.50
0361	Mad Max 2	Adventure	18	£2.00
0422	City Slickers	Comedy	15	£1.25
0744	Die Hard 2	Adventure	18	£1.50
0813	Blackadder	Comedy	15	£1.50

Write down the instructions or steps that you might use if you wanted the FILMS datable to display a list of Adventure films which are rated 18 and cost less than £2.00 to hire.

(a) Choose suitable items of information for the MEMBERS database file from the list below.

Address of the club	Film name	Member's name
Original cost of film	Film number	Name of club manager
Membership number	Date of birth	Film category
Hire date	Phone number	Length of hire

ITEM1	ITEM2	ITEM3	ITEM4

FILMS HIRED FILE

(b) When new members join the video club they complete an application form. The form is used to enter information into the MEMBERS database file. Design a suitable form.

(NEAB/WJEC Spec Option R)

5 A company uses a computer to put buyers of second-hand cars in touch with people who are selling cars. It collects information from sellers by getting the sellers to complete a form. Buyers can then ring up and ask for a list of people who have the sort of car they want.

(a) Design a form for the input of information from a SELLER. (5 marks)

(b) Describe clearly the processes required to get a list (in price order) of all Ford Escort cars less than 5 years old in the price range £3000 to £4000. (5 marks)

(c) Explain why a manual card index might be better than a computer for a second-hand car dealer who usually has between 8 and 10 cars for sale. (2 marks)

(SEG NT HT Spec)

Your local tourist board has decided to produce a database of attractions within a 20 mile radius of where you live. Some of the information they would need would include:

name of attraction

location

admission costs

opening hours.

Use the Guinness Book Of British Hit Singles to compile a database which may be used by a person asking the questions in a music quiz. You need to hold as much information about each artist and their records as you can find.

Think about what questions might be asked using the database such as:

• What was the highest chart position by the record XYZ?

• What year did the group XYZ have a hit with VWX?

• Who had a hit with the song XYZ?

You have been asked to write an article on database packages for inclusion in a computer magazine. The article is aimed at the 14–18 years age group. You need to outline what a database is and how useful it can be. Also, you need to outline some of the facilities of the more popular database packages so that the reader can choose one.

Ecctis is a database held on CD-ROM about all the higher education courses in the UK. It is used mainly by sixth formers when they are applying for courses and it is updated yearly. If your school has a sixth form then the school is likely to use this system.

Use the Ecctis database (you will find it very straightforward to use) to search for courses in areas that interest you. Produce a report with evidence of what you have found out. How easy did you find it? Produce a written evaluation.

With some database packages you can design your own input screen but with others the screen has the fields in the same order as in the database structure. See whether you can design an input screen. Produce a manual design to start with. Fully document your solution.

Interrogate a monarchs (kings and queens) database either on disk or on CD-ROM and find out any interesting facts. Produce a report on what you have managed to find out. Things you could find out include the answers to questions such as:

- Who was the youngest monarch?
- Who reigned for the shortest period?
- Who lived the longest?

 Use an electronic organiser or similar computer package to store information on your friends' names, addresses and birthdays. Compare and contrast this method with the old manual address book.

 You have been asked to design an information system for a video library. Assume that the library has around 2000 members and 1400 videos, and that at present, it uses a manual system for recording details of members and videos.

It would be a good idea to arrange to visit a video library to see how such a system works. It might be hard to find a video library that uses a manual system, so try to find out how a manual school library system works, as the system will be similar.

 One of the largest databases in the country is the Driver and Vehicle Licensing Authority (DVLA) database which contains the registration details of all the cars, motorcycles, lorries, etc. In addition to this information, it also contains the details of all the people who hold driving licenses in the country.

Look at two documents: a registration document for a vehicle and a driving licence, and note the data that they contain.

You have been asked to develop a system that can be used to hold information about a company fleet of vehicles and their drivers. It is important to model this on the DVLA database and also put in some other information, such as the cost of the vehicles, service records, accidents, driver penalty points, etc.

Don't forget to fully document the system.

 Investigate and then develop and implement an information system centred around one of the following:

(a) a database of members of a health club

(b) a database of books held in a library

(c) a database of pupils in a school

(d) a database held by a mail order computer games company.

 Investigate and then develop a system to hold information about the prices of branded goods at different supermarkets. This could be used by prudent shoppers so that they can go to different supermarkets and buy just those goods that were cheaper than anywhere else.

Fully develop and document the system.

Using database software

Describe how you would perform the following, using the database software you are going to use:

(a) load the database

(b) create a new database and design the structure

(c) save the structure and print it out

(d) add records to the database

(e) save the database

(f) go back to the structure and make changes, such as delete a field and insert a new field

(g) go back to the database and

    (i) edit a record

    (ii) delete a record

(h) perform a simple search (searching on a single field)

(I) search on several fields using the logical operators (AND, OR and NOT)

(j) produce a report containing selected fields

(k) change the format of a report.

A car stock list

A large second hand car company keeps details of all its cars in stock using a series of records held in a filing cabinet. It is decided that the data should be transferred to a database held on computer. Here is part of the file:

Make	Model	Price	Year	Type	Mileage
Nissan	Sunny 1.4L	£7000	93	Saloon	24000
Nissan	Sunny 1.4GL	£6200	92	Saloon	35000
Ford	Mondeo	£8300	94	Saloon	34000
Ford	Escort	£3500	92	Saloon	56000
Nissan	200SX	£10995	92	Sports	34000
Nissan	300ZX	£14995	92	Sports	25000
Nissan	Primera 2.0GL	£8995	93	Saloon	19000
Nissan	Micra 1.0L	£4995	94	Saloon	23000
Nissan	Micra 1.3GL	£5500	94	Saloon	12000
Ford	Probe (24v)	£13995	95	Sports	5000
Honda	Prelude (2.3)	£14995	94	Sports	13995
Honda	Civic	£7995	92	Saloon	10000
Honda	Accord	£12999	93	Saloon	11000
Ford	Probe (16v)	£9999	94	Sports	6000
Nissan	Sunny	£3000	91	Estate	38000
Mercedes	230	£20000	95	Saloon	23000
Nissan	Micra	£3500	93	Saloon	40000
Ford	Escort	£2900	90	Saloon	56000

1 Load your database software.

2 Create a structure for your database file (use only character and numeric fields), with suitable widths. When you are happy with your structure, save it and print a copy.

SKILLS BUILDING

3 Enter the above data, verify it by proof reading and then save and print a copy.

4 Reload your database and make the following amendments:
- the Nissan Sunny for £7000 is actually a Nissan Sunny 1.4GLX
- the Mercedes 230 needs its price reducing to £18 995
- the Ford Escort is a 1.8GL and is a 91 model
- the Sunny Estate needs its price reducing to £2500.

Make these amendments and save and then print a copy of the database.

5 The following cars have come in, so they should be added to the database:

Nissan	Micra	£4500	94	Saloon	32000
Ford	Escort 1.6	£6000	94	Saloon	25000
Nissan	Primera 1.6	£8995	95	Saloon	4000

Add them and then save the database.

6 The following cars have been sold so their details need deleting from the database.

Ford	Probe (16v)	£9999	94	Sports	6000
Nissan	Sunny 1.4GL	£6200	92	Saloon	35000
Nissan	Micra 1.0L	£4995	94	Saloon	23000

After deleting these records, save the database.

7 Sort the cars file
- (a) alphabetically according to make, with the As at the top of the file
- (b) numerically according to price, with the most expensive car at the top
- (c) using an index (if your database has one) according to make and then within this, according to price.

Produce a printout for each one to check that it has been sorted correctly.

8 Search for
- (a) details of all cars costing less than £3000
- (b) details of all Ford cars costing less than £7000
- (c) details of all cars costing between £5000 and £6000
- (d) details of all sports cars.

You should produce a printout to provide evidence that the search is correct.

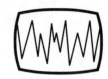

Before reading this chapter you should look at Chapter 21, especially the section on pseudo-code. In this chapter we will look at monitoring, data logging and using computers for control.

Turtle graphics

In this section we will look at how you can use a series of instructions to move a turtle around on the screen of a computer. As the turtle moves, it can be instructed to leave a line behind it showing its path.

Turtle graphics is just one of the features of a programming language called LOGO. Ask you teacher how to load the LOGO software and get the turtle to appear on the centre of the screen. We can now instruct the turtle to move and leave a line drawn behind it to show its path.

Moving the turtle

When the turtle is facing a certain way, it can move only in that direction. To move in another direction you have to turn the turtle before moving it.

Let's now look at some of the commands;

FORWARD 30   moves the turtle 30 units forward. How far this is depends on the screen you are using. Notice also that a line is not drawn showing its path.
BACKWARD 10   moves the turtle 10 units backward.
PENUP   raises the pen and stops the line being drawn.
PENDOWN   puts the pen down so that a line is drawn behind the turtle.

Turning the turtle

The turtle turns by giving it a direction of turn (LEFT or RIGHT) and an angle of turn in degrees. The angle is measured from the

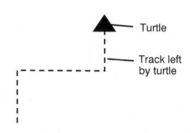

Figure 32.1 *With LOGO you control a movable turtle*

line the turtle would take if it proceeded normally. Figure 32.1 helps explain this. Here are some commands and explanations;

LEFT 90   turns the turtle to the left by 90 degrees.
RIGHT 60   turns the turtle to the right by 90 degrees.
CLEARSCREEN   clears the screen.

Making a program

A program is a list of instructions arranged in a logical order that can be obeyed by a computer. We will now look at how to put some of the commands together that we have already learnt.

We can draw a square using the following program:

```
CLEARSCREEN
FORWARD 20
RIGHT 90
FORWARD 20
RIGHT 90
FORWARD 20
RIGHT 90
FORWARD 20
```

This method is tedious so there is an easier way:

REPEAT 4 (FORWARD 20 RIGHT 90)

The above instruction tells LOGO to draw four lines, each 20 steps long and to turn 90 degrees between lines.

Suppose we want to draw many squares. How do we do this?

Well, we can use what is called a procedure. This is a series of instructions to which we give a name. We can make up the procedure for the square like this;

TO SQUARE
REPEAT 4 (FORWARD 20 RIGHT 90)
END

Each time we refer to SQUARE it will repeat this section of program called a procedure. Sometimes what actually happens is not always what you think will happen. Take the following, for instance:

REPEAT 4 (SQUARE)

You might have expected this to draw the square and then go over it another three times. What actually happens is shown in Figure 32.2. Try to use the instructions with a piece of paper and pen, but when you do remember that it is important to know in which direction the turtle is pointing. What you are actually doing is performing a DRY RUN. A DRY RUN means working through a program with a pen and paper to see if it produces the expected results.

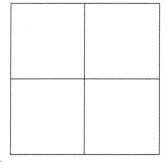

Figure 32.2

QUESTIONS

1 See if you can work out, using pen, paper and a protractor what happens in the following procedure.
TO PATTERN
FORWARD 50
RIGHT 150
FORWARD 60
RIGHT 100
FORWARD 30
RIGHT 90
END
Draw an accurate diagram of what you would see (assume that the pen is down).

2 Repeat the above pattern using the program:
REPEAT 20 (PATTERN)
Explain why it did not go over the drawing in the first question 20 times.

3 Write a LOGO program to draw an equilateral triangle on the screen with sides of length 50. (N.B. In an equilateral triangle, all the sides are the same length and all the angles are 60°.)

4 A polygon is a many sided figure. All of the interior angles in a regular polygon are the same size and the sides are the same length. Write a series of programs to produce the following shapes:
(a) a square
(b) a pentagon (five sides)
(c) a hexagon (six sides)
(d) a heptagon (seven sides)

1 The following instructions will draw a shape.

REPEAT 4 [FORWARD 5 RIGHT 90]

(a) Show clearly on squared paper the shape drawn.

(b) Write a similar list of instructions to draw a rectangle with sides of length 4 and 6.

(SEG IS FT)

2 A robot is used to retrieve fuel rods from a nuclear reactor. To get the rod labelled X, the following instructions could be given:

FORWARD 3

TURN RIGHT

FORWARD 1

TAKE

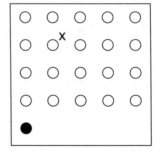

(a) The robot has an instruction (INPUT var) that allows numbers to be input into variables, which can then be used instead of the numbers indicated above. Write a program so that it will allow any rod to be retrieved. Make sure you clearly identify the use of your variables.

(b) Why would a robot be used for this job?

(SEG IS IT)

3 The pen on a graph plotter can be controlled by a computer using a simple set of commands which are stored as a program:

PEN UP

PEN DOWN

FORWARD x moves the pen forward x cm

RIGHT x turns x degrees to the right

LEFT x turns x degrees to the left

STOP

(a) You will need a protractor to measure the angles in the following program using the above commands:

PEN DOWN

FORWARD 10

RIGHT 90

FORWARD 10

RIGHT 90

FORWARD 10

RIGHT 90

FORWARD 10

STOP

Using a pen, paper, ruler and protractor, trace the shape that the plotter would draw using the above instructions.

(b) Write a program using the list of commands shown above to produce an equilateral triangle of side 15. (An equilateral triangle has equal sides and all the interior angles are 60°.)

(c) So that a series of instructions can be repeated, there are the following commands:

254

REPEAT n TIMES

....

....

....

....

AGAIN

The dotted lines are used to represent the lines of commands that are repeated.

Write a program to draw a regular hexagon with sides of length 10 like the one shown in the diagram, using the REPEAT command.

4 A computer can control a turtle on the screen. When the turtle moves it leaves a line on the screen. Some of the commands are:

FORWARD steps

BACK steps

RIGHT angle

LEFT angle

For example, FORWARD 50 moves the turtle forward 50 steps in a straight line. RIGHT 45 turns the turtle 45° to the right.

Here are the commands which are needed to draw the S shape.

FORWARD 50 LEFT 90

FORWARD 50 LEFT 90

FORWARD 100 RIGHT 90

FORWARD 100 RIGHT 90

The turtle starts from the position shown in the diagram.

Arrange these commands in the right order to draw the S shape.

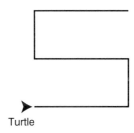

Turtle

(NEAB/WJEC Spec Level P)

Monitoring physical quantities (temperature, pressure, etc.) using a computer

Monitoring temperature

If we wanted to look at how coffee cooled when placed in a polystyrene cup we could just use a stop clock and a thermometer and take a reading every minute over a period of an hour.

Doing it this way, we would need to sit with the whole apparatus for an hour and remember to take a reading of the thermometer every minute. Clearly this is tedious, even for one hour. If we needed to

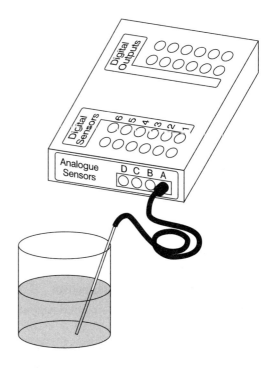

Figure 32.3 *Analogue to digital conversion is necessary with a temperature sensor*

take more frequent readings over a longer period of time, we would probably give up.

Help is at hand though in the form of data logging (see Chapter 15). Here, we can use a computer (desktop or portable), an interface, suitable software and a temperature sensor to perform this experiment easily.

Once we have loaded the software and told the computer which sensors we have connected (some systems can do this automatically) we then need to tell the computer how frequently the measurements are to be made and over what period. We can then go away and do something else while the computer gets on with the job.

Most data loggers will record the data in the form of a table which can be imported into other software, such as spreadsheet or graphics packages for further work. You can usually display your readings graphically at the end of the experiment or while the experiment is taking place since the readings are taken automatically by the sensor.

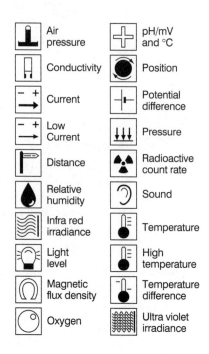

Figure 32.4 *The range of sensors available from Philip Harris*

TASKS

Data logging

Here is a variety of tasks you can perform using data logging equipment. It is impossible to give exact instructions of how to use any particular piece of apparatus, because the instructions are different for different makes. This means you will have to find out from your teacher how do the following:

1 Connect the sensor, interface and computer as instructed by your teacher.

2 Load the data logging software (if necessary).

3 Specify how frequently the readings are taken (most packages allow you to vary this from about one ten thousandth of a second to around 30 minutes).

4 Specify the total recording time (i.e. the total time over which the readings are taken). For most packages this can be from a fraction of a second to almost three weeks.

5 Display the data as a list on the screen.

6 Produce a display of the data plotted against time.

7 Save the data to disk for use later.

8 Plot the graph in real time so that, as a reading is taken, it is automatically plotted on the screen.

9 Export the previously saved data into other software packages such as spreadsheet or wordprocessing packages.

Temperature variation of water

Use datalogging equipment to find out how the temperature of a glass beaker of boiling water varies with time when it is left to cool.

You will need to think about the following:

• how frequently the temperature reading needs to be taken and over what period

• what can be done to increase the time over which the water cools.

• try the experiment using different types of mugs. Do tall thin mugs keep the water hotter than tall thin mugs? Does the surface area in contact with the air matter? Try other similar experiments.

Moisture content of soil

Monitor the change in the moisture content of the soil surrounding a house plant with time.

- What sensor or sensors will you use (hint: you will need to measure the moisture and any other physical properties on which the drying out of the soil will depend)?
- How often does the data logger need to obtain a reading?
- Drying out is a slow process, so over what total time should the data logger operate? Why have you chosen this period?
- Explain exactly what you did and the reasons for doing it.

Conditions in a fish tank

Monitor the conditions in a tropical or marine fish tank over a period of 24 hours.

You could use a variety of sensors such as:

- light
- temperature
- pH
- oxygen

In a tropical or marine fish tank the temperature should be kept constant using the heater and the thermostat. From your readings, how successful was this system in keeping the temperature constant? You could try plotting physical quantities against each other rather than against time. For example, try plotting the amount of oxygen against the amount of light. Do they follow each other? Again fully document your experiment, paying particular attention to the use of the data logging equipment.

Wind chill factor

You may have heard the term wind chill factor being used by weather forecasters. We all know that, even on a warm day, it can feel a lot cooler if there is a wind.

One way of cooling a drink is to wrap a damp towel around the bottle and place it in a draughty place. The water evaporates and cools the bottle. Could this we use this principle to make a device to give us a measure of the wind chill factor?

See what you can come up with and fully describe your solution.

Advantages of data logging

Data logging can be used for recording data about fast events that would happen too quickly for you to take readings manually. It can also be used for very slow events where recording them manually would be tedious and time consuming.

Because the readings are taken automatically accurate measurements are made without human error and exactly at the right time.

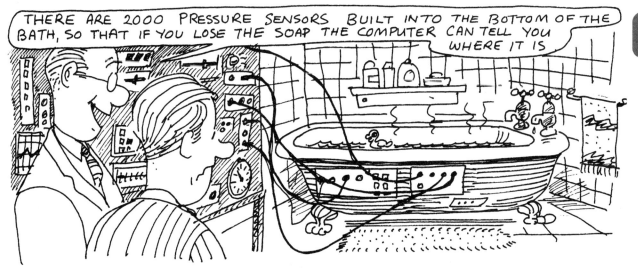

Figure 32.5 *The uses of sensors are limited only by your imagination*

Other examples of computer control

In this section we will look at how computers can be used to control devices and perform useful tasks.

Cold tea?

The problem

Make a system that warns you when your hot tea has cooled enough and is ready to drink. You should be able to cancel the alarm when you go to your drink.

Questions

- What temperature is the tea when it is cool enough to drink?
- What kind of a warning do you need?
- What will you use to tell the computer you have now received the warning and got your drink?

Solution

Tea at temperatures of around 55–70°C might be suitable for drinking. A buzzer would give a suitable warning. The buzzer would continue until a push button is pressed to cancel the alarm. The sensors may be connected to the interface along with a special module which is used for control. The buzzer is connected as number 6 and the push switch as input 1. If the temperature is less than 70°C the buzzer should be switched on. When the push button is pressed the buzzer stops. Using IF and WHEN, the computer tests the temperature and waits until the temperature condition is met.

Here is the control program:

```
WHEN TEMPERATURE IS
BELOW 70 THEN SWITCH ON 6
WHEN INPUT 1 IS ON
THEN SWITCH OFF 6
```

Here is another program which does the same thing

```
REPEAT FOREVER
IF TEMPERATURE IS
BELOW 70 THEN SWITCH
ON 6
AGAIN
```

Alternatively, both solutions can be built as procedures to give the same results:

```
BUILD tealarm
WHEN TEMPERATURE IS
BELOW 70 THEN SWITCH
ON 6
WHEN INPUT 1 IS ON
THEN SWITCH OFF 6
END
```

or

```
BUILD teatwo
REPEAT FOREVER
IF TEMPERATURE IS
BELOW 70 THEN SWITCH
ON 6
AGAIN
WHEN INPUT 1 IS ON
THEN SWITCH OFF 6
END
```

Further work

1 If the freezer breaks you need to know if the food starts to thaw out.

2 You have just put a bottle of warm Cola in the fridge. You need a cold drink and want to know as soon as it's ready to drink. Make an alarm system.

Wake up

The problem

Make an alarm clock which switches on at dawn and switches off when you shout at it.

Questions

- How will the computer know if it is morning?
- How will the computer detect you have shouted at it?
- How loud do you need to shout to stop the alarm?
- What can you use to set the alarm?
- How could you tell that the alarm has been set?

Solution

The light sensor can measure the light level. When the light reaches a certain level the alarm will be switched on. A sound sensor is used to detect the sound of a voice. The sound level at which the alarm switches off should be set high enough so that it is not switched off by the alarm itself. Use the push switch to set the alarm and switch on a green light to indicate it is set. Connect the sound sensor and the module to the interface. Connect the light and sound sensors to the interface. the push switch is connected as input 1 and the green indicator lamp is connected as number 3.

Here is the control program. This program is written as a procedure.

```
BUILD alarm
REPEAT FOREVER
WHEN INPUT 1 IS ON
THEN SWITCH ON 3
WHEN LIGHT IS ABOVE 40
THEN SWITCH ON 6
WHEN SOUND IS ABOVE
80 THEN SWITCH OFF 6
SWITCH OFF 3
AGAIN
END
```

To make this procedure run, type the line below:

```
DO alarm
```

Further work
1 Make an alarm that tells you when you're playing your music too loud.

2 Make a burglar alarm that can be triggered by the noise level. The alarm sound can be on and off like a siren.

Shop

The problem
Make a buzzer for a shop that works when you go in and step on the door mat.

Questions
• What can you use to tell if the mat has been stepped on?
• What should the buzzer do – should it stay on all the time or should it switch off after a certain time?
• What should happen if another customer enters the shop?

Solution
Use the push switch to tell if the mat has been stepped on. If the push switch has been pressed the buzzer should be switched on. The buzzer should stay on for a few seconds then it should be switched off. Go back and check if the push switch has been pressed, in case another customer enters the shop. This will be repeated over and over. Connect the module to the interface. The buzzer is connected as number 6 and the push switch as input 1.

Here is the control program.

```
REPEAT FOREVER
WHEN INPUT 1 IS ON
THEN SWITCH ON 6
WAIT 20
SWITCH OFF 6
AGAIN
```

Alternatively, we can use a procedure called shop to do the same.

```
BUILD shop
REPEAT FOREVER
WHEN INPUT 1 IS ON
THEN SWITCH ON 6
WAIT 20
SWITCH OFF 6
AGAIN
END
```

To make this procedure run, type the line below

```
DO shop
```

Further work
Make the buzzer produce an intermittent sound. As an alternative to the push switch it is possible to make a pressure 'switch' by attaching a near flat balloon to a pressure sensor. Use the same procedure as above but replace the lines that read:

```
WHEN INPUT 1 IS ON
THEN SWITCH ON 6
```

with

```
WHEN PRESSURE IS
ABOVE 20 THEN SWITCH
ON 6
```

You may need to experiment with the value of the pressure to make the buzzer work in the way that you want.

Lighthouse

The problem
Make a flashing warning light for a lighthouse.

Questions
- Which colour will you use for the warning light? Give your reason.
- What should the warning light do?

Solution
Use a red light, LED number 1, as red light is a good warning colour. The warning light should come on for a second then go off for a second. This should repeat over and over. Connect the module to the universal interface.

Here is the control program:

```
REPEAT FOREVER
SWITCH ON 1
WAIT 5
SWITCH OFF 1
WAIT 5
AGAIN
```

Alternatively, you could build a 'procedure' called flash to do the same thing:

```
BUILD flash
REPEAT FOREVER
SWITCH ON 1
WAIT 5
SWITCH OFF 1
WAIT 5
AGAIN
END
```

To run this procedure type the line below:

```
DO Flash
```

Further work
Use two flashing lights as the warning signal.

Go away

The problem
People keep ringing your door buzzer at night. Make a door buzzer that works only in the daytime.

Questions
- What will you use as a push button?
- How will the door bell know whether it is night or day?
- What should the light level be for the door buzzer to work – above 60, above 40 or something else?

Should the buzzer work:

1 when it is pressed or the light level is low?
2 when it is pressed or the light level is high?
3 when it is pressed and the light level is low?
4 when it is pressed and the light level is high?

When should the door buzzer stop buzzing – when you stop pressing it, after a few seconds or when you answer the door?

Solution
Use the push switch as the door push button. Use a light sensor to find out whether it is night or day. Trial and error will determine the most suitable light level for the buzzer to work. The door buzzer should work only if two conditions are met: if the push switch has been pressed and if the light level is high. The buzzer should be switched off a few seconds after the button has been pressed. Next go back and check if the push switch has been pressed again. This will be repeated forever.

Connect the light sensor and module to the universal interface. The buzzer is connected as number 6 and the push switch as input 1.

Here is the control program:

```
REPEAT FOREVER
IF LIGHT IS ABOVE 50
AND INPUT 1 IS ON THEN
SWITCH ON 6
WAIT 20
SWITCH OFF 6
AGAIN
```

Alternatively you could use a procedure called buzzer:

```
BUILD buzzer
REPEAT FOREVER
```

IF LIGHT IS ABOVE 50
AND INPUT 1 IS ON THEN
SWITCH ON 6
WAIT 20
SWITCH OFF 6
AGAIN
END

Further work

Porch light
You want a light to come on at your front
door whenever it is dark and switch off
when it gets light. To save electricity, you
also want to be able to switch the light off
when you go to bed.

Welcome home
You want a light to come on at your front
door when you arrive home at night.
Obviously it doesn't come on during the day.

Chapter 33

Modelling

Modelling coursework

There is a series of coursework tasks at the end of this chapter for you to choose. It is best to choose one that interests you. Ask your teacher if the task is a suitable one for you to do. You don't have to use any of the ones given and you could make up your own. Either way, you need to provide evidence for the modelling strand. To provide this evidence you need a fairly structured approach to the documentation. For this reason it is best for you to adopt a format along the lines of the one shown below.

Identify

The first step is to identify the problem. You need to express clearly what the problem is for which you are trying to produce a model. You also need to say why you have chosen particular software rather than something else. Mention software you thought of choosing but you later rejected with reasons why you rejected it.

Analyse

At the analysis stage, you need to plan out your approach to the problem and also include any simplifications or assumptions you have made. Also include the variables you need to enter and the output you need from the system.

Design

When dealing with the design, you can describe what the model as a whole will look like and then go into greater detail. At this stage you can start to plan the layout of the spreadsheet if you are using one.

Use/implement

At this stage you provide evidence that you have produced some solution to the problem or are well on the way of getting nearer to a solution. Remember, it is very difficult and in many cases impossible to produce a perfect model. If you have had to alter your design for whatever reason then you need to say why you have altered it. Always include every piece of your work as evidence, even the parts which you did completely wrong.

You need to test your model. In some cases this will just be comparing some of the answers with those obtained using a calculator, but in others you may be able to test the system against reality. For instance if you had to produce a model for the population growth in Britain over the last century, you could obtain actual figures and see how good your model is.

Evaluation

When you evaluate your model you need to say whether you are happy with it. Given more time, what further adjustments would you make to it? Could you have approached the problem in a different way?

Refinement

If you are unhappy with your model you can refine it. Sometimes you can call each version attempt 1, attempt 2, etc., until you get your final version. At the end you can include a final evaluation.

Modelling a supermarket queue

In this example we will look at the problem of making a model of a supermarket queue. The way the model is written up is the same

Figure 33.1 *The other queue always moves faster*

as that outlined before. When doing any coursework on modelling, make sure that you adopt a similar format.

Identifying the problem

Suppose we are opening a new supermarket. How do we decide how many tills or point-of-sale terminals to use? If the supermarket is part of a chain like Tescos, then past experience may help us. But if this is our first supermarket we haven't any others to make a comparison with. Some other method will need to be used.

Analysing the situation

Why do we need to get it right?
If we don't get the number of tills right the consequences could be:

1 either we could buy too many POS terminals and thereby waste money
2 or we could buy too few and cause long queues which might make the shoppers reluctant to shop at the store again.

What software do we need to use to perform this task?
Since we are trying to understand how a real system operates, we could use a spreadsheet. We do need to think carefully about the problem before we start trying to design the spreadsheet. We are going to construct a model of the queue using numbers.

We need first to decide:

1 the inputs to the system
2 the calculations that need to be performed on these numbers
3 the outputs from the system.

The advantage of constructing such a model is that we can make changes to the inputs and see what effects they have on the output. For example, the supermarket owner/manager can immediately see the effect of altering the number of tills on the lengths of queues and the average waiting times.

What are the inputs to the supermarket model?
The inputs include:

1 how many people are waiting
2 how many POS terminals or tills there are
3 how long each person takes to be served. This will have to be an average time, since the time depends on the number of items the person is buying and the method of payment (e.g. credit card, debit card, cheque or cash).

Always produce the simplest model to start with. This will help you get a grasp of the problem and you can refine it later. Make sure that you include all your work if you are including a modelling/simulation project for your coursework.

Design

In this section we have to start designing our model. In this case we will be using a spreadsheet so we can either design it straight onto the spreadsheet or plan it on paper first. If you are designing the model straight onto the spreadsheet, make sure that you know enough about the commands to move things around if you need to alter them.

In this problem we can have a heading and then divide the spreadsheet into two parts for the inputs and the outputs. Calculations are performed on the inputs to produce the output. Figure 33.2 shows the design.

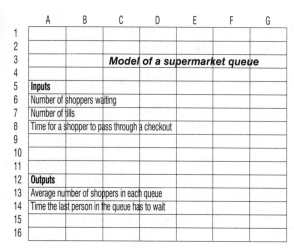

Figure 33.2 *Design of the model*

Suppose that there are 40 shoppers waiting to pay for the goods and there are 20 checkouts. Let us also assume that, on average, it takes a shopper two minutes to pass through the checkout. We will have to assume that the shoppers will distribute themselves equally in the queues. We can then calculate the average number of shoppers in each queue using the formula:

$$\text{average number of shoppers in each queue} = \frac{\text{number of shoppers waiting}}{\text{number of tills}}$$

Using our figures we get:

$$\text{average number of shoppers in each queue} = 40/20 = 2$$

Now, the last shopper in one of these queues will have to wait a time which is given by the following formula:

time last person in queue has to wait = average time for a person to go through the checkout in minutes × the average number of shoppers waiting in each queue.

Using our figures we get:

$$\text{time last person in each queue has to wait} = 2 \times 2 = 4 \text{ min}$$

Now, the beauty of using a spreadsheet is the ease with which we can carry out the calculations. However, we must make sure that we link the outputs to the inputs using formulae.

Figure 33.3 shows the formulae that have to be used. You should be able to print your spreadsheet out showing any formulae placed in each cell. Produce this as evidence in your project.

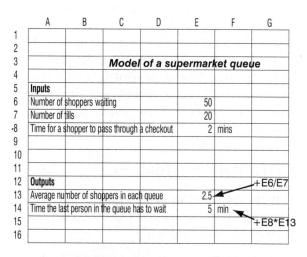

Figure 33.3 *Spreadsheet showing the inputs, outputs and the formulae used to calculate the outputs*

Implementation

Implementation involves actually using the model. In other words we have to perform a simulation by putting in number to see what happens.

Figure 33.4 shows the effect of altering the inputs to the system. Try to use the model you have created to explore the effect of changing the variables and rules and to test hypotheses.

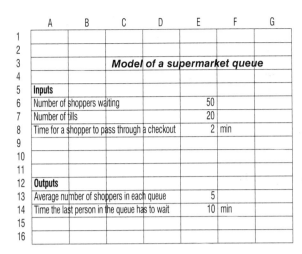

	A	B	C	D	E	F	G
1							
2							
3			*Model of a supermarket queue*				
4							
5	**Inputs**						
6	Number of shoppers waiting				50		
7	Number of tills				20		
8	Time for a shopper to pass through a checkout				2	min	
9							
10							
11							
12	**Outputs**						
13	Average number of shoppers in each queue				5		
14	Time the last person in the queue has to wait				10	min	
15							
16							

Figure 33.4 *Spreadsheet showing the effect of altering the number of tills*

Evaluation

We have to look carefully at the model we have produced. Maybe we could have made it better. Here we describe whether we are happy with the model, any improvements that could be made to it and whether it solves the problem that we started with.

Refinement

If the model is a good one, then no refinement is needed. If we need to alter the model in any way to reflect the real situation more accurately, then we need to say why and provide evidence of having done this, which would include printouts of the improved model. Obviously you could go on forever making changes and trying to get things right but there has to be a point where you stop. Finally, perfection is impossible to achieve especially if human behaviour is to be taken into account.

QUESTIONS

1 One of the assumptions used in the model was that queues consist of equal numbers of people. Does this always happen? Why not? What changes could be made to the model to reflect this?

2 Can you produce a better model of a supermarket queue than this? Remember that this is only an initial model. If you were

submitting this as a piece of coursework you would need to refine it. See what you can do. Write up your report using the above headings and subheadings as a guide.

Break-even analysis

Beatbox is a new company set up by a brother and sister to manufacture small loudspeakers. They hope to sell the small speakers to people who want to attach their personal stereos or CDs to them, or who need speakers for multimedia applications.

They realise that things will be hard to start with so, to give themselves some light at the end of the tunnel, they would like to find out how many speakers they would need to sell to break even.

When a business is started, money has to be paid out for equipment, parts, premises, etc., before the company starts making the products. So money goes out of the business but there is none coming in. Once the product begins to be made and sold, the money starts coming back into the business. Eventually, when Beatbox has sold a certain number of loudspeakers, the company will break even. This point, called the break-even point, occurs when the money coming in from the sale of the loudspeakers balances the money that has been paid out. In other words, the company is neither making a profit nor a loss. There will be a certain number of loudspeakers for which this will occur. Once past this point, the sale of the speakers will start to produce a profit.

Break-even analysis is important when starting a business since the banks that lend the company money to start up will want to know when the borrower will start to make a profit.

In order to produce a model for break-even analysis, Beatbox needs to work out the fixed costs and the variable costs. The company's accountant tells the owners the following information.

Fixed costs

Fixed costs are any costs that do not depend on the number of loudspeakers sold. Fixed costs would include rent of buildings, rates, salaries and finance costs. It is important to note that fixed costs do not stay fixed forever. They are only fixed over the short term and over a certain range of production.

Variable costs

Variable costs are the costs that depend on the number of speakers produced. So, the costs of the parts which make up the speakers and the electricity used would be classed as variable costs.

Beatbox has worked out the following figures:

fixed costs	= £1000
variable costs per speaker	= £12.50
selling price per speaker	= £18.00

Variable costs are the costs of making a certain number of speakers and sales revenue is the money which comes in when the same number of speakers is sold. So:

total cost of producing speakers = variable costs + fixed costs

variable costs = variable costs per speaker × number of speakers

sales revenue = selling price per speaker × number of speakers

We can now produce a table with the column headings shown below using spreadsheet software.

Number of speakers	Variable costs	Fixed costs	Total cost	Sales revenue

You will now perform a series of tasks which will determine the break-even point.

First attempt

The first attempt is used to obtain the very rough range that the break-even point could lie within.

In the first attempt to find the break-even point you can use numbers of speakers from 50 to 500 going up in steps of 50. Make sure that you key in the all the information except that in the following columns: variable costs, total costs and sales revenue. You should work these out using suitable formulae and then copy them down the relevant columns. Check that your final model looks like the one in Figure 33.5.

The break-even point occurs where the sales revenue and the total costs are equal. As you can see there is no such value on our

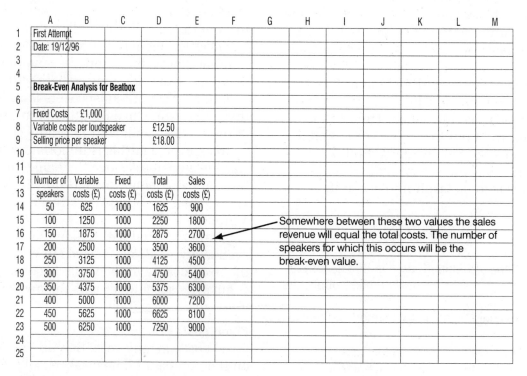

	A	B	C	D	E	F	G	H	I	J	K	L	M
1	First Attempt												
2	Date: 19/12/96												
3													
4													
5	Break-Even Analysis for Beatbox												
6													
7	Fixed Costs	£1,000											
8	Variable costs per loudspeaker			£12.50									
9	Selling price per speaker			£18.00									
10													
11													
12	Number of	Variable	Fixed	Total	Sales								
13	speakers	costs (£)	costs (£)	costs (£)	costs (£)								
14	50	625	1000	1625	900								
15	100	1250	1000	2250	1800		Somewhere between these two values the sales						
16	150	1875	1000	2875	2700		revenue will equal the total costs. The number of						
17	200	2500	1000	3500	3600		speakers for which this occurs will be the						
18	250	3125	1000	4125	4500		break-even value.						
19	300	3750	1000	4750	5400								
20	350	4375	1000	5375	6300								
21	400	5000	1000	6000	7200								
22	450	5625	1000	6625	8100								
23	500	6250	1000	7250	9000								
24													
25													

Figure 33.5 *First attempt at finding the break-even point*

	A	B	C	D	E	F	G	H	I	J	K	L	M
1	Second Attempt												
2	Date: 19/12/96												
3													
4													
5	**Break-Even Analysis for Beatbox**												
6													
7	Fixed Costs	£1,000											
8	Variable costs per loudspeaker			£12.50									
9	Selling price per speaker			£18.00									
10													
11													
12	Number of	Variable	Fixed	Total	Sales								
13	speakers	costs (£)	costs (£)	costs (£)	costs (£)								
14	150	1875	1000	2875	2700								
15	160	2000	1000	3000	2880								
16	170	2125	1000	3125	3060								
17	180	2250	1000	3250	3240								
18	190	2375	1000	3375	3420								
19	200	2500	1000	3500	3600								
20	210	2625	1000	3625	3780								
21	220	2750	1000	3750	3960								
22	230	2875	1000	3875	4140								
23	240	3000	1000	4000	4320								
24	250	3125	1000	4125	4500								
25													

Break-even value of number of speakers lies between 180 and 190.

Figure 33.6 *Second attempt at finding the break-even point*

	A	B	C	D	E	F	G	H	I	J	K	L	M
1	Third Attempt												
2	Date: 19/12/96												
3													
4													
5	**Break-Even Analysis for Beatbox**												
6													
7	Fixed Costs	£1,000											
8	Variable costs per loudspeaker			£12.50									
9	Selling price per speaker			£18.00									
10													
11													
12	Number of	Variable	Fixed	Total	Sales								
13	speakers	costs (£)	costs (£)	costs (£)	costs (£)								
14	180	2250.00	1000	3250.00	3240								
15	181	2262.50	1000	3262.50	3258								
16	182	2275.00	1000	3275.00	3276								
17	183	2287.50	1000	3287.50	3294								
18	184	2300.00	1000	3300.00	3312								
19	185	2312.50	1000	3312.50	3330								
20	186	2325.00	1000	3325.00	3348								
21	187	2337.50	1000	3337.50	3366								
22	188	2350.00	1000	3350.00	3384								
23	189	2362.50	1000	3362.50	3402								
24	190	2375.00	1000	3375.00	3420								
25													

Figure 33.7 *Third attempt at finding the break-even point*

spreadsheet so we look for where the sales revenue goes from being smaller than the total costs to where it is greater. Looking at the spreadsheet you can see that this occurs between sales of 150 to 200 speakers. We need to investigate this region more closely to get a more accurate picture. We therefore produce a second spreadsheet just covering this area.

Second attempt

Produce another spreadsheet by altering the first one to go from 150 speakers to 250 speakers in steps of 10. Check with Figure 33.6 that you get the same values. It should reveal that the break-even point lies somewhere between 180 and 190 speakers.

Third attempt

Now repeat the process using the numbers of speakers from 180 to 190 in steps of one speaker.

What value do you get for the number of speakers to break even? What do you think you should do if it is not a whole number?

Check that your spreadsheet looks like the one in Figure 33.7.

Finding the break-even point graphically

We can find the break-even point graphically by plotting the sales revenue and total costs against the number of speakers sold. You can do this either using graph paper or get the computer to draw two line graphs like the one shown in Figure 33.8. The break-even point is where the two straight line graphs cross. The number of speakers sold to break-even can be read from the graph.

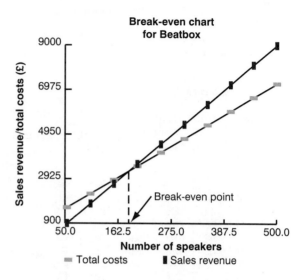

Figure 33.8 *Finding the break-even point graphically*

QUESTION

John enjoys woodwork and has decided to make a bird table for his parents. The first table he makes is seen by his neighbours, who ask him if he can make them one. The word travels around and before long he has a book full of orders. He even starts to get the odd order from a garden centre.

He would like to speed up the construction of the tables by using more power tools. He has £400 in the bank, which he spends on the latest woodworking equipment. His variable and fixed costs are:

fixed costs (woodworking equipment) = £400
variable costs   = £15.00 per bird table
selling price   = £25.00 per bird table

Using a spreadsheet, work out how many bird tables he would need to sell before he breaks even.

IT TASK

Use a spreadsheet to solve a pair of simultaneous equations such as the pair:

$3x + 4y = 25$
$3x + 2y = 17$

There is a variety of ways you could approach this problem.

(a) You use the spreadsheet to set up a table for each equation and then use each table to plot a graph. Where the two straight line graphs cut, the x and y co-ordinates will give the solution to the above pair of equations.

(b) You could develop a method on the spreadsheet using trial and error.

(c) You could use matrices. Some spreadsheets have a function where you can solve simultaneous equations. See if yours has and find out how to use it.

Suzanne is 25 and lives at home with her parents. She is bored with her present job working in an office and would like a challenge. Her present job is quite well paid and brings her in £150 per week.

She has just seen an advertisement in her local newspaper advertising a training course to become a driving instructor. Tuition for the fees and final examination are £1300. She can drive at the moment but does not have her own car. She therefore needs to buy a car with dual controls. Suzanne sees a car she likes and with the dual controls it will cost her £8000.

In order to get established Suzanne reckons she will need to undercut the fees charged by the other driving schools. She therefore decides to charge £12 per hour. To attract customers, she decides to advertise in the local paper and this will cost £30 per week. Also, her mother, who is at home all day, will answer the phone calls and make bookings and Suzanne will give her mother £20 per week for doing this.

Before giving up her job and going ahead with the venture she decides to work out how many hours she would need to work each week in order to break even. To do this she must work out her fixed and variable costs. This she has done and the following figures are obtained.

Fixed costs

Advertising in the local paper = £30.00 per week

Payment to her mother = £20.00 per week

Borrowing to buy the car and pay for tuition fees for course = £40.00 per week

Depreciation of the car = £80.00 per week

Variable costs

The only variable costs will be the running costs of the car. These include petrol, repairs, etc. She works out these variable costs to be 20p per mile. On average, in a one hour lesson she estimates that she will travel about 15 miles. Hence, the variable costs for one lesson will be 15 × 20p = £3.00.

Task

Suzanne has asked for your help in making her decision.

You have your own computer and have told Suzanne that you will help her by making use of appropriate computer software.

1 Set up a model of the business and use your model to determine the number of lessons she would need to do each week in order to break even.

2 Suggest some improvements she might make and show them as printouts.

3 Write a brief report on the proposed business. Should she quit her job or stick with it? What do you think on the basis of your figures?

In mathematics you often come across equations such as:

$x^2 - x - 6 = 0$

We would normally solve this by factorisation like this:

$(x - 3)(x + 2) = 0$

giving values of x; $x = 3$ or -2.

Some equations are difficult to solve. For instance the quadratic equation

$x^2 + 6x - 2 = 0$

has the solutions $x = 0.32$ or -6.32 to two decimal places, so we can't solve it by simple factorisation. We could however use a spreadsheet and try various values of x in the equation to see if we can get zero.

Here is an equation to solve using a spreadsheet. Do not try to factorise it because it cannot be factorised.

$$x^2 - 8x - 6 = 0$$

Now, you can use the same method to solve a cubic equation. With cubic equations, there are three solutions. See if you can find all the solutions for the following cubic equation:

$$x^3 - 6x^2 + 3x + 10 = 0$$

To give you a clue, all the solutions lie somewhere between -2 and $+6$.

You may also like to plot the equations using a graphics, curve sketching or spreadsheet package. Can you spot your solutions on the graph?

You are the promoter for a pop concert. You are going to organise a concert with a famous group or singer. You have certain overheads such as the costs of the group, singer, etc., as well as costs of rental of the hall, printing of tickets, security guards, refreshments, programmes, etc.

You are to produce a model of the business and simulate a variety of different situations e.g. very few people turning up, a sell out concert, etc.

Produce a report showing examples of your model and explain any assumptions you made in making your model. Give a conclusion explaining, how closely your model mimics the real situation and outline any improvements you could make.

In this task you will be required to solve a pair of equations simultaneously.

Here is the pair of equations:

$$y = x^2 - 4x + 7$$
$$y = x + 1$$

The first equation is called a quadratic equation and the second is called a linear equation. The solution to the simultaneous equations will be a value of x when put into either of the equations, that will give the same value of y. There are two such values of x for which this will happen and you, using a spreadsheet model will have to find them.

If you are submitting this task as part of your coursework, you need to make sure that you have fully documented both the initial problem and its solution. The structure of your solution should fall under the following headings:

- Identify
- Analyse
- Design
- Use or implement
- Evaluate.

You have been asked to produce a model for electricity usage in a house over a year. Quantity of electricity is measured in a unit called a kilowatt hour (written as kWh). A 1 kWh appliance, such as a one bar electric fire, used for one hour would consume 1 kWh of electricity. Used for half an hour, it would consume 0.5 kWh. If you are unsure how to calculate amounts of electricity from the power of an appliance and the time it is used, consult your physics teacher.

Things to think about

- Design a document on which you could record the names of the appliances owned and their power consumption.

- Use this document to collect the information.
- Interview the people who use the appliance, find out how long they use it for each week or month and then use this figure to work out the daily usage. You need to do this, because not every appliance will be used each day.
- You will need to find the cost of a 1 kWh unit of electricity.
- Design a spreadsheet to model the situation with suitable column and row headings.
- You will need to calculate the total cost per day and the total cost per year.

Explore the prepared model of traffic flow at a crossroads with traffic lights. Find out the best timing of the NS and EW lights to minimise the queues of traffic for particular rates of traffic flows in each direction. Produce a brief report, including at least one printout to support your conclusions.

Model a set of temporary traffic lights, one at each end of some road works 100 m long. Only one line of traffic can pass, so the lights must be set to allow safe passage of traffic. Investigate the effect of different lengths of time on green on the length of queues for particular rates of traffic flows. Produce a brief report, including printouts of your model and of the queue graphs for different values of variables.

(RSA Spec)

Chapter 34

Graphics Packages

Graphics

Graphics is a word used for all types of artwork, including line diagrams, bitmap images made up of lots of tiny dots, photographs, graphs and charts.

Graphics packages

For most of us, graphics packages can mean just a simple paint package where you can draw line diagrams, flood fill, and produce a variety of shadings. You can also produce text in a variety of fonts and typefaces. These simple but very useful packages can be used as an alternative to specialist and more complicated desktop publishing packages. Producing diagrams is extremely difficult using a mouse so some professional artwork is hand drawn and then scanned into a graphics package. A great deal of professional artwork is now drawn with software packages which do not use a mouse.

Some graphics packages allow you to scan a photograph or diagram directly into the computer so that you can subsequently manipulate it in some way. Using special equipment and software it is possible to capture pictures from a television screen or from a video camera. The extra equipment needed to do this is called a video grabber.

If you need to use pictures then you can use clip art.

Bit map and vector graphics

There are two formats that a graphics file can have; it can represent the image as a bit map or as a vector graphic.

A bit map file represents each dot or pixel on the screen as a single bit of information in a file. If the pixel is in colour, then additional bits will need to be stored. Many

paint packages such as PC Paintbrush and MacPaint create bit mapped images. One of the main disadvantages of bitmapped images is that they are difficult to change because they have to be altered a pixel at a time.

With vector graphics, the lines are stored as equations inside the computer. They are expressed in vector format so they have a starting point, a length and a direction. The main advantage of vector graphics is that they are easy to change without any loss of resolution. With bit mapped graphics, if the image is enlarged, the number of pixels used stays the same. As a result of this the pixels move further apart and this makes the image

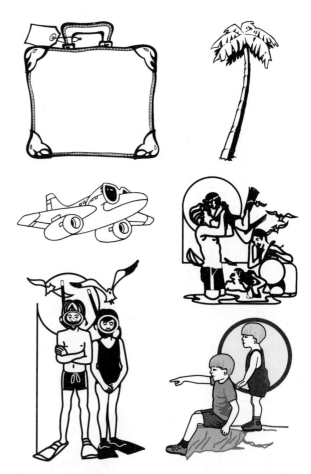

Figure 34.1 *Some holiday clip art*

look grainy. When a vector graphics image is enlarged, the number of pixels used to make up the image increases in proportion and the resolution stays the same.

CAD packages make use of vector graphics.

Clip art

For those without an artistic streak, the thought of having to draw pictures to be placed in an important document can bring on a cold sweat. Anyone who has tried to use a mouse to draw pictures using a paint or draw package will know how hard it is. Help is at hand however with clip art. Clip art illustrations are copyright-free drawings which you can place in your documents. These documents could be wordprocessed, desktop published or could be a diagram drawn using a graphics package. Some clip art is shown in Figure 34.1.

Because clip art is accurately predrawn when imported into your documents, it gives a professional look to the documents. Disks containing clip art can be bought separately or as part of a graphics or DTP package. CorelDraw!, which is the most popular graphics package in use, has over 23 000 pieces of clip art. With this number, the hardest part is choosing the most suitable. Clip art is available covering all manner of subjects. Anglia Television, whose address is at the back of this book, produces a huge variety of clip art on GCSE subjects. See Figures 34.2 and Figure 34.3.

Presentation software

Pictures are able to communicate ideas and concepts to an audience much better than the written or spoken word alone. Presentations are used to sell products, services or just ideas to someone else. Good presentations use visual aids such as slides or transparencies on a projector. The visual aids are used to backup what the presenter is saying. Graphs are usually included in such presentations. If the work is displayed attractively, then the audience will be more able to digest the key points.

Figure 34.2 *Examples of clip art*

Ancient Egypt (KS2)
Aztecs (KS2)
Birds of New Zealand and Australia
Britain 1750–1900 (KS3)
Britain since 1930 (KS2)
Castles (KS2/3)
Clothing through the Ages
Explorers of Australia and New Zealand
Famous Faces 1
Famous Faces 2
Farm Animals (KS2/3)
The Greeks (KS2)
Human Biology (KS2/3)
Invaders (KS2)
Mediaeval Realms (KS3)
Music and Instruments
Natural History of Britain
North American Animals
Prehistoric Animals
The Romans Romans (KS3)
Shakespearean Characters (KS3/4)
Ships through the Ages (KS2/3)
United Kingdom 1500–1750 (KS3)
World War II (KS3)

Figure 34.3 *List of clip art disks available from Anglia Television*

While a projector is needed for a large audience, for smaller audiences a rolling slide show can be produced on the screen of a computer.

Multimedia (hypermedia) presentations

Multimedia is sometimes called hypermedia. Multimedia presentations are useful for training since students can see demonstrations onscreen and can also interact with the software. It is hard to explain the capabilities of multimedia and you should look at different packages for yourself.

Colour

Colour printing is affordable if you use an ink-jet printer, but colour laser printers are expensive both to buy and to run. When producing graphics you need to decide whether they are to be printed out. It you do not have a colour printer then there is no point in worrying about colour when planning your design on the screen. You will find that much clearer graphics are produced on black and white printers if you use black and white on the screen.

Computer aided design

Computer aided design or CAD for short, is used by engineers, architects, etc. to produce high quality technical drawings drawn to scale. The sorts of diagram produced by these packages include plans of houses, maps, circuit diagrams, engineering drawings, 3D plans of kitchens, etc. Figure 34.5 shows a stairway design which has been produced using CAD.

Before computers were used, if a drawing needed a simple modification then it was often necessary to completely redraw it. Now, with the use of CAD software modifications can be made at the press of a button.

Architects can produce a plan view of a building and then immediately view it in three dimensions and even rotate it to see

TASK

Using a mouse and drawing package
When people want to find you, it is handy to give them a map. Here is a map for you to copy.

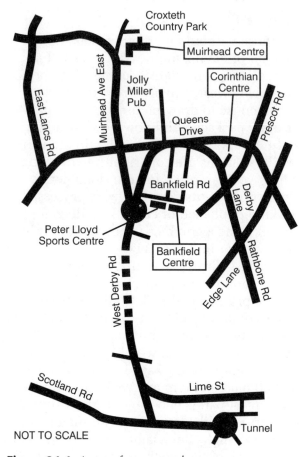

Figure 34.4 *A map for you to draw*

Use appropriate software such as a painting, drawing or art package to perform the following tasks:

1 copy the map shown in Figure 34.4. Try to make it exactly the same and use a mouse to draw the roads

2 add the landmarks such as the Jolly Miller Pub, Peter Lloyd Sports Centre, etc.

3 add the text to your diagram, making sure that the size and font are suitable

4 add the boxes around the text as shown in the diagram

5 save your work using a suitable file name

6 print a copy of your map.

Now design and draw your own map, showing directions either to your house or to your school or college.

what it looks like from different angles. The most popular CAD package is AutoCAD, which is quite expensive, so you are unlikely to see it in schools. There is a cut down version available at a much lower price.

Advantages of using CAD:
1 it saves a lot of time
2 it produces accurate scale diagrams
3 you can easily manipulate the images on the screen
4 you can produce drawings in 3D, which is especially useful for diagrams of kitchens, gardens, buildings, etc.
5 images can be saved on disk and retrieved at a later date
6 drawings can easily be scaled up and down.

Figure 34.5 *Stairway design produced using CAD software*

THINGS TO DO

1 (a) Explain what is meant by the abbreviation CAD.

(b) Give three advantages of using CAD against performing the same task manually.

2 A friend of your family knows of your interest in computers and has asked you your opinion regarding buying a multimedia computer system.

(a) What makes a multimedia system different from an ordinary computer system?

(b) Describe two of the multimedia packages that you have used.

3 Many people find it easier to use clip art than use their own diagrams.

(a) Explain what is meant by 'clip art'.

(b) Why is it easier to use clip art?

(c) What are the disadvantages of using clip art?

Pick one of the following, and use any graphics, paint or other package to help you with your design.

1 Design a package that could be used to hold a single golf ball. You will need to design the shape of the package and design the net.

2 You have been asked by a fabric manufacturer to come up with a new design for a fabric. Use appropriate software to do this.

3 A friend of yours is a question master in a local pub quiz. He decides that it would be nice to include a page of flags of different countries of the world in the quiz. The idea is that each contestant will be given a sheet with the flags on and the contestant has to write the name of the country underneath. If you do not have access to a colour printer then you could try taking a photograph of the screen. You could find the designs of the flags with an atlas such as World Atlas held on CD-ROM.

Many companies use logos as part of their advertising. These logos are cleverly thought out and enable people to recognise the company or their products.

To see how important they are, can you draw the logos for the following companies:

• MacDonald   • BT

- Acorn Computers
- Shell
- the National Lottery.
- Peugeot Cars
- the Bradford & Bingley Building Society

Choose a company which does not use a logo at the moment and design a logo for it using graphics software. You should include several designs, so that the company could be able to choose between them. Also include a wordprocessed report outlining the ideas behind your logos.

You have been asked by the teacher of a local primary school to produce diagrams of a series of objects that can be coloured in by the pupils. Underneath each diagram will be the name of the object in large print so that the pupils can be taught to read.

Produce, using appropriate software, a series of suitable diagrams for this purpose. Remember that the diagrams will need to be quite large, otherwise they will be too difficult to colour in.

Look through a selection of clip art using a drawing, painting or graphics package for any clip art connected with transport. The clip art should be grouped into the following:

- road: cars, bicycles, vans, lorries and motorbikes
- rail: locomotives and carriages
- air: balloons, gliders, spacecraft, jets and helicopters
- water: pleasure craft, ferries, tankers, yachts and freight ships.

Produce an attractive display of clip art images under each of the above headings. A small piece of text should be added about each one.

A teacher in a junior school has approached you for some help in designing a sheet to be used by pupils for explaining the names and properties of certain shapes. The shapes they would like you to include are as follows:

- rectangle
- rhombus
- kite •
- right-angled triangle
- isosceles triangle.
- square
- parallelogram

trapezium
- equilateral triangle

Remember, as well as drawing these shapes, you have to name them and write a small piece explaining their properties.

You could try doing a similar task involving 3D shapes, such as cuboids, cylinders, etc.

You have been asked by your history teacher to find out about one of the following events:

(a) the English Civil War

(b) the American Civil War

(c) the First World War

(d) man landing on the Moon for the first time.

Produce sample illustrations, such as photographs from encyclopaedias held on CD-ROMs, appropriate clip art, scanned artwork from a book or even a drawing you have produced yourself using a suitable package. In the chapter on desktop publishing, there is an exercise to incorporate these illustrations in the text.

Produce a heart shape for a Valentine's card using the LOGO programming language. Fully document your solution by providing explanations of the methods you used to try to solve the problem. Evidence of your work should be provided in the from of program listings and screen dumps onto a printer. Include all your work, including the parts that you rejected. Now try to use an art package to do the same thing. What functions in the drawing package did you use? Make comparisons between the two ways of solving the problem. Which one was the easiest to use? Again, fully document your solution.

 This task requires a knowledge of chemistry.

Using suitable software, produce a selection of hazard symbols (see Figure 34.6).

Figure 34.6

Using a selection of clip art images and the cut, paste and copy facilities, come up with repeating designs for one of the following:

- Christmas wrapping paper
- birthday wrapping paper
- wallpaper.

 There is a variety of diagrams that can be used to describe a system, such as system flowcharts, structure diagrams and data flow diagrams. The diagrams make use of a variety of different shaped boxes. Some graphics packages have these boxes included with them as clip art.

Find out if your graphics package has any of these shapes; and if not produce a selection and store each one in a separate file to be used later.

Finally, produce a systems flowchart (use the one on page 89 if you cannot make one up of your own) using your graphics package.

 Produce a garden design using a painting or other suitable package. Remember that certain plants are in bloom at different times of the year so you could try to incorporate this fact in some way.

It is Christmas and the police are worried about people drinking and driving. There have been several fatal accidents involving people who have been drinking. Produce a poster which can be placed on pub walls outlining the horrors or the consequences of drinking and driving.

You have decided to sell your home computer or games console. Use DTP software to produce an advert for the system you are selling which will be placed on a school or college notice board. Try to make your design as eyecatching as possible, by using special text effects, boxes and graphics.

Design and print a ticket for any one of the following:
- a disco
- a school concert
- a party for a special occasion
- a garden fete.

You have been asked by your local hospital to draw people's attention to personal hygiene. You decide to produce a series of posters. The sorts of topics you might consider could include:
- washing hands after using the toilet
- keeping food covered while left out.

Any health or hygiene message can be used. Go for a catchy phrase to help get your message across.

SKILLS BUILDING

You have been asked to produce a picture of birthday cake like the one shown in Figure 34.7 using a drawing/paint package.

Happy
Birthday
John

Figure 34.7

1 Load your software.
2 Draw a single candle with the flame at the top and save it to disk so that it can be copied as many times as you like.
3 Draw the rest of the cake.
4 Using suitable commands, copy and position the required number of candles on the top of the cake.
5 Select suitable fonts for the text and place the text in position on the diagram.
6 Save your design and then print it out.

Could you produce a better diagram of the cake shown? Have a go and print out your effort.

Preparing for the Exam

Revising

Most people think of revision as just reading notes and trying to remember them. This is true to some extent but there are some ways of revising more effectively. We will look at several ways of revising and some of the likely questions you would want to ask about revision.

Where should you revise?

Choose a room where there will be no distractions. Work at a table or desk, make sure that there is a bright light on the table and that the room is warm. Some students like to work in a local library. This can be quite a good idea but there can be distractions, such as people moving around. However there won't be the other distractions that you may have at home such as brothers, sisters, radios and TVs. Try to work in silence. Your revision will be a lot more effective and you will not need to revise for as long (Figure 35.1).

You should make a timetable and decide how long to revise for, then you will have earned your free time. Planned breaks in revision increase the amount of information you retain.

How often should you revise?

Revision should be a constant process throughout the years of your course (Figure 35.2). Try not to leave your revision to the few weeks before the exam. Divide your work into topics and then revise a topic at a time. Don't move on to a new topic until you have mastered the old one. It is better to have a thorough knowledge of a few topics than a skimpy knowledge of the whole syllabus.

When is the best time to revise?

Most people are at their peak early in the morning. Near exam time try to get up earlier. If you are on holiday then early morning is an ideal time, because you will have fewer distractions from other people in the house. Early evening is a good time, before you get tired.

Figure 35.1 *It is important to revise in the right surroundings*

Figure 35.2

What shall I revise?

Ideally it would be best if you could revise the whole syllabus. If you have difficulty with certain topics then you could leave them out but you would need to know the other topics really well.

Obtain a copy of your syllabus either by asking your teacher or by sending off to the examination board for their price list. The names and addresses of the examination boards are in the list of suppliers at the back of the book.

Using the syllabus to guide you, make a revision checklist of all the topics you need to study and tick them off as you complete your revision of each topic.

Syllabus and past papers

It will help a lot if you get your own copy of the examination syllabus. Since there are many different examination boards and sometimes different syllabuses even for the same subject with some examination boards, you should ask you teacher which board and syllabus you are following.

When you buy your own copy of the syllabus you will also be able to buy some copies of recent examination papers. You

may also find that your local library or school library has copies of these publications. If you can't find them, ask the librarian in the reference section.

Near the time of the exam, check to see how much of the syllabus you have covered. Sometimes your teacher may not have time to cover the whole syllabus. If this happens, look at your syllabus to see which parts have been left out. You could then study the missing parts on your own. Having a set of past papers will enable you to see the way the exam is set out. You can familiarise yourself with the structure of the paper.

You can use the exam papers as an aid to your revision. Give yourself mock exams to see how your revision is going. Check your answers using this book or ask your teacher to have a look at them. Once you can answer most of the questions from the past papers, you will have nothing to fear about the actual exam.

Figure 35.3 *Get yourself a syllabus so that you know what to revise*

Programme of Study	Content		Statements of Attainment
Pupils should be taught to:	Related to Technology Theme	General	Pupils should be able to:
understand that simulations using IT can be used for dangerous, costly or long timescale investigations, and those that are difficult to measure	investigate the use of simulation software for aircrew training, and explore the realism of flight simulators for small computer systems	investigate the use of simulation software for industrial chemistry; genetic simulations; economic forecasting	7f understand that dangerous or costly investigations, or those not easily measured can be simulated using IT
model a process or situation that is controlled by a number of variable factors, and identify the relationships between these variables	create a computer model to show projected traffic flows in a new development which includes residential, commercial and industrial building	create a computer model of population growth in the UK from the 18th century, and alter factors such as birth and death rates, immigration and emigration	8d use software to represent a situation or process with variables, and show the relationship between them
know that the mathematical basis of a computer representation of a situation determines how accurately the model reflects reality	design a program to estimate the stopping distances of vehicles of differing sizes at differing speeds in different weather conditions; a spreadsheet to anticipate trends in passenger travel	design a model to simulate breeding of Drosophila to demonstrate monohybrid inheritance; a model of the British economy	9a evaluate a software package or a complex computer model; analyse the situation for which it was developed; assess its efficiency, ease of implementation and appropriateness and suggest refinements
analyse a situation and then design, implement, assess and refine a complex model to present it	design a system to model and investigate the movement of individual items of freight for a haulage company	design a system to model and investigate production schedules and stockholding strategies for a company making and distributing fast foods	9b design, implement and document a system for others to use
analyse systems to be modelled using information technology, make choices in designing, implementing and testing them, and justify the methods they have used	develop a system to test a person's readiness to take a driving test	develop a system to notify an insurance broker's clients that their policies are due for renewal; design a system to operate a heated greenhouse in an energy-efficient way	10a decide how to model a system, and design, implement and test it; justify methods used and choices made
Strand D **Measurement and Content** know that programmable devices can be controlled using sequences of instructions, and use such devices	use a programmable vehicle	use pre-defined procedure in Logo	3b give a sequence of direct instructions to control movement

Figure 35.4 *Page from the Southern Examining Group's syllabus*

Things to check just before the exam

1 Collect the necessary equipment: two pens, in case one dries up; two pencils; a sharpener; a rubber; and a ruler. You may be allowed to use a flowchart template but check first. You might not be able to use one with the names of the boxes on it.
2 Always take a watch into the exam. There will be a clock in the exam room but if you are at the back of the room you might not be able to see it.
3 Go to the toilet before the exam; this avoids the embarrassment of having to leave the room under supervision.
4 Check to see if you have to wear school uniform.

Things to check in the exam room

1 Check that you have the correct exam paper in front of you. Several different exams may be going on at the same time.
2 Check that there are no pages missing from the paper. It is not unknown for a page to be blank. If there is anything wrong with the paper, such as your not being able to read the print, then you should ask for a new paper.

The exam

The following list gives some hints on things you should do when actually taking the exam.

1 Always read the instructions on the front of the paper carefully. In particular, note the time you are allowed.
2 Time yourself. Don't spend too much time on a question that you can answer well at the expense of other questions.
3 Try to write neatly. The examiners have hundreds of scripts to mark and it is not worth risking annoying an examiner by making her waste time deciphering an untidy script.
4 Only do what the question asks. If it asks for two reasons, make sure that you give two: not three or one. Always check that, in an answer to a question with two parts, you have not written similar answers to both parts. If you have, you will only obtain marks on one of them.
5 Use the mark scheme at the side of the questions as a guide to how much you should write. If there are, say, two marks, there must be two points you need to mention in order to get both marks.
6 After you have answered a question, read it through again to make sure that you have not missed part of it out.

Examination Questions

Here are a variety of recent examinations covering material present on all the examination board's syllabuses.

1 An experiment is set up to investigate the rate at which boiling water cools. It has been decided to use data-logging equipment connected to a microcomputer to collect this data.
   (a) What type of sensor would be used to collect this data?
   (b) A suitable time interval and period of logging have to be chosen.
       (i) What is meant by the term "time-interval"?
       (ii) What is meant by the term "period of logging"?
       (iii) From the lists below, choose the most suitable time interval and period of logging for this experiment.
           Possible time intervals: 30 sec, 30 mins, 10 hrs, 24 hrs, 48 hrs
           Possible periods of logging: 30 sec, 30 mins, 10 hrs, 24 hrs, 48 hr
           Most suitable time interval   Most suitable period of logging
       (iv) State **two** suitable ways in which the data collected from this experiment could be displayed on the screen (VDU).
       (v) Give **two** advantages of using data-logging for this experiment rather than taking manual readings with a thermometer.

   (NEAB June 95 Option Q)

2 Give **three** reasons why it might be easier to misuse personal information stored on computer files rather than the same information stored on paper files.

   (NEAB June 95 Option Q)

3 The widespread use of IT in the workplace has had a great effect on employment.
   (a) Give **two** examples of jobs which have been created by the introduction of IT.
   (b) Give **two** examples of jobs which may have been lost by the introduction of IT.

   (NEAB June 95 Option Q)

4 Computer simulation can be used to test the potential performance of aeroplanes during their design.
   (a) Give **two** reasons why computer simulation is used in this situation.
   (b) Name and briefly describe **two** other situations in which computer simulation might reasonably be used.

   (NEAB June 95 Option Q)

5 A tyre manufacturer uses a computer-based model to work out the stopping distances of cars.
   (a) Give **two** reasons why a tyre manufacturer would use a computer-based model.
   (b) You are asked to design a computer-based model to work out the stopping distances of cars.
       One factor that will need to be considered is the condition of the tyres.
       Identify **three** other factors that will affect stopping distance once braking has started.
   (c) Your model will be based on rules that link the different factors.
       One rule might be:
       "A car with bald tyres takes longer to stop".
       Describe **two** possible rules for the factors you have identified in your answer to (b).
   (d) (i) Explain how you would check that **one** of your suggested rules is correct.
       (ii) Explain how you would test the whole model.

   (SEG June 95 HT)

6 GoSun travel agency arranges day trips.

This is a fax sent to the station manager at Nelson railway station.

FAX

TO: The station manager, Nelson railway station.

FROM: GoSun travel agency.

On 1/7/95 at 8.00 a.m., there will be a daily trip by train from Nelson to Blackpool. The return fare is £3.50.

Please arrange local advertising.

The station manager has asked you to design a poster to advertise this day trip.

(a) Explain why the fax itself is not suitable for advertising this day trip.

(b) From the list, write down **two** forms of information that could be in the poster.

formulae

pictures

graphs

sound

words

(c) Write down **four** items of information in the fax that must be included in the poster.

(d) Tick **one** box to choose the software you would use to produce the poster.

Software	Tick **one** box
Database	
Desk Top Publishing (DTP)	
Games	
Spreadsheet	
Viewdata	

(e) Give **two** reasons why the software you choose is better than a wordprocessor for producing a poster.

(f) You can print out the poster on **one** of these printers.

  daisy wheel

  dot matrix

  laser

 (i) From the list, write down the type of printer that would produce the best black and white poster.

 (ii) Give **two** reasons for your choice.

(g) GoSun keeps the information about all its day trips on a database.

This is part of the database:

Trip number	From	To	Date	Transport
027	Leeds	Chester	27/10/95	Rail
369	Watford	Bradford	01/01/96	Bus
041	Guildford	Plymouth	14/12/95	Rail
333	Colchester	Plymouth	16/11/95	Rail
502	St. Ives	London	02/03/96	Bus
691	Leeds	London	11/09/95	Rail
413	London	Reading	11/09/95	Rail

(i) Write down the name of the field that would be used as the key field.

(ii) Write down the **Trip Number** of the day trips selected by these search conditions

Search Condition 1: **Date** is 14/12/95

Search Condition 2: **Transport** is Rail AND **To** is London

Search Condition 3: **From** is Colchester OR **To** is Reading

(iii) State **three** more fields that should be included in each record.

(iv) Complete the sentences using terms from the list.

amend

delete

insert

search

sort

You remove a record from the database when you .... the record.

The records are arranged in the order you asked for when you .... the file.

You change the data in a field when you .... the field.

(v) Explain why the database should be a direct access file.

(vi) GoSun has 800 day trips on the database.

Give **two** advantages to GoSun in using a database instead of writing down the information about the day trips.

(SEG June 95 IT)

7 Mail order companies store personal data about their customers on computer files. The Data Protection Act is designed to protect customers from data misuse.

(a) Give **three** rights that this Act gives to the customer. (3 marks)

(b) Give **five** requirements concerning data that the company must meet to comply with the Act. (5 marks)

(c) Some data is granter exemption from some of the provisions of the Act. Give three grounds for partial exemption, stating the type of exemption allowed. (6 marks)

(NEAB Tier R June 95)

8 The owners of a chain of video shops are considering using a computer system to handle stock records and loans of videos. You are asked to produce a feasibility report.

(a) Describe **three** ways in which you could find out about the existing system. (6 marks)

(b) As a result of this study, you are asked to design a new computerised system.

Give **three** items the design should include. (3 marks)

(c) When the new system is installed, a User Guide is provided for the shop staff. Describe **three** topics you would expect to be covered in this guide. (3 marks)

(d) When the system is installed, the staff may not be able to use it straight away. Give **two** reasons why they might not be able to switch to the new system immediately. (2 marks)

(NEAB Tier R June 95)

9 The temperature and soil moisture of a greenhouse must be controlled and must remain in a certain range. The temperature must be kept between 5°C and 30°C and the soil must not get too dry.

Describe, in detail, how a computer system could be used to monitor and control both the temperature and soil moisture in the greenhouse. In your answer state what items of hardware or equipment could be needed. (12 marks)

(WJEC May 95 P1 Option R q4)

10 The Science department in a school uses software to demonstrate the working of a nuclear reactor. The pupils find the graphics and animation more attractive than written explanations.

Give one other reason for using this software to explain the process. (1 mark)

(WJEC May 95 P1 Option R q5)

11 The headteacher of a school wants to use an Information System for school administration. In particular, pupils' school records would be kept on the system.

(a) Design a capture form for parents to complete so that basic pupil information can be set up. (5 marks)

(b) Some of the fields could be fixed and others of variable length.

(i) Give **one** advantage of using fixed length fields. (1 mark)

(ii) Give **one** disadvantage of using fixed length fields. (1 mark)

(c) Explain how you could verify that the entries in the pupil file are correct. (1 mark)

(d) The software package used enables validation to be carried out on certain fields.

Explain the term validation. (2 marks)

(e) Name three different types of validation that can be carried out on setting up a pupil record. (3 marks)

(f) The database file on pupil records is very large. What method can be used to minimise storage requirements when archive copies are made? (2 marks)

(WJEC June 95 P2 Option R q4)

12 What method of data capture would be most suitable for the following situations?

(a) (i) Data from football pools coupons.

(ii) The loan of a book from a library. (2 marks)

(b) (i) What do banks use M.I.C.R. for ?

(ii) Give one advantage of M.I.C.R. over other methods of data capture. (2 marks)

(WJEC June 95 Option Q Paper 2 q2)

13 Priory National is a bank.

A certain high street branch of Priory National has eight cashier service windows for customers to use.

Many aspects of the business of the branch are controlled by a computer system customers to use.

Many aspects of the business of the branch are controlled by a computer system called BILL.

Above each of the cashier windows there is a pair of lights:

A green light on indicates that the cashier is available.

A red light on indicates that the cashier is busy.

No lights on indicates that there is not a cashier at the window.

The lights for each window are controlled by the cashier at that window.

The states of all the lights are recorded by the states of two specific eight bit bytes in BILL.

(a) The byte that records the states of the eight red lights is called **R** and the type that controls the states of the eight green lights is called **G**.

A bit set to 1 would mean that the light was **on** and a bit set to 0 would mean that the light was **off**.

(i) Complete the table below to show the state of the lights:

Colour	Byte Name	Byte Pattern	State of Lights
Red	**R**	11100101	–,–,–,–,–,–,–,–
Green	**G**	00010010	–,–,–,–,–,–,–,–

(2 marks)

(ii) In the table below, write down ONE combination of patterns of **R** and **G** that should not be allowed.

Colour	Byte Name	Byte Pattern
Red	**R**	
Green	**G**	

(2 marks)

(b) BILL has been programmed recently to record how long each individual cashier spends with a customer.

(i) Describe how BILL could "know" which cashier is at any particular service window. (2 marks)

(ii) A the end of each month the SERVICE TIME file is processed to produce two reports.

REPORT 1. A list of the average service time for each cashier in alphabetical order of the name of the cashier.

REPORT 2. The name of the cashier who services the largest number of customers.

Explain how the processes of sorting and searching are used in the production of these reports. (4 marks)

(iii) Design a suitable testing procedure for the program that records how much time cashiers spend servicing customers.

(3 marks)

(iv) Some of the members of the management are not happy that BILL should be programmed to record how much time cashiers spent servicing customers.

Give TWO arguments that the managers may have stated against BILL being programmed in this way. (4 marks)

(ULEAC June 95 Higher Tier P2 q3)

14 State THREE ways in which computers are useful in the prevention or detection of crime. (3 marks)

(MEG Syll A Intermediate Tier p2 q2)

15 A database program can do the following tasks:

Create or load a datafile

Ask a single question

Display results

Save a file

(a) Describe THREE other tasks which a database program should be able to do. (3 marks)

(b) The program uses a graphical user interface (GUI). Write down TWO features in a GUI. (2 marks)

(c) Give TWO reasons why it is better to use a graphical user interface rather than to type commands. (2 marks)

(MEG Syll A Intermediate Tier p2 q5)

16 A mechanical arm is connected to a computer. The arm selects objects of different shapes and sizes from a box and places them in separate boxes. Describe how the computer uses sensors to perform the task.   (4 marks)

(MEG Syll A Intermediate Tier p2 q7)

17 A satellite dish on the roof of a school is connected to a computer.

Describe how this system could be used to collect and store pictures of weather over the UK.   (3 marks)

(MEG Syll A Intermediate Tier p2 q3)

18 Describe THREE sensors that are used in an automatic washing machine.   (3 marks)

(MEG Syll A Intermediate Tier p2 q14)

19 A supermarket has several point-of-sale (POS) checkouts connected to a minicomputer in the same building. All goods in the supermarket have bar codes on their labels.

(a) Explain how a bar code is automatically read and accepted at a checkout.   (2 marks)

(b) Describe how each bar code is validated. (2 marks)

(c) Prices are not shown on most of the bar codes. Give a reason for this.   (1 mark)

(d) Some customers pay for their shopping using EFTPOS (Electronic Funds Transfer at Point Of Sale).

Explain how this method of payment works. (4 marks)

(e) Details of the daily sales are stored on the minicomputer. At the end of each day this data needs to be sent to another computer at Head Office many miles away. Describe how this transfer takes place.   (3 marks)

(MEG Syll B Intermediate Tier p2 q3)

20 A group of sales representatives has to decide how to hold an important meeting. The representatives work in different parts of the UK. The two options open to them are either to meet at a hotel or to hold an electronic conference. Compare the two methods of holding the meeting.   (4 marks)

(MEG Syll B Higher Tier p3 q10)

21 Discuss the apparent association between new technology and unemployment.   (6 marks)

(MEG Syll B Higher Tier p3 q15)

22 Describe TWO parts of the Data Protection Act that try to protect us from the misuse or personal data held on computer files.   (2 marks)

(MEG Syll A Higher Tier p3 q8)

23 Computer sometimes hold information about the public. Describe TWO ways in which incomplete or false information can affect individuals and how these problems should be avoided.   (4 marks)

(MEG Syll A Higher Tier p3 q9)

24 Describe THREE sensors that are used in an automatic washing machine.   (3 marks)

(MEG Syll A Higher Tier p3 q6)

25 The management of a supermarket uses a computer for various activities.

Two of these activities are:
Stock Control
Monitoring and controlling Anti-Theft devices.

(a) (i) State the type of software that could be used for each of these activities.

Stock Control   (1 mark)

Anti-Theft   (1 mark)

(ii) Describe how the output from the computer would be presented for each of these activities.

Stock Control   (2 marks)

Anti-Theft   (2 marks)

(b) Otto is the manager of a supermarket.

Otto thinks that more of a particular item are sold if more are displayed on the shelves.

Otto decides to put his thoughts to the test.

On odd numbered weeks he will display two full shelves of YUMYOG yoghurt, but on even numbered weeks only one full shelf of YUMYOG is displayed.

Below is part of a spreadsheet that Otto uses to record the sales of YUMYOG over a ten week period.

	A	B	C
1	Week Number	Number of Sales	
2	1	621	
3	2	407	
4	3		
5	4		
6	5		
7	6		
8	7		
9	8		
10	9		
11	10		
12	Total Number Sold during Odd Weeks	=	
13	Average Number Sold during Odd Weeks	=	
14	Total Number Sold during Even Weeks	=	
15	Average Number Sold during Even Weeks	=	

(i) Explain how Otto must design his spreadsheet to allow the required results to appear in cells C12, C13, C14 and C15.

C12 (2 marks)

C13 (2 marks)

C14 (1 mark)

C15 (1 mark)

(ii) Otto hopes that the total sales during the odd numbered weeks will be at least 500 greater than those during the even numbered weeks.

Describe how the spreadsheet could display the messages:

Otto is right

or   **Otto is wrong**

depending on the current state of the data stored.   (3 marks)

(c) Otto wants to predict the total sales of YUMYOG for the whole year.

He uses the results from his sales experiment to produce a new spreadsheet that will give him this prediction.

(i) Explain why this new spreadsheet that Otto produces is a model of the sales of YUMYOG.   (2 marks)

(ii) State ONE reason why this model might be unreliable.   (2 marks)

(ULEAC June 95 Intermediate Tier P2 Section B q2)

Glossary

Access   To obtain data from the computer.

Actuators   Hardware devices, such as motors, which react according to signals given to them by the computer.

ADC   See analogue-to-digital converter.

Applications package   A program or a set of programs to carry out a particular application, such as accounts or payroll.

Algorithm   A set of rules that gives a sequence of operations for solving a problem.

ALU   See arithmetic and logic unit.

Analogue computer   A computer that works on data represented by some continuous physical quantity such as electric current.

Analogue-to-digital converter   ADC. A device that changes continuously changing quantities (such as temperature) into digital quantities.

Application   What a computer can be used to do.

Archiving   Storing copies of important files for back-up or reference purposes.

Arithmetic and logic unit   Part of the central processing unit. It performs all the arithmetic and logic operations.

Artificial intelligence   The science of developing computers that 'think' like humans.

ASCII   American Standard Code for Information Interchange. A code for representing characters in binary.

Assembler   A program that converts assembly language into machine code.

Assembly language   Low-level language where one programming instruction corresponds to one machine code instruction.

Automation   The automatic control of a process or system without requiring a human operator.

Backing store   Memory storage outside the CPU. It is non-volatile which means the data does not disappear when the computer is switched off.

Backup file   A copy of a file which is used in the event of the original file being corrupted (damaged).

Barcode   A code of lines on the side of goods, luggage, etc.

Barcode reader   An input device used to scan a series of lines (called a barcode).

BASIC   A high-level programming language.

Batch processing   A method of processing where programs are run in batches and data is processed in batches.

Baud rate   A data transmission rate: the number of bits per second.

Bit   Binary digit 0 or 1.

Bitmap   A image represented by patterns of tiny dots called pixels.

Bitmap graphics   Graphics formed by a pattern of pixels. The whole picture is stored as a series of dots.

Buffer   A storage area where data is temporarily stored. Printers have buffers so that the data can wait to be printed while the user can get on with something else.

Bug   A mistake or error in a program.

Byte   The amount of memory needed to store one character, such as a letter or a number. See also kilobyte and megabyte.

C++   A general purpose programming language which is easier to understand than assembly language but runs almost as fast. It is a development of the programming language C.

CAD   Computer aided design. A method of using the computer to produce technical drawings.

CAL (Computer Assisted Learning)   The process of using computers for the instruction, training or testing of learners.

CD-ROM   Compact disk-read only memory.

Cell   An area on a spreadsheet produced by the intersection of a column and a row in which data may be placed.

Central processing unit   CPU. The computer's brain. It stores and processes data. It has three parts: the ALU, the control unit and the memory.

Character   Any symbol that you can type from the keyboard.

Check digit   A number placed after a string of numbers to check that they have all been correctly input to the computer.

Chip   An integrated circuit etched onto a thin slice of silicon.

Clones   The name given to computers that are copies of the original IBM Personal Computer.

COBOL   A high-level programming language used mainly in business because of its good file handling facilities. COBOL is an abbreviation for COmmon

Business Orientated Language.

Compiler   Software that converts a high-level language program into machine code.

Configuration   The hardware that is needed to set up a certain computer system.

Continuous stationery   Stationery in continuous sheets, for use, for example, with a dot matrix printer. It may be pre-printed with company logos etc.

CPS   Characters per second. A measure of the speed of data transfer between hardware devices.

CSV   Comma separated variables. A way of holding data so that it can be transferred into databases or spreadsheets.

Data   Information in a form that a computer can understand.

Database   A series of files stored in a computer which can be accessed in a variety of different ways.

Data capture   The way the computer obtains its data for processing.

Data compression   Taking files on a disk and using software to reduce their size so that they take up less space on the disk.

Data logging   A system that automatically collects data over a certain period of time. Remote weather stations use data logging.

Data processing   Doing something with raw data to produce some form of useful output.

Data Protection Act, 1984   A law that restricts the way personal information is stored and processed on a computer.

Debugging   Removing all the errors in a program.

Decollate   To separate the sheets of continuous stationery.

Desktop publishing   Software that can be used to combine text and pictures on a screen to produce neat looking posters, newsletters, brochures, etc.

Digital computer   A computer that works on data represented by numbers. Most ordinary computers are digital.

Directory   A list of the names of programs and files stored on a disk. The directory enables files to be retrieved from backing store by the operating system.

Disk   A storage medium used to hold data.

Document   A text file produced by a wordprocessor.

Documentation   The paperwork that accompanies an information system explaining how the system works. The manuals that accompany a program.

DOS   Disk Operating System. A program that tells a computer how to work. Controlling data storage on the disk drives is one of the many tasks it performs.

Dot matrix printer   An impact printer that produces characters by using a print head with either 24 or 9 pins that punch through a ribbon onto the paper.

DPI   Dots per inch. The term is used to describe the resolution of printers. A 600 DPI laser printer will produce a sharper image than a 300 DPI printer.

Dry run   Writing down the results of each program step manually to check that the program is correct.

e-mail   Electronic mail. With e-mail messages and documents can be created, sent and read without the need for them to be printed out.

EDI   Electronic data interchange. A network link that allows companies to pay suppliers electronically without the need for invoices and cheques.

Edit   Changing something stored on a computer.

EFT   Electronic fund transfer. The process of transferring money electronically without the need for paperwork or the delay that using paperwork brings.

EFTPOS   Electronic fund transfer point of sale. Where electronic fund transfer takes place at a point of sale terminal.

Electronic mail   See e-mail.

Encrypt   Sensitive files can be encrypted, which means coding them. To be read they have to be decoded.

EPOS   Electronic point of sale. A computerised till which can be used for stock control.

Ergonomics   The science of the correct design of working equipment and the working environment.

Execution errors   Errors detected during the running of a program.

Evaluation   The process of determining the quality of software or hardware.

Expert system   A program that behaves in the same way as a human expert in a specialist field.

Fact finding   The investigation of a system prior to performing a feasibility study.

Fax   A machine capable of sending and receiving text and pictures sent along telephone lines.

Feasibility study   A study carried out by experts before a new system is developed to see what type of system is needed.

Fibre optics   Thin strands of glass along which light signals pass for communication purposes.

Field   A space in a database used for inputting data. For instance, you could have fields for surname, date of birth, etc.

Field check   A check performed by a computer to see if the data is the right type to be put into a field. It would be able to check that only numbers are entered into numeric fields.

File   A collection of related data; for example, a student file would contain details of all students in a school.

File server   A network computer used for storing all the users' programs and data.

Flat-file database A database that is able to use only one file at a time unlike a relational database, which is able to use two or more files at a time.

Floppy disk A magnetically coated disk used to store data. The 3.5 inch disk is inside a hard case.

Flowchart Flow diagram. A chart or diagram used to break down a task into smaller parts.

Font A style of type.

FORTRAN A high-level programming language.

Gateway The connecting computer link that translates between two different kinds of computer networks.

Generation of files Every time a file is updated, a new generation of the file is produced.

GIGO Garbage in garbage out. It means that if you put rubbish into the computer then you get rubbish out.

Grammar checker A program (usually part of a wordprocessing package) that checks a document for grammatical errors and provides suggestions for the corrections.

Graph plotter A device that draws by moving a pen. It is useful for scale drawings and is used mainly with CAD packages.

Graphics Diagrams, charts or graphs either on the screen or printed out.

GUI Graphical User Interface. A way of allowing users to communicate with a computer that makes use of icons and pull-down menus. Windows is a GUI and Macintosh computers use a GUI.

Hacker A computer enthusiast who tries to break into a secure computer system.

Hard copy Printed output from a computer which may be taken away and studied.

Hard disk A rigid magnetic disk which provides more storage and faster access than a floppy disk.

Hard drive A unit containing a hard disk.

Hardware The components of the computer system that you can actually touch. These would include the visual display unit, processor, printer, modem, etc.

Hash total A meaningless total of numbers used to check that all the numbers have been entered into the computer.

Hexadecimal A number base system used by computers. Hexadecimal numbers use a number base of 16, compared with the number base of 10 that we normally use.

High-level language A programming language where each instruction corresponds to several machine code instructions.

Icons Symbols displayed on the screen in the form of a menu.

Immediate access store Storage in the memory of the central processing unit.

Impact printer Any printer that relies on a character pressing against an inked ribbon for its operation.

Implementation The process of converting over to a new system.

Information What we get from a set of data.

Information retrieval The process of recovering information after it has been stored.

Information technology The application of a combination of computing, electronics and communications.

Ink-jet printer A printer that works by spraying ink through nozzles onto the paper.

Input Data fed into a computer for processing.

Integrated circuit Semiconductor circuits inside a single crystal of semiconductor.

Interactive A program or system that allows the user to respond to questions from the computer (and vice versa) and immediately acts on the answers.

Interface The hardware and software used to enable devices to be connected together. (e.g. an interface would be needed to connect a joystick to a computer)

Internet Worldwide computer network of networks. The Internet forms the largest connected set of computers in the world.

Interpreter A program that converts a high-level language into machine code. An interpreter is different from a compiler because it translates each instruction and then carries it out. Compilers translate the whole of the program first and then carry out each instruction separately.

Interrogation The process of getting information from a file.

Invoice A bill.

Joystick An input device used instead of the cursor keys or mouse as a way of producing movement on the screen.

K Kilobyte or 1024 bytes. Often abbreviated as KB. A measure of the storage capacity of disks and memory.

Keyboard A computer keyboard consists of the standard typewriter keys plus calculator keys and some special keys.

Key-to-disk A way of inputting data directly into a computer and onto disk using the keyboard.

Kimball tag A piece of card with holes punched in it which represents a code. When something is bought, the card is removed and input to a computer. It is used mainly in clothes shops for stock control.

LAN Local Area Network. A network of computers on one site

Laptop   A portable computer small enough to fit in your lap. Laptop computers use rechargeable batteries.

Laser printer   A printer which uses a laser beam to form characters on the paper.

LOGO   A simple computer language which enables a 'turtle' to move according to the instructions given to it.

Loop   A sequence of steps in a program which repeat more than once.

Low-level language   A programming language very similar to the machine language of the computer. Each low-level instruction can easily be converted into a machine code instruction.

Machine code   The language the computer can understand without it being translated. Each type of computer has its own machine code.

Magnetic ink character recognition   MICR. Method of input that involves reading magnetic ink characters on certain documents. MICR is used on cheques by banks.

Magnetic media   Media such as tape and disk where the data is stored as a magnetic pattern.

Magnetic stripe reader   Reads the data contained in magnetic stripes, such as those on the back of credit cards.

Magneto optical disk   Combines the technologies of magnetic media and CD-ROM to produce a disk looking like a CD-ROM but with the difference in that you can read and write to it, and data on it can be erased

Machine readable   Data that can be input directly into a computer without any data preparation. For example, the magnetic ink characters on cheques are machine readable.

Mainframe   A large computer system with many dumb terminals attached.

Mainstore   Memory inside a CPU.

Master file   The main source of information and the most important file.

Medium   The material on which data can be stored, such as magnetic disk, tape, etc.

Memory   Area of storage inside silicon chips. ROM and RAM are two types of memory.

Merge   The combination of data from two different sources.

Megabyte   One million bytes.

Megahertz (MHz)   One million cycles per second. The speed of the internal clock which controls the speed of the pulses in the computer is measured in megahertz. Chip design and clock speed determine the overall performance of the CPU.

Microcomputer   A cheap but relatively slow computer that is able to work only on one program at a time. The memory is usually limited.

Modem   MODulator/DEModulator. A modem converts data from a computer into a form that can be passed along a telephone wire.

Monitor   Another name for a VDU.

Mouse   An input device which, when it is moved over a table, moves a cursor on the screen. Buttons on a mouse are pressed to make a selection from a menu.

MS-DOS   Microsoft Disk Operating System. An operating system used by personal computers.

Multi-access system   A system which allows many different users to gain access to a computer. Each user appears to have sole access because of the speed of the CPU, although in actual fact the time is being shared amongst the users.

Multimedia   Software that combines more than one medium for presentation purposes, such as sound, graphics and video.

Network   A group of computers which are able to communicate with each other. See also LAN and WAN.

OCR   Optical character recognition. A combination of software and a scanner which is able to read characters into a computer.

OMR   Optical mark reader/recognition. A reader that detects marks on a piece of paper. Shaded areas are detected and the computer can understand the information contained in them.

On/off-line   When a device is under the control of the computer it is said to be on-line.

Operating system   The software that controls the hardware and also runs the programs.

Output   The results from processing data.

Package   Sometimes called an applications package. A set of programs, with documentation, used to perform a task or a set of tasks.

Peripheral   A device connected to and under the control of a CPU.

PIN   Personal identification number. The secret number that needs to be keyed in to gain access to a cash dispenser.

Piracy   The illegal copying and use of software.

Privacy   The rights of individuals to decide what information about them should be known by others.

Programmer   A person who writes computer programs.

Protocol   A set of standards that allow the transfer of data between computers on a network.

Pseudocode   A combination of English and a programming language used to express the flow of a program.

RAM   Random access memory. A fast temporary memory area where programs and data are stored while the computer is switched on.

Range check   A data validation technique which checks that the data input to a computer is within a certain range.

Real time   A real time system accepts data and processes it immediately. The results have a direct effect on the next set of available data.

Record   A set of related information about a thing or individual. Records are subdivided into fields.

Relational database   A database that consists of several files. It is possible to use a single file and access data in several of the other files.

Remote sensing   The process where sensors are connected via communication lines to a main computer.

Robot   A machine or device that has been programmed to carry out some (usually mechanical) process automatically.

ROM   Read only memory. Computer memory that cannot be changed by a program.

Run time error   An error detected during the running of a program (e.g. division by zero).

Screen dump   A printout of what appears on the screen.

Search   To look for an item of data.

Sensors   Devices which measure physical quantities such as temperature, pressure, etc.

Serial access   Accessing the data in sequence. The time it takes to locate an item depends on its position.

Simulation   The imitation with a computer program of some system (e.g. an aircraft flight simulator) or some phenomenon that can be described mathematically (e.g. how the economy of the country works).

Smartcard   A plastic card which is 'intelligent' because it contains its own chip.

Software   The programs used in a computer.

Source documents   The original documents from which the data is taken.

Spellchecker   A program usually found with a wordprocessor which checks the spelling in a document and suggests correctly spelt words.

Spreadsheet   A software package which consists of a grid used to contain text, numbers or formulae. Spreadsheets are used to produce financial predictions.

Syntax error   An error reported by a computer due to the incorrect use of the rules governing the structure of the language.

Systems analyst   A person who studies the overall organisation and implementation of a business system.

Tape   Magnetic media used to store data.

Telecommunications   The field of technology concerned with communicating at a distance (e.g. telephones, radio, cable, etc.)

Terminal   A computer on a network, or a keyboard and VDU connected to a mini or mainframe computer.

Test data   Data used to test a program or flowchart for logical errors.

Thesaurus   Software which suggests words with similar meanings to the word highlighted in a document. Thesauruses are found mainly with wordprocessors.

Time slice   The time given to a terminal.

Toner   Tiny black plastic particles used by laser printers as the 'ink'.

Trace   Check performed by a computer program, where it follows the program, writing down the line numbers of each step as it is carried out. Tracing is useful for checking the logic of a program.

Tracker ball   An input device which is rather like an upside down mouse.

Transaction file   A file on which all the transactions (items of business) over a certain period of time are kept. A transaction file is used to update a master file.

Translator   A program used to convert a program written in a high- or low-level language into machine code.

Turnaround document   A document produced by a computer, filled in manually and then used as the input to the computer.

UNIX   An operating system used in multi-user computing.

Update   The process of changing information in a file that has become out of date.

User   A person who uses a computer.

Validate   A check performed by a computer program to make sure that the data is allowable.

VDU   Visual display unit. The screen on which data is displayed. Also called a monitor.

Vector graphics   Graphics which are defined using co-ordinate geometry. They are easy to scale (made bigger or smaller) without any loss of resolution.

Viewdata   A computer based information retrieval system such as Teletext or Prestel, which uses screen messages to display information.

Virtual reality   Computer technology which creates a simulated multidimensional environment for the user.

Virus   A nasty program that has been created to do damage to your computer system.

Visual display unit   See VDU.

Voice recognition   The ability of a computer to

'understand' spoken words by comparing them with stored data.

WAN   Wide area network. A network where the terminals are remote from each other and telecommunications are used to communicate between them.

WIMP (**W**indows **I**cons **M**enus **P**ointing devices) The graphical user interface (GUI) way of using a computer rather than typing in commands at the command line.

Windows   A graphical user interface which provides a common way of using programs.

Wordprocessor   A wordprocessor allows text to be typed and displayed on a VDU and to be edited before being printed out.

Write-protect notch   A notch found on a 3.5 inch floppy disk which when, opened, will not allow data to be stored on the disk.

Names and Addresses

Equipment Suppliers

For data logging systems, sensors and control equipment used in Chapter 32 contact
Philip Harris Education
Lynn Lane, Shenstone, Lichfield
Staffordshire WS 14 OEE
Tel 01543 480077

'The Weather Reporter' fully automatic datalogging weather station is available from
AU Enterprises Ltd
126 Great North Road, Hatfield Herts AL9 5JZ
Tel 01707 266714

The World Development Database is available from
Worldaware
The Centre for World Development Education
1 Catton Street, London WCIR 4AB
Tel 0171 831 1746

For Weather Satellite Systems contact
Timestep
PO Box 2001, Newmarket CB8 8XB
Tel 01440 820040

Dartcom
Powdermills, Postbridge, Yelerton
Devon PL20 6SP
Tel 01822 88253

The material needed for managing BT engineers (page 174) may be obtained from
BT Education Service
PO Box 10, Wetherby
West Yorkshire LS23 7EL
Tel 01937 844443

Model Builder, Expert Builder and Energy Expert as mentioned on pages 175–176, can be obtained from
National Council for Educational Technology
Milburn Hill Road, Science Park
Coventry CV4 7JJ
Tel 01203 411418

Examination Boards

NEAB
Northern Examinations & Assessment Board
Devas Street, Manchester M15 6EX
Tel 0l61 953 1180

MEG
Midland Examining Group
I Hills Road, Cambridge CBl 2EU
Tel 01223 61111

SEG
Southern Examining Group
Stag Hill House, Guildford
Tel 01483 506505

ULEAC
University of London Examinations & Assessment Council
Stewart House, 32 Russell Square
London WC1 5DN
Tel 0171 331 4000

NISEAC
Northern Ireland Schools Examinations & Assessment Council
Beechill House, 42 Beechill Road
Belfast BT8 4RS
Tel 01232 704666

WJEC
Welsh Joint Education Committee
245 Western Road, Cardiff CF5 2YX
Tel 01222 561231

Index

Real time processing 71
Record 60
Record design 61
Remote sensing 47
Repetitive strain injury (RSI) 162
Reports (database) 243
Reproductive hazards 162
Revising 279
Robots 150
ROM 26
RSI 162

Satellites 107
Scalable fonts 229
Scanner 18, 228
Schools Information Management System 4
Search conditions 240
Security files 64
Security (Physical) 120, 124
Sensors 18, 104, 152
Sequential access 63
Sequential files 63
Serial access 63
Serial files 63
SIMS 4
Simulations 172, 177
Smart cards 139
Social effects of IT 143
Software 6, 31
Software piracy 140
Sorting 65
Sorting a database 242
Sound 81, 195
Sound sampling 196
Spell checking 55, 209
Spreadsheets 216
Stepper motor 154
Structure diagrams 85
Style sheets 229
Supermarkets 192
Synthesisers 195
System design 96, 244
System evaluation 99
System flowcharts 88
System security 120
System software 31
System tasks 202
Switch card 17

Tailormade software 33

Teamwork 245
Technical documentation 99, 245
Telecommunications 113
Telecommuting 169
Teleconferencing 169
Teletext 168
Templates 229
Testing 42, 97
Theft of computers 120
Thesaurus 209
Timesharing 72
Top down approach 85
Touch screen 14
Tracker ball 13
Traffic light control 46
Transaction files 64
Transaction processing 72
Transcription errors 55
Translation programs 33, 35
Transposition errors 55
Turnaround document 47
Turtle graphics 252

Unemployment 146
Updating 65
User documentation/guide 98
User interfaces 31, 32
Utility programs 32

Validation 54, 240
Variable length fields 64
Vector graphics 272
Verification 52, 240
Video 83
Video digitiser 17
Viewdata 168
Virtual reality 83
Viruses 121
Visual display unit 19, 228
Voice output 21
Voice recognition 17

WAN 112
Weather forecasting 103
Weather satellites 107
Wide area network (WAN) 112
Wordprocessing 207
World Wide Webb (WWW) 114

Zip files 77